CO CDY 447

JOURNAL FOR THE STUDY OF THE NEW TESTAMENT
SUPPLEMENT SERIES

227

Sheffield Academic Press
A Continuum imprint

The Anecdote in Mark, the Classical World and the Rabbis

Marion C. Moeser, osf

Journal for the Study of the New Testament
Supplement Series 227

Published by Sheffield Academic Press Ltd
The Tower Building, 11 York Road, London SE1 7NX
370 Lexington Avenue, New York, NY 10017-6550

www.SheffieldAcademicPress.com
www.continuum-books.com

British Library Cataloguing-in-Publication Data
A catalogue record for this book is available from the British Library

Typeset by Sheffield Academic Press
Printed on acid-free paper in Great Britain by Bookcraft Ltd, Midsomer Norton, Bath

ISBN 0-8264-6059-3

CONTENTS

Acknowledgments

This work is a minor revision of my 1998 doctoral dissertation in the Christianity and Judaism in Antiquity program at the University of Notre Dame, Indiana. I am indebted to Harry Attridge, Mary Rose D'Angelo and Michael Signer, who read the manuscripts of my dissertation and offered helpful suggestions. Roger Brooks and John R. Donahue, although no longer at Notre Dame, stimulated and guided my research. Gene Ulrich offered me the opportunity to study and work with the Dead Sea Scrolls and encouraged me throughout the enterprise of doctoral studies.

I am most indebted to Adela Yarbro Collins, who served as my mentor and who directed the original dissertation. The sage responsible for Prov. 8.14 has Lady Wisdom describe herself thus: 'I have good advice and sound wisdom; I have insight, I have strength.' Adela guided me with good advice, wisdom, insight and strength; I am privileged to have worked with her. More than this, Adela and her husband John extended to me the warmth of their friendship, their family and their home; I offer them my gratitude and deep appreciation.

Moreover, I am grateful for the support of my religious congregation, the Sisters of Saint Francis of Williamsville, NY, and to the many colleagues and friends who encouraged my efforts, particularly four marvelous story-tellers, Lois Paha, OP, Gabriel Scarfia, ofm, Daniel Lanahan, ofm, and William R. Bigelow.

Finally, I wish to express my thanks to my associates at the Franciscan School of Theology, Berkeley, CA: to the Administration and Board of Regents for granting me the sabbatical leave that enabled me to prepare this work for publication; to Simon and Cynthia Rebullida who helped copy-edit the manuscript; to the faculty and staff whose vision of our enterprise incorporates that of Francis and Clare of Assisi; and to our students, whose eagerness to hear 'the story' that is contained in the New Testament continues to touch my research and teaching with satisfaction and joy.

Needless to say, from all of this...anecdotes abound!

Abbreviations

ABD	David Noel Freedman (ed.), *The Anchor Bible Dictionary* (New York: Doubleday, 1992)
AJT	*American Journal of Theology*
ANRW	Hildegard Temporini and Wolfgang Haase (eds.), *Aufstieg und Niedergang der römischen Welt: Geschichte und Kultur Roms im Spiegel der neueren Forschung* (Berlin: W. de Gruyter, 1972–)
ASNU	Acta seminarii neotestamentici upsaliensis
ATAbh	Alttestamentliche Abhandlungen
BDB	Francis Brown, S.R. Driver and Charles A. Briggs, *The New Brown-Driver-Biggs-Gesenius, Hebrew and English Lexicon with an Appendix Containing the Biblical Aramaic* (Peabody, MA: Hendrickson, 1979)
BDF	Friedrich Blass, A. Debrunner and Robert W. Funk, *A Greek Grammar of the New Testament and Other Early Christian Literature* (Cambridge: Cambridge University Press, 1961)
BETL	Bibliotheca ephemeridum theologicarum lovaniensium
BibRes	*Biblical Research*
BJS	Brown Judaic Studies
BNTC	Black's New Testament Commentaries
BR	*Bible Review*
BTB	*Biblical Theology Bulletin*
BZNW	Beihefte zur *ZNW*
CBQ	*Catholic Biblical Quarterly*
ConBNT	Coniectanea biblica, New Testament
CRINT	Compendia rerum iudaicarum ad Novum Testamentum
EncJud	*Encyclopaedia Judaica*
ExpTim	*Expository Times*
FRLANT	Forschungen zur Religion und Literatur des Alten und Neuen Testaments
HAR	*Hebrew Annual Review*
HR	*History of Religions*
HSCL	Harvard Studies in Comparative Literature
HTR	*Harvard Theological Review*
Int	*Interpretation*

JAAR	*Journal of the American Academy of Religion*
JAOS	*Journal of the American Oriental Society*
JBL	*Journal of Biblical Literature*
JJS	*Journal of Jewish Studies*
JQR	*Jewish Quarterly Review*
JSJSup	*Journal for the Study of Judaism*, Supplement Series (formerly SPB)
JSNT	*Journal for the Study of the New Testament*
JSNTSup	*Journal for the Study of the New Testament*, Supplement Series
JSOTSup	*Journal for the Study of the Old Testament*, Supplement Series
KlPauly	K. Ziegler and W. Sontheimer (eds.), *Der Kleine Pauly: Lexicon der Antike* (5 vols.; Stuttgart: Alfred Druckmüller, 1967)
LAW	Carl Anderson *et al.* (eds.), *Lexicon der Alten Welt* (Zürich: Artemis, 1965)
LCL	Loeb Classical Library
LSJ	H.G. Liddell, Robert Scott and H. Stuart Jones, *Greek–English Lexicon* (Oxford: Clarendon Press, 9th edn, 1968)
NA	Eberhard Nestle, Erwin Nestle and Kurt Aland *et al.* (eds.), *Novum Testamentum Graece* (Stuttgart: Deutsche Bibelgesellschaft, 27th edn, 1993)
NHS	Nag Hammadi Studies
NICNT	New International Commentary on the New Testament
NovT	*Novum Testamentum*
NovTSup	*Novum Testamentum*, Supplements
NTAbh	Neutestamentliche Abhandlungen
NTS	*New Testament Studies*
OCD	*Oxford Classical Dictionary*
PTMS	Pittsburgh Theological Monograph Series
PW	August Friedrich von Pauly and Georg Wissowa (eds.), *Real-Encyclopädie der classischen Altertumswissenschaft* (Stuttgart: Metzler, 1894–)
PWSup	Supplement to PW
RAC	*Reallexikon für Antike und Christentum*
SBL	Society of Biblical Literature
SBLDS	SBL Dissertation Series
SBLMS	SBL Monograph Series
SBLSBS	SBL Sources for Biblical Study
SBLSP	SBL Seminar Papers
SBLTT	SBL Texts and Translations
SCHNT	Studia ad corpus hellenisticum Novi Testamenti
SJLA	Studies in Judaism in Late Antiquity
SNTSMS	Society for New Testament Studies Monograph Series

SPB	Studia postbiblica
TRE	*Theologische Realenzyklopädie*
WUNT	Wissenschaftliche Untersuchungen zum Neuen Testament
ZNW	*Zeitschrift für die neutestamentliche Wissenschaft*

INTRODUCTION

The Nobel laureate, Elie Wiesel, recounts the story of the great Rabbi Israel Baal Shem-Tov, who saw that misfortune was threatening the Jews. Rabbi Israel went to a certain part of the forest to meditate, light a fire and say a special prayer. When he did this a miracle occurred and the misfortune was averted. A generation later the Rabbi of Mezritch had occasion to intercede with God to avert hardship for the Jewish people. He went to the same place in the forest and told God that he did not know how to light the fire, but he did know the prayer. And God listened to him and the miracle happened. Many years later, Rabbi Moshe-Leib sought to save his people. When he went into the forest he said, 'I do not know how to light the fire, I do not know the prayer, but I know the place and this must be sufficient.' It was sufficient; the miracle was accomplished.

> Then it fell to Rabbi Israel of Rizhyn to overcome misfortune. Sitting in his arm chair, his head in his hands, he spoke to God: 'I am unable to light the fire and I do not know the prayer; I cannot even find the place in the forest. All I can do is to tell the story, and this must be sufficient.' And it was sufficient.
>
> God made man because he loves stories.[1]

Human persons of all times and places also love stories. This holds true for people of the early Christian era. As one New Testament scholar has observed:

> The brief stories and sayings which Christians used both in speech and writing to communicate their commitment to God's activity through the prophets, John the Baptist, Jesus and the disciples were a powerful and natural form of communication in Mediterranean culture.[2]

1. Elie Wiesel, *The Gates of the Forest* (trans. Frances Frenaye; New York: Holt, Rinehart & Winston, 1966; French original, 1964), pp. vi-x.

2. Vernon K. Robbins, 'The Chreia', in David Aune (ed.), *Greco-Roman Literature and the New Testament: Selected Forms and Genres* (SBLSBS, 21; Atlanta: Scholars Press, 1988), pp. 1-23 (22).

The claim for the existence of such brief stories is confirmed by the following examples taken from three different literary worlds of that Mediterranean culture, namely one found in a work of the Greek author Lucian, another in the early Christian Gospel of Mark and a third in the *Mishnah* of early rabbinic Judaism:

> Once the Sidonian sophist was distinguishing himself in Athens and voicing his own praise to the effect that he had examined all philosophy—but it is well to cite the very words he used: 'If ever Aristotle calls me to the Lyceum, I shall attend; if Plato calls me to the Academy, I shall arrive; if Zeno calls, I shall spend my time in the Poecile (great hall); if Pythagoras calls, I shall keep silence'. Demonax arose in the midst of the audience and said, calling him by name, 'Pythagoras is calling you' (*Demonax*, 14.1-4).[3]

> When the Pharisees and some of the scribes who had come from Jerusalem gathered together about him [Jesus], they saw some of his disciples eating meals with defiled, that is, unwashed, hands... The Pharisees and the scribes asked him, 'Why do your disciples not live according to the tradition of the elders, but eat their meal with defiled hands?'... Then he called the crowd to himself again and said to them, 'Listen to me, all of you, and understand: there is nothing from outside a person which by going into a person can defile that person; but the things which come out of a person are what defile the person' (Mk 7.1-2, 5, 14-15).[4]

> Perqlos b. Pelosepos asked Rabban Gamaliel in Akko, when he was washing in Aphrodite's bathhouse, saying to him, 'It is written in your Torah, "And there shall cleave nothing of a devoted thing to your hand" (Deut. 13.18). How is it that you are taking a bath in Aphrodite's house?' He said to him, 'They do not give answers in a bathhouse'. When he went out, he said to him, 'I never came into her domain. She came into mine! They don't say, 'Let's make a bathhouse as an ornament for Aphrodite'. But they say, 'Let's make Aphrodite as an ornament for the bathhouse' (*'Abod. Zar.* 3.4).[5]

An investigation of the brief stories of these three literary worlds is the subject of this book. For each literary world the genre of the anecdote, as it appears in writings of that world, is discussed and anecdotes from a specific literary work of that world are analyzed. The purpose of the study

3. Lucian, *Demonax*, in *Lucian*, LCL edition. Unless otherwise noted all Greek and Latin authors are cited from the LCL editions.

4. From the Greek of Eberhard Nestle, Erwin Nestle and Kurt Aland *et al.* (eds.), *Novum Testamentum Graece* (Stuttgart: Deutsche Bibelgesellschaft, 27th edn, 1993). All translations from the New Testament are my own.

5. *The Mishnah: A New Translation* (trans. Jacob Neusner; New Haven: Yale University Press, 1988), p. 665.

is to clarify the genre, that is, the form, content and function, of the anecdotes of Mark's Gospel, in particular Mk 8.27–10.45, through a comparison of these anecdotes with those of a Greek work and a rabbinic text.

Toward the middle of this century, R.O.P. Taylor urged New Testament form critics to investigate 'the careful studies of literary form which were made by writers of the first centuries of our era'.[6] The first such study that Taylor presents is the Greek grammarian Theon of Alexandria's definition of the χρεία, that is, 'A Chreia is a concise and pointed account of something said or done, attributed to some particular person.'[7] Taylor then remarks that 'the definition exactly fits the detachable little stories of which so much of Mark consists'.[8] Despite Taylor's urging, it was not until the last decade, with the renewed study of Greek and Roman rhetoric, that biblical scholars were again drawn to first-century writers, and specifically to their work on the χρεία, in relationship to New Testament anecdotes.

Scholars had already given attention to the 'detachable little stories' in the Gospels earlier in this century. In 1919, in his *Die Formgeschichte des Evangeliums*, Martin Dibelius identified an anecdotal gospel 'form' which he named 'paradigm'.[9] Major contributions to the study of New Testament anecdotes were made by Rudolf Bultmann in his programmatic study of the history of New Testament 'forms', including the 'biographical apophthegm', the 'controversy dialogue' and the 'scholastic dialogue', and by Martin Albertz in his work on the 'controversy dialogue'.[10] To his credit Bultmann looked for analogies to the Gospel stories in rabbinic and Greek anecdotes. However, the rabbinic analogies Bultmann gave were almost all from late rabbinic texts, and he gave only brief mention to Greek analogies. Albertz also made reference to rabbinic anecdotes, specifically those that took the form of debates; however, Albertz discussed only four rabbinic units and these were from texts of a late date.

In the second edition of his book (1933), Dibelius included a com-

6. R.O.P. Taylor, 'Form-Criticism in the First Centuries', *ExpTim* 55 (1943–44), pp. 218-20 (218).

7. Taylor, 'Form-Criticism', p. 218. This is Taylor's translation of Theon.

8. Taylor, 'Form-Criticism', p. 218.

9. Martin Dibelius, *Die Formgeschichte des Evangeliums* (Tübingen: J.C.B. Mohr, 1919).

10. Rudolf Bultmann, *Die Geschichte der synoptischen Tradition* (FRLANT, 29; Göttingen: Vandenhoeck & Ruprecht, 2nd edn, 1931 [1921]); English: *The History of the Synoptic Tradition* (trans. J. Marsh; New York: Harper & Row, 3rd rev. edn, 1963); Martin Albertz, *Die synoptischen Streitgespräche: Ein Beitrage zur Formengeschichte des Urchristentums* (Berlin: Trowitzsch, 1921).

parison of the 'paradigm' to the Greek and Roman χρεία, although he used his own definition for a χρεία, referring only in a footnote to the definition of Theon.[11] Dibelius's comments on the differences between the Gospel paradigm and the Greek χρεία indicate that he had not studied the Greek genre completely. This second edition of his work also included comments on rabbinic analogies. Like Bultmann and Albertz, Dibelius used late rabbinic texts for his anecdotes. Moreover, his conclusions as to the significant differences between rabbinic anecdotes and his Gospel paradigms were not based on the two generic expressions of the brief story; these differences flowed from his suppositions about the nature of the literature involved.

Scholarly interest in brief gospel narratives continues down to the present in the recent studies of the χρεία and rabbinic anecdotes by Burton Mack and Vernon Robbins.[12] However, even these recent works do not adequately investigate early rabbinic expressions of the anecdote, and hence do not provide an adequate basis for a comparison of Gospel and rabbinic anecdotes.

It is important to note the starting point of the method employed by Martin Dibelius (1933) and indeed by almost all subsequent scholarship on these short narrative units. Dibelius identified a particular literary unit within the Gospels, worked on its 'form' and function and sought analogies to this particular Gospel 'form' in other literary worlds.[13] There is validity to this method, namely to ascertain whether works of another contemporary literary world contain the exact same or a very similar 'form' as a particular Gospel 'form'. However, there is also a drawback; it is possible to become too focused on the particularities of one expression of a literary genre and thereby overlook other similar genres in different literary worlds.

This book pursues a more universal starting point for a study of the 'brief stories' of the Gospels. First, the basic literary genre 'anecdote', common to many narrative worlds, ancient and modern, oral and literate, is identified, and then the expression of this genre in each of three ancient literary worlds is investigated. On the basis of these investigations,

11. Martin Dibelius, *From Tradition to Gospel* (trans. B.L. Woolf; New York: Charles Scribner's Sons, rev. edn, 1965), p. 152 n. 1 (German: *Formgeschichte des Evangeliums* [Tübingen: J.C.B. Mohr, 2nd edn, 1933]).

12. Burton L. Mack and Vernon K. Robbins, *Patterns of Persuasion in the Gospels* (Sonoma, CA: Polebridge Press, 1989), and the essays in Vernon K. Robbins (ed.), *The Rhetoric of Pronouncement* (Semeia, 64; Atlanta: Scholars Press, 1993).

13. Note that while Dibelius rejected the notion that Gospel anecdotes had exact analogies in Greek and Roman literary genres, he nevertheless sought such analogies.

similarities and differences among these expressions are presented. This approach employs modern literary theories of narrative genres along with a study of the literary genres of the first century.[14] This method provides a broader basis for comparison and a clearer understanding of the particularities of a 'form' in a specific literary world; hence, the drawback mentioned above is overcome.

This volume therefore encompasses an examination of the genre 'anecdote' as it appears in Mark's Gospel, in Greek and Roman literature, as well as in early rabbinic literature; the focus is on the literary form, the content and the function of the 'anecdote'. Such an investigation will offer a proper basis for an evaluation of Robbins's statement that 'brief stories...were a powerful and natural form of communication in Mediterranean culture'.

Chapter 1 provides a foundation and context for the studies of ancient literature that follow. This chapter defines and discusses not only the narrative entity 'anecdote', but also, indeed begins with, the notion of 'genre'. Furthermore, the oral-aural-literary character of the socio-cultural worlds of the first century is discussed as well as the extent of the 'Hellenization' of first-century Palestine.

Chapter 2 investigates the genre 'anecdote' as it was understood or defined by grammarians, rhetoricians and writers of the Greek and Roman worlds. The anecdotes of Lucian's *Demonax* are studied both as to their genre and their function within the *Demonax*. The *Demonax* was chosen because of its similarity in length and style, that is, popular literary, to Mark's Gospel, as well as its focus on an exemplary individual. Chapter 3 pursues a similar study of rabbinic anecdotes. First the rabbinic expression of the genre is described and then the anecdotes of one division of the *Mishnah*, *Mo'ed Qaṭan*, are studied. All of the anecdotes in the *Mishnah* that feature Rabbi Gamaliel II are also examined. The anecdotes on Rabbi Gamaliel II were chosen because he was an important figure in early rabbinic Judaism and because there are a sufficient number of brief stories centered on him to form the basis of a statistically valid study. This chapter concludes with a discussion of the function of the anecdotes within the tractate *Mo'ed Qaṭan* as well as the portrait of Gamaliel that is presented in the Mishnaic anecdotes.

14. For a similar method see Richard A. Burridge, who approaches his subject using 'an interdisciplinary study involving gospel studies, literary theory of genre and proper understanding of literature which was contemporary with the gospels...' (*What Are the Gospels? A Comparison with Graeco-Roman Biography* [SNTMS, 70; Cambridge: Cambridge University Press, 1992], p. 105).

Chapter 4 presents a review of the scholarship on New Testament anecdotes. In Chapter 5 attention is turned to Mark's Gospel and the evangelist's use of 'brief stories' in the section from 8.27 to 10.45. This Markan material is chosen, first, because it is a recognizable section of the gospel and, secondly, it contains a significant number of anecdotes. These anecdotes are analyzed as to their form, content and function both within the Gospel narrative and as a vehicle for Mark's portrait of Jesus. Finally, the Conclusion compares the anecdotes of the *Demonax*, the *Mishnah* and Mark's Gospel and discusses the results of this comparison.

Chapter 1

The Anecdote in the Framework of Literary Criticism

The term 'anecdote' connotes different things to different people, even within the discipline of literary criticism. For some, 'anecdote' suggests 'amusing triviality'; hence, Winston Churchill could remark that anecdotes are 'the gleaming toys of history'.[1] Others attach to 'anecdote' a connotation of gossip or humor. Thus it has been recorded: 'The dress designer Edith Head, who knew Grace Kelly in Hollywood, was, at the time of Miss Kelly's marriage, asked for anecdotes about the princess. Said Miss Head, "Grace doesn't allow anecdotes to happen to her".'[2] Therefore, in order that anecdotes, or 'brief stories', can be seen to function as 'powerful' means of communication,[3] both in the first century CE and at the present time, the genre 'anecdote' must be defined and discussed carefully so that the definition includes 'serious' functions as well as those mentioned above. This first chapter develops such a definition beginning with a discussion of the notion of 'genre'.

1. *Genre*

The importance of a study of 'genre' for biblical exegesis was recognized by the Society of Biblical Literature in the early 1970s with its Task Force on Genre of the Seminar on the Gospels. William Doty's article, 'The Concept of Genre in Literary Analysis', written for that Task Force in 1972, proceeded, as he himself notes, 'from the understanding that clarity is lacking within biblical criticism with respect to identifications of primitive Christian (and other) literary genres'.[4] Likewise, Doty notes that

1. Clifton Fademan, 'Introduction', in *The Little, Brown Book of Anecdotes* (Boston: Little, Brown, 1985), p. xiii.

2. Fademan, 'Introduction', p. xx.

3. See the citation from Vernon Robbins in the Introduction.

4. William G. Doty, 'The Concept of Genre in Literary Analysis', in Lane C.

the concept of genre 'has not had an easy history' among literary critics and that '[w]ithin literary criticism unanimity is as rare as within biblical criticism, and uniformity with respect to the term "genre" is hardly to be considered'.[5]

The discussion of genre in literary criticism revolves around what are sometimes seen to be two opposing positions, namely that genre is a principle of classification, either prescriptive or descriptive,[6] based upon literary form or structure, or that genre is a principle of meaning concerned with communication.[7] Consider the following definitions of genre taken from two different contemporary literary critics:

> Genre. Used to designate the types or categories into which literary works are grouped according to form, technique, or, sometimes, subject matter.[8]

McGaughy (ed.), *SBL Proceedings* 2 (Missoula, MT: Scholars Press, 1972), pp. 413-48 (414-15). For additional reading on the importance of the concept of genre for biblical exegesis see George W. Coates, 'Introduction. Genres: Why Should They Be Important?', in *Saga, Legend, Tale, Novella, Fable: Narrative Forms in Old Testament Literature* (JSOTSup, 35; Sheffield: JSOT Press, 1985), pp. 7-15; Mary Gerhart, 'Generic Studies: Their Renewed Importance in Religious and Literary Interpretation', *JAAR* 45 (1977), pp. 309-25; *idem*, 'Generic Competence in Biblical Hermeneutics', in Mary Gerhart and James G. Williams (eds.), *Genre, Narrativity, and Theology* (Semeia, 43; Atlanta: Scholars Press, 1988), pp. 29-44; John S. Kloppenborg, 'Introduction: Forms and Genres', in *The Formation of Q: Trajectories in Ancient Wisdom Collections* (Studies in Antiquity and Christianity; Philadelphia: Fortress Press, 1987), pp. 1-8; Christopher Tuckett, 'Genre', in *Reading the New Testament: Methods of Interpretation* (Philadelphia: Fortress Press, 1987), pp. 68-77.

5. Doty, 'Concept of Genre', pp. 415-16.

6. Generally, one can say that classical genre theory looked upon genres as regulative and prescriptive, whereas modern genre theory tends to be almost purely descriptive and attempts to avoid generic hierarchies. See Brian C. Lee, 'genre', in Roger Fowler (ed.), *A Dictionary of Modern Critical Terms* (London: Routledge & Kegan Paul, rev. edn, 1987), pp. 104-105; M.H. Abrams, *A Glossary of Literary Terms* (Chicago: Holt, Rinehart & Winston, 5th edn, 1988), pp. 72-75; René Wellek and Austin Warren, 'Literary Genres', in *The Theory of Literature* (New York: Harcourt Brace Jovanovitch, 3rd edn, 1977), pp. 226-37.

7. See Alastair Fowler, 'Concepts of Genre', in *Kinds of Literature: An Introduction to the Theory of Genres and Modes* (Cambridge, MA: Harvard University Press, 1982), p. 37.

8. C. Hugh Holman and William Harmon, *A Handbook to Literature* (New York: Macmillan, 6th edn, 1992), p. 212. See also Seymour Chatman, *Story and Discourse: Narrative Structure in Fiction and Film* (Ithaca, NY: Cornell University Press, 1978), p. 18, and Wellek and Warren, 'Literary Genres', pp. 226-27.

> Genres are no longer taxonomic classes but groups of norms and expectations which help the reader to assign functions to various elements in the work, and thus the 'real' genres are those sets of categories or norms required to account for the process of reading.[9]

Since literary criticism, including genre theory, deals with actual texts one can ask, 'Does the concept of genre arise out of the text alone, out of the author-reader(or hearer)-relationship alone, or out of both at the same time?' If out of the text alone, one might see genre merely as a principle of classification of forms, and use such a classification as a means to establish a set of historical influences on or similarities among texts. If, however, one considers the triple complex of author-reader(or hearer)-text as the 'place' of origin of a genre, then one is able to see that genre provides both a classification of a work as a particular type and an associated 'world of meaning'.

It is helpful here to ask oneself, 'How does one arrive at a notion of a particular genre?' 'How does one know what one means by saying that a particular work of literature is a murder mystery? a particular work of art is an impressionistic piece?' It is asserted that it is through the experience of one or more examples of a similar 'kind' of literary work or work of art that one comes to expect certain conventions, elements, in a work of that 'kind' and that these conventions can be named.[10] The repeated experience of this set of conventions, as a whole or in large number, provides the reader or viewer with an interpretive background with which to approach

9. Jonathan Culler, *The Pursuit of Signs: Semiotics, Literature, Deconstruction* (Ithaca, NY: Cornell University Press, 1981); cited in Thomas Kent, *Interpretation and Genre: The Role of Generic Perception in the Study of Narrative Texts* (London and Toronto: Associated University Presses, 1986), p. 59. Likewise, Abrams (*Glossary*, pp. 74-75) holds: 'By structuralist critics...a genre is conceived as a set of constitutive conventions between writer and reader. These sets of conventions are what make possible the writing of a particular work of literature, though the writer may play against, as well as with, the prevailing generic conventions. For the reader, such conventions function as a set of expectations, which may be converted rather than satisfied, but enable the reader to make the work intelligible...' See also Fowler, 'Concepts of Genre', pp. 37-53, and Adrian Marino, 'Toward a Definition of Literary Genres', in Joseph P. Strelka (ed.), *Theories of Literary Genre*. III. *Yearbook of Comparative Criticism* (University Park: Pennsylvania State University Press, 1978), pp. 41-53.

10. As Kent (*Interpretation and Genre*, p. 15) points out, there is circularity to this notion of the origin of a generic class, 'Our recognition that a specific text is a member of a particular genre creates, in turn, certain generic expectations, so that...we expect to discover certain elements common to this particular genre'.

another work.[11] This concept of a set of texts that display similar conventions is known as a genre.[12] It is important to note that 'genre' remains an abstract notion, a concept, in much the same way as the mathematical concept 'number'.[13]

In a brief essay, Tzvetan Todorov discusses the origins of genres; he defines a genre simply as a 'class of texts'. Todorov's presentation provides a helpful distinction between genres and their function when he asserts, 'Genres communicate with the society in which they flourish by means of institutionalization… It is because genres exist as an institution that they *function* as "horizons of expectation" for readers, and as "models of writing" for authors.'[14] Todorov is correct in tying the institutionalization of a particular genre within a culture to the function of that genre. The notion of 'genre as a principle of meaning' is likewise bound up with the cultural world that perceives the 'meaning' and hence 'genre as a principle of meaning' corresponds to the 'function' of a genre.

Heather Dubrow, in her brief monograph *Genre*, introduces her study, engaging the reader from the outset, by asking that a paragraph of descriptive text be read first as the opening paragraph of a murder mystery

11. On a very mundane level, one is reminded of the 'convention' among American pre-teens beginning with the words 'Knock knock?' After a child has experienced one or two of these jokes, the words 'Knock knock?' immediately signal an expected pattern of response, i.e., 'Who's there?' 'So-and-so.' 'So-and-so who?' '*So-and-so…*' The words 'Knock knock?' signal a world of meaning, i.e., this is a joke, a pun or play on words, involving a specific pattern of dialogue in which the 'punch line' reflects a mispronunciation of, a repositioning of the syllables in, and or a change in spelling of the words of the original response. In fact, the conventions are so stereotyped that a list of 'knock-knock jokes' could be written with nothing more than the two responses 'So-and-so' and '*So-and-so…*'; e.g., 'Sultan'/'*Sultan pepper*' or 'Esther'/'*Esther a doctor in the house?*'

12. See Tzvetan Todorov: 'In a society, the recurrence of certain discursive properties is institutionalized, and individual texts are produced and perceived in relation to the norm constituted by this codification. A genre, literary or otherwise, is nothing but this codification of discursive properties' ('The Origin of Genres', *New Literary History* 9 [1976], pp. 159-70 [62]).

13. Here, for example, one may think of the concept of 'three-ness', which is represented by various numerals, including 3, iii and the English word 'three'. No matter how one represents 'three-ness' or posits that some entity contains 'three' elements, 'three-ness' itself remains a concept. The act of counting is the application of the concept of a number to an entity or entities. In a similar fashion, one identifies a piece of literature as a particular genre.

14. Todorov, 'The Origin of Genres', p. 163, emphasis mine.

and then read as the first lines of a *Bildungsroman* (a narrative that traces the maturation and education of its hero).[15] Dubrow is assuming that her readers would have had previous experiences with the kinds of literature known as a murder mystery and *Bildungsroman*. This previous familiarity leads the reader to interpret the details of the brief text differently given the two different 'horizons of expectation' for the text. The effect of this exercise is striking and prepares the reader to accept Dubrow's thesis that a 'genre functions much like a code of behavior established between the author and his reader'.[16] Details of the description would be intended differently by the author and interpreted differently by the reader in different contexts; for successful communication both author and reader must share the interpretive context.

The literary critics René Wellek and Austin Warren combine both principles under discussion above, that is, genre as a principle of categorization and genre as a principle of meaning, when they state, 'Genre should be conceived, we think, as a grouping of literary works based, theoretically, upon both outer form (specific metre or structure) and also upon inner form (attitude, tone, purpose—more crudely, subject and audience).'[17] When one moves to include the audience of a work in the definition of a genre, one has moved to include the 'function' of a work in the definition.

For this study, I will use the definition of genre given by David Aune in *The New Testament in its Literary Environment*:

> A *literary genre* may be defined as a group of texts that exhibit a coherent and recurring configuration of literary features involving form (including structure and style), content, and function.[18]

15. The descriptive text reads as follows: 'The clock on the mantelpiece said ten thirty, but someone had suggested recently that the clock was wrong. As the figure of the dead woman lay on the bed in the front room, a no less silent figure glided rapidly from the house. The only sounds to be heard were the ticking of that clock and the loud wailing of an infant' (Heather Dubrow, *Genre* [New York: Methuen, 1982], p. 1). For another example of the influence of context on interpretation see Tuckett, 'Genre', pp. 68-70.

16. Dubrow, *Genre*, p. 2. See also Norman R. Petersen: 'Genres are cultural media (codal elements or conventions) which function on levels of linguistic competency beyond the scope of the sentence, i.e., supra-sententially, within every linguistic community' ('On the Notion of Genre in Via's "Parable and Example Story: A Literary-Structuralist Approach"', in Robert W. Funk (ed.), *A Structuralist Approach to the Parables* [Semeia, 1; Missoula, MT: Scholars Press, 1974], pp. 134-81 [137]).

17. Wellek and Warren, 'Literary Genres', p. 231.

18. David Aune, *The New Testament in its Literary Environment* (Library of Early

There remain two final points for consideration before applying the concept of genre to a brief story, that is, how is the word 'form' used in the present study and can such a 'small' literary unit as the brief story be considered a genre?

Modern form criticism (*Formgeschichte*) of the Bible originated among German scholars, for the Hebrew Bible with Hermann Gunkel's study of the legends of the book of Genesis and for the New Testament with the work of Karl Schmidt, Martin Dibelius and Rudolf Bultmann.[19] In subsequent scholarship one finds an ambiguity in the use of the German terms *Form* and *Gattung*, translated as 'form' and 'genre', respectively, occasioned in part by the use of 'form' to mean both a genre and the structural elements of a genre. In 1966, Gene Tucker noted:

> Though th[e] word *Form* is used very commonly as a synonym for *Gattung*, the two terms point to two distinct concepts. *Gattungen*, on the one hand, are the different kinds or types of literary and preliterary material, some of which had ancient names, but most of which require modern categories. *Form*, on the other hand, refers to the structure, the schema, the outline, or

Christianity; Philadelphia: Westminster Press, 1987), p. 13. It should be noted that this definition grew out of the discussion of the Apocalypse Group of the Society of Biblical Literature's Genres Project. A first definition of genre used by this group did not include the element 'function'; in fact, this element was specifically excluded. See John J. Collins, 'Introduction: Towards a Morphology of a Genre', in *Apocalypse: The Morphology of a Genre* (Semeia, 14; Missoula, MT: Scholars Press, 1979), pp. 1-20 (1-2). Cogent arguments for the inclusion of 'function' in a definition of genre were made by David Hellholm ('The Problem of Apocalyptic Genre and the Apocalypse of John', in Adela Yarbro Collins [ed.], *Early Christian Apocalypticism: Genre and Social Setting* [Semeia, 36; Atlanta: Scholars Press, 1986], pp.13-64 [13-19]) and David Aune ('The Apocalypse of John and the Problem of Genre', in Adela Yarbro Collins [ed.], *Early Christian Apocalypticism: Genre and Social Setting* [Semeia, 36; Atlanta: Scholars Press, 1986], pp. 65-96 [65-67]). See also the summary of the discussion by Adela Yarbro Collins, 'Introduction', in *Early Christian Apocalypticism: Genre and Social Setting* (Semeia, 36; Atlanta: Scholars Press, 1986), pp. 1-11 (6-7).

19. Hermann Gunkel, *Genesis, übersetzt und erklärt* (Göttingen: Vandenhoeck & Ruprecht, 3rd edn, 1917). For a summary of the history of form criticism see Gene M. Tucker, *Form Criticism of the Old Testament* (Guides to Biblical Scholarship, Old Testament Series; Philadelphia: Fortress Press, 1971), pp. 1-21; Edgar V. McKnight, *What Is Form Criticism?* (Guides to Biblical Scholarship, New Testament Series; Philadelphia: Fortress Press, 1969), pp. 1-16; and *idem*, 'Form and Redaction Criticism', in E.J. Epp and G.W. MacRae (eds.), *The New Testament and its Modern Interpreters* (The Bible and Its Modern Interpreters, 3; Atlanta: Scholars Press, 1989), pp. 149-74.

> the pattern of a given piece of literature or a given oral type... Consequently, if the term *Form* is to be used, as many use it, to refer to *Gattungen*, it must be made clear that the word [form] has thereby taken on a secondary connotation.[20]

Doty suggests three additional causes for the confusion: the identification of a genre solely by its literary structure (form) while neglecting its content and function; the lack of stable English equivalents for the German *Gattung* and *Form*; and the use of *Gattungen* by earlier Old Testament form-critics to refer to pre-literary types or units, while early New Testament form-critics used *Gattungen* to refer to literary types or units and *Formen* to designate pre-literary expressions of a tradition.[21]

There are 18 entries for the English noun 'form' in *Webster's Third New International Dictionary*, including: '2a. the shape and structure of something as distinguished from the material of which it is composed'; and '9. one of the different modes of existence, action, or manifestation of a particular thing or substance... (the democratic ~ [form] of government)'.[22] These two usages are both commonly found in scholarly discussions of biblical literary units. For example, the definition of 'genre' given above involves the use of 'form' in the sense of 'shape and structure'. Hans Peter Müller, noting the different uses of like concepts in form criticism of the Hebrew Bible, accepts a 'solution' employing *Form* as a particular manifestation of a *Gattung*, reflecting usage '9' above. In this Müller follows G. Fohrer who writes, '*Form* is assigned to a single text; *Gattung* refers to a text-type.'[23]

20. Gene M. Tucker, review of *Was is Formgeschichte? Neue Wege der Bibelexegese* (Neukirchen–Vluyn: Neukirchener Verlag, 1964), by Klaus Koch, in *Dialog* 5 (1966), pp. 145-47 (145). See Tucker's further comments on this confusion in *Form Criticism of the Old Testament*, p. 12.

21. Doty, 'Concept of Genre', pp. 433-36. However, even in this last area of confusion, some Old Testament scholars use 'form' to refer to pre-literary units of tradition. See J. Coert Rylaarsdam, 'Editor's Foreword', in Gene M. Tucker, *Form Criticism of the Old Testament* [Guides to Bible Scholarship, Old Testament Series; Philadelphia: Fortress Press, 1971), pp. iii-vii.

22. *Webster's Third New International Dictionary of the English Language Unabridged* (editor-in-chief Philip B. Gove; Springfield, MA: Webster, Inc., Publishers, 1986), pp. 892-93. The German–English dictionary, *Langenscheidts*, gives 34 usages for the German word *Form* (*Langenscheidts Enzyklopädische Wörterbuch: Der Englische und Deutschen Sprache. Teil II. Deutsch-Englisch. 1. Band A–K* [ed. Otto Springer; Berlin: Langenscheidt, 1974], p. 592).

23. Georg Fohrer *et al.*, *Exegesis des Alten Testaments: Einführung in die Methodik*

Finally, somewhat similarly to the New Testament scholars who employ 'form' for pre-literary units of tradition, other clarifications of terminology are offered.[24] Consider first the suggestion of Petersen, namely that 'while *Formen* are the media by which pre-literary traditions are shaped, genres are the media by which formed traditions are transformed into what we may call...literary functions within extended texts'.[25] E.P. Sanders would differentiate between two usages of *Gattung*. When *Gattung* refers to a 'larger' literary work, Sanders translates this as 'genre'; however, if *Gattung* refers to a smaller component, he retains the German word.[26] Many other critics designate 'larger' literary units as 'genres' and their components, which are themselves independent units, as 'forms'.[27]

(Uni-Taschenbücher, 267; Heidelberg: Quelle & Mayer, 1976), p. 54 (cited in Hans Peter Müller, 'Formgeschichte/Formenkritik. I. Altes Testament', *TRE* XI [1983], p. 276). This usage of the German *Form* as a 'manifestation', *Erscheinung*, is given as usage '9' in *Langenscheidts*, p. 592.

24. Morton Smith attributes a very distinct meaning to 'literary form' in his discussion of 'Parallels of Literary Form' in *Tannaitic Parallels to the Gospels* (SBLMS, 6; Philadelphia: Society of Biblical Literature, rev. edn, 1968), pp. 78-114. Smith holds that the 'customary use of the word form...is apt to be misleading for the essential parallelism of the passages [he discusses]...is one of meaning'. He proceeds to say that 'parallels of literary form' are actually 'parallels of meaning' and emphasizes 'that literary form, 'the form of the thought', has no direct connexion with the forms of the sentences in which the thought is expressed' (p. 78, Smith's emphasis). Smith uses the English word 'form' in three different ways in this sentence. Not only is the sentence confusing but his stated use of 'literary form' is somewhat unique among biblical scholars. Smith's work presents yet another instance affirming the necessity for a clarification in the use of the term 'form'. See also Jacob Neusner's caustic critique of Smith's work, especially Neusner's appraisal of Smith's concept of 'literary form' in *Are There Really Tannaitic Parallels to the Gospels? A Refutation of Morton Smith* (South Florida Studies in the History of Judaism, 80; Atlanta: Scholars Press, 1993), pp. 34-35.

25. Petersen, 'Notion of Genre', p. 157.

26. E.P. Sanders, 'The Genre of Palestinian Jewish Apocalypses', in David Hellholm (ed.), *Apocalypticism in the Mediterranean World and the Near East: Proceedings of the International Colloquium on Apocalypticism, Uppsala, August 12–17, 1979* (Tübingen: J.C.B. Mohr, 1983), pp. 447-59 (453).

27. This is a common usage of these terms. For example, see Aune (*New Testament in its Literary Environment*, p. 13), who, after his definition of 'literary genre', writes the following: '*Literary forms*, on the other hand, while exhibiting similar recurring literary features, are primarily constituent elements of the genres which frame them.' See also Doty, 'Concept of Genre', p. 439; David Hellholm, 'Die Unterscheidung zwischen Gattung und Form', in *Das Visionenbuch des Hermas als Apokalypse:*

In this book I follow the distinction between *Form* and *Gattung*, translated as 'form' and 'genre', respectively, employed by Klaus Berger: 'Form is the sum of the stylistic, syntactic and structural characteristics of a text... A genre is a group of texts based on common characteristics...'[28] Throughout this study I attempt to use the English word 'form' only in this sense. Pre-literary or oral units of tradition are referred to as pre-literary or oral units or genres.

The question as to the appropriateness of applying the concept 'genre' to the brief story arises not only from the fact that often it is the major types of literature that are referred to as genres, for example, the classifications of lyric, epic and drama attributed to Aristotle.[29] The literary works dealt with in this study are themselves also 'larger' texts that include brief stories as one component of their overall composition; for example, the Gospel of Mark contains not only brief stories but other components, such as parables and proverbs. Furthermore, the brief story itself may make use of another genre, such as maxim or proverb spoken by a character in the narrative. Hence, even a brief story can be a 'larger' genre. It is apparent that either the use of the term and concept 'genre' should be reserved for the 'larger' units and a new term employed for the 'smaller' components or the use of the term or concept 'genre' both for a 'larger' structure and for its 'smaller' components must be clarified carefully. Since the confusion resulting from the use of the different term 'form' for a 'smaller'

Formgeschichtle und Texttheoretische Studien zu einer literarischen Gattung. 1. *Methodologische Vorüberlegungen und makrostrukturelle Textanalysis* (ConBNT, 13:1; Lund: C.W.K. Gleerup, 1980), pp. 68-69; and Helmut Köster, 'Formgeschichte/Formenkritik. II. Neues Testament', *TRE*, XI, pp. 286-87. In another work ('The Problem of Apocalyptic Genre', pp. 20-21), Hellholm also distinguishes among 'communication situation', 'mode of writing', 'genre', 'subgenre' and 'form'.

28. Klaus Berger, *Formgeschichte des Neuen Testaments* (Heidelberg: Quelle & Meyer, 1984), p. 9. See Ian H. Henderson ('Gnomic Quatrains in the Synoptics: An Experiment in Genre Definition', *NTS* 37 [1991], pp. 481-98), who also works using this distinction. I, however, view a genre as the 'concept' of a group of texts and read Berger's definition of 'genre' with this in mind.

29. Later literary critics developed this tripartite schema from Aristotle's discussion of three different manners of representing human beings: epic being Aristotle's manner where the narrator proceeds 'partly by narrative and partly by assuming a character other than himself'; lyric where the narrator remains himself 'without any such change'; and drama where 'the characters carry out the whole action themselves' (*Poetics* 3.1-2). See also the discussion of this point in Wellek and Warren, 'Literary Genres', pp. 227-28.

component that is itself a 'genre' has been pointed out and rejected above, the latter approach is presented here.

The critic Thomas Kent, commenting upon literary studies of the folktale, refers to what he calls a 'pure' genre, that is:

> a genre that cannot be reduced to a more fundamental generic category. For example, the fairy tale or dime novel cannot be reduced to a generic category more fundamental than 'fairy tale' or 'dime novel' and still retain its identity as a narrative unit... A pure genre may be reduced to basic narrative or linguistic components, like a scene or a paragraph or image pattern, but it cannot be reduced to another recognizable generic category.[30]

Since a 'brief story'[31] does not contain within itself another *narrative* genre, it is possible to look upon this narrative unit as a 'pure genre'. Hence, the application of the notion 'genre' to a 'brief story' is acceptable.

David Hellholm applies text-linguistic analysis in his studies of the genre of apocalyptic texts. Using text linguistics as applied to the concept of 'chair' to discuss the levels of abstraction of a concept, Hellholm demonstrates a 'hierarchy of concepts' based on the rule: the higher the concept the fewer the characteristics of that concept.[32] He then speaks of the similar process of identifying levels of abstraction of the concept 'genre' as found in literary criticism. These levels are: the 'communication situation'; the 'mode of writing and type of writing', such as the narrative, the epic, the dramatic; the 'genre' or 'historic and concrete realization' of the mode or type of writing, for example, a novel as a historic, concrete realization of the narrative; and, finally, the 'subgenre', that is, the realization of a genre on a lower level of abstraction, such as the 'love-story' as a subgenre of the 'novel'.[33]

In his application of this process to apocalypses, Hellholm identifies two additional levels of abstraction, one between 'mode of writing' and 'genre', namely 'type of text', and another after 'subgenre', namely 'single text'. The schema Hellholm then sketches for a hierarchy of generic concepts with respect to apocalypses, for example, *2 Enoch*, is as follows: *Mode of writing*: narrative; *Type of text*: revelatory writing; *Genre*: apocalypse; *Subgenre*: apocalypse with other-worldly journey (versus apocalypse without other-worldly journey); *Single text*: *2 Enoch*. A similar schema for the Gospel of Mark might read: *Mode of writing*: narrative; *Type of text*:

30. Kent, *Interpretation and Genre*, pp. 67-68.
31. See the definition of 'anecdote' in section 2, p. 20.
32. Hellholm, 'The Problem of Apocalyptic Genre', p. 15.
33. Hellholm, 'The Problem of Apocalyptic Genre', p. 20.

historiography; *Genre*: gospel; *Subgenre*: synoptic; *Single text*: Mark.[34] To include the situation of a 'brief story' within a gospel, one could add yet another lower level of abstraction to the hierarchy. After 'single text' one could add 'component unit', specifying such an entity to be any literary unit in the specific text that is itself an example of a particular genre. For the Gospel of Mark, 'component units' would include such genres as parable, hymn[35] or 'brief story'. The actual hierarchy of generic concepts developed for a single text would depend upon the focus of one's study.

Hellholm's hierarchy of generic concepts clarifies our discussion in that it places the 'brief stories' in Mark's Gospel within a framework of other levels of 'generic abstraction', namely Synoptic Gospel, historiography and narrative; thus, for the Gospel itself one can be clearer upon which literary level a question focuses. Additionally, such a hierarchy provides a reminder that the three elements in any genre-designation, namely content, structure and function, must be identified and held in balance for both the 'larger' and the 'smaller' units.

Keeping in mind this hierarchy of generic concepts, the notion of 'host genre' presented by Heather Dubrow provides a simpler, working, clarification of terms. Despite the fact that Dubrow uses the term 'form' in a sense that I reject, her definition of 'host genre' is useful, that is, 'those forms one of whose roles is to provide a hospitable environment for the other form or forms that are regularly incorporated within them'.[36] David Aune uses the terminology of 'host genre' when he deals with the tension between 'larger' and 'smaller' units in his work on the book of Revelation. Aune discusses the two styles of literary macro-structures in Greek and Roman literature, namely periodic and paratactic. He points out that the paratactic style of a literary work gave it an elastic quality and that 'the inclusion of a wide variety of constituent literary forms within larger, more encompassing "host" or "inclusive" genres became commonplace'.[37]

34. Specifying Mark's Gospel as a 'type' of historiography in this schema follows the identification of Mark's Gospel as an 'apocalyptic historical monograph' developed by Adela Yarbro Collins ('Is Mark's Gospel a Life of Jesus? The Question of Genre', in *The Beginning of the Gospel Probings of Mark in Context* [Philadelphia: Fortress Press, 1992], pp. 1-38 [repr. of *Is Mark's Gospel a Life of Jesus? The Question of Genre* (Pere Marquette Lecture in Theology, 1989; Milwaukee: Marquette University Press, 1990)]).

35. Mk 11.9-10 contains an adaptation of Ps. 118.25-26.

36. Dubrow, *Genre*, p. 16.

37. Aune, 'Apocalypse of John', pp. 80-81.

Adela Yarbro Collins speaks of 'the various *genres* of the Jesus tradition' being integrated into a larger work that itself became a 'host-genre to those smaller forms'.[38]

Instead of employing the terms 'genre' and 'form' or engaging completely in Hellholm's levels of abstraction, I distinguish 'larger' and 'smaller' literary units using 'host genre' and 'genre', respectively. With this clarification, then, it is appropriate to apply the concept 'genre' to the 'brief story' in Mark's Gospel.

There is additional precedent for using the notion of 'genre' for smaller units in biblical studies. After he made the distinction between 'genre' and 'form', Gene Tucker used the term 'genre' to refer to such narratives as the myth, legend and saga.[39] In her 1988 essay, 'Generic Competence in Biblical Hermeneutics', Mary Gerhart uses the term 'genre' to include all levels of categorization, that is, 'large "modes of cognition", such as narrative, philosophical argument, history…science…as well as "major" genres, such as dramas, the epic, the lyric; "sub-genres", such as tragedy, comedy, dialogue; and components of all of these, such as conversation, aphorism, anacoluthon'.[40] The 'brief story' is included in this last grouping of 'components'. Likewise, Ian Henderson, studying a small unit, the 'gnomic quatrain', which occurs seven times in the Synoptic Gospels, has justified the use of genre theory in reference to these brief narrative 'Synoptic sayings-types'.[41]

The concept of genre, then, is essential for a comparison of the literary shapes and functions of the 'brief story' in the three ancient literary worlds under consideration in this book. Genre, as defined above, offers a clearer

38. Adela Yarbro Collins, 'Narrative, History, and Gospel', in Mary Gerhart and James G. Williams (eds.), *Genre, Narrativity, and Theology* (Semeia, 43; Atlanta: Scholars Press, 1988), pp. 145-53 (146), emphasis mine.

39. Tucker, *Form Criticism of the Old Testament*, p. 26.

40. Gerhart, 'Generic Competence', p. 34. This published title of the essay differs from the first heading of the paper, which reads, 'Genric Competence in Biblical Hermeneutics'. From the author's footnote on 'Genric', one wonders if the title is misstated. Gerhart states, 'I use the adjectival form "genric" to emphasize the functions of the concept of genre in interpretation. The conventional form "generic" has come to connote aspects such as non-specificity and common variety, aspects unrelated to the process of interpretation. The term "generic" recalls only the taxonomic function of genre whereas the term "genric" points also to its productive function' (pp. 411-42 n. 1).

41. Henderson, 'Gnomic Quatrains', pp. 481-83.

concept to discuss than the notion 'form' with all its ambiguities. Moreover, in a definition of a particular literary genre, all three elements of a genre, namely content, form and function, must be employed.[42] In the formation of typologies, while all three of these elements should be kept in mind, a typology for a particular genre may be based on just one of these elements, for example, a typology based on 'form'. The notion of genre also allows one to investigate any change, particularly in function, which a narrative unit undergoes when it is incorporated into a host-genre. Finally, genre criticism affords a valid method of cross-cultural comparison of a given genre. Thus, a literary critical approach based on the concept of genre offers a background for the critique of past definitions and typologies, both ancient and modern, of 'brief stories' and is a necessary background to evaluate critically the methods and the conclusions of scholarship on these narrative units.

2. *The Anecdote—a Definition*

As a designation for the literary genre of the 'brief story' I employ the term 'anecdote'. The *Oxford English Dictionary* gives the following definitions for the term 'anecdote': '1. *pl.* Secret, private, or hitherto unpublished narratives or details of history... 2. The narrative of a detached incident, or of a single event, told as being in itself interesting or striking.'[43] The first definition referring to 'secret' or 'unpublished narratives' reflects the etymology of the word 'anecdote'. Our English word is adopted from the French word *anecdote*, which itself derives from the Greek ἀνέκδοτος. *A Greek–English Lexicon* gives 'unpublished' as the second meaning of ἀνέκδοτος (the first meaning being 'not given in

42. On this point see the excellent remarks of Coates ('Introduction: Genres: Why Should They Be Important?', pp. 13-14): 'If a genre observation isolates characteristics that are fundamentally a part of the unit under consideration, and if those characteristics can be identified in other pieces of literature, then the common patterns of the pieces can come to light. Moreover, the common patterns will show a tendency for the genre, a tendency that illuminates the typical function of the genre. The student of exegesis can then ask whether the particular piece under investigation also reveals the generic function or some distinct, unique function. These fruits open the particular intention of the piece, and they arise primarily from investigation of genre.'

43. *The Oxford English Dictionary* (ed. J.A. Simpson and E.S.C. Weiner; Oxford: Clarendon Press, 2nd edn, 1989), p. 454.

marriage').[44] ἀνέκδοτος, in turn, is derived from the privative ἀ(ν) prefixed to the Greek verb ἐκδίδωμι, 'to give out', which, mainly in the passive, means 'to put out, to publish'.[45]

The second English usage of anecdote, that of a 'narrative of a detached incident', apparently grew out of the original meaning of the word. Procopius used the term for his 'Unpublished Memoirs' of the Emperor Justinian. Since these memoirs contained many stories of the private life of the court, the term 'anecdote' came to be applied to short stories.[46] This second English definition of anecdote is useful as a designation for the literary genre of the narrative units under discussion. I note, however, that the word ἀνέκδοτος did not have the usage of 'narrative of a detached incident' in antiquity.[47] This is a later usage, which I use as an 'umbrella' term with which to name the various manifestations of the genre 'brief story' in the cultural worlds of antiquity.

With further refinements to suit the context of this study, the following is a definition of the literary genre 'anecdote':

> a brief narrative, either oral or written, describing an incident, including its setting, which involves one or more persons and which focuses on an action, saying, or dialogue; the function of an anecdote is to entertain, instruct, relate an historical incident, characterize a person, or authoritatively

44. *A Greek–English Lexicon* (compilers Henry G. Liddell and Robert Scott; revised and augmented by Henry S. Jones; Oxford: Clarendon Press, supplemented 9th edn, 1968), p. 131, col. 1 (hereafter LSJ). Ancient evidence of ἀνέκδοτος, used in the sense of 'unpublished material', can be found in the writing of the first century BCE historian, Diodorus of Sicily, *Bib. Hist.* 1.4.6; Cicero also uses the Greek word ἀνέκδοτον in his correspondence with Atticus, *Att.* 14.17.

45. LSJ, p. 504, col. 2. This usage is attested in the writings of Isocrates, *Philippus* 11 and in Aristotle, *Poetics* 15.12. For ἀνέκδοτος as 'unpublished writings' see Diogenes Laertius, 'Lyco', *Lives Phil.* 5.73.4.

46. *Oxford English Dictionary*, p. 453.

47. This despite modern references to Momigliano's statement: 'Perhaps he [Aristoxenus, fourth century BCE] was also the first to make anecdotes an essential part of biography… I suspect that we owe to Aristoxenus the notion that a good biography is full of good anecdotes' (Arnaldo Momigliano, *The Development of Greek Biography* [Cambridge, MA: Harvard University Press, 1971], p. 76). Momigliano never defines what he means by 'anecdote'. Furthermore, it is clear from the fact that he gives Aristotle's descriptive characterization of Hippodamus (*Politics* 2.5.1-4) as an example of an anecdote (p. 69) that Momigliano does not have in mind a restriction of the term 'anecdote' to a 'brief story'. See references to Momigliano's statement in Joseph Epstein, 'Literary Biography', *The New Criterion* 1 (1983), pp. 27-37 (32), and Clifton Fademan, 'Introduction', p. xiii.

> legitimate a specific opinion, a specific practice, or a broader view of reality.[48]

a. *Brief Narrative, Oral or Written*

Some clarifying comments on this definition are in order here. First, what is meant by a 'narrative'? Literary critics Holman and Harmon characterize 'narrative' as an 'account of events' and distinguish between 'simple narratives' that describe events chronologically and 'narratives with a plot', often arranged according to a principle determined by the plot rather than chronologically.[49] An anecdote is an account of a single episode and differs from other narratives, such as the short story, in that it lacks a plot, that is, 'the outline of the events'.[50] Even though the anecdote lacks a plot, it does exhibit a completeness; any passage of time indicated in the single episode is likely to be perceived as chronological because of this completeness. Hence, the anecdote can be classified as a simple narrative.

The notions of 'story' and 'story-teller' are included in the definition of narrative given by Scholes and Kellogg, that is, 'By narrative we mean all those literary works which are distinguished by two characteristics: the presence of a story and a story-teller.'[51] Unfortunately, these critics do not define what they mean by 'story' or 'story-teller'; they presume a shared understanding of these terms with their readers.

The narrative structure laid out by Seymour Chatman in his *Story and Discourse* contains a careful discussion of both 'story' and 'story-teller' or 'author'. Using structuralist theory,[52] Chatman first distinguishes between 'story' and 'discourse' as follows:

> Structuralist theory argues that each narrative has two parts: a story (*histoire*), the content or chain of events (actions, happenings), plus what may be called existents (characters, items of setting); and a discourse (*discours*), that is, the expression, the means by which the content is communicated.[53]

48. This definition of anecdote was developed with the assistance of Adela Yarbro Collins.

49. Holman and Harmon, *Handbook*, p. 308.

50. Robert Scholes and Robert Kellogg, *The Nature of Narrative* (New York: Oxford University Press, 1966), p. 12. This definition of 'plot' is based on Aristotle's definition in his *Poetics* 6.8. Scholes and Kellogg further develop the concept of 'plot' to show that it is 'the dynamic, sequential element in narrative literature' (p. 207).

51. Scholes and Kellogg, *Nature of Narrative*, p. 4.

52. Seymour Chatman, *Story and Discourse*, p. 20. Chatman cites the French structuralist Claude Bremond ('Le message narratif', *Communications* 4 [1964], pp. 4-32).

53. Chatman, *Story and Discourse*, p. 19.

The story, then, is the *what*, while the discourse is the *how*. Furthermore, the story exists only at the abstract level.[54] Any communication of this story moves to the concrete level of discourse. It is important to see a story, its oral expression and its written expression as three distinct notions. In the definition of anecdote given above, the incident is the story and the 'anecdote' is the expression or discourse. The phrase 'either oral or written' refers to the discourse level of a story, to its oral expression or to its written expression. The incident itself, however, is equivalent to neither the oral anecdote nor the written anecdote. Additionally, the oral expression of a story and the written expression of that story are distinct entities; hence, one needs to distinguish between the oral anecdote and the written anecdote. They need not be the same.

Chatman's study of narrative literature contains detailed comments on the notion of the 'story-teller'. Working with what he notes is 'a commonplace of literary theory', Chatman first distinguishes between the real author of a narrative, that is, the historical person who speaks or writes a narrative, and the 'narrator'. The narrator is the 'speaker' within a literary text whom the reader hears as she or he moves through the text.[55] For example, in the anecdote from Mark cited in the Introduction above (7.1-2, 5, 14-15), the real author is the evangelist and the narrator is that 'someone' within the text who is telling the reader that the Pharisees and scribes asked a question of Jesus. The real author has created this narrator. In the case of oral discourse, such as the relating of an anecdote, the author and the narrator can be one and the same person, or a narrator may be relating an anecdote learned from another. Even in the latter instance the narrator is an 'author' in the sense of interpreter, if only through voice inflection and/or gesture.[56]

Embedded in the general concept of the 'story-teller' of a narrative is a third notion, that which Wayne Booth has called the 'implied author'.[57]

54. Chatman, *Story and Discourse*, p. 37.

55. Chatman, *Story and Discourse*, pp. 147-48; see also his Chapter 4, 'Discourse: Nonnarrated Stories', and Chapter 5, 'Discourse: Covert Versus Overt Narrators'.

56. With regard to the gospel parables, Bernard Brandon Scott comments that the actual words of Jesus' parables would not have been remembered, but rather their structure. He continues: 'Traditional storytellers, preachers, teachers, and evangelists were not simply passive memory receptacles but performers, shaping and adapting the structure in a concrete performance' (*Hear Then the Parable: A Commentary on the Parables of Jesus* [Philadelphia: Fortress Press, 1989], p. 40).

57. Wayne C. Booth, *The Rhetoric of Fiction* (Chicago: University of Chicago Press, 2nd edn, 1983), esp. pp. 70-77.

This is the abstract, literary version of himself or herself that the author creates and which the reader reconstructs from the narrative. Chatman writes, 'We can grasp the notion of implied author most clearly by comparing different narratives written by the same real author but presupposing different implied authors.'[58] In this respect, the author and the 'implied author' are much like an actress and the characters she portrays. An actor can convincingly portray several different characters, none of whom exactly matches the historical person of the actor himself or herself.[59]

The contemporary concept of the implied author may be compared to the ἦθος of a speaker in ancient rhetorical theory. In Aristotle's *Rhetoric* one reads, 'The orator persuades by ἦθος when his speech is delivered in such a manner as to render him worthy of confidence…this confidence must be due to the speech itself, not to any preconceived idea of the speaker's character' (1.2.4).[60] During a speech or oral presentation the hearer can project a 'persona' onto the speaker based simply on the speech. Hence, it is possible to speak of the 'implied author' as present in both written and oral narratives.

In the anecdote in Mk 7.1-2, 5, 14-15, a reader would sense that the implied author knew the Pharisaic concept of ritual purity and the food laws. The author, through the narrator, explains that 'defiled' (κοινός) hands are 'unwashed' (ἄνιπτος) hands. The narrator's comments continue in the next two verses (not cited in the Introduction), which read:

> [3]For the Pharisees and all the Jews do not eat unless they wash their hands thoroughly, since they observe the tradition of the elders [4]also they do not eat things from the marketplace unless they wash them; and there are many other observances which they have inherited, such as the washing of cups, pots, and copper vessels.

It is clear that the author of the gospel presents himself as one who is knowledgeable of these Jewish practices.

In general, however, the anecdote is a relatively short genre. Thus, when one is dealing with these narrative units it may be difficult to discern a

58. Chatman, *Story and Discourse*, p. 148. Here he cites Wayne Booth's example of three works of Henry Fielding that have clearly different implied authors (see Booth, *The Rhetoric of Fiction*, p. 72).

59. On this point one can consider the actress Lily Tomlin and the cast of characters she portrays in her enactment of Jane Wagner's *The Search for Signs of Intelligent Life in the Universe*.

60. See also 'Implied Author' in Holman and Harmon (*Handbook*, p. 243): '[E]thos is the image of the speaker projected by the speech itself.'

great deal about the implied author, for example, the anecdote cited from Lucian's *Demonax* in the Introduction. When an anecdote is contained within a host genre, however, its placement as well as the selection and arrangement of other anecdotes or small genres will also reveal the implied author.[61]

A story and a story-teller presuppose an audience. Here again one must distinguish among the narratee, the implied hearer or reader and the real hearer or reader. The narratee is that person to whom the narrator is thought to be addressing her or his remarks. The narratee may be a character in the narrative or, more often, the narratee is a stand-in for an implied hearer or reader. Like the implied author, the implied hearer or reader is a construct and is immanent to the text. The implied hearer or reader is envisaged as a member of the audience presupposed by the narrative itself, responding to the text at every point. The real hearer or reader, on the other hand, is any flesh and blood person, outside the narrative transaction, who actually hears or reads the narrative.[62] In the Markan anecdote discussed above, the narratee is a stand-in for the implied reader. The anecdote itself presupposes a Greek-speaking reader who may not be familiar with Jewish purification laws and customs. The real reader of this anecdote is anyone reading or hearing the anecdote at any time. This may be a first-century person, even a contemporary person.

This rather lengthy discussion of the concept of narrative can be summarized in the following citation from Chatman:

> Narratives are communications…from author to audience. But we must distinguish between real and implied authors and audiences: only implied authors and audiences are immanent to the work, constructs of the narrative-transaction-as-text. The real author and audience of course communicate, but only through their implied counterparts. What is communicated is *story*, the formal content of narrative; and it is communicated by *discourse*, the formal expression element.[63]

61. In regard to implied author and Mark's Gospel see Mary Ann Tolbert, *Sowing the Gospel: Mark's World in Literary-Historical Perspective* (Philadelphia: Fortress Press, 1989), pp. 51-52, and Robert Fowler, *Let the Reader Understand: Reader-Response Criticism and the Gospel of Mark* (Philadelphia: Fortress Press, 1991), pp. 61-154.

62. See the discussion of these distinctions in Chatman. *Story and Discourse*, pp. 149-51. See also Robert Fowler, 'The Implied Reader of the Gospel of Mark', in *Loaves and Fishes: The Function of the Feeding Stories in the Gospel of Mark* (SBLDS, 54; Chico, CA: Scholars Press, 1981), pp. 149-57.

63. Chatman, *Story and Discourse*, p. 31.

What then of a 'brief' narrative? In his book, *Hear Then the Parable*, Bernard Brandon Scott defines a parable as 'a *mashal* that employs a short narrative fiction to reference a symbol'.[64] Scott mentions the lack of precision in the term 'short' and proceeds to ask, 'When does a story become so long that it is no longer a parable?' He notes, '"Short" hints at the primarily oral character of parables. The parables are among the smallest complete narrative units of oral tradition.' Scott then designates 'short' as 'what one can hold in the ear, much like a joke'.[65] It is obvious that Scott's characterization of 'short' is derived from his understanding of the oral background of parables. It is argued that the genre 'anecdote', with its limitation to a single incident, fits the observations of Scott regarding the parable, that is, an anecdote is a small, complete narrative unit often used in oral communication. Therefore, 'brief' in the definition of an anecdote is also that 'size' of a story that 'one can hold in one's ear'.

b. *Incident, Person(s) or Character(s), Setting*

The next elements of the definition of anecdote that necessitate discussion are 'incident', 'person(s)' and 'setting'. In exploring the meaning of the term 'incident' one is speaking on the story level of the narrative structure. What is an incident? *Webster's* defines it as 'an occurrence of an action or situation felt as a separate unit of experience'.[66] Keeping in mind the time-dimension of an incident, that is, a 'separate unit of experience', Chatman's concept of story as 'event' is helpful to this discussion. He posits that an 'event' is either an 'action' where a person brings about a change of state, or a 'happening' in which a change of state affects a person. The person involved in an action is called an 'agent'; the one involved in a happening is referred to as a 'patient'. Chatman includes in actions the speech, thoughts and feelings attributed to a person.[67] An incident, then, may be described as a separate event, on the level of story, that is either an action or a happening. On the level of discourse, an anecdote is the narrative expression of an incident.

On the level of story one speaks of person(s), on the level of discourse

64. Scott, *Hear Then the Parable*, p. 35.

65. Scott, *Hear Then the Parable*, p. 35. One wonders if Scott is influenced in his notion of 'short' by the comments of Quintilian on the *sententia*, 'short, witty saying', i.e., 'their brevity makes them cling to the memory' (*Inst.* 12.10.48).

66. *Webster's New Third International Dictionary*, p. 575. See also 'Episode', in Holman and Harmon, *Handbook*, pp. 174-75.

67. Chatman, *Story and Discourse*, pp. 44-45.

one speaks of 'character(s)'. 'Character' here is taken to mean 'one of the persons of a drama or a novel'.[68] 'Character' also includes any group of persons who are presented as a single entity, such as 'the Pharisees and some of the scribes' or 'the crowd' of the anecdote in Mk 7.1-2, 5, 14-15. The anecdote is a relatively brief and simple genre, hence two uses of 'character' found in literary criticism are excluded in this study: the more abstract use of 'character' as an idea of the moral constitution of the human personality[69] and Chatman's use of 'character' as a designation applied to an 'agent' or a 'patient' only when the action involving that person is 'plot significant'.[70]

On the level of the narrative discourse of an anecdote, one also encounters the notion of 'setting'. Setting describes the 'space' of an event; it is the narrative background against which the action takes place.[71] This background information may contain descriptions or allusions to an occasion, physical space, occupations or manner of living, time periods or general environment. An anecdote, as defined above, must then contain some indication of the background of the character's actions or sayings.

Since the occasion of the speech is presented, the following incident from Plutarch's *Cato the Elder* fits the definition of an anecdote: 'He once wished to dissuade the Roman people from insisting unseasonably upon a distribution of corn, and began his speech with these words: "It is a hard matter, my fellow citizens, to argue with the belly, since it has no ears"' (*Cat. Maj.* 8.1). However, in the same work one reads of Cato, 'Wise men, he said, profited more from fools than fools from wise men; for the wise shun the mistakes of fools, but fools do not imitate the successes of the wise' (9.4). This narrative contains no hint of a setting. Hence, it is not an anecdote, but rather an attributed saying.

c. *Action, Saying, Dialogue*

An anecdote focuses on an action, saying, or a dialogue. Action here is taken as a change of state and includes both Chatman's definition of 'action' and his definition of 'happening'. Thus, an anecdote may focus on a change of state where a character is either an 'agent' or a 'patient'. The

68. *Webster's New Collegiate Dictionary* (Springfield, MA: G. & C. Merriam Company, 1981), p. 185.

69. See Holman and Harmon, *Handbook*, pp. 78-79.

70. Chatman, *Story and Discourse*, p. 44.

71. Holman and Harmon, *Handbook*, p. 440. See also Chatman, *Story and Discourse*, pp. 138-45.

narrative focus may also be a saying attributed to one of the characters and this saying may be reported in either direct or indirect speech. Additionally, the narrative may center on a dialogue between two or more characters. Furthermore, an anecdote may contain a combination of the above foci. For example, the anecdote from *m. 'Abodah Zarah* cited in the Introduction contains a dialogue and an action, both of which are essential to the narrative.

The three possible foci of an anecdote assist one in a discussion of the levels of communication within the narrative. Cilliers Breytenbach discusses such levels in his essay, 'The Gospel of Mark as Episodical Narrative'.[72] He identifies four narrative levels of communication present in Mark's text, namely: the normal level of narration of facts between narrator and implied reader;[73] the meta-narrative level 'where the narrative is interpreted, elucidated, or underlined' by the narrator for the implied reader; the embedded level, that is, the level of communication between characters of the narrative, such as a dialogue; and finally, the level of direct speech.[74] The level of direct speech is that level where a character is cited directly in her or his speech to another character in the narrative, but where this speech is also directed to the implied reader. Breytenbach admits that it is difficult to separate this fourth level sharply from the embedded level.[75]

The anecdote in Mk 7.1-15 serves as an excellent example of these four levels of communication. The presentation of the characters and their actions found in vv. 1, 5a and 14a represents the first level, the narration of facts from the narrator to the reader. On the other hand, the explanations given the reader in vv. 3 and 4 and the aside in 11d function on the meta-narrative level.[76] The anecdote presents a dialogue between the 'Pharisees

72. Cilliers Breytenbach, 'The Gospel of Mark as Episodical Narrative: Reflections on the "Composition" of the Second Gospel', *Scriptura* S (special issue) 4 (1989; German original, 1985), pp. 171-97.

73. Although Breytenbach initially uses the term 'reader', further on in his discussion he clarifies that this is the 'implied reader' ('Mark as Episodical Narrative', p. 17). As noted above, the narratee is often a stand-in for the implied reader.

74. Breytenbach, 'Mark as Episodical Narrative', pp. 16-18, esp. p. 16.

75. Breytenbach, 'Mark as Episodical Narrative', p. 16. Breytenbach gives as one criterion that an entire pericope may be viewed as an insertion into the narrative sequence and hence the communication may be viewed as direct speech to the reader. However, his 'insertion' argument is weak.

76. Verses 3 and 4 read: '[3] For the Pharisees and all the Jews do not eat unless they wash their hands thoroughly, since they observe the tradition of the elders [4]also they do

and some of the scribes' (taken together as a single character) and Jesus in vv. 5 through 13 which are used on the embedded level. The first level communication of v. 14a, 'And calling the crowd again, he said to them', signals a change in narrative levels.[77] The remarks of Jesus to the crowd move from the preceding embedded level of the dialogue to the level of direct speech, where the remarks are also directed to the implied reader. Thus, in this instance, the crowd is a stand-in for the implied reader.

Furthermore, the levels of communication in Mk 7.1-15 enable one to see a relationship between the focus of an anecdote and the level of communication present within it. As stated above, the three possible foci of an anecdote are action, saying and dialogue. With respect to the levels of communication one can posit the following relationships: the description of an action indicates the level of narration of facts; the report of a saying, if reported indirectly is on the level of narration of facts, while if reported directly it may be the level of direct speech; and the account of a dialogue indicates the embedded level. The example of Mk 7.1-15 further illustrates the possibility of combined foci and combined levels of communication. Finally, the relationship between the focus of an anecdote and the level of communication present may offer important clues to the function of an anecdote within a host-genre.

d. *Function*

The final element in the definition of an anecdote to be clarified is that of 'function'. In general, what does it mean to inquire about the 'function' of a genre? David Hellholm's text-linguistic approach begins by asking about the function of a concept. He points out that the function of a concept encompasses both 'for whom' it functions and 'what way' or 'how' it functions.[78] Both of these aspects are related to the 'communication situation' of a genre. Hellholm describes the communication situation as those

not eat things from the marketplace unless they wash them; and there are many other observances which they have inherited, such as the washing of cups, pots, and copper vessels'. Verses 6, 10-12 read: '[6]He said to them, "Rightly did Isaiah prophesy of you hypocrites... [10]For Moses said, 'Honor your father and your mother'; and, 'Whoever speaks evil of father or mother, let him surely die'. [11]But you say, 'If anyone tells father or mother, whatever support you might have received from me is Corban'" (that is, a gift to God) [12]"then you no longer allow that person to do anything for father or mother..."'

77. See Breytenbach, 'Mark as Episodical Narrative', p. 16, where he discusses the use of narrative sentences to indicate a change in narrative level.

78. Hellholm, 'Problem of Apocalyptic Genre', p. 17.

'factors characterizing the relationship between a sender and a receiver in which a speech-act is carried out'.[79] In the field of biblical scholarship, Hellholm posits that the concept of *Sitz im Leben*, that is, the social setting within Israel or the early Church, is roughly equivalent to the communication situation.[80] In both the communication situation and the *Sitz im Leben* one is referring to an aspect of the story-telling situation. Therefore, the 'social setting' of a narrative genre should not be confused with the background setting of an incident described within the narrative itself.

Given a particular narrative genre, is it always possible to determine that narrative's social setting? Christopher Tuckett questions what he calls a 'fundamental axiom' of biblical form criticism, that is, 'that there is a correlation between the way in which a unit of tradition is told, its form and the type of situation where it is being used'.[81] Tuckett criticizes the assumption on which the application of this principle is based, namely that there is always, or usually, a one-to-one correspondence between a particular genre and a specific *Sitz im Leben.* To counter this assumption, he points out that a cultic situation can give rise to hymns, creeds, etc. and that a hymn can function also within a paraenetic letter.[82]

Tuckett's point is legitimate in regard to what I have been naming 'small' genres, and hence in the case of an anecdote. On this point, I am reminded of a lecture I attended recently. The presenter regularly used an anecdote as a transition device to move to the next topic of his lecture. One of these anecdotes reported an incident involving a certain rabbi who, when approached by the speaker, collected money for a needy graduate student thus enabling the student to avoid a burdensome bank loan. This particular anecdote may have first been related as an example of the communitarian aspect of contemporary Judaism. It may just as easily have

79. Hellholm, 'Problem of Apocalyptic Genre', p. 20.

80. On *Sitz im Leben*, see Richard N. Soulen, *Handbook of Biblical Criticism* (Atlanta: John Knox Press, 2nd edn, 1981), pp. 178-79.

81. Christopher Tuckett, *Reading the New Testament: Methods of Interpretaion* (Philadelphia: Fortress Press, 1987), p. 95. It should be noted that Bultmann (*Geschichte der synoptischen Tradition*, p. 395; English: p. 370), in reference to the transmission of oral tradition and its 'forms', says: '[I]t is difficult to say which precise pieces of tradition [i.e. 'forms'] played a role in the concrete situations of the community.' See also the critique of the search for a specific *Sitz im Leben* by Douglas A. Knight, ('The Understanding of "*Sitz im Leben*" in Form Criticism', in George MacRae [ed.], *SBL Seminar Papers 1974* [ed. George MacRae; 2 vols.; Cambridge, MA: Scholars Press, 1974], I, pp. 105-25 [112-17]).

82. Tuckett, *Reading the New Testament*, p. 100.

originated in a situation where the life of the rabbi involved was being commemorated and praised.

For a narrative genre, it is possible to posit an equivalence between the 'for whom' of a narrative unit and its 'implied reader or hearer', including that reader or hearer's circumstances. Likewise, the 'what way' or 'how' relates to the intention of the implied author.[83] Once again, however, given the brevity of the anecdote, these equivalences do not necessarily enable one to move to the actual story-telling situation of a particular anecdote.

For the independent anecdote, then, it is difficult, if not impossible, to pinpoint the original story-telling situation. However, drawing upon life experience one can say that the author's intention is generally one of those purposes given in the above definition of anecdote, namely 'to entertain, instruct, relate an historical incident, characterize a person, or authoritatively legitimate a specific opinion, a specific practice, or a broader view of reality'. This is as close as one can come to the function of an anecdote as an independent narrative unit.

The function of an anecdote must be discussed separately for the case where the anecdote appears as a component of a host genre. The anecdote within a host genre takes on the story-telling situation or the communication situation of the host work. Thus, the implied reader or hearer of the anecdote is the implied reader or hearer of the whole work. Moreover, while the authorial intention for a component-anecdote includes the intention of the work as a whole, the component-anecdote may have a specific literary function within the larger composition that differs from its originating function. For example, in the *Mishnah* one finds anecdotes that serve the purpose of legitimating, by the authority of a named rabbi, a previously stated legal lemma. Such an anecdote is found in *m. Kil.* 4.9 B-E.[84] Further study shows that this anecdote had an independent existence, since the content of the anecdote does not match completely the content of

83. See also Coates, 'Introduction: Genres', p. 13.

84. *m. Kilaim* 4.9 A-E: 'A. He who plants his vineyard by [intervals of] sixteen *amah*, sixteen *amah* [in rows sixteen *amoth* apart]—it is permitted to put seed into it [the area between the rows.] B. Said R. Judah, "*M'SH B*: In Salmon one planted his vineyard by [intervals of] sixteen *amah*", C. "and he would turn the foliage of two rows to one side and sow the cleared land." D. "And in the next year he would turn the foliage to another place [to the area which he had sown in the previous year] and sow the uncultivated land." E. "And the case came before the sages and they permitted [his actions]"' (*Mishnah*, trans. Neusner), p. 58. See also Irving Mandelbaum, *A History of the Mishnaic Law of Agriculture: Kilayim* (BJS, 26; Chico, CA: Scholars Press, 1982), pp. 158-61.

the preceding lemma (4.9A).[85] There is no way of knowing the exact setting of the original anecdote; however, in this tractate it is specifically cited to provide an authoritative opinion and serves one of the authorial intentions of the editor(s) of the *Mishnah*.

In an anecdote, then, one encounters a brief narrative genre that appears both independently and as a unit within a host-genre. Both the definition of anecdote given above and the accompanying comments are construed so as to permit a cross-cultural comparison of a similar genre.

3. *The Anecdote in Modern Literary Studies*

In modern literary studies, comments on the anecdote occur in the scholarship of literary critics and that of folklorists. Many English-speaking literary critics give only passing reference to the anecdote, with no detailed discussion. For example, J.A. Cuddon tersely describes an anecdote as ‘a brief account of or a story about an individual or an incident’.[86] An often cited study, *The Anatomy of the Anecdote* by Louis Brownlow, is almost ‘anecdotal’ in its treatment of the literary genre. Brownlow approaches a definition of anecdote in the following:

> The anecdote does demand the classic unity of a beginning, a middle, and an end, but it finds its beginning in the memories and minds of its hearers, devises no plot for its middle and, therefore, needs no dénouement for its end. For its end it needs only the jolt of ‘finis’—with sometimes a little after-play for savor.[87]

Brownlow makes no further remarks on the anecdote as a literary entity; instead, he proceeds to detail the story of why and how he came to write his book.

An exception to this cursory treatment of the anecdote is the much earlier, 1793, treatise of Isaac D’Israeli, *Dissertation on Anecdotes*.[88] This long essay is D’Israeli’s attempt to persuade his contemporaries to treat

85. The anecdote does not concern the space between the rows as does 4.9 A, but rather the turning of the foliage of the vines.

86. J.A. Cuddon, ‘anecdote’, in *A Dictionary of Literary Terms and Literary Theory* (Oxford: Basil Blackwell, 3rd edn, 1991), p. 42. See the brief remarks on anecdote in Abrams, *Glossary*, p. 73, and Holman and Harmon, *Handbook*, p. 23.

87. Louis Brownlow, *The Anatomy of the Anecdote* (Chicago: University of Chicago Press, 1960), p. 2.

88. Isaac D’Israeli, *Dissertation on Anecdotes* (facsimile copy; New York: Garland Publishing, 1972) (original: London: Kearsley and Murray, 1793).

the anecdote as a serious literary entity. He 'defines' the anecdote as 'a minute notice of human nature and of human learning'.[89] In addition to amusement, the author presents the following functions of the anecdote: to illustrate the history of manners; to discover the character of eminent persons; to become acquainted with human nature; to lead one's mind into reflection; to illustrate literary themes; to strengthen opinion; and to enliven writing.[90] D'Israeli's essay is influential even today;[91] the essay, however, lacks attention to the content and the form, or structure, of an anecdote.

The most straightforward discussion of the anecdote among English-speaking scholars is the work of Lawrence Epstein. In his 'Introduction' to *A Treasury of Jewish Anecdotes*, Epstein defines the anecdote as 'a story with a point. The story is a brief account of a biographical incident. It is usually about a famous person and often reveals a little known aspect of the person's life.'[92] The last phrase of his definition of anecdote reflects the etymology of the word anecdote. With regard to the functions of an anecdote, Epstein paraphrases those given by D'Israeli and adds, 'Anecdotes humanize individuals and turn abstract concepts into concrete ones. They make complex ideas immediately clear.'[93] The author continues with a discussion of the content of anecdotes, that is, the historicity and the significance of the material narrated in anecdotes. The value of Epstein's discussion, although brief, is both its clarity and its pursuit of a genre-study of the anecdote, that is, a study of its form, content and function.

A German critic, Jürgen Hein, provides a straightforward generic study of the anecdote. Noting the difficulties in the definition of the anecdote, he points out that these difficulties are due, in part, to the original meaning of the Greek word ἀνέκδοτος and to the relationship of the oral anecdote to the written anecdote.[94] To overcome the difficulty encountered in defining

89. D'Israeli, *Dissertation on Anecdotes*, pp. 80-81.

90. D'Israeli, *Dissertation on Anecdotes*, pp. 6-67.

91. See Fademan, 'Introduction', pp. xiii-xxii.

92. Lawrence Epstein, *A Treasury of Jewish Anecdotes* (Northvale, NJ: J. Aronson, 1989), p. xix.

93. Epstein, *A Treasury of Jewish Anecdotes*, p. xix.

94. Jürgen Hein, 'Die Anekdote', in Otto Knörrich (ed.), *Formen der Literatur in Einzeldarstellugen* (Stuttgart: Alfred Kröner, 1981), pp. 14-20 (14). Hein notes other difficulties as well, namely the anecdote's use in historiography and biography as well as in epic short genres, for example, the novella; the relationship of the poetic anecdote to the published anecdote; and the attempt to determine 'inner' criteria of form for the anecdote (p. 14). See also the earlier German monograph of Heinz Grothe, *Anekdote*

the anecdote, Hein presents some 'recurrent criteria' for an anecdote. These criteria include: a differentiated incident, a lesser occurrence of special realism; a claimed historic dimension; the characterization of a well-known, usually historical personality; a dramatically shaped action or saying; a clever or humorous structure to the narrative; and an incident that often has political significance.[95]

In a summary paragraph, the author presents what is clearly a generic definition of an anecdote, namely:

> the anecdote is a short prose form originating in and transmitted through a social, story-telling situation. It narrates, in a pivotal manner, an historically true or possible, humanly significant event to which it corresponds in substance, form, and speech. Its functions extend from plain, social entertainment...through a narrative of a piece of advice or information...up to the symbolic or critical presentation of a characteristic situation of human nature, history, or society.[96]

An investigation of the anecdote in folklore studies reveals that formal genre-studies, as literary critics know them, are only recently finding their way into the scholarship of folklorists.[97] In 1970, the folklorist Archer Taylor wrote an essay entitled 'The Anecdote: A Neglected Genre'.[98] Taylor speaks of the anecdote as 'narrative folk tradition of its own special kind', and provides a definition of the anecdote, that is, 'a brief narrative current in oral tradition that tells something unusual about a person, an event, or a thing. It may involve quotation of a witty remark or description of a remarkable situation.'[99] Taylor devotes the remainder of his essay to a comparison of the anecdote with the *Märchen* (folk tale), the German *Sage* (local legend) and the *Witz* (joke). Regrettably, he provides no clear

(Realien zur Literatur, Sammlung Metzler B, 101; Stuttgart: J.B. Metzlersche, 1971), esp. pp. 5-10.

95. Hein, 'Die Anekdote', p. 15.

96. Hein, 'Die Anekdote', p. 18.

97. See Dan Ben-Amos, 'Introduction', in *Folklore Genres* (Bibliographical and Special Series [Publications of the American Folklore Society], 26; Austin: University of Texas Press, 1976), pp. x-xvii. Here Ben-Amos chronicles the use of the notion of genre from the beginning of folklore studies with the initial collections of folklore 'types'. He points out, however, that this use of a genre-notion served as a means of classification and did not represent a critical use of the concept of genre.

98. Archer Taylor, 'The Anecdote: A Neglected Genre', in Jerome Mandel and Bruce A. Rosenburg (eds.), *Medieval Literature and Folklore Studies: Essays in Honor of Francis Lee Utley* (New Brunswick, NJ: Rutgers University Press, 1970), pp. 223-28.

99. Taylor, 'The Anecdote', p. 223.

distinctions among these genres and offers no conclusions from this comparison for the study of the anecdote.[100]

'Folk Narrative', a 1972 essay by Linda Dégh, begins with a definition of folk narratives as 'all genres of oral literature in prose'.[101] Dégh also writes of the difficulties one encounters in developing a typology for oral narratives:

> Because of their oral existence, narrative genres float in an unlimited number of variants around a limited number of plots. Hence a perfect classification based on form, content, and function would hardly be possible... Identical stories can be found within different genres. They may be shaped into fictitious, credible, revered, or ridiculed treatments. What is a tale for one culture may be an origin legend for another...[102]

Mindful of these limitations, Dégh develops a threefold typology for these oral narratives consisting of tale genres, legend genres and true experience stories.[103] Under the genre 'tales' one finds two subgenres, namely complex tales and simple tales. The anecdote appears, grouped with the joke, in the second category of simple tales. Dégh defines the anecdote as follows: '[It] characterizes a person, a memorable event, or a place through a representative personal episode. As a brief and funny experience story it resembles a *Schwank* [longer humorous narrative] not fully developed...'[104] The remainder of her comments in this section relate to *der Schwank.*[105] The narrow focus the author gives to the function of an anecdote, that is, its role in humor, is repeated in her section on the true experience story. There Dégh states, 'Humorous stories bear a strong resemblance to improvised anecdotes but are usually narrower, centering

100. Evidently, Taylor's work was meant only to present the need for a further, full-scale study of the anecdote and not provide such a study. Early in the essay, after his definition of anecdote, he writes: 'I leave the task of a more elaborate definition to another occasion or another hand' ('The Anecdote', p. 224).

101. Linda Dégh, 'Folk Narrative', in Richard M. Dorson (ed.), *Folklore and Folklife: An Introduction* (Chicago: University of Chicago Press, 1972), pp. 53-83 (58).

102. Dégh, 'Folk Narrative', p. 59.

103. In constructing her own typology, Dégh comments upon and reworks the well-known motif-based typology presented by Aarne and Thompson. See Antti Aarne and Stith Thompson, *The Types of the Folk-Tale: A Classification and Bibliography* (Folklore Fellows Communications, 184; Helsinki: Suomalainen Tiedeakatemia, Academia Scientarum Fennica, 1961), cited by Dégh ('Folk Narrative', p. 60 and *passim*).

104. Dégh, 'Folk Narrative', p. 70.

105. *der Schwank* is a German term used in literary criticism. See Cuddon, *Dictionary of Literary Terms*, p. 594.

on one comic incident.'[106] Her limiting of the oral anecdote to a comical or humorous function weakens Dégh's presentation of the anecdote.

For the most part, folklore studies of narratives are dealing with oral expressions. Folklorists are interested not only in the somewhat 'fluid' genres of oral narratives, but also in the origins of such genres. An important work for both literary critics and folklorists is André Jolles's *Einfache Formen.*[107] Jolles studies what he termed the 'einfache Formen', the simple or primary genres of the *Legend* (religious legend), *Sage* (local legend), *Myth, Rätsel* (riddle), *Spruch* (saying, proverb), *Kasus* (moral case), *Memorabile* (report of a fact), *Märchen* (folktale) and *Witz* (joke).

Jolles sought to classify these basic genres of oral folk narratives, and at the same time to describe the animating forces that contributed to their formation. His study is based upon the following fundamental concepts: first, that one of the properties of language is its inherent ability to transform words into genres through a process involving 'mental activity' or 'mental concern', *Geistesbeschäftigung*; secondly, that such activity takes place within a certain 'field of meaning', *Bedeutungsfeld*; thirdly, that each simple genre represents a particular 'speech-gesture' or the verbal formulation of a particular 'mental activity', *Sprachgebärde*; fourthly, that a simple genre could be transformed into a more complex genre, yet the 'mental activity', 'field of meaning' and the 'speech-gesture' would remain the same; and finally, that simple genres occur across cultures and across time.[108]

Regarding the *Memorabile*, for example, Jolles posits the mental activity to be a concern for factuality, the field of meaning to be the concrete portrayal of actual events and the speech-gesture to be the historical document. He also discusses the growth of the simple genre *Memorabile* into the *Kunstform* of the history.[109] In addition to the *Memorabile*, Jolles deals with other simple genres that are similar to the anecdote, namely the *Spruch, Kasus* and *Witz*. Their respective 'fields of meaning' and 'speech-gestures' are: *Spruch*, human experience and the summation of a certain chain of human experience; *Kasus*, the weighing of standards and a norm or legal paragraph; and *Witz*, comedy and disengagement from the present and a release of tension.[110]

106. Cuddon, *Dictionary of Literary Terms*, p. 78.

107. André Jolles, *Einfache Formen: Legend, Sage, Myth, Rätsel, Spruch, Kasus, Memorabile, Märchen, Witz* (Tübingen: Max Niemeyer, 3rd edn, 1965).

108. Jolles, *Einfache Formen*, pp. 262-65.

109. Jolles, *Einfache Formen*, pp. 211-17.

110. Jolles, *Einfache Formen*, pp. 160-63 (*Spruch*), 179-83 (*Kasus*) and 252-54 (*Witz*).

In some ways, the concepts *Geistesbeschäftigung*, *Bedeutungsfeld* and *Sprachgebärde* employed by Jolles can be related to the notion of genre. One can compare Jolles's *Geistesbeschäftigung* (mental activity) to the intention of the speaker and the interpretation of the hearer in a communication act, his *Bedeutungsfeld* (field of meaning) to the shared world of meaning or context of a genre, and the *Sprachgebärde* (speech-gesture), in general, to the form, content and function of an individual genre. The *Geistesbeschäftigung* and the *Bedeutungsfeld*, then, would be components of what Dubrow calls the 'code of behavior established between the author and reader' or what Welleck and Warren refer to as the 'inner form' of a genre. What is not certain, however, is Jolles's claim that these concepts represent inherent properties of language. It would seem that they are properties of the human person and hence are brought to bear within a communication situation. The concept of genre, including the 'mental activity' and the 'field of meaning', arises out of the experience of a certain communication situation and its formalized elements.

Kurt Ranke continued the discussion of Jolles's *einfache Formen* with his 1959 address to the International Congress of Folklorists.[111] In this address, Ranke notes the critics of Jolles who attack his overemphasis on 'the independently creative character of language'.[112] Ranke posits that Jolles's study went only 'half-way' in his attempts to elucidate the creative forces beneath the various folk narrative genres. He would move beyond Jolles's *Geistesbeschäftigung* to the impulses of the human psyche. Ranke maintains that 'this unconscious productivity, these spiritual energies, should be added, as the most important ingredient…to the complex forces animating *einfache Formen*'.[113] Thus he see the simple genres as 'forms expressive of certain psycho-intellectual attitudes and the concomitant creative powers [enérgeia] of mankind'.[114] These *einfache Formen*, according to Ranke, have their origins in the 'basic needs of the human soul'; thus, these simple genres are 'dictated by necessity'.[115] Ranke's additions to the concepts of Jolles move one much closer to the communication situation spoken of by literary critics. Whether or not the necessity to express basic needs accounts fully for the appearance of simple genres

111. Kurt Ranke, '*Einfache Formen*' (trans. William Templer and Eberhard Alsen), *Journal of Folklore Institute* 4 (1967), pp. 17-31.

112. Ranke, '*Einfache Formen*', p. 23.

113. Ranke, '*Einfache Formen*', p. 23.

114. Ranke, '*Einfache Formen*', pp. 24-25.

115. Ranke, '*Einfache Formen*', p. 27.

across cultures and across time needs further discussion beyond the scope of the present study.

The anecdote is not among Jolles's *einfache Formen*. Undoubtedly that is because the anecdote has more than one function, as seen not only from the definition of the anecdote developed for this book, but also from the definitions of the anecdote offered by modern writers. In fact, the functions of the anecdote encompass those of at least four of Jolles's *einfache Formen*, namely the *Spruch*, the *Memorabile*, the *Kasus* and the *Witz*. In his essay, the literary critic Hein notes that the anecdote is not a 'simple genre' but a *Kunstform*. He holds that the anecdote is often considered as one of three closely related literary entities, that is, as a 'popular, pre-literary element of daily narratives', as a literary genre, or as a *Zweckform* in historiography, biography or even in the mass media of our own time.[116]

Folklorists raise another criticism of Jolles's work, namely that he treated the *einfache Formen* as precursors of the complex genres, usually understood to be written narratives. Rather than studying oral narratives for the information that they can give regarding a written narrative, folklorists wish to have oral narratives studied purely for their own sake. Dan Ben-Amos notes, 'The genres of folklore are no longer "*einfache Formen*"...but are intricate forms of verbal art with their own dramatic, syntactic and semantic structures, the complexity of which is yet to be discovered.'[117]

116. Hein, 'Die Anekdote', pp. 15-16.

117. Dan Ben-Amos, 'Forward', *Genre* 2 (1969), pp. iii-iv. Francis Lee Utley's 'Oral Genres as Bridges to Written Literature' (*Genre* 2 [1969], pp. 91-103) represents the usage criticized by Ben-Amos. One recent attempt to deal with an oral narrative precisely as an 'oral' unit of literature is found in the work of Elizabeth Fine (*The Folklore Text: From Performance to Print* [Bloomington, IN: Indiana University Press, 1984], esp. pp. 166-95). She challenges the validity and accuracy of a written text as a recording of a performance. In the last section of her monograph, Fine attempts to translate elements of the performance style of an oral narrative to print style. She illustrates her method using a brief narrative whose main character is Stagolee, a southern African American male. Here one brief line is presented, paying attention to only voice intonation. The line describes what Stagolee sees when he arrives in hell: 'It was cool. Brothers and Sisters had put in wall-to-wall carpeting, stereo system, and best of all, air-conditioning.' Fine uses the following vocal characterizers to indicate several paralinguistic features of the line: all caps for words spoken with greater emphasis; ~~~~ over a word for a raspy voice; hyphens between letters in a word to indicate that the preceding vowel is held longer than usual; '/' to indicate a rising pitch on the last syllable; and underlining to indicate a sustained pitch. Fine's record of the above line reads: 'It was COol. Brothers and Sisters had put in WA-LL-to-WALL CARpeting / STER--eo SYS-tem / and BEST of all -A~IR conditioning' (pp. 193-94).

While the anecdote does not receive widespread study in either modern literary criticism or folklore studies, some attempts have been made to discuss the form, function and to a lesser degree, the content of this genre. As noted, Jürgen Hein does offer a straightforward generic definition of the anecdote. Folklorists, too, pay little attention to the anecdote in their work on the basic genres of folk narratives. However, they draw attention to the orality of folk genres and point out the necessity to treat these oral genres in their own right rather than merely as pre-literary genres. Such attention to the features of orality has found a place in recent scripture studies.

4. *From Orality to Literacy*

The call for an appreciation of the 'forms of verbal art' has been sounded in recent years by those scholars who point out the 'residual orality' of the New Testament literature. For example, Paul Achtemeier writes of a neglect of 'the fact that we have in the culture of Western antiquity a culture of high residual orality which nevertheless communicated significantly by means of literary creations'.[118] He further posits the 'need to keep in mind the essentially oral communication of the written texts of the New Testament and shape our examination of those texts, and their interpretation, accordingly'.[119]

118. Paul J. Achtemeier, '*Omne Verbum Sonat*: The New Testament and the Oral Environment of Late Western Antiquity', *JBL* 109 (1990), pp. 3-27 (3). One should note a partial corrective to Achtemeier's essay, namely Frank D. Gilliard's, 'More Silent Reading in Antiquity: *Non Omne Verbum Sonabat*', *JBL* 112 (1993), pp. 689-94. Gilliard contends: 'The evidence strongly suggests that a person not only might but sometimes did [read silently]' (p. 693). Gilliard himself admits that this demonstrable fact does not contradict Achtemeier's main thesis, stated above.

119. Achtemeier, '*Omne Verbum Sonat*', p. 3 n.1. See also the following works: Joanna Dewey, 'Mark as Interwoven Tapestry: Forecasts and Echoes for a Listening Audience', *CBQ* 53 (1991), pp. 221-36; *idem*, *Markan Public Debate: Literary Techniques, Concentric Structure and Theology in Mark 2:1–3:6* (Chico, CA: Scholars Press, 1979), pp. 5-39; *idem*, 'Oral Methods of Structuring Narrative in Mark', *Int* 43 (1989), pp. 32-44; *idem* (ed.), *Orality and Textuality in Early Christian Literature* (Semeia, 65; Atlanta: Scholars Press, 1995); Birger Gerhardsson, *Memory and Manuscript: Oral Tradition and Written Transmission in Rabbinic Judaism and Early Christianity* (ASNU, 22; Lund: C.W.K. Gleerup, 1961); Erhardt Güttgemanns, *Candid Questions Concerning Gospel Form Criticism: A Methodological Sketch of the Fundamental Problematics of Form and Redaction Criticism* (trans. W.G. Doty; PTMS, 26; Pittsburgh: Pickwick, 1979; German original, 2nd edn, 1971), esp. 'Part II. Problems of the Oral and the Written and Their Relation to the Gospel Form', pp. 95-

Many of the English-speaking scholars who deal with the oral[120] background of New Testament texts express an indebtedness to previous studies of oral literature by classicists, folklorists and sociologists. Such studies include those of Milman Parry and Albert Lord. Parry worked on Homer's epic poems, showing that these poems demonstrate certain oral methods of composition, that is, they employ stock phrases and formulas to fit the metrical needs of the hexameter line.[121] Lord employed Parry's insights in his own studies of Serbo-Croatian epic singers. Lord concluded that these singers produced their songs by utilizing groups of standard patterned themes; he designated this process as 'composition by theme'.[122] He also demonstrated, through use of audio-taped records, that an oral song differed at each performance, yet the singer still preserved the basic story.[123] Furthermore, Lord points out that the transition from an oral song to a written record of that oral performance involves a change in emphasis 'from stability of the essential story, which is the goal of an oral tradition, to stability of text, of the exact words of the story'.[124] Finally, he cautions that some of the features of an oral composition are changed in the transition to a written composition and, in fact, that such a transition might involve the use of borrowed or foreign literary genres.[125]

In his *Preface to Plato*, Eric Havelock contends that Plato excluded poets from his republic because of their role as agents and instruments of an oral tradition. Poetic works contained *doxa*, or 'opinion', a word that

267; Werner H. Kelber, *The Oral and Written Gospel: The Hermeneutics of Speaking and Writing in the Synoptic Tradition, Mark, Paul, and Q* (Philadelphia: Fortress Press, 1983); the essays in Lou H. Silberman (ed.), *Orality, Aurality and Biblical Narrative* (Semeia, 39; Chico, CA: Scholars Press, 1987); and the essays in Henry Wansbrough (ed.), *Jesus and the Oral Gospel* (JSNTSup, 64; Sheffield: JSOT Press, 1991). For comments on orally formulated and orally transmitted traditions prior to the written documents of early rabbinic literature see Jacob Neusner, *Oral Tradition in Judaism: The Case of the Mishnah* (Albert Bates Lord Studies in Oral Tradition, 1; New York: Garland Publishing, 1987).

120. I employ 'oral' to include also the notion of 'aural', that is, the fact that texts were meant to be read aloud and to be heard.

121. Milman Parry, *The Making of Homeric Verse: The Collected Papers of Milman Parry* (ed. Adam Perry; Oxford: Clarendon Press, 1971), pp. xix-xv.

122. Albert B. Lord, *The Singer of Tales* (HSCL, 24; Cambridge, MA: Harvard University Press, 1960), pp. 92, 98.

123. Lord, *The Singer of Tales*, p. 123.

124. Lord, *The Singer of Tales*, p. 138.

125. Lord, *The Singer of Tales*, p. 138.

Plato used both as 'the label of the non-abstract mind' and as a name for the knowledge-content of poetry.[126] Havelock asserts that in the *Republic* Plato is arguing for philosophy and against the preserved knowledge that was built up in the community memory through an oral process and communicated by oral poetry. Such *doxa* is characterized by a knowledge of happenings that are separate, visually concrete units not connected by cause and effect.[127]

In his Chapter 10, 'The Content and Quality of the Poetised Statement', Havelock discusses aspects of the oral performance of epic poetry. Here he emphasizes that to communicate with the audience, the poet used as many bodily 'reflexes' as possible. Believing that it is easiest for a speaker to involve the whole body when relating actions, Havelock concludes that the 'content of the *epos* [epic poem] should, therefore, itself consist preferably of a series of doings'.[128] Oral memorization and oral record, likewise required that the content be a set of actions or events: 'A doing or a happening can occur quite obviously only in the context of what we might call an episode, a little story or situation.'[129] A 'great story' might also contain a 'connected series' of little stories, brief anecdotes.[130]

For the cultural world of the New Testament, the gospels represent a movement from a predominantly oral to a written record of the Jesus tradition. Hence, studies on the transition from orality to literacy, including the work of Jack Goody and Walter Ong, are important for New Testament scholarship. As a sociologist, Goody has studied the cultures of West Africa, including aspects of the movement from orality to literacy.[131] His observations on this movement, along with those of Ian Watt, are

126. Eric A. Havelock, *Preface to Plato*. I. *A History of the Greek Mind* (Cambridge, MA: Harvard University Press, 1963), pp. 180-81, 248-49. See also Havelock's 'Oral and Written: A Reappraisal', in *The Literate Revolution in Greece and its Consequences* (Princeton, NJ: Princeton University Press, 1982), pp. 3-38, esp. p. 5.

127. Havelock, *Preface to Plato*, p. 180. Joanna Dewey relies heavily on Havelock's work on *doxa* in her essay, 'Oral Methods of Structuring Narrative in Mark'.

128. Havelock, *Preface to Plato*, p. 167.

129. Havelock, *Preface to Plato*, p. 174. In 'Oral Composition in the *Oedipus Tyrannus* of Sophocles', *New Literary History* 16 (1984), pp. 175-97, Havelock reiterates these points, adding that 'it is the tale that we are biologically programmed to remember most easily' (p. 182). One should note also the reference to Quintilian's remarks on this point found in n. 65 above.

130. Havelock, *Preface to Plato*, p. 291.

131. Jack Goody, 'Restricted Literacy in Northern Ghana', in *Literacy in Traditional Societies* (Cambridge: Cambridge University Press, 1968), pp. 198-264.

presented in the essay 'The Consequences of Literacy'.[132] One especially relevant element of their work is what they assert to be the social function of memory and or forgetting, namely the 'homeostatic organization of the cultural tradition in non-literate society'.[133] They conclude:

> In oral societies the cultural tradition is transmitted almost entirely by face-to-face communication; and changes in the content are accompanied by the homeostatic process of forgetting or transforming those parts of the tradition that cease either to be necessary or relevant.[134]

Walter J. Ong has written extensively on the transformation from primary oral cultures to literate ones.[135] Of particular interest to this discussion is his illuminating chapter, 'Some Psychodynamics of Orality', in *Orality and Literacy.* Here Ong discusses ten characteristics of orally based thought and expression, namely that experience is intellectualized mnemonically; thought and expression are additive rather than subordinate; they are aggregate rather than analytic; they are redundant or 'copious'; they are conservative or traditionalist; they are close to the life world; they are agonistically toned; they are empathetic and participatory rather than objectively distanced; they are homeostatic (Ong refers to Goody and Watt); and they are situational rather than abstract.[136] Finally, Ong, like Lord, discusses the transformation from an oral to a predominantly written culture. He points out that the writing down of a previously oral tradition involves an act of interpretation, namely the preservation of one particular version of an oral performance and/or the interpretive shaping that takes

132. Jack Goody and Ian Watt, 'The Consequences of Literacy', in Jack Goody (ed.), *Literacy in Traditional Societies* (Cambridge: Cambridge University Press, 1968), pp. 27-68.

133. Goody and Watt, 'The Consequences of Literacy', p. 30. 'Homeostatic' is derived from 'homeostasis', which is defined as 'a relatively stable state of equilibrium or a tendency toward such a state between the different but interdependent elements or groups of elements of an organism or group' (*Webster's New Collegiate Dictionary*, p. 542).

134. Goody and Watt, 'The Consequences of Literacy', p. 67.

135. Among Ong's works see: *The Presence of the Word: Some Prolegomena for Cultural and Religious History* (New Haven, CT: Yale University Press, 1967); *Interfaces of the Word: Studies in the Evolution of Consciousness and Culture* (Ithaca, NY: Cornell University Press, 1977); *Orality and Literacy: The Technologizing of the Word* (New Accents; London: Methuen, 1982); and 'Text as Interpretation: Mark and After', in Lou H. Silberman (ed.), *Orality, Aurality and Biblical Narrative* (Semeia, 39; Atlanta: Scholars Press, 1987), pp. 7-26.

136. Ong, *Orality and Literacy*, pp. 33-57.

place in any longer work that uses several oral traditions.[137]

In his *Oral Tradition and the Gospels*,[138] Barry Henaut warns against an uncritical appropriation, by New Testament scholars, of the conclusions of studies on oral folklore and oral transmission. He validates the central insight of the Parry–Lord studies, namely that for an oral tradition 'it is impossible to establish an original text'.[139] However, Henaut critiques the use of their other conclusions on formulaic epic poetry from social contexts presumed to be illiterate for narrative gospels from an 'urban Hellenistic milieu'.[140] In particular he argues against any clear-cut distinction between orality and literacy in the social context of the gospels. Citing Ruth Finnegan's work on the interplay between written and oral channels of communication in societies that are primarily oral,[141] Henaut concludes that, given the highly literate context of the gospels, 'interaction between orality and literacy is a far more appropriate model for the synoptic transmission'.[142] He does allow for aspects of so-called 'residual orality' when he deals with the 'aural' dimension of gospel literature. On this point Henaut admits that since the Gospels were an 'aural medium' they may contain oral structuring devices; however, rather than guaranteeing prior oral traditions, such devices 'might simply reflect the "literary style" appropriate to a Gospel composed with an emphasis upon the spoken word'.[143]

Henaut speaks of the difficulty of recovering any element of an oral tradition behind a Gospel passage. He warns that 'the oral phase [of Gospel tradition(s)] is lost to us because, even assuming a prior oral history for a unit, the very communal, anonymous and changeable nature of this medium makes it impossible to trace a tradition's history through this transmission'.[144] Not only are there no 'ground rules' for oral transmission, but one cannot assume that a Gospel unit is a direct transcription

137. Ong, 'Text as Interpretation', p. 11.

138. Barry W. Henaut, *Oral Tradition and the Gospels: The Problem of Mark 4* (JSNTSup, 82; Sheffield: JSOT Press, 1993).

139. Henaut, *Oral Tradition*, p. 91.

140. Henaut, *Oral Tradition*, p. 117; see also pp. 76-86.

141. Ruth Finnegan, *Oral Poetry: Its Nature, Significance and Social Context* (Cambridge: Cambridge University Press, 1977).

142. Henaut, *Oral Tradition*, p. 117; see also pp. 95-96.

143. Henaut, *Oral Tradition*, p. 52. See also Øivind Andersen, 'Oral Tradition', in Henry Wansbrough (ed.), *Jesus and the Oral Gospel* (JSNTSup, 64; Sheffield: JSOT Press, 1991), pp. 17-58, esp. pp. 45-50.

144. Henaut, *Oral Tradition*, p. 15.

of an oral narrative.[145] Furthermore, Henaut argues against assuming that a distinctive 'form' (genre) in a written Gospel is a 'guarantee of an oral history'; he would allow for composition of a unit by the evangelist.[146] Given these circumstances, the search for an 'original' version of a Gospel unit can be futile.[147]

What then of the anecdotes in Mark's Gospel? Given the universality of anecdotes, this genre was probably present among pre-Markan oral or written Jesus traditions. 'Residual orality' with respect to an anecdote has been noted in the discussion on the brevity of this genre and 'brief' has been defined to be that size that 'one can hold in the ear'. Given the insights and cautions just presented, further remarks on 'residual orality' in Mark, with applications to the Markan anecdotes, can be made.

With respect to the style of Mark's Gospel itself, Vincent Taylor states, 'Mark's Gospel is written in a relatively simple and popular form of Greek which has striking affinities with the spoken language of everyday life as it is revealed to us in the papyri and inscriptions.'[148] Taylor goes on to cite Mark's frequent use of καί-paratactic, his failure to use the longer Greek period and his vivid details and concrete phrases.[149]

On this topic I note the description of 'Plain Style' (ὁ ἰσχνός χαρακτῆρ) by the ancient literary critic Demetrius (dated variously from the third century BCE to the first century CE). What is of interest to me is the over-lap of some of the qualities of Demetrius's 'plain style' with those that Ong attributes to orally based expression. Demetrius directs that the subject matter of the 'plain style' should be 'homely and appropriate' to the style, the diction must be 'current and familiar' and 'above all, the style should be lucid [σαφές]' (*Style* 4.191). In pursuit of lucidity, Demetrius advises using

145. On this lack of 'ground rules', see also Wansbrough's summary introduction to papers from two symposia on oral tradition in which he states: 'We have been unable to deduce or derive any marks which distinguish clearly between an oral and a written transmission process' (*Jesus and the Oral Gospel*, p. 12).

146. Henaut, *Oral Tradition*, p. 73.

147. Henaut, *Oral Tradition*, pp. 115-18. Here I note that even in the search for the 'form' of a written Gospel unit one must proceed with caution since the literary structure of a larger section may influence the 'form' of an individual unit. See J. Dewey's work on the chiastic structure of Mk 2.1–3.6 and its implications for the 'form' of 3.1-6 ('The Literary Structure of the Controversy Stories in Mark 2:1–3:6', *JBL* 92 [1973], pp. 397-400 [399]).

148. Vincent Taylor, *The Gospel According to St. Mark: The Greek Text with Introduction, Notes and Indexes* (London: Macmillan, 2nd edn, 1966), p. 52.

149. Taylor, *The Gospel According to St. Mark*, pp. 52-53.

current words and phrases as well as repetition, following the natural order of words, avoiding the use of dependent clauses and long members, employing limited amplifications and striving for 'vividness' (*Style* 4.192-209). Vividness, according to Demetrius, arises from exact narration, repetition, the mention of the accompanying circumstances of any action and from onomatopoetic words (*Style* 4.209-21). These stylistic features can be compared to Ong's 'close to the life world', 'additive', 'aggregative', 'redundant' and 'situational'. Furthermore, Demetrius's note on vividness arising from 'the mention of the accompanying circumstances of any action' may be equated with what Havelock presents as a requirement for an oral record, that is, an episode or anecdote. It may well be that Demetrius's 'plain style' reflects 'residual orality' in texts meant to be read aloud and heard by an audience. No doubt certain features of the style of Mark's Gospel reflect the 'residual orality' of the culture of the early Christian community.

The homeostatic process in an oral society, that is, the process of forgetting or transforming parts of the tradition, necessitates that a distinction be made between accurately transmitting 'authentic content' and the verbatim repetition of a tradition. With respect to the parables, Scott notes:

> The parables' orality makes our quest for the parables of Jesus problematic… We have no parable of Jesus as he performed it. All extant parables ascribed to Jesus show traces of performances by others… Traditional storytellers, preachers, teachers, and evangelists were not simply passive memory receptacles but performers, shaping and adapting the structure (of a parable) in a concrete performance.[150]

What Scott says of the parables of Jesus can be applied to eyewitness accounts of happenings involving Jesus. We have no original eyewitness accounts of these happenings. At most we can say that the written stories we have may have been based on oral stories; these in turn may have been based, directly or through a chain of oral tradition, on eyewitness accounts. In all these narrations we must allow for the shaping and adapting of an account by the narrator. A Markan anecdote, then, if based on oral tradition at all, is far removed from the actual event. Furthermore, the difference between 'story' and 'discourse', the 'what' and the 'how', as presented above, reinforces the necessary distinctions among a historical event involving the historical Jesus, an oral anecdote relating that event and a written anecdote based on the oral tradition. As noted, the event

150. Scott, *Hear Then the Parable*, pp. 40-41.

itself is equivalent to neither the oral anecdote nor the written anecdote. Eyewitness accounts, oral or written, are only partial representations of the event. These distinctions reinforce Henaut's comments on the futility of a search for an 'original' version of a Gospel unit.

In an oral culture, or a culture of high 'residual orality', traditional information is often transmitted through the narrative of a situation or an event. This feature comes into play when one distinguishes between a saying and an anecdote containing that saying. One might ask if the setting was composed, in an oral or a written account, to 'make sense' of a saying, to make it relevant to an audience, or to enable easy memorization.[151] The creation of situations or events for the transmission of traditional information adds another note of caution to any search for the exact words of a pre-Markan oral tradition, including the exact words of the historical Jesus and their 'original' settings.[152]

Furthermore, the genre employed in a written record of an oral tradition cannot be assumed to be a pure continuation of the oral genre of that tradition.[153] An oral anecdote may take, at least, a different *form* when it is written. Moreover, as Lord's studies demonstrate, a 'foreign' or literary genre may be used.[154] This second point is important with respect to any statements about the genre of pre-Markan oral anecdotes when such statements are derived from the Greek literary anecdotes in our present Gospel. Additionally, specific oral and literary genres are often tied to a specific language; hence, a brief digression on the languages spoken in first-century CE Palestine is presented here.

Studies abound that make it clear that Hellenism influenced the cultural

151. On this point see Dewey ('Oral Methods of Structuring Narrative in Mark', p. 35) who holds: 'The embedding of teaching in event is characteristic of Mark.'

152. Stylistic arguments can also be questioned. For example, Taylor (*Gospel According to St. Mark*, p. 53) asserts that the vivid details in Mark's Gospel belong not to the evangelist but to the historical 'tradition he records'. See also pp. 135-49. John P. Meier correctly questions the conclusions of Taylor: 'Perhaps the vividness of narration gets us behind Mark to his oral tradition. But does it get us back to Jesus?' (*A Marginal Jew: Rethinking the Historical Jesus*. I. *The Roots of the Problem and the Person* [New York: Doubleday, 1991]), p. 181.

153. See Helmut Köster ('Written Gospels or Oral Tradition?', *JBL* 113 [1994], pp. 293-97 [296]) who argues that 'the establishment of a biographical framework [written gospels] may fundamentally change the form and function of a piece of tradition because it is now transferred from its situation in the life of the community into the context of the life of Jesus'.

154. Kloppenborg also makes this point in 'Introduction: Forms and Genres', p. 7.

world of first century CE Judaea and Galilee.[155] The question of the use of the Greek language as a measure of Hellenistic influence has received much attention in these studies. Epigraphic, archaeological and literary evidence confirms that a knowledge of Greek existed at this time; the question is, 'How much and how widespread was this knowledge?' Meier correctly points out the ambiguity of the data and that the evidence is often mistreated. The ambiguity lies in the fact that the data, particularly building and ossuary inscriptions, are indicative mostly of the upper class. Moreover, the evidence is often presented, as in Mussies's, treatment, without proper attention to early and late datings. A further caution on this

155. See: Elias J. Bickerman, *The Jews in the Greek Age* (Cambridge, MA: Harvard University Press, 1988); Sean Freyne, *Galilee from Alexander the Great to Hadrian, 323 B.C.E. to 135 C.E.: A Study of Second Temple Judaism* (University of Notre Dame Center for the Study of Judaism and Christianity in Antiquity, 5; Notre Dame, IN: University of Notre Dame Press, 1980); Martin Hengel, *Judaism and Hellenism: Studies in their Encounter in Palestine during the Early Hellenistic Period* (trans. John Bowden; 2 vols.; London: SCM Press, 1974; German 2nd rev. edn, 1973); Martin Hengel with Christoph Markschies, *The 'Hellenization' of Judaea in the First Century after Christ* (trans. John Bowden; London: SCM Press, 1989; German original, 1989); Meier, *Marginal Jew*; G. Mussies, 'Greek in Palestine and the Diaspora', in Shmuel Safrai *et al.* (eds.), *The Jewish People in the First Century: Historical Geography, Political History, Social, Cultural and Religious Life and Institutions* (CRINT, 1.2; Atlanta: Scholars Press, 1976), pp. 1040-64; Chaim Rabin, 'Hebrew and Aramaic in the First Century', in Shmuel Safrai *et al.* (eds.), *The Jewish People in the First Century: Historical Geography, Political History, Social, Cultural and Religious Life and Institutions* (CRINT, 1.2; Atlanta: Scholars Press, 1976), pp. 1007-39; Emil Schürer, *The History of the Jewish People in the Age of Jesus Christ (175 B.C.–A.D. 135)* (rev. and ed. Geza Vermes *et al.*; 4 vols.; Edinburgh: T. & T. Clark, 1973–87); and J.N. Sevenster, *'Do You Know Greek?' How Much Greek Could the First Jewish Christians Have Known?* (NovTSup, 19; Leiden: E.J. Brill, 1968). For epigraphic, archaeological and literary evidence see Richard A. Horsley, 'The Historical Jesus and the Archaeology of Galilee: Questions from Historical Jesus Research to Archaeologists', in Eugene H. Lovering (ed.), *SBLSP 1994* (SBLSP, 33; Atlanta: Scholars Press, 1994), pp. 129-35; Mussies, 'Greek in Palestine and the Diaspora', pp. 1042-54; and Schürer, *The History of the Jewish People*, I, pp. 1-81. While Saul Lieberman's writings concern Hellenistic influences in Jewish Palestine, he draws his evidence from later rabbinic texts. See his 'How Much Greek in Jewish Palestine?', in Alexander Altmann (ed.), *Biblical and Other Studies* (Studies and Texts, 1; Cambridge, MA: Harvard University Press, 1963), pp. 123-41, and *Hellenism in Jewish Palestine: Studies in the Literary Transmission, Beliefs and Manners of Palestine in the I Century BCE–IV Century CE* (Text and Studies, 18; New York: Jewish Theological Seminary of America, 1950), pp. 83-99.

matter is the need to distinguish geographical areas.[156]

One can say confidently that Greek was certainly spoken among the educated, upper classes of many large urban centers, including Jerusalem and the Galilean cities of Tiberias and Sepphoris.[157] However, there are questions as to the fluency of the Greek of this class. Hengel holds that in the first century, Jerusalem, with Greek-speaking synagogues, was a center of the Greek language, established as a language in local use for over 300 years.[158] Further on in his essay, Hengel posits that the upper class had a knowledge of Greek, but only a few possessed literary skills.[159] Feldman discusses the work of the Jewish historian Josephus, who needed assistants 'for the Greek language' when composing the Greek version of *The Jewish Wars* (*Apion* 1.50). From the poor quality of the Greek on ossuaries, and from the fact that Josephus continued to use Aramaic, Feldman also concludes that 'few attained the competence in the language necessary for reading and understanding Greek literature'.[160]

Persons residing in areas outside Jerusalem, for example, in the villages of Galilee, would have had a rudimentary knowledge of Greek also since the administrative and commerical life of the country was probably conducted in Greek.[161] However, outside the range of the Greek-speaking cities 'there seems little doubt that Aramaic remained the most commonly spoken language of the vast majority of the inhabitants of Galilee throughout the whole period of this survey (323 BCE–135 CE)'.[162] Again, it is important to ask about the fluency in Greek of these rural persons, particularly those in the areas around Nazareth. While two Hellenistic cities, Sepphoris and Tiberias, were nearby, this does not imply that inhabitants of other smaller villages would be fluent in speaking Greek, let alone possess literary skills. To posit that Jesus of Nazareth or his early follow-

156. See the cautions given by Horsley, 'The Historical Jesus and the Archaeology of Galilee', p. 113.

157. See Freyne, *Galilee from Alexander the Great to Hadrian*, p. 139; Mussies, 'Greek in Palestine and the Diaspora', p. 1052, and Schürer, *History of the Jewish People*, I, p. 79.

158. Hengel and Markschies, *'Hellenization' of Judaea*, pp. 12-13.

159. Hengel and Markschies, *'Hellenization' of Judaea*, pp. 16-17.

160. Louis H. Feldman, *Jew and Gentile in the Ancient World: Attitudes and Interactions from Alexander to Justinian* (Princeton, NJ: Princeton University Press, 1993), p. 1056.

161. Freyne, *Galilee from Alexander the Great to Hadrian*, p. 141.

162. Freyne, *Galilee from Alexander the Great to Hadrian*, p. 144. There is general agreement among scholars that this was the case.

ers were fluent and literate in Greek goes beyond the evidence available to us.[163] The most that can be said is that, while Aramaic was their mother tongue, they would know enough Greek to get along in the market place. This has led Meier to assert, 'I remain doubtful that any body of Jesus' sayings existed from the very beginning in Greek, needing no translation as it passed into our Greek Gospels.'[164] Thus, the evidence indicates that at least some of the original oral traditions involving the historical Jesus probably would have circulated in an Aramaic-speaking cultural world.

Returning now to the genre of pre-Markan traditions, the significance for this study of Lord's comment on the adoption of 'foreign' or literary genres for the written record of an oral tradition is clearer. Not only would this be true within the same cultural world, but perhaps even more so when one moves to another cultural milieu. Given the cultural world of first century CE Galilee and Judea, it is probable that oral anecdotes about Jesus were transmitted in Aramaic. In Mark's Gospel some of these oral traditions may appear in the Greek literary genre, the χρεία. Inasmuch as a specific literary genre is often tied to a specific language, there is no way to posit with total assurance that the first telling of an original anecdote was an oral Greek χρεία, or for that matter, that there were oral Greek χρεία about Jesus circulating before Mark's Gospel.

Finally, the transition to a written expression from previous oral tradition(s) involves an act of interpretation; this is also true of the gathering together of prior oral or written traditions into a longer, coherent narrative. In his *The Oral and Written Gospel*, Werner Kelber writes that despite the fact that 'Mark's text is rooted in and surrounded by orality', the Gospel

163. In their *'Hellenization' of Judaea*, Hengel and Markschies move from the position that Jesus could carry on a conversation in Greek (p. 17) to ask, in reference to Cynic anecdotes in the Gospels: 'Why should not the craftsman Jesus, who grew up in the neighborhood of Sepphoris, have made contact with Cynic itinerant preachers, especially as he himself spoke Greek?' (p. 44). However, they seem to contradict themselves, since earlier in the monograph they had written: 'As Jesus came from a pious Jewish craftsman's family, with country origins, there are reasons which tell *against* too close a connection with the largely Hellenistic (Sepphoris)' (p. 74 n. 90).

164. Meier, *Marginal Jew*, I, p. 262. See a similar opinion of Joseph Fitzmyer, *A Wandering Aramean: Collected Aramaic Essays* (SBLMS, 25; Missoula, MT: Scholars Press, 1979), p. 10 (reprinted in *The Semitic Background of the New Testament: Combined Edition of Essays on the Semitic Background of the New Testament and A Wandering Aramean: Collected Aramaic Essays* [Biblical Resource Series; Grand Rapids, MI: Eerdmans, 1997]).

'transformed, absorbed but reconstructed the collective memories of oral tradition'.[165] This reconstruction holds true, even if Mark used written sources. Walter Ong also comments on Mark's interpretative achievement:

> He undertook to produce and did produce a unified narrative, with some items thoughtfully and programmatically subordinated to others, with a focus or point of view shaped...by his sense of the way the kerygma had to be organized to make it most effective for Christians generally who had been through the sacking of Jerusalem and the destruction of the Temple.[166.]

In conclusion, one can say that what we have in Mark's Gospel is a written work undoubtedly meant to be read aloud to a listening audience of early Christians. As such it contains 'residual orality' in its style; its author may have employed some prior oral traditions about Jesus that were cast in anecdotes. However, the nature of oral transmission makes it difficult to produce any such oral anecdotes. Moreover, the written genre of an anecdote in the Gospel need not represent the same genre of the tradition in a pre-Markan oral or written source. In light of these conclusions, the present study will concentrate on the text of Mark's Gospel as 'evidence for the time of writing rather than as evidence for the events referred to',[167] or as clear evidence of pre-Markan oral genres.[168] Therefore, I limit myself to a study of the written anecdotes in Mk 8.27–10.45, their literary shape, content and function within the host-genre of this Gospel.

165. Kelber, *Oral and Written Gospel*, p. 184. Kelber then attributes a motive to Mark, that is, Mark produced a written Gospel precisely as a 'counterform to, rather than extension of, oral hermeneutics' (p. 185). A critique of this imputed motive is beyond the scope of the present study.

166. Ong, 'Text as Interpretation', p. 13. Although Ong's projected audience for Mark is debatable, nonetheless his point is well taken.

167. Norman R. Petersen makes this point in *Literary Criticism for New Testament Critics* (Guides to Biblical Scholarship, New Testament Series; Philadelphia: Fortress Press, 1978), p. 17.

168. Jacob Neusner reaches a similar conclusion with respect to the *ipsissima verba* of pre-Mishnaic masters. He admits to the existence of oral traditions prior to the Mishnah; however, he asserts: '[W]hether the transmitted pericopae derive from originally oral materials is a question that cannot be settled, one way or the other, by the character of the materials we now have only in written form.' See his 'The Rabbinic Traditions about the Pharisees before 70 C.E.: The Problem of Oral Transmission', in *Early Rabbinic Judaism: Historical Studies in Religion, Literature and Art* (SJLA, 13; Leiden: E.J. Brill, 1975), pp. 73-89 (79) (reprint of 'The Rabbinic Traditions about the Pharisees before 70 C.E.: The Problem of Oral Transmission', *JJS* 22 [1971], pp. 1-18).

Chapter 2 studies the anecdote as it was understood and defined by grammarians, rhetoricians and writers of the Greek and Roman worlds. Having investigated the Greek and Latin anecdote in general, I examine the form, content and function of the anecdotes of a specific text, Lucian's *Demonax*.

Chapter 2

THE ANECDOTE IN GREEK AND ROMAN WRITERS

In his *The Development of Greek Biography*, Momigliano spoke of 'the obvious delight which Aristotle and his pupils took in anecdotes'.[1] To illustrate this point Momigliano presented one such 'anecdote', a passage from Aristotle concerning a Milesian, Hippodamus son of Euryphon,

> who invented town planning and laid out Piraeus and had odd theories about other aspects of life which he liked to make himself known for: accounts of his foibles mention his long hair and expensive personal possessions and also the cheap but warm clothes he wore in summer as well as in winter, and his desire to be an expert in all the sciences (*Politica* 2.5.1).[2]

This unit is clearly not an anecdote as I have defined it above in Chapter 1.[3] Momigliano proceeded to comment on the use of anecdotes among Aristotle's followers down through Aristoxenus (c. 370 BCE) whom Momigliano 'suspects' is responsible for 'the notion that a good biography is full of good anecdotes'.[4]

Unfortunately, Momigliano never defined what comprises the unit he would classify as an anecdote. It is clear from the references he cited and the terms he employed that for him the concept 'anecdote' included not only the description of Hippodamus just mentioned, but also an ἀπόφθεγμα, a παράδειγμα, a γνώμη, and a χρεία. Moreover, he held that Valerius Maximus, in his *Factorum et dictorum memorabilium* (c. 31 CE), gave us

1. Arnaldo Momigliano, *The Development of Greek Biography*, p. 68.
2. Cited by Momigliano, *The Development of Greek Biography*, p. 69.
3. That is, '[A] brief narrative, either oral or written, describing an incident, including its setting, which involves one or more persons and which focuses on an action, saying, or dialogue; the function of an anecdote is to entertain, instruct, relate an historical incident, characterize a person, or authoritatively legitimate a specific opinion, a specific practice, or a broader view of reality.'
4. Momigliano, *The Development of Greek Biography*, p. 76.

'a precise idea of the genre'.[5] Indeed, Valerius's collection contains many examples of what I term an anecdote, but it also records other much longer narratives.[6] Momigliano's use of the single term 'anecdote' to include such a group of different terms or genres is representative of the fluid state of the usage of these terms among the ancient Greek and Roman writers themselves.

As I stated in Chapter 1, the word ἀνέκδοτος referred to 'unpublished materials' in ancient literature. ἀνέκδοτος was not used by Greek or Roman writers to designate the brief story. There was no one, unique term consistently employed by the ancients for what I call the anecdote. Instead, a 'range of terms', including ἀπομνημόνευμα, ἀπόφθεγμα, παράδειγμα and χρεία was used for units some of which may be anecdotes. Furthermore, terminology designating an attributed or unattributed saying without a narrated setting was not consistent; ἀπόφθεγμα, ἀφορισμός, γνώμη and χρεία were all used at times for such a unit. For example, in his *Lycurgus*, Plutarch offered a selection of ἀποφθέγματα, 'apophthegms', as proof of the Spartans' aversion to long speeches (20.1-2). His illustrations included both attributed sayings without settings and anecdotes. He then referred to other 'pointed remembrances', τῶν πικῶν ἀπομνημονευμάτων, and, as illustrations, cited anecdotes (20.2-4). Moreover, it is not at all clear that Plutarch meant to distinguish an ἀπόφθεγμα from an ἀπομνημόνευμα, or for that matter that he employed the terms to identify genre categories.[7]

Since ancient rhetors and writers first encountered the rhetorical or literary genres in their academic training, this chapter begins with an account of the educational curriculum in the Greek and Roman worlds. There follows a discussion of the ancient use of various terms that could apply to the brief story. Because the brief stories often contain a saying, the discussion begins by clarifying terms for a saying when it appears

5. Momigliano, *The Development of Greek Biography*, pp. 72-74.

6. Valerius Maximus, *Factorum et dictorum memorabilium Libra IX* (ed. Carolus Kempf; 2 vols.; Leipzig: Teubner, 2nd edn, 1888; repr. Stuttgart: Teubner, 1966; English: *Valerius Maximus: Memorable Deeds and Sayings* [trans. Samuel Speed; London: Booksellers, 1678]).

7. See also the opening of 'Sayings of Kings and Commanders' (172C), attributed to Plutarch, which contains the terms ἀπόφθεγμα (in the title), ἀπομνημόνευμα and χρεία. While this last is clearly meant to indicate the 'usefulness' of the ἀπομνημονεύματα that the author recorded, nonetheless, the appearance of this word along with the other two terms points to the fluidity of these terms.

without a narrative context. The study of terms leads to the χρεία as a genre that included anecdotes. Thus, the third section focuses on the χρεία, including its place in the educational curriculum. Finally, a literary study of the anecdotes among the χρεῖαι of Lucian's *Demonax*, a second century CE Greek work, is undertaken to provide a point of comparison for the study of the anecdotes in Mark's Gospel.

1. *Ancient Education and the* Προγυμνάσματα

Formal literary criticism, as we know it today, was not recognized as a separate art in the Greek and Roman worlds. Instead, as John Atkins maintained in the last century, 'the main current of ancient [literary] criticism flowed in the channel of rhetorical theory'.[8] Moreover, since the goal of ancient education was the training of an orator, rhetorical theory was the basis of the curriculum in Greek and Roman schools. However, such training was considered equally important for writers. Theon, a first century CE grammarian, wrote:

> practice in the exercises [of rhetorical training] is absolutely necessary, not only for those who intend to be orators, but also if someone wants to be a poet or prose-writer, or if he wants to acquire facility with some other form of writing. For these exercises are, so to speak, the foundation stones for every form of writing (2.140-43).[9]

Theon's opinion is confirmed by the Roman orator Quintilian (c. 40–96 CE) who held that 'there is absolutely no difference between writing well and speaking well' (*Inst.* 12.51).[10] Hence, one can seek elements of literary criticism, including generic definitions, in the Greek and Roman rhetorical manuals used in the schools as well as in treatises on rhetoric.[11]

Little is known about the courses of study in the ancient Greek and Roman schools prior to the first century CE. A possible reference to 'pre-

8. J.W.H. Atkins, *Literary Criticism in Antiquity: A Sketch of its Development*. I. *Greek* (Cambridge: Cambridge University Press, 1934), p. 6.

9. All references to and citations of Theon are from James R. Butts, 'The "Progymnasmata" of Theon: A New Text with Translation and Commentary' (PhD dissertation, Claremont Graduate School, 1986).

10. For evidence supporting these dates for Quintilian see George A. Kennedy, *Quintilian* (New York: Twayne Publishers, 1969), pp. 15-30.

11. Furthermore, given the oral background of the first Christian works, rhetorical criticism not only can be used in the study of this literature, but in fact it must. In a primarily oral culture, the authors of works that were intended to be read to an audience undoubtedly employed rhetorical principles and techniques.

liminary exercises', προγυμνάσματα, is found in Anaximenes's *Rhetoric to Alexander* (c. 300 BCE).[12] In relation to the elements of argumentation and figures of thought, the author stated: '[I]f we accustom and train ourselves to repeat them on the lines of our προγυμνάσματα, they will supply us with plenty of matter both in writing and in speaking' (28.1436a). Seneca (c. 4 BCE–62 CE), while presenting his views on liberal studies in his *Epistle 88* included brief comments on the task of the *grammaticus*. In his *De Oratore* (1.42.187-88), Cicero appears to list the elements of a curriculum, although he did not describe it as such.

In Books 1 and 2 of his *Institutio Oratoria*, Quintilian provided the first full description of education in the ancient world. There were three stages: that which took place before formal schooling under the supervision of a *paedagogus* (1.1.8-37), the first level of formal education with a grammarian, *grammaticus* (1.4-11), and the advanced school conducted by a rhetorician, *rhetor* (2.4). Under the *paedagogus*, the young person was taught to 'read and write without difficulty' (1.1.4). This stage also included the development of the skill of memorization, using *dicta* of famous persons and some familiarity with poetry (1.2-3). The chief responsibilities of the grammarian were to teach first, 'the art of speaking correctly', *methodicen* (μεθοδική), which included the art of writing, and second, 'the interpretation of poets', *historicen* (ἱστορική), which was necessarily preceded by correct reading (1.4.2-3; 1.9.1). This level of instruction also included the paraphrasing of fables and the writing of *sententiae*, *chriae* and *aetiologia* (1.9.2-4).[13] Under the rhetorician the student learned the composition of historical, fictitious, realistic and poetic narratives, then the task of refuting and confirming these narratives, praise and denunciation in general, the commonplace, the thesis, praise and blame of particular laws, and finally, declamation (2.4-6). In the opening of Book 2, Quintilian indicated that Latin grammarians were taking over the work of rhetoricians and teaching all of the exercises prior to that of declamation. Quintilian disapproved of this practice, saying that such was not the custom among the Greeks, and urged that the grammarians and the rhetoricians cover their 'proper spheres' as he had outlined them (2.1.1).

12. This work is attributed to Anaximenes by Quintilian (*Inst.* 3.4.9).

13. See F.H. Colson, 'Phaedrus and Quintilian I.9.2', *Classical Review* 33 (1919), pp. 59-61, and 'Quintilian I.9 and the "Chria" in Ancient Education', *Classical Review* 35 (1921), pp. 150-54. For the reading *aetiologia* as opposed to *ethologia* (LCL) see Colson, 'Quintilian 1.9 and the "Chria"', pp. 150-54. In short, there is no manuscript evidence for *ethologia*.

a. Προγυμνάσματα

At whatever level they were taught, it is clear that Quintilian described a series of graded exercises on various rhetorical units employed by the grammarians and rhetoricians. These exercises moved from the simple to the moderately sophisticated, providing an opportunity for the composition of preliminary genres before the writing of actual speeches. Suetonius (c. 69–122 CE) indicated that certain exercises were in use in Roman rhetorical schools from the first century BCE (*Rhet*. 1).[14] That the exercises were taught at this earlier date is further evidenced by *Rhetorica ad Herennium* (c. 86–82 BCE) 4.44.57, which presented an exercise, *expolitio*, used on a maxim that was very similar to one of the handbook exercises, the ἐργασία.[15] Eventually, near the end of the fourth century CE, works presenting these exercises came to be called προγυμνάσματα.[16]

The earliest extant 'Book of Exercises', προγυμνάσματα, is that of Theon, although he himself noted that his was not the first such manual (1.15-16). The work is entitled Προγυμνάσματα, but this title is probably a later addition.[17] Theon has been identified as Aelius Theon of Alexandria

14. Among others, Suetonius mentioned the exercises of expanding and condensing narratives and confirming and refuting both myths and theses. The exercises on the thesis are missed in the translation by Rolfe who renders the Latin *quod genus thesis et anasceuas et catasceuas Graeci vocant* as 'an exercise which the Greeks call "destructive" and "constructive" criticism' (Suetonius, *De Rhetoribus* [trans. J.C. Rolfe; LCL; 2 vols.; Cambridge, MA: Harvard University Press, 1930]).

15. For the date of this work, see Erling B. Holtsmark, 'Auctor Incertus [*Ad Herennium*]', in Donald C. Bryant (ed.), *Ancient Greek and Roman Rhetoricians: A Biographical Dictionary* (Columbia, MO: Artcraft Press, 1968), pp. 18-19. For ἐργασία and *expolitio* see below, section d, pp. 82-87.

16. A history of the development of the προγυμνάσματα is found in Ronald F. Hock, 'General Introduction to Volume I', in Ronald F. Hock and Edward N. O'Neil, *The Chreia in Ancient Rhetoric*. I. *The* Progymnasmata (SBLTT, 27, Graeco-Roman Religion Series, 9; Atlanta: Scholars Press, 1986), pp. 10-22, and in Kathryn M. Thaniel, 'Quintilian and the Progymnasmata' (PhD dissertation, McMaster University, 1973), pp. 1-33. See also Stanley F. Bonner, *Education in Ancient Rome: From the Elder Cato to the Younger Pliny* (Berkeley: University of California Press, 1977), pp. 250-76, and D.L. Clark, *Rhetoric in Greco-Roman Education* (New York: Columbia University Press, 1957), pp. 170-81.

17. For 'exercise', Theon used γυμνασία (1.40) or γύμνασμα (1.46). For the sequence of the exercises, the Walz manuscript reads γυμνάσματα (1.157) while Butts's Greek text reads προγυμνάσματα (1.77). Butts gives no note for this reading nor does his own introduction to the work contain a discussion of it. In fact, his intro-

who lived in the latter half of the first century CE.[18]

Theon's Προγυμνάσματα, presented here as a sample of its type, opened with an introductory chapter discussing the reasons for the study of the preliminary exercises, claiming that the majority of the orators of his day were lacking in proper training (1.1-11). In this chapter Theon named and briefly described the rhetorical units and the exercises with the units, as well as the order he would follow in their presentation.[19] In Chapter 2, Theon discussed successful teaching methods used not only to impart the content of the exercises but also to influence the attitude of the students. The first two chapters, coupled with the remaining detailed chapters on each unit, its definition, typologies and its exercises, replete with examples, produced a work that served both as a teaching manual and a student textbook.

Theon presented ten rhetorical units for study, namely the χρεία, 'chreia', μῦθος, 'fable', διήγημα, 'narrative', τόπος, 'commonplace', ἔκφρασίς, 'description', προσωποποιΐα, 'speech-in-character', ἐγκώμιον, 'encomium', συγκρισίς, 'comparison', θέσις, 'thesis', and the νόμος, 'law'. Several of Theon's treatments of these units approached genre definitions. For example, 'A fable is a fictional story depicting a truth' (4.3), and one function of a fable was its use in the construction of a speech (4.106-163). The rhetorical unit of interest in the search for an ancient entity like the anecdote is the χρεία.

These brief comments on the curriculum of Greek and Roman schools indicate that one can study the rhetorical handbooks, including the προγυμνάσματα, for elements of genre definitions of rhetorical units. Addition-

ductory remarks indicate that this probably is not Theon's term ('The "Progymnasmata" of Theon', p. 8).

18. Quintilian mentions a 'Stoic Theon' in his *Inst.* 9.3.6 (cf. 3.6.48). An argument can be made, although not a conclusive one, that this is the Theon of the Προγυμνάσματα. For a discussion of the identity and date of Theon see Butts, 'The "Progymnasmata" of Theon', pp. 1-6; Ronald F. Hock and Edward N. O'Neil, 'Aelius Theon of Alexandria', in Ronald F. Hock and Edward N. O'Neil (eds.), *The Chreia in Ancient Rhetoric*. I. *The* Progymnamata (SBLTT, 27, Graeco-Roman Religion Series, 9; Atlanta: Scholars Press, 1986), pp. 63-78; George A. Kennedy, *The Art of Persuasion in Greece* (Princeton, NJ: Princeton University Press, 1963), p. 270; and W. Stegemann, 'Theon (5)', PW, V.A.2, cols. 2037-2039.

19. Theon's introductory chapter placed the χρεία first (1.175-76) in the order of exercises to be taught while the extant Greek manuscripts of his text place the chapter on the χρεία third. However, the Armenian manuscript has the chapter on the χρεία first. Theon's introductory statement and the order of the Armenian text led Butts to place the chapter on the χρεία first in his edition of Theon. See Butts, 'The "Progymnasmata" of Theon', pp. 11-20.

ally, writers themselves often made reference to various rhetorical or literary units within their works; such comments shed light on the form, content and function of the literary units named.[20] In the next section of this chapter I clarify, using the προγυμνάσματα and the literary works themselves, any generic terms the ancients employed for the anecdote.

2. *Terms and Definitions*

This section opens with comments on three terms, παράδειγμα, γνώμη and ἀφορισμός, that are clearly not used by the ancients to designate a genre 'anecdote', but which sometimes appear in the secondary literature dealing with brief stories.

a. παράδειγμα *or* exemplum

In 1919 Martin Dibelius identified anecdotes or brief Gospel 'example-narratives' from the deeds of Jesus as 'paradigms' and referred to the Greek term παράδειγμα.[21] Dibelius chose this term since he believed that these units functioned as supports or illustrations for the preaching of the early Christian community. Indeed, the comments of the ancient writers on the παράδειγμα and *exemplum* concentrate almost exclusively on its persuasive or functional aspects.[22] However, the following study shows that the παράδειγμα, or *exemplum*, was not presented as a genre by the ancient writers, nor was it studied as one of the προγυμνάσματα in the schools.

Etymologically, παράδειγμα comes from the verb παραδείκνυμι, 'to exhibit side by side'. Five meanings are found in the LSJ: a pattern, model; a precedent, example, sample; a lesson, warning; an argument, as in 'proof from example'; and in law, a leading case, precedent.[23] The Latin *exemplum*, from *exemplare*, 'to copy', has English meanings that are parallel to those of παράδειγμα, namely sample; imitation, image;

20. Bennett J. Price ('Paradeigma and Exemplum in Ancient Rhetorical Theory' [PhD dissertation, University of California at Berkeley, 1975], p. 215) concluded his study on the *exemplum* with the comment that a more complete investigation should be based not just on rhetorical theorists but on 'the practices in the orators'.

21. Martin Dibelius, *From Tradition to Gospel*, p. 10.

22. Two helpful contemporary studies on the παράδειγμα are Price, 'Paradeigma and Exemplum' and John D. Thomas, 'The Exemplum in Ancient Rhetorical Theory' (MA thesis, University of Florida, 1960). See also A. Lumpe, 'Exemplum', *RAC*, VI, cols. 1229-57, and Heinrich Lausberg, 'Exempla', in *Handbuch der literarischen Rhetorik* (Munich: Max Hueber, 1960), I, §406-26.

23. LSJ, pp. 1307, col. 2-1308, col. 1.

pattern, model; proof; instruction; and precedent, case.[24] Greek and Latin writers used the terms παράδειγμα and *exemplum* most often in the senses of pattern or model, precedent, sample or illustration, and proof from example.[25]

In his *Rhetoric,* Aristotle (384–322 BCE) presented the παράδειγμα as a mode of argument. Distinguishing between proof by syllogism and proof by induction, he considered παράδειγμα to be 'rhetorical induction', ἐπαγωγὴν ῥητορικήν (1.2.8), that is, a proof from a number of cases (1.2.9). He held that the παράδειγμα was more suited to deliberative oratory (1.9.40; 3.17.5) and that, for a superior argument, the παράδειγμα should stand after the enthymeme where it 'resembles evidence' (2.20.9). A παράδειγμα may also form part of the enthymeme wherein one 'assumes the general and then concludes the particular by example' (2.35.8). These remarks constitute a 'functional' description of the παράδειγμα. Aristotle did approach a description of the contents of a παράδειγμα when he stated, 'There are two kinds of examples: namely one which consists in relating things that have happened before [πράγματα], and another in inventing them oneself'. πράγματα could include anecdotes under Aristotle's classification; however, he gave no indication of the 'form' πράγματα would take. Hence, given that a literary genre consists of form, content and function, παράδειγμα is not defined as a literary genre by Aristotle.

The author of *Rhetoric to Alexander* treated the παράδειγμα under the first of two types of proofs, that which was 'drawn from words and actions and persons themselves' (3.1428a.7). He defined παραδείγματα as 'actions that have occurred previously and are similar to, or opposite of those which we are now discussing'. The παραδείγματα are to be used as illustrations in an argument, where they lend greater credibility to the speaker. The author gave illustrations of this use, but none of the illustrations given were anecdotes; rather, the units may best be described as 'brief historical accounts'. This author's short presentation on the παράδειγμα also dwelt on the function of the unit; it was not a description of a literary genre.

24. *A Latin Dictionary* (ed. Charlton T. Lewis and Charles Short; Oxford: Clarendon Press, 1966), p. 682.

25. For example, for pattern or model see Plato, *Meno* 77b, Plutarch, *Lib. ed.* 16 and *Rhet. Her.* 4.44.57. For precedent see Plato, *Laws* 9.876E and *Rhet. Her.* 3.4.9. For illustration see *Rhet. Alex.* 7, Theon, Προγυμνάσματα 2.79, Plutarch, *Mulier. virt.* 243.A and Cicero, *Inv.* 1.12.16. For proof see Aristotle, *Rhet.* 1.2.8 and Cicero, *Inv.* 1.30.49.

As for Greek writers, they referred to various literary units as παραδείγματα. For example, in his essay Περὶ ἀοργησίας, 'On the Control of Anger', Plutarch presented a number of units, which he referred to as παραδείγματα, to illustrate outbursts of anger (454C.3-457C.9). In the course of his description of lack of control of one's anger, the παραδείγματα were used as 'evidence' of his points. For example, Plutarch remarks that even a simple jest can rouse a person to anger and then proves his point by presenting the example of Helen provoking her niece Electra with the remark, 'Electra, virgin for so long a time' (454D.3). These παραδείγματα that Plutarch employed included attributed sayings without a narrative setting and anecdotes. Thus, Plutarch used anecdotes as παραδείγματα; however, he too did not define the παράδειγμα.

While Roman rhetors and grammarians considered the *exemplum* to be a form of argument, they also treated the *exemplum* under the heading of 'figures of thought'. The author of *Rhetorica ad Herennium* discussed the *exemplum* when describing the *exornatio* or 'embellishment' of a judicial speech. The purpose of the *exornatio* is to adorn and enrich the argument after the proof was established (2.17.28) and one means of such enrichment was the use of *exempla* (2.19.46). In Book 4, on figures of thought, the *exemplum* is defined as 'the citing of something done or said in the past, along with the definite naming of the doer or author' (4.49.62). The qualification that the doer or author must be named resonates with the definition of an anecdote; yet 'citing of something done or said' is too general to limit an *exemplum* to an anecdote. Additionally, an *exemplum* was to be used to render 'a thought more brilliant...clearer...more plausible...[and] more vivid' (4.49.62). This author viewed the *exemplum* from a functional perspective whether in relation to a proof or to a figure of thought.

Cicero (106–43 BCE) also discussed the *exemplum* in relation to the proof of an argument and as a figure of thought.[26] Additionally, he noted the role of the *exemplum* as an ornament: '[T]he mention of antiquity and the citation of examples gives the speech authority and credibility as well as affording the highest pleasure to the audience' (*Or. Brut.* 34.120). Cicero's treatment added the element of pathos, or the stirring of

26. For Cicero an *exemplum* could support or weaken a case 'by appeal to precedent or experience, citing some person or historical event' (*Inv.* 1.30.49). He held that an *exemplum* is the greatest corroboration for a probable truth (*Part. or.* 11.40) and that it may be a historical event or a fictitious narrative (*Top.* 10.44-450). As a figure of thought, the *exemplum* served as an amplification within the *peroratio*, particularly in exhortations (*Part. or.* 17.58).

emotions, to the function of an *exemplum.* However, like the preceding authors, he did not present the *exemplum* as a literary genre.

One final Latin rhetor to be considered is Quintilian. Like the Greek authors mentioned above, Quintilian dealt with *exemplum* under the topic of proofs. He viewed the *exemplum* as an induction, equated the term *exemplum* with the Greek παράδειγμα, and appeared to be citing Aristotle when he wrote, in Greek, 'παράδειγμα ῥητορικὴν ἐπαγωγήν' (*Inst.* 5.11.2).[27] Quintilian defined an *exemplum* as 'the adducing of some past action, real or assumed, which may serve to persuade the audience of the truth of the point which we are trying to make' (5.11.6). He did not limit *exempla* to accounts of historical events but included poetic fiction and fables (5.11.17-21). In his illustrations of historical *exempla* Quintilian used an anecdote (5.11.15), an attributed saying (5.11.16) and an unattributed saying (5.11.14). Once again, his discussion of the *exempla* was that of a functional entity and not a specific literary genre. Thus the ancients, both Greeks and Romans, did not use the terms παράδειγμα or *exemplum* to mean, exclusively, the genre I define as an anecdote.[28]

b. ἀφορισμός

Transliterated into English as 'aphorism', the word ἀφορισμός comes from the verb ἀφορίζω, meaning 'to mark off boundaries'. In the LSJ ἀφορισμός is taken first to mean 'a delimitation or assignment of boundaries'. The fourth meaning given is 'a pithy sentence', and reference is made to 'those of Hippocrates'.[29] This undoubtedly refers to Ἀφορισμοί, a work attributed to Hippocrates and dated to the fifth century BCE.[30] Ἀφορισμοί is a collection of statements concerning various diseases and

27. See Aristotle's ἐπαγωγὴν ῥητορικήν, *Rhet.* 1.2.8.

28. For this reason, I question the arguments put forward by Elizabeth Haight (*The Roman Use of Anecdotes in Cicero, Livy and the Satirists* [New York: Longmans, Green, 1940], pp. 2-9) in which she equates *chria*, *exemplum* and anecdote. Richard Saller ('Anecdotes as Historical Evidence for the Principate', *Greece and Rome*, 2nd series, 27 [1980], pp. 69-83) and S. Perlman ('The Historical Example, Its Use and Importance as Political Propaganda in the Attic Orators', in Alexander Fuks and Israel Halpern (eds.), *Scripta Hierosolymitana*. VII. *Studies in History* [Jerusalem: Magnes Press, 1961], pp. 150-66) both argue persuasively for caution in using historical anecdotes or examples from ancient Greek and Latin writings to obtain historical facts. Saller, however, equates anecdotes and *exempla* without adequate nuance, while Perlman avoids any definition of an 'example'.

29. LSJ, p. 292, col. 2.

30. See W.H.S. Jones, 'Introduction', in *Hippocrates* (LCL), IV, p. xxxv.

includes descriptions of symptoms, procedures for treatment, and prognoses.[31] All the units of this work are statements without a narrative setting and none are individually attributed to Hippocrates. While ancients considered Hippocrates to be the author of the statements, more recent scholarship has shown that Ἀφορισμοί contains both units that appear in other works attributed to Hippocrates and units that are later additions. In fact, Ἀφορισμοί may be a collection of statements made by Hippocrates or one of his followers and then expanded over time.[32]

Philo of Alexandria (c. 20 BCE–CE 45) employed ἀφορισμός in *De somniis* 1.16.101 within the context of his comments on Exod. 22.26-27a: 'If you take your neighbor's cloak in pawn, you shall restore it before the sun goes down; for it may be your neighbor's only clothing to use as cover.' Philo distinguished 22.27a as an ἀφορισμός, 'explanatory statement', of the precept in v. 26 rather than a further exhortation. There is no specific attribution given for the ἀφορισμός; in a general way, however, this section of Exodus is attributed to God through Moses.[33]

Vernon Robbins has argued recently for the use of the term aphorism to designate 'a saying attributed to a specific person'.[34] Robbins reasons from two words of Theon's definition of a χρεία as a 'statement [ἀπόφασις] attributed...to a specific [ὡρισμένον] person'.[35] Robbins holds that 'aphorism' captures the ἀπο of ἀπόφασις (an assertion 'from') and by the fact of its being attributed, aphorism deals with the specificity of person. His arguments, while persuasive for a contemporary use of aphorism for this type of literary unit, do not find confirmation in the ancient sources. The term is neither defined nor widely utilized by the Greek writers for an attributed saying. The use of ἀφορισμός for statements attributed only in a general way in Hippocrates' Ἀφορισμοί and in Philo's *De somniis*, does not confirm, conclusively, Robbins's use of the term for an attributed state-

31. E.g., 'Sleep or sleeplessness, in undue measure, these are both bad symptoms' (*Aph.* 2.3); 'In every movement of the body, to rest at once when pain begins relieves the suffering' (*Aph.* 2.48); and 'When sleep puts an end to delirium it is a good sign' (*Aph.* 2.2).

32. Jones, 'Introduction', IV, pp. xxxiv-xxxvi.

33. The LSJ entry on ἀφορισμός as 'pithy sentence' also refers to Hermogenes, Περὶ ἰδεῶν 1.6. The word ἀφορισμός is not found there. What one does find, however, is a general statement on a person's rhetorical ability (*On Ideas of Style*, in *Hermogenis opera* [ed. Hugo Rabe; Rhetores Graeci, 6; Stuttgart: Teubner, 1913]).

34. Vernon Robbins, 'Picking up the Fragments', *Foundations and Facets Forum* 1.2 (1985), pp. 30-64 (35-36).

35. Theon, Περὶ Χρείας 3.2-3.

ment among the Greeks. They more often use ἀπόφθεγμα, ἀπομνημόνευμα or χρεία to refer to an attributed saying.

Latin writers, too, did not define one specific term for the attributed saying. At times they employed the terms *sententia*, *chria* and *dictum* to describe such sayings. They included both sayings and actions under the term *chria* and, as I argue below, the term *sententia* designated an unattributed saying. The noun *dictum* is tied to the Latin verb *dico*, 'to speak', and as such carries with it the sense of a particular speaker. R.O.P. Taylor alluded to the use of *dictum* for an attributed saying in his comments on the Greek γνώμη and χρεία. Referring to the fact that an unattributed saying, a maxim (γνώμη), must be attributed to be included under the term χρεία, Taylor stated that 'the maxim was required to be a *dictum*'.[36]

Keeping in mind that these are modern classifications, I nonetheless follow Robbins's and Taylor's lead and employ ἀφορισμός and *dictum* for an attributed saying that does not have a narrative setting. I do so only for ease of classification within the context of this investigation.

c. γνώμη *or* sententia

Since a great many ancient anecdotes contain sayings, some remarks are in order concerning what is termed the 'maxim' or 'gnome'. The Greek γνώμη, 'means of knowing', also carried the sense of an 'opinion or judgment'; hence, the plural, γνῶμαι can be translated as 'practical maxims'.[37] Quintilian equated the Greek γνώμη with the Latin *sententia* (*Inst.* 8.5.3). *Sententia* derives from the verb *sentio*, 'to perceive, to know'. The noun has the meaning of 'a thought expressed in words…a maxim'.[38] Aristotle defined a γνώμη as 'a general statement…which deals with the objects of human actions and what should be chosen or avoided with reference to them'. He held that a γνώμη can be used as a thesis or a premise on which to build an argument or as the summary of a previous argument (*Rhet.* 2.21.2-9). All but one of the examples Aristotle included in his discussion of the γνώμη are unattributed sayings. The one exception, a saying of Steisichorus, Aristotle identified as a Laconic ἀπόφθεγμα (2.21.8); it should be noted that this ἀπόφθεγμα lacks a narrative setting. Later, the author of *Rhetorica ad Alexandrum* defined γνώμη as 'the expression of an individual opinion about general matters of conduct' (3.1430a-b.11).

36. R.O.P. Taylor, 'Greek Forms of Instruction', in *The Groundwork of the Gospels with Some Collected Papers* (Oxford: Basil Blackwell, 1946), pp. 79-80.

37. LSJ, p. 354, cols. 1-2.

38. *Latin Dictionary*, pp. 1671-72.

The examples presented there are all unattributed sayings. Theon, in his Προγυμνάσματα, commented on the γνώμη within his chapter on the χρεία. There he asserted that a γνώμη is a general statement, always unattributed, and concerned with matters useful in life (3.7-14). Theon is the first extant source to state explicitly that the γνώμη is an unattributed saying.

The treatments of the *sententia* by the Latin authors were similar to those of the Greek authors on the γνώμη. The author of *Rhetorica ad Herennium* wrote: 'A *sententia* is a saying drawn from life which shows concisely either what happens or ought to happen in life' (14.17.24). The author's examples are all unattributed sayings. Quintilian devoted almost a full chapter to the *sententia*; however, the closest he came to a definition was the statement that *sententiae* are 'striking' statements (*Inst.* 8.5.2). He held that the term is 'most correctly applied' to the Greek γνώμη, but did not define the Greek term. There is no mention by Quintilian that the contents of a *sententia* should be of a general, utilitarian nature. Quintilian further differed from Theon, and possibly others, by including attributed sayings as well as anecdotes in his examples of *sententiae*.[39]

Thus, in Greek writers the γνώμη was unattributed, while in the history of the use of the *sententia* by Latin writers it came to be attributed, at least occasionally. In this book, I follow the Greek writers and consider the γνώμη and the *sententia* to be unattributed, general statements about the conduct of life. Since the γνώμη and *sententia* are distinguished from the attributed saying (aphorism), they are also different from an anecdote that refers a saying to a specific person.

A brief comment is made here on παροιμία. This word is used in the

39. For further remarks on the γνώμη and *sententia* see: O. Gignon and K. Rupprecht, 'Gnome', *LAW*, cols. 1099-1100; Paul A. Holloway, 'Paul's Pointed Prose: The *Sententia* in Roman Rhetoric and Paul', *NovT* 40 (1998), pp. 32-53, esp. 34-45; Konstantin Horna, 'Gnome, Gnomendichtung, Gnomologie', PWSup, VI, cols. 74-87; Heinrich Lausberg, 'Sententia', in *Handbuch der literarischen Rhetorik* (2 vols.; Munich: Max Hueber, 1960), I, §1121; Rollin A. Ramsaran, 'More Than Opinion: Paul's Rhetorical Maxim in First Corinthians 7:25-26', *CBQ* 57 (1995), pp. 531-34; W. Spoerri, 'Gnome', KlPauly, II, cols. 823-29; Walter T. Wilson, 'The Ancient Genres of Gnomic Wisdom', in *The Mysteries of Righteousness: The Literary Composition and Genre of the 'Sentences' of Pseudo-Phocylides* (Texte und Studien zum antiken Judentum, 40; Tübingen: J.C.B. Mohr [Paul Siebeck], 1994), pp. 15-41, and 'The Gnomic Saying in Antiquity', in *Love without Pretense: Romans 12.9-21 and Hellenistic–Jewish Wisdom Literature* (WUNT, 2nd series, 46; Tübingen: J.C.B. Mohr [Paul Siebeck], 1991), pp. 9-39.

plural ΠΑΡΟΙΜΙΑΙ in the LXX to translate the title of the Hebrew book משלי. The title appears as *Prouerbia* in Latin, hence the English title 'Proverbs'. The book consists of several collections, including collections of sayings. An example of one of its sayings is, 'Better is a dry morsel with quiet than a house full of feasting with strife' (17.1). While the entire work is ascribed to Solomon, the book contains wisdom instructions and collections of sayings. Two of these collections are attributed to Solomon, those found in 10.1–22.16 and those in 25.2–29.27, which were collected by 'officials of King Hezekiah of Judah' (25.1). A third collection of proverbs, 22.17–24.34, is introduced as 'the words of the wise'. As in the case of the sayings in Hippocrates' Ἀφορισμοί, the sayings in these collections are attributed to individuals or a group only in a general way.

The Hebrew משל is also attested for the unattributed saying in 1 Sam. 24.14 (Heb.), which reads: 'As the משׁל says, "Out of the wicked comes forth wickedness".' παροιμία is likewise attested for a general saying in Plato's *Symposium* 174B.

A study of the sayings in 'Proverbs' leads to the following definition of a proverb: 'A short popular saying that communicates a familiar truth or observation in an expressive and easily remembered form.'[40] The sayings are most often drawn from experience and comment on human behavior. This description of the content of a proverb is similar to Theon's comment that a γνώμη is concerned with 'matters useful in life'. Thus, on the one hand, the ancients attributed some proverbs or collections of proverbs to individuals in a manner akin to the way they attributed aphorisms to one person. There is, however, a similarity in the content of the משׁל, or παροιμία, to that of the γνώμη.

The reminder of this section of the chapter deals with the terms ἀπομνημόνευμα or *commemeratio*, ἀπόφθεγμα, and the χρεία or *chria*, all of which the ancients used as terms for units, some of which are anecdotes.

d. ἀπομνημόνευμα *or* commemeratio

Derived from the Greek verb ἀπομνημονεύω, 'to relate from memory', the noun ἀπομνημόνευμα meant a 'memorial' or a 'record'. The plural, ἀπομνημονεύματα was used in the sense of 'memoirs' or 'reminiscences'.[41] As 'memoirs', ἀπομνημονεύματα occurs as the title of Xenophon's book

40. Roland E. Murphy, 'proverb', in P.J. Achtemeier (ed.), *Harper's Bible Dictionary* (San Francisco: Harper & Row, 1985), pp. 831-32.

41. LSJ, pp. 209-10. See E. Schwartz, 'Apomnemoneumata', PW, II.A.1, cols. 170-71.

about his teacher Socrates and in Plutarch's reference to a small book about Brutus written by Bilbus (*Brut.* 13.3).[42] Justin Martyr also used the term in the sense of memoirs, whether oral or written, in his 'First Apology' (c. 138–161 CE), when he wrote of the Gospels as 'ἀπομνημονεύματα τῶν ἀποστόλων' (67.3).[43] The term ἀπομνημόνευμα also referred, in a very general sense, to a sort of narrative unit. As noted above, Plutarch seems to have interchanged the terms ἀπομνημονεύματα and ἀποφθέγματα in his *Life of Lycurgus* and included under both terms units that were aphorisms, anecdotes and longer narratives.[44]

In his Προγυμνάσματα, Theon briefly mentioned the ἀπομνημόνευμα when he distinguished it from a χρεία. Stating that, like the χρεία, the ἀπομνημόνευμα is an action or saying useful for living (3.5-6), it nevertheless differs from the χρεία in that the ἀπομνημόνευμα need not be brief as required for the χρεία (3.15-18). In the second century CE, Hermogenes also held that an ἀπομνημόνευμα 'may occur in greater length' than a χρεία (*Prog.* 6.15-17). The third century CE fragment on rhetoric, *Oxyrhynchus Papyrus 85*, records that the χρεία was a concise ἀπομνημόνευμα. Moreover, it contains this line: 'Why is the χρεία an ἀπομνημόνευμα? Because it is kept in mind (ἀπο-μνημονεύεται) in order that it may be quoted.'[45] It appears that the grammarians considered

42. ἀπομνημονεύματα is used in this same sense by Diogenes Laertius who recounted the following anecdote about Plato: 'Being asked whether there would be any memoirs [ἀπομνημονεύματα] of him as of his predecessors, he replied, "A man must first make a name and then there will be many"' (*Lives Phil.* 3.38).

43. τοῦ ἁγίου Ἰουστίνου Ἀπολογία ὑπὲρ Χριστιανῶν πρὸς Ἀντωνίνον, *Saint Justin: Apologies* (ed. André Wartelle; Paris: Études Augustiniennes, 1987). Schwartz ('Apomnemoneumata', p. 170) suggested that the word ἀπομνημονεύματα carried with it a connotation of a personal remembrance by the narrator or at least a personal acquaintance with the tradition being related. While a discussion of whether or not the narrator of an ἀπομνημονεύματα had such personal acquaintance with the material being related is beyond the scope of this book, such a discussion is important for the interpretation of Justin Martyr's use of the term ἀπομνημονεύματα. See the discussion in Detlev Dormeyer, *Evangelium als literarische und theologische Gattung* (Erträge der Forschung, 263; Darmstadt: Wissenschaftliche Buchgesellschaft, 1989), pp. 11-16.

44. The same interchange of Greek terms for similar contents occurs in Plutarch's *Cato Major* (20.1.2, 4).

45. *Oxyrhynchus Papyrus 85*. Greek text published in R.O.P. Taylor, *The Groundwork of the Gospels with Some Collected Papers* (Oxford: Basil Blackwell, 1946), p. 82. See also the comments on this fragment in James Moulton and George Milligan, *The Vocabulary of the Greek New Testament Illustrated from Papyri and Other Non-*

the ἀπομνημόνευμα to be a narrative, longer than a χρεία, which was remembered because of its significance. Given the uses of the term by Plutarch mentioned above, one can observe that the distinctions the grammarians laid out were not necessarily observed by all Greek writers. The conclusion can be drawn that the ἀπομνημόνευμα was not a clearly describable, unique literary unit for the Greeks of antiquity.

Latin writers likewise did not have a single term for the reminiscence. The title of Xenophon's Ἀπομνημονεύματα appears as *Memorabilia* in the later Latin translation of the title. Valerius Maximus's collection of deeds and sayings of famous persons is entitled *Factorum et dictorum memorabilium*, where *memorabilia* is an adjective. The noun *memorabilia* does not appear to have been used in early Latin sources for a narrative unit.[46] Priscian, in his *Praeexercitamina*, a late fifth or early sixth century CE translation of Hermogenes's Προγυμνάσματα, translates ἀπομνημόνευμα as *commemeratio* (194.2).[47] I use *commemoratio* for memoir and reminiscence in this investigation when necessary.

e. ἀπόφθεγμα

No clear definition of ἀπόφθεγμα exists in the extant works of the ancient Greek and Latin writers. The nearest one comes to a definition is this statement of Diogenes Laertius (3rd century CE) in his 'Aristotle', 'For many other works and ἀποφθέγματα, pointed oral sayings (ἀγράφου φωνῆς εὐστοχήματα), are attributed to him' (*Lives Phil.* 5.34.9-10).

Derived from the verb ἀποφθέγγομαι, 'to speak one's opinion plainly', ἀπόφθεγμα is defined in the LSJ as a 'terse pointed saying'.[48] The first extant work containing ἀπόφθεγμα is Xenophon's *Hellenica* (fifth–fourth century BCE) where reference is made to two sayings of Theramenes. Referring to these sayings first using the Greek noun ῥῆμα, Xenophon recounted them as follows:

Literary Sources (London: Hodder & Stoughton, 1914–30), p. 67 (repr. Grand Rapids: Eerdmans, 1974).

46. See the comments of Theodor Klauser, 'Apophthegma', *RAC*, 1, col. 545.

47. For the text of Priscian see *Praeexercitamina*, in *Prisciani* (ed. Henricus Keil; Grammatici Latini; 4 vols.; Hildesheim: Georg Olms, 1961), 3.430-40; also the edition by Edward N. O'Neil, 'The Chreia Discussion of Priscian', in Ronald F. Hock and Edward N. O'Neill, *The Chreia in Ancient Rhetoric*. I. *The* Progymnasmata (SBLTT, 27, Graeco-Roman Religion Series, 9; Atlanta: Scholars Press, 1986), pp. 194-97. O'Neil's text is cited in my work.

48. LSJ, p. 226, col. 2.

> When Satyrus told him [Theramenes] that if he did not keep quiet, he would suffer for it, he asked [ἔφη]: 'Then if I do keep quiet, shall I not suffer?'
>
> And when, being compelled to die, he had drunk the hemlock, they said that he threw out the last drops, like a man playing *kattabos*, and exclaimed: 'Here's to the health of my beloved Critias [who had condemned him]' (2.3.56).

It is noteworthy for this study that the first narrative is an anecdote containing a saying and that the second narrative, also an anecdote, contains both a saying and an action.

Aristotle referred to a saying attributed to Anaxagoras, namely 'Things would be for them [his students] as they judged them to be', as an ἀπόφθεγμα (*Metaph.* 4.5.12). Thus Aristotle applied ἀπόφθεγμα to an aphorism, as he also did in his *Rhetoric* at 2.12.7, 8 and 3.11.6. Cicero employed the Greek word ἀπόφθεγμα in reference to witty aphorisms in the phrase '*multaque multorum facete dicta*', that is, 'many witty sayings of many men' (*Off.* 1.39.104).

Among Greek writers, Plutarch, as mentioned above, used ἀπόφθεγμα to describe sayings, anecdotes and longer narratives. There are also three works found in Plutarch's *Moralia* that are entitled ἀποφθέγματα, namely 'Ἀποφθέγματα βασιλέων καὶ στρατηγῶν', 'Ἀποφθέγματα Λακωνικά' and 'Λακαινῶν ἀποφθέγματα'.[49] All three works are comprised of aphorisms and anecdotes that highlight both sayings and actions. Diogenes Laertius in his *Lives of Eminent Philosophers* also employed the term ἀπόφθεγμα in reference to both aphorisms and anecdotes.[50]

The grammarian Theon did not give a definition of an ἀπόφθεγμα; however, in his chapter on the thesis he did speak of the 'useful apophthegm' as a way of confirming a thesis. There ἀπόφθεγμα occurs in a series of units that include the γνώμη, the χρεία and the story (11.19-22). Given Theon's careful use of terms, it appears that he meant to distinguish the ἀπόφθεγμα from the χρεία. Yet such a distinction is not found when one studies the use of ἀπόφθεγμα by Greek authors themselves.

49. It is not certain whether these works were compiled by Plutarch or by someone shortly after his death. For a summary of the discussion on this point see L.A. Trittle, 'Plutarch's "Life of Phocion": An Analysis and Critical Report', *ANRW*, 2.33.6, pp. 4287-90. See also Theodor Klauser, 'Apophthegma', *RAC*, 1, cols. 546-47, and Vernon K. Robbins, 'Pronouncement Stories from a Rhetorical Perspective', *Forum* 4.2 (1988), pp. 3-32 (3).

50. See *Thales* (1.35), *Pittacus* (1.79), *Bion* (4.47), *Aristotle* (5.16) and *Theophrastus* (5.39).

A brief comment on the 'classical form' of an ἀπόφθεγμα is in order here. Modern authors often follow the work of Wilhelm Gemoll (1924), who described the 'classic form' of an ἀπόφθεγμα as 'ἐρωτηθεὶς εἶπε' and cited four classical examples for such a form.[51] Only two of his examples actually use the verb form ἐρωτηθεὶς, from the verb ἐρωτάω.[52] The other two examples, Xenophon's *Memorabilia* 3.13.14 and Lucian's *Demonax* 25, employ a different verb, εἴρομαι.[53] Thus, Gemoll must have intended his classic form to be that of a question asked and answered. If such a classic form did exist, one would expect to find it as the predominant form used by Greek writers; this is not the case. Moreover, such a form is never defined by ancient writers, and, Gemoll's two examples aside, the fact remains that other forms for the ἀπόφθεγμα exist, such as the two units from Xenophon's *Hellenica* cited above. Hence, one must reject Gemoll's assertion of a classic form for the ἀπόφθεγμα.

From a consideration of the use of the term ἀπόφθεγμα by Greek writers, it can be said that the ἀπόφθεγμα was an oral or written unit that could take the form of an aphorism or an anecdote containing a saying or an action. Often, but not always, the sayings involved were 'pointed' or 'witty'. Since one type of ἀπόφθεγμα is the anecdote, it can be concluded that the term ἀπόφθεγμα was an ancient Greek term for an anecdote. It remains true, however, that this ἀπόφθεγμα was not a technical term with a precise meaning.

f. Χρεία *or* chria

The final Greek and Latin terms to be considered are χρεία and *chria*.[54] The χρεία was one of the rhetorical units studied in the προγυμνάσματα.

51. Wilhelm Gemoll, *Das Apophthegma: Literar-historische Studien* (Vienna: Hölder–Pichler–Tempsky, 1924), p. 2. For modern scholars who follow Gemoll, see Richard Spencer, 'A Study of the Form and Function of the Biographical Apophthegms in the Synoptic Tradition in Light of Their Hellenistic Background' (PhD dissertation, Emory University, 1976), pp. 84-85, 120; Klauser, 'Apophthegma', col. 545; and O. Gignon and H. Rupprecht, 'Apophthegma', *LAW*, col. 222.

52. The examples are from two Greek ostraca, that is, Nr 1226 and Nr 1310 from Wilcken, *Griechische Ostraka aus Ägypten und Nubien* (1899), as cited in Gemoll, *Das Apophthegma*, p. 2.

53. However, ἐρωτάω was used in Attic for the present indicative of ἔρομαι (in Ionic εἴρομαι) (LSJ , p. 691, col. 1 and p. 696, col. 1).

54. For ease of reading in the remainder of this investigation, the Greek term χρεία is used to include its Latin transliteration, *chria*. *Chria* is employed only when directly referring to a Latin writer or if a distinction is necessary.

Of all the extant προγυμνάσματα, Theon's, the earliest, contains the fullest presentation of the χρεία. Therefore, for this section I follow Theon's work.[55]

Theon considered the χρεία in Chapter 3 of his Προγυμνάσματα, where he gave this definition:

> Χρεία ἐστὶ σύντομος ἀπόφασις ἢ πρᾶξις μετ᾽ εὐστοχίας ἀναφερομένη εἴς τι ὡρισμένον πρόσωπον ἢ ἀναλογοῦν προσώπῳ (3.2-3).
>
> The χρεία is a concise statement or action which is attributed with aptness to some specified character or to something analogous to a character.[56]

Theon described the χρεία further when he distinguished it from both the γνώμη and the ἀπομνημόνευμα. In these sections one finds that the χρεία 'sometimes makes a general statement and sometimes a specific one' (3.9-11), is 'witty, sometimes containing nothing useful for living' (3.11-12) and may be attributed to 'various characters', τινα πρόσωπα (3.17-18).[57]

Furthermore, Theon explained, this unit had the name χρεία 'because of its excellence, for more than the others (exercises) it is useful [χρειώδης] for life' (3.19-20). This statement is a play on the word χρεία as well as a comment on its function, that is, to present the teaching or behavior contained in the χρεία as a model for life. The 'aptness' of the attribution contributed a persuasive element to the χρεία since the specific personage cited lent the argument of authority for the behavior(s) or attitude(s) portrayed in the χρεία.[58] To produce or employ an 'aptly' attributed χρεία therefore indicated a nascent ability to persuade others using an 'argument from authority'. Thus, Theon could assert that the material of a χρεία that was 'useful for life' produced 'a virtuous character' in students (1.40-42)

55. The treatment of the χρεία in other προγυμνάσματα as well as in Quintilian's writing is discussed in the next section of this chapter.

56. Greek text and translation from Butts, 'The "Progymnasmata" of Theon'. Note that Butts's critical edition of the Greek text is also used as the text of Theon's chapter on the χρεία in Hock and O'Neil, 'Aelius Theon', pp. 81-112.

57. For example, the χρεία in Theon 3.91-92, that is, 'Bion the sophist used to say that love of money is the mother-city of every evil', is attributed to Diogenes the Cynic philosopher by Diogenes Laertius (*Lives Phil.* 6.50).

58. See Vernon K. Robbins ('Progymnastic Rhetorical Composition and Pre-Gospel Traditions: A New Approach', in Camille Focant (ed.), *The Synoptic Gospels: Source Criticism and the New Literary Criticism* [BETL, 110; Leuven: Leuven University Press, 1993], pp. 121-23), who writes of the 'culture-transmitting' usage of specific personages in an oral culture.

as well as, no doubt, in readers and hearers. Several functions of the χρεία, therefore, were to entertain (witty), to instruct, to persuade and to influence behavior.

A study of the numerous examples of χρεῖαι provided by Theon serves to clarify further which, if any, of the other units discussed previously in this chapter Theon would have considered to be χρεῖαι. There are 30 examples of χρεῖαι in Theon's chapter on this unit: 7 are aphorisms and the other 23 include narrative settings. Among those with settings, one finds that 18 contain sayings alone, 4 relate actions alone, and 1 has both an action and a saying. For example, there is this aphorism:

> The poet Euripides has said that the mind of each of us is a god (3.203-204);

a narrative containing only a saying:

> Socrates the philosopher, when a certain student named Apollodorus said to him, 'The Athenians have unjustly condemned you to death', said with a laugh, 'But, did you want them to do it justly?' (3.104-106);

a narrative containing only an action:

> Pythagoras the philosopher, on being asked how long human life is, went up to his bedroom, and peeked in for a short time (3.79-81);

and a narrative containing both an action and a saying:

> Alexander, the Macedonian king, on being asked by someone where he kept his treasures, pointed to his friends and said: 'In these' (3.116-118).

Theon's definition of χρεία and these examples lead to three conclusions. First, his treatment of the χρεία indicates that it was a defined rhetorical entity. From a modern perspective, since its definition includes form, content and function, one can say that the term χρεία describes a genre.

Secondly, consider the definition of an anecdote I gave in Chapter 1:

> A brief narrative, either oral or written, describing an incident, including its setting, which involves one or more persons and which focuses on an action, saying, or dialogue; the function of an anecdote is to entertain, instruct, relate an historical incident, characterize a person, or authoritatively legitimate a specific opinion, a specific practice, or a broader view of reality.

One type of χρεία, that which includes a narrative setting, fits this definition of an anecdote. Therefore, one ancient Greek and Latin generic term for the anecdote is the χρεία or *chria*.

Finally, from the above discussions of the ἀπόφθεγμα and the χρεία, as well as the examples given of each, it is clear that both terms described units, some of which are anecdotes. However, since the χρεία is the more clearly defined and commented upon term in both Greek and Latin sources, I, along with other contemporary form critics, choose the χρεία or *chria* as the name for the ancient anecdote.

This study has distinguished among the units termed ἀφορισμός, γνώμη, ἀπομνημόνευμα, ἀπόφθεγμα and χρεία. Using the conclusions drawn thus far, I present the following typologies for these units as a schema of the relationships I have clarified. The first typology is based upon the type of narrative unit the terms described; the second typology concentrates on the type of saying involved in the unit.

- I. Based on the narrative
  - A. ἀπομνημόνευμα
    - 1. 'longer' narrative[59]
    - 2. brief: χρεία or ἀπόφθεγμα = ANECDOTE
      - a. anecdotal saying-χρεία
      - b. anecdotal action-χρεία
      - c. anecdotal mixed-χρεία: both action(s) and saying(s)
  - B. Other narratives (not the subject of this investigation)[60]
- II. Based on the saying
  - A. γνώμη (unattributed)
  - B. attributed saying
    - 1. ἀφορισμός (without setting)
    - 2. χρεία or ἀπόφθεγμα (with a brief setting) = ANECDOTE
      - a. saying–χρεία
      - b. mixed–χρεία, i.e., saying(s) and action(s)

Thus far the ancient terms used for various rhetorical units have been clarified and their relationship to one another has been demonstrated. The ἀπόφθεγμα and the χρεία have been shown to be units that overlap with the anecdote as I have defined it. The χρεία was chosen as the most appropriate term for the anecdote because it was clearly defined and extensively treated in the προγυμνάσματα of the Greek and Latin grammarians.

59. A discussion of 'longer' is not found in the ancients. However, in section a, p. 25, I discussed 'brief' as involving only one incident and defined it as 'that "size" of a story which "one can hold in one's ear"'. 'Longer' would contrast with this either in the number of incidents involved or in the length of the narrative itself.

60. Another type of narrative would be the 'fable', μῦθος, that is, 'a fictional story depicting a truth', one of the rhetorical units treated by Theon (Ch. 4). See also his 'narrative', διήγημα (Ch. 5), and 'description', ἔκφρασις (Ch. 7).

However, thus far I have dealt only with the definition of the χρεία from the Προγυμνάσματα of Theon. In the next section I further explore Theon's chapter and the writings of Quintilian and other προγυμνάσματα dealing with any variations in the definition of the χρεία, with various typologies developed for the χρεία, and with the school exercises on the χρεία.

3. *The* Χρεία *or* Chria *in Quintilian and Greek and Latin* Progymnasmata

In addition to Theon of Alexandria, other Greek and Latin rhetoricians wrote treatises on the χρεία.[61] The writings of Quintilian and the προγυμνάσματα of Hermogenes, Priscian, Aphthonius and Nicolaus of Myra will be discussed here.[62]

The Roman orator Marcus Fabius Quintilian (c. 40–96 CE), a contemporary of Theon, was born in Spain, studied rhetoric in Rome and then returned home to practice law until he was brought back to Rome by the Emperor Galba in 68 CE. There Quintilian established a school of rhetoric and delivered judicial speeches in the law courts. He was chosen by Vespasian to be the first rhetorician to receive a state subsidy; later, Domitian appointed him tutor to his two great-nephews. After his retirement, c. 90 CE, Quintilian wrote his 12 book *Institutio Oratoria*, 'On the Training of an Orator'.[63]

The *Institutio Oratoria* is not a προγυμνάσματα; rather, the work deals with the education of an orator from young child to grown man. It is in Quintilian's report on the first level of formal education with a *grammaticus* that one finds a brief treatment of the preliminary exercises,

61. For a discussion of the χρεία in the ancient προγυμνάσματα, see Klaus Berger, 'Hellenistische Gattungen im Neuen Testament', *ANRW*, 2.25.2, pp. 1092-93; *idem*, *Formgeschichte des Neuen Testaments*, pp. 82-82; Hock, 'General Introduction to Volume I', pp. 1-60; and Vernon K. Robbins, 'Introduction: Using Rhetorical Discussions of the Chreia to Interpret Pronouncement Stories', in Vernon K. Robbins (ed.), *The Rhetoric of Pronouncement* (Semeia, 64; Atlanta: Scholars Press, 1993), pp. vii-xvii (xii-xvi).

62. Edward N. O'Neil ('The Vatican Grammarian', in Ronald F. Hock and Edward N. O'Neil (eds.), *The Chreia in Ancient Rhetoric.* I. *The* Progymnasmata (SBLTT, 27, Graeco-Roman Religion Series, 9; Atlanta: Scholars Press, 1986), pp. 271-93, also presents the χρεία discussion of the Vatican Grammarian (15th–16th century CE). Due to its late date it is not discussed in this book.

63. For the life of Quintilian, see Kennedy, *Quintilian*, pp. 15-30, and Grube, *The Greek and Roman Critics*, pp. 284-307.

including the *chria* (1.9.3–10.1). His cursory treatment of the *chria* is important since it is the earliest extant Latin source on the unit.

The second century produced Hermogenes of Tarsus (b. 161 CE), who, at the age of 15, declaimed before the emperor Marcus Aurelius.[64] Hermogenes is credited with a five-part work on the constituents of rhetoric, that is, Περὶ τῶν στάσεων, Περὶ εὑρέσεως, Περὶ ἰδέων, Περὶ μεθόδου δεινότητος and a Προγυμνάσματα. Only Περὶ τῶν στάσεων and Περὶ ἰδεῶν, however, are universally accepted as authentic.[65] The Προγυμνάσματα appears to have been written in the time period between Theon and the rhetorician Aphthonius (late fourth century CE); Burton Mack and Edward N. O'Neil argue that 'on balance' the evidence favors Hermogenes as the author.[66] What is important about this προγυμνάσματα, whether authored by Hermogenes or a near contemporary, is that it gives us a clear presentation of one of the exercises on the χρεία, namely that of ἐργασία, 'elaboration'.[67]

A Latin translation of Hermogenes's προγυμνάσματα was produced by Priscian Caesariensis (c. 450–530 CE), a Christian rhetorician in Constantinople.[68] Priscian's *Praeexercitamenta* follows Hermogenes very closely and sometimes explains the Greek writer. Hence, Priscian's work serves as a check on Hermogenes.

A work that exerted a later influence 'all out of proportion to its size' is the Προγυμνάσματα of Aphthonius of Antioch (late fourth century CE).[69]

64. See Philostratus, *Vitae sophistarum* 2.7.

65. So Malcolm Heath, *Hermogenes 'On Issues': Strategies of Argument in Later Greek Rhetoric* (Oxford: Clarendon Press, 1995), p. 241; Hugo Rabe (ed.), *Hermogenis opera* (Rhetores Graeci, 6; Stuttgart: Teubner, 1913), pp. ix-xii; and Ludwig Radermacher, 'Hermogenes (22)', PW, VIII, cols. 872-73. Burton L. Mack and Edward N. O'Neil ('Hermogenes of Tarsus', in Ronald F. Hock and Edward N. O'Neil (eds.), *The Chreia in Ancient Rhetoric*. I. *The* Progymnasmata [SBLTT, 27, Graeco-Roman Religious Studies, 9; Atlanta: Scholars Press, 1986], pp. 156-57) would also grant that Περὶ μεθόδου δεινότητος was written by Hermogenes.

66. Mack and O'Neil, 'Hermogenes', pp. 158-60.

67. See the discussion of ἐργασία below, section d, pp. 82-87. The text of Hermogenes Προγυμνάσματα can be found in Rabe (ed.), *Hermogenis opera*, pp. 1-27. An English translation of the entire Προγυμνάσματα is given in Charles S. Baldwin, *Medieval Rhetoric and Poetic (to 1400): Interpreted from Representative Works* (New York: Macmillan, 1928), pp. 23-38.

68. On Priscian, see Edward N. O'Neil, 'Priscian', in Ronald F. Hock and Edward N. O'Neil (eds.), *The Chreia in Ancient Rhetoric*. I. *The* Progymnasmata (SBLTT, 27, Graeco-Roman Religion Series, 9; Atlanta: Scholars Press, 1986), pp. 185-88.

69. James R. Butts and Ronald F. Hock (eds.), 'Aphthonius of Tarsus', in Ronald

Little is known of Aphthonius other than that he was a student of Libanius at Antioch. A letter of Libanius (*ep.* 985), written in 392 CE, mentions Aphthonius, indicating that he wrote 'many things'.[70] His Προγυμνάσματα survived and received prominence because of its incorporation into the *Corpus Hermogenianum* in the sixth century, perhaps because Aphthonius's exercises were accompanied by clear examples. The influence of the *Corpus Hermogenianum*, including Aphthonius's Προγυμνάσματα, continued down through the eighteenth century, having been in use in the American colonies at Harvard College.[71] The chapter on the χρεία is important because it presents a more detailed ἐργασία of a χρεία than had been given in previous προγυμνάσματα.[72]

Nicolaus of Myra (c. 430–500 CE) studied in Athens and taught rhetoric in Constantinople.[73] His is the latest of the extant Greek προγυμνάσματα. Although listed in the *Suda*, the text of Nicolaus's προγυμνάσματα was not discovered until the second half of the nineteenth century and even then not the complete text.[74] The chapter on the χρεία is well preserved and, although much of its contents are familiar, it contains noteworthy nuances. Unique to Nicolaus's presentation, moreover, is a section on the usefulness of the χρεία and the χρεία-exercises for rhetorical training.[75]

The above-mentioned works will be compared, along with that of Theon and the *Oxyrhynchus Papyrus 85*, first to clarify the definition of the

F. Hock and Edward N. O'Neil (eds.), *The Chreia in Ancient Rhetoric*. I. *The* Progymnasmata (SBLTT, 27, Graeco-Roman Religion Series, 9; Atlanta: Scholars Press, 1986), pp. 212-22.

70. Cited in Butts and Hock, 'Aphthonius', p. 219 n. 7. See also Julius Brozoska, 'Aphthonius (1)', PW, I, cols. 2797-2800.

71. For a discussion of the influence of the *Corpus Hermogenianum* and the προγυμνάσματα in general, see Butts and Hock, 'Aphthonius', pp. 212-16, and D.L. Clark, 'The Rise and Fall of *Progymnasmata* in Sixteenth and Seventeenth Century Grammar Schools', *Speech Monographs* 19 (1952), pp. 259-63.

72. The Greek text of Aphthonius is found in *Aphthonii Progymnasmata* (ed. Hugo Rabe; Rhetores Graeci, 10; Leipzig: Teubner, 1926), pp. 1-51. An English translation is given by Ray Nadeau, 'The Progymnasmata of Aphthonius', *Speech Monographs* 19 (1952), pp. 264-85.

73. See W. Stegemann, 'Nikolaos (21)', PW, XVII, cols. 424-57.

74. See the discussion of the discovery in Lester L. Grabbe and Ronald F. Hock, 'Nicolaus of Myra', in Ronald R. Hock and Edward N. O'Neil (eds.), *The Chreia in Ancient Rhetoric*. I. *The* Progymnasmata (SBLTT, 27, Graeco-Roman Religion Series, 9; Atlanta: Scholars Press, 1986), pp. 238-39.

75. The text of Nicolaus' Προγυμνάσματα is found in *Nicolai Progymnasmata* (ed. J. Felten; Rhetores Graeci, 11; Leipzig: Teubner, 1913), pp. 1-60.

χρεία, then to present the different typologies for χρεῖαι worked out by these authors and, finally, to discuss the exercises with the χρεία.

a. *Definitions*

Although the actual definitions of the χρεία differ somewhat in the early writers, if one considers also their clarifying comments on the χρεία, their presentations are substantially the same. Therefore, what follows are brief remarks on each writer's nuances.

Theon's discussion on the χρεία is the longest of our extant sources. Theon began with a definition of the χρεία and followed this with a differentiation of the χρεία from other units, a comment on the name 'χρεία', typologies for the unit, and, finally, exercises with the χρεία along with examples. It is to be noted that in his definition,[76] Theon identified the χρεία as a statement, ἀπόφασις, or an action. He distinguished the χρεία from the ἀπομνημόνευμα, but it is not clear that Theon would have considered the χρεία a subtype of the ἀπομνημόνευμα as did some others. Also, while it is not a major difference, Theon was the only Greek writer who used the word ἀπόφασις· for the 'saying' that sometimes occurs in a χρεία; others used the term λόγος.

Quintilian's remarks on the *chria* did not include a definition. Instead, he merely stated that the *chria* was different from the *sententia*, the *aetiologia* and the *narratiuncula* (*Inst.* 1.9.3-4, 6). Since the text is corrupt in the lines concerning the *aetiologia* and the *chria*, it is difficult to glean exactly what he meant except that the *sententia* was a 'general' statement. Any further distinction would involve a reconstruction of the text.[77] Thus, all one can actually conclude is that, for Quintilian, a *chria* was somehow different from the 'general statement'.

Hermogenes, and all the grammarians who followed him, discussed the χρεία as the third exercise after μῦθος and διήγημα. Hermogenes's presentation on the χρεία, while much shorter than that of Theon, contains the same basic components, that is, definition, typologies, differentiations,

76. The definition is repeated here: 'The χρεία is a concise statement or action which is attributed with aptness to some specified character or to something analogous to a character.'

77. For the problems with the text of Quintilian in this passage, see Edward N. O'Neil, 'Marcus Fabius Quintilianus', in Ronald F. Hock and Edward N. O'Neil (eds.), *The Chreia in Ancient Rhetoric*. I. *The* Progymnasmata (SBLTT, 27, Graeco-Roman Religion Series, 9; Atlanta: Scholars Press, 1986), pp. 122-28. The suggested reconstructions all depend on the definition of the χρεία found in other sources.

and one exercise, ἐργασία. Hermogenes defined the χρεία as 'a reminiscence of some saying or action or a combination of both which has a concise resolution, generally, for the purpose of something useful' (6.3-5). Hence, Hermogenes classified the χρεία as a subtype of the ἀπομνημόνευμα. Moreover, his definition included the 'combination-χρεία', a concise 'resolution', δήλωσις, within the χρεία instead of the whole unit's conciseness, and the χρεία's function as 'useful'. The χρεία's attribution to a character, missing from the definition, is picked up by Hermogenes when he distinguished the χρεία from the γνώμη (7.4-6). However, the 'aptness', εὐστοχία, of the χρεία is missing from Hermogenes altogether. Priscian's Latin translation of Hermogenes followed the latter's definition exactly. Priscian is the only extant source who used the Latin *usus* for the Greek χρεία (194.1).

The third-century papyrus fragment, *Oxyrhynchus Papyrus 85*, adds two factors to the discussion of the χρεία. First, the definition of the χρεία as 'a concise reminiscence which praises a certain person', contributes the idea that the χρεία commends the character involved. Secondly, as noted above, this fragment asserted that the χρεία was memorized so that it could be quoted. Similar to the definition of *Oxyrhynchus Papyrus 85* is that of Aphthonius, namely that 'A χρεία is a concise reminiscence aptly attributed to some character.' The only other comment on the χρεία itself by Aphthonius was simply that the unit received its name because it was useful. Finally, Nicolaus's definition is the most like that of Theon, since Nicolaus also defined the χρεία as a saying or action rather than an ἀπομνημόνευμα.[78] Unique to Nicolaus is a clause on the function of the χρεία as 'correcting [ἐπανόρθωσιν] some aspect of life' (19.10).

Theon's definition of the χρεία, therefore, stands as adequate for the purposes of this book. What I would add to Theon is that the χρεία is a subtype of the ἀπομνημόνευμα. That the χρεία functioned as praise of the character involved (*Oxyrhynchus Papyrus 85*) is not always the case; nor does the χρεία always serve as 'correcting some aspect of life'. It is clear that this unit consisted of either an attributed saying or a narrative of the setting of an attributed saying, attributed action, or both. The unit had three characteristics: (1) it was brief; (2) it was aptly attributed to a character; and (3) it was useful for living.

78. Nicolaus defined the χρεία as 'a saying or action which is apt and concise, attributed to some specified character and employed for the purpose of correcting some aspect of life' (19.7-10).

b. *Typologies of the* χρεία

The προγυμνάσματα all discussed one or more typologies for the χρεία. The first of Theon's typologies, his most detailed,[79] contained the general categories that the others followed, namely the three 'classes', γένη: (1) 'saying-χρεῖαι', λογικαί; (2) 'action-χρεῖαι', πρατικαί; (3) or 'mixed (both action and saying)-χρεῖαι', μικταί (3.22-24).[80] The typology was based on the content of the χρεία, that is, whether the unit narrated a statement, an action, or both.

Theon further divided both the λογικαί and the πρατικαί into 'species', εἴδη. He gave three species of λογικαί: the 'statement', ἀποφάτικον; the 'response', ἀποκριτικόν; and the 'double', διπλοῦν. Theon further subdivided the statement into (a) that which was unprompted, for example, 'X said…' or 'X used to say…'; and (b) that which arose out of a specific situation, for example, 'On seeing Y, X said…' (3.28-33). The first subdivision, the unprompted statement, is what I have called an aphorism.

The response-species was subdivided into those which responded (a) to a simple question answerable with a 'yes' or a 'no'; (b) to an inquiry that required a longer answer; (c) to a question calling for an explanation, that is, where a reason was given; and, finally, into the (d) 'responsive' species, that which contained some remark or action to which the main character responded (3.34-61).[81]

Theon subdivided the action-χρεῖαι, πρατικαί, into these two species: (1) active, wherein the character acted, and (2) passive, which merely pointed out something experienced by the character (3.71-77). Theon gave no species for the mixed-χρεῖαι, μικταί. He simply commented that mixed χρεῖαι 'make their point with the action' (3.79).[82] Finally, the

79. Theon also gave examples for each element of his typology.

80. See: Hermogenes, 6.7-14; Priscian, 194.7-15; Aphthonius, 4.2-13; and Nicolaus, 20.6–21.1. Quintilian's discussion does not include the 'mixed' *chria*. Instead, he spoke of statements, responses and a third 'chria-like' unit, which he named with the Greek term, χρειῶδες. He gave this example of a χρειῶδες: 'Milo used to carry the bull which he had grown accustomed to carry as a calf' (*Inst.* 1.9.5). See the comparison of Quintilian's classification with that of Theon in Otmar Schissel, 'Die Einteilung der Chrie bei Quintilian', *Hermes* 68 (1933), pp. 245-48.

81. Theon gave this example of a 'responsive' species: 'Once when Diogenes invited him to lunch, Plato said: "Diogenes, how charming your unpretentiousness would be, if it were not so pretentious".' Theon explained that Diogenes had not questioned Plato but simply invited him to lunch (3.55-61).

82. For example, 'A Laconian, when someone asked him where the Lacedaemonians consider the boundaries of their land to be, showed his spear' (Theon, 3.82-83).

double, διπλοῦν, species was defined by Theon as one in which two characters utter statements and one statement makes the exchange a χρεία. He specified that the unit was already a χρεία before the second statement.[83] This first of Theon's two typologies will be employed in the classification of the anecdotes in Lucian's *Demonax* pursued later in this chapter.

Having laid out this general classification, Theon produced a second typology based on the different ways χρεῖαι are expressed, that is, as a maxim; as an explanation; with wit; with a syllogism; with an enthymeme; with an example (παράδειγμα); with a wish; in a symbolic manner; in a figurative manner; with double entendre; with a change of subject; and in a combination of the preceding 11 forms. A study of the examples Theon gave for each of these 'expressions', yields 10 saying-χρεῖαι and 1 mixed-χρεία. The mixed-χρεία reads: 'Alexander, the Macedonian king, on being asked by someone where he kept his treasures, pointed to his friends and said: "In these"' (3.116-18). Theon cited this anecdote as an example of a χρεία expressed in a symbolic manner; the meaning of the χρεία would be conveyed with the symbolic gesture alone; the saying is superfluous.[84]

At a later time, Nicolaus of Myra spoke of two other classifications for the χρεία: the first distinguished the units according to function, that is, those which were witty and those which were useful. He admitted, however, that this was not a satisfactory division since wit could also be useful (21.1-17). His second classification dealt with whether a χρεία demonstrated 'the way things are' or 'the way things should be' (22.10-22). Nicolaus commented that this classification would aid the argumentative exercises of refuting and confirming the χρεία.

These then are the typologies for the χρεία that one finds in the ancient sources. The most general was that of saying-χρεῖαι, action-χρεῖαι and mixed-χρεῖαι. Theon's further subdivision into species was the most detailed presented in the προγυμνάσματα. Other typologies of Greek or Latin χρεῖαι that appear in the secondary literature of this century are the result of later literary studies on the χρεία, or anecdote, as employed by the ancient writers.[85]

83. For example, 'A Roman knight was once drinking at the games, and Augustus sent him the following message: "If I want to dine, I go home". To which the other replied, "Yes, but you are not afraid of losing your seat"' (Quintilian, *Inst.* 6.3.63).

84. This contradicts the statement of Hock that Theon limited his classification of 'expressions' to saying-χρεῖαι alone (Hock, 'General Introduction', pp. 32-33).

85. For example, the typology based on the life-cycle of the human person used by Vernon K. Robbins in the arrangement of the anecdotes in his edited work *Ancient*

c. χρεία *Exercises*

The third part of Theon's chapter on the χρεία presented the exercises with the χρεία. At the outset, Theon named the eight exercises he would discuss and then explained each, providing examples. The first two exercises, the simplest, are 'recitation', ἀπαγγελία, and 'inflection', κλίσις. Recitation involved repeating the χρεία in the same or similar words. Earlier, Theon had commented that the purpose of recitation was so to familiarize the students with the units that they could later imitate them in their own compositions (2.147-48).[86] This ἀπαγγελία presupposed the memorization of the appropriate units. There is ample evidence in the ancient writings that educated persons did in fact memorize anecdotes. Seneca referred to children memorizing *chriae*, although he urged the educated adult to produce *dicta* and not to memorize them (*Ep.* 33.7).[87] Plutarch advised the new bride Eurydice to adorn herself with the 'rare and precious jewels' of the ἀποφθέγματα of wise and good persons which she had memorized, ἀνελάμβανες, when she was young (*Conj. praec.* 48). Such wise and good persons included women, since Plutarch suggested nine women, six by name. Plutarch proposed that Eurydice do this so as to give joy to her husband and to win the admiration of other women. Hence, the χρεία could also function to enhance the ἦθος of the speaker or writer who employed it.

On the other hand, for Theon, inflection was a simple grammatical exercise for parsing skills and involved changing the characters 'into three numbers', that is, into singular, dual and plural (3.146-99). Thus, for example, 'Isocrates the rhetor used to say that gifted students are children of gods', became, in the singular, 'Isocrates the rhetor used to say that the gifted student is a child of gods.' In inflection the χρεία was also changed into each of the five cases in reference to the character.[88]

The third exercise, 'adding a comment' or 'approving', ἐπιφώνησις, was paired with the fourth exercise, that of 'objecting', ἀντιλογία. One

Quotes and Anecdotes: From Crib to Crypt (Sonoma, CA: Polebridge Press, 1989), and the thematic typology used by Catherine Hezser in 'Die Verwendung der hellenistischen Gattung Chrie im frühen Christentum und Judentum', *JSJ* 27 (1996), pp. 371-439 (414-24).

86. In the same passage Theon spoke of the proper manner of recitation so that one's words were 'attractive to the mind of the listeners' (2.154-77).

87. Seneca also spoke of the memorization and recitation of *fabulae* (*Ep.* 24.6).

88. The many possibilities for this exercise are each accompanied by an example from Theon. Quintilian spoke of this exercise a *declination*, but without specification (*Inst.* 1.9.5).

approves of the saying in a χρεία by adding the simple comment that it is 'true, or noble, or advantageous, or has appealed to other men of distinction' (3.200-16). The objecting was to be done 'from the opposite points of view' (3.217-23). These two basic exercises prepared the student for the later exercises of confirming and refuting a χρεία.

'Expanding', ἐπεκτείνωσις, and 'condensing', συστολή, the fifth and sixth exercises, were also paired. As their names imply, expanding meant to amplify or enlarge upon the questions, responses or descriptions contained in the χρεία. Condensing was the opposite. Theon gave a lengthy example of an expansion of the χρεία: 'Epameinondas, as he was dying childless, said to his friends: "I have left two daughters—the victory at Leuctra and the one at Mantineia".' Theon amplified each member of the χρεία by adding other descriptive remarks. For example, the expansion begins, 'Epameinondas, the Thebian general, was of course a good man in time of peace…' (3.224-40). That orators and writers were trained in these two exercises is important to note in relation to the search for the 'original tradition', oral or written, that stands behind any anecdote in ancient literature.[89]

The last two exercises, again seen as pairs, were 'refuting', ἀνασκευή, and 'confirming', κατασκευή. According to Theon, one refuted a χρεία using the most appropriate of these arguments: obscurity, pleonasm, ellipsis, impossibility, implausibility, falsity, unsuitability, uselessness or shamefulness (3.241-76).

When Theon commented on the eighth exercise, 'confirming', κατασκευή, he failed to use its name or to provide examples. Instead he wrote, 'It is necessary also to offer proofs, ἐπιχειπεῖν, for each detail of the χρεία, beginning with the first ones, using as many commonplace arguments, τόπων, as possible' (3.277-78). He then spoke of arranging arguments as 'in the order of commonplace arguments', but gave no such order. However, Theon noted that the 'same commonplace arguments could be used for refuting and confirming (κατασκευή) maxims (γνωμῶν)'. Since Theon had no chapter on the γνώμη, this remark can be considered an aside; however, from his use of κατασκευή it can be inferred that in regard to the χρεία-exercise of confirming, 'to offer proofs' is a description of and is equivalent to κατασκευή. Theon's chapter on the fable, μῦθος, affords

89. This point is a major argument in the works of Saller ('Anecdotes as Historical Evidence for the Principate') and Perlman ('The Historical Example'). See also the comments on historicity and the χρεία in Hock, 'General Introduction', pp. 41-46.

clarification on the missing 'commonplace arguments'.[90] In that chapter he discussed refuting and confirming the fable (4.100-63), and his arguments for refuting the fable are almost identical to those he gave for refuting the χρεία. As for confirming the fable, Theon stated that 'one should confirm from the opposite arguments [to those for refuting it]' (4.103-105). It can be argued, therefore, that in confirming a χρεία, 'the commonplace arguments' would be the opposite of those Theon gave for refuting the χρεία.[91] These arguments then would be: clarity, exactness, completeness, possibility, plausibility, truth, suitability, usefulness and worthiness. Such arguments would be appropriate for beginning students.

Finally, at the close of his whole discussion, indeed the chapter on the χρεία, Theon gave a three-part structure for the confirmation of a χρεία as follows: (1) an introduction tailored to each χρεία by using some of its main ideas; (2) the statement of the χρεία itself; and finally (3) the commonplace arguments also using 'expansion, digressions, and character delineations, where there is an opportunity for them' (3.284-91).

Immediately before this structure, Theon made the remark that for more advanced students the exercise of κατασκευή should start from the many additional commonplace arguments presented in his chapter on the 'thesis', θέσις. There he gave 27 topics for confirming the thesis, beginning with 'possibility', and including from 'the opposite', from 'the similar', 'many others do it' or example, and ending with 'testimony of famous men' (11.42-76). These particular arguments from Theon are highlighted here since they are the specific ones presented in later προγυμνάσματα as the elements of the argumentation in an 'elaboration', an ἐργασία.

It is tempting to conclude that this more advanced level of confirming was in actuality the elaboration, but such a conclusion is not justified.[92]

90. Hock, 'General Introduction', pp. 72-74.

91. A further argument for this conclusion is found in Hermogenes's Προγυμνάσματα. Hermogenes did not discuss refuting and confirming the χρεία itself; however, he had a separate chapter on these two exercises in general (11.1-20). There, after giving the commonplace arguments for refuting (similar to those Theon gave for refuting the χρεία), Hermogenes concluded his discussion with, 'while confirming is from the opposites [of these]' (11.19-20).

92. Contrary to the conclusions of Robbins ('The Chreia', pp. 19-20) and Burton L. Mack ('Elaboration of the Chreia in the Hellenistic Schools', in B.L. Mack and V.K. Robbins (eds.), *Patterns of Persuasion in the Gospels* [Sonoma, CA: Polebridge Press, 1989], pp. 31-67 [40]). I also take exception to Robbins's use of the terms 'first-level elaboration (ἐργασία)' and 'second-level elaboration (ἐργασία)' ('Progymnastic Rhetorical Composition', pp. 121-23, and 'Introduction', p. xiv). Robbins uses the

Nowhere did Theon indicate this. Moreover, while the present Greek manuscripts of Theon's work do not contain a chapter on the ἐργασία, internal and external evidence indicates that his original version did have such a chapter. In his opening chapter Theon mentioned the exercises he would treat and there one finds the ἐργασία (1.172-74, 199-201). Five of Theon's planned exercises, including the ἐργασία, are missing from the Greek manuscripts. The Armenian manuscripts, however, do contain four of these five missing exercises, the ἐργασία being one of them.[93] With this information, and given Theon's careful presentations, it is best merely to indicate similarities between his second level of confirming a χρεία and the exercise of elaboration and to consider this second level as a preparation for the more difficult elaboration, as indeed Theon himself indicated in his opening chapter (1.199-201).

Theon's eight exercises with the χρεία were designed to introduce students to the art of persuasion. In his opening chapter, Theon commented that those who could refute and confirm were 'not far behind those who deliver speeches' (1.30-33). Thus the progression in argumentation, using the χρεία, went from objecting and approving to refuting and confirming on two levels, to the elaboration, and finally to the speech itself. For the exercise of elaboration, however, one must consider later προγυμνάσματα.

d. ἐργασία—*The Elaboration of the* χρεία

Hermogenes's Προγυμνάσματα is our first extant source on the method of the elaboration of a χρεία. The ἐργασία, which Hermogenes referred to as 'the chief matter' of his chapter, is the only χρεία-exercise he presented. He began with the first three parts: a short encomium for the one who spoke or acted, a paraphrase of the χρεία, and then the 'rationale', αἰτία (7.10-13). There followed the sketch of an ἐργασία on the χρεία (aphorism): 'Isocrates said that education's root is bitter, its fruit is sweet' (7.13–8.13). In this sketch, Hermogenes indicated five additional elements of the ἐργασία after the rationale so that the final arrangement consisted of these eight elements:

former for the confirming exercise found in Theon and the latter for the actual εργασία, 'elaboration', as found in the later handbooks. The authors of the ancient handbooks do not present the confirming exercise as a 'first-level ἐργασία'.

93. See Butts's discussion of these points ('The "Progymnasmata" of Theon', pp. 8-20).

1. ἐγκώμιον, encomium;
2. παράφρασις, paraphrase of the χρεία with amplification;
3. αἰτία, rationale;
4. κατὰ τὸ ἐναντίον, argument from the opposite;
5. ἐκ παραβολῆς, argument from analogy;
6. ἐκ παραδείγματος, argument from example;
7. ἐκ κρίσεως, argument from authority; and
8. παράκλησις, exhortation to heed the one who spoke or acted.

In his illustration Hermogenes did not write out the ἐργασία completely; this is particularly true for steps two, seven and eight. The later Προγυμνάσματα of Aphthonius, however, did contain a complete illustration of an ἐργασία, using the same aphorism of Isocrates as did Hermogenes (4.16–6.19).[94]

Nicolaus of Myra's fifth-century Προγυμνάσματα also contained a pattern for the elaboration, which he termed the διαίρεσις (17.23; διῄρηται in 24.3). Unfortunately, Nicolaus did not illustrate his pattern, which included six heads: (1) encomium, (2) paraphrase of the χρεία, (3) the probable and the true, (4) examples, (5) opinion of others and (6) brief exhortation. Additionally, he allowed that 'analogy' sometimes followed after 'the true' (24.4-15). One can interpret Nicolaus's 'opinion of others' to be the same as Aphthonius's 'testimony of the ancients' and Hermogenes's 'authority', and thus any difference in Nicolaus's elaboration is in his 'the probable and the true', and may reflect a development in the exercise of elaboration, since his text is later than the others.[95]

Of further importance for my study is Nicolaus's observation that some of the προγυμνάσματα were partial speeches, including the χρεία, since 'it cannot fulfill the purpose of a complete speech alone' (23.6-8). Nonetheless, Nicolaus stated that 'the χρεία'[96] contributed to the practice of

94. Aphthonius's pattern for the ἐργασία has eight 'heads', κεφαλαῖοι, which are essentially the same as those of Hermogenes (4.13-16). His seventh head, μαρτυρία παλαιῶν, 'testimony of the ancients', is equivalent to Hermogenes's 'authority' and Ἐπιλόγῳ βραχεῖ, 'short epilogue', Aphthonius's last head, when studied in the illustration he provided, is in fact an exhortation as in the last step of Hermogenes's ἐργασία.

95. It is not clear what Nicolaus intended by the two heads 'the probable' and 'the true' since he did not explain this step nor provide an example. See Grabbe and Hock, 'Nicolaus of Myra', pp. 244-45.

96. It is clear from his comments that by the 'χρεία' Nicolaus meant the elaboration exercise with the χρεία, although his detailing of this exercise followed his comments on the χρεία as a practice for the parts of a speech.

the three types of rhetorical speech, 'deliberative' (συμβουλευτικοῦ), 'epideictic' (πανηγυρικοῦ) and 'forensic' (δικανικοῦ). In that it urged one to do something good or refrain from something evil, the χρεία belonged to deliberative rhetoric; when praise was given, the χρεία was encomiastic or epideictic; and where thc elaboration of the χρεία involved argument from the probable or from examples one was concerned with forensic rhetoric (23.9-17). Nicolaus did not claim that the elaboration of the χρεία was a complete speech or argument of any type, but rather that practice with the elaboration in some way prepared the student to compose such speeches.

Furthermore, the elaboration of the χρεία provided training in each of what Nicolaus gave as the five parts of the public speech, that is, the 'introduction' (προοίμιον), 'statement of the facts' (διήγησις), 'antithesis' (ἀντίθεσις), 'resolution' (λύσις) and 'epilogue' (ἐπίλογος) (23.9–24.3). Praise of the one speaking or acting in the χρεία served as an 'introduction'; the paraphrase of the χρεία was a partial 'statement of the facts'; confirming (κατασκευάζομεν) what has been said or done constituted 'arguing the case' (ἀγωνιζόμεθα), even without 'attacking a counter proposition' (ἀντιθέσεως ἁπτώμεθα); and the exhortation served as an epilogue. Again, it must be stated that Nicolaus did not hold that the elaboration of the χρεία in itself contained all the parts of a complete speech, only that the elaboration furnished training for each part of a speech.[97]

The first extant προγυμνάσματα to present the χρεία-elaboration, that of Hermogenes, is dated to the second century. Therefore, before inquiring whether or not the anecdotes of the first-century Gospel of Mark display any elements of the elaboration of a χρεία, it is important to investigate works that predate Hermogenes for evidence of such an ἐργασία or a similar exercise. For this reason two earlier rhetorical handbooks are considered here.[98]

The *Rhetorica ad Alexandrum* (300 BCE) furnishes us with an early

97. This point is stressed since several modern scholars hold that the elaboration pattern of Hermogenes represents a 'complete argument'. See my comments on the work of Burton Mack and Vernon Robbins in section a, pp. 175-80, below.

98. These two handbooks are discussed here since they figure prominently in the arguments put forth by Burton L. Mack in his 'Decoding the Scriptures: Philo and the Rules of Rhetoric', in F.E. Greenspahn, E. Hilgert and B.L. Mack (eds.), *Nourished with Peace: Studies in Hellenistic Judaism in Memory of Samuel Sandmel* (Denver: University of Denver [Colorado Seminary], 1984), pp. 83-115; *idem*, 'Anecdotes and Arguments: The Chreia in Antiquity and Early Christianity', *Occasional Papers of the Institute for Antiquity and Christianity* 10 (1987), pp. 1-48; and 'Elaboration of the Chreia in the Hellenistic School'.

pattern of argumentation. The treatise begins its discussion of 'the principles of political oratory' by identifying three classes [γένη] of public speech, that is, parliamentary or deliberative, epideictic and forensic (1.1420a.6-9). The author then asserted that each class was divided into the same seven species (εἴδη), namely exhortation, dissuasion, eulogy, vituperation, accusation, defense and investigation (1.1421b.7-11). Beginning with the deliberative speech of exhortation, the author presented a pattern for the speech as follows: (a) presentation of the course of action being urged; (b) rationale for the course of action using one of seven commonplace topics: that it is just, lawful, expedient, honorable, pleasant, practical or necessary; (c) analogies; (d) opposites; and (e) 'previous judgments of time made by the gods or by men of repute or by judges, or by our opponents' (1421b.21-1422a.27). There followed an illustration of parts two through five for each of the seven topics. The author concluded the discussion of the pattern of speeches by saying that all the other speeches are similarly structured (1423a.12). This early arrangement of the argumentation of a speech (parts two through five) is very similar to the χρεία-elaboration pattern of Hermogenes (parts three through seven), lacking only his encomium, example and final exhortation. Thus one can see that the practice of the elaboration of a χρεία indeed might be preparation for a speech, at least the pattern of argumentation found in *Rhetorica ad Alexandrum*. There is no sample of the elaboration pattern itself used in this handbook, however, that could allow one to make this a definite claim for such an early date for this work.

A closer parallel to the ἐργασία of a χρεία is found in the *Rhetorica ad Herennium* (86–82 BCE).[99] In Book 4 the author considered the principles of 'Style' (*elocutio*), dealing first with the kinds of style and then with the qualities of finished style. Under the quality of 'distinction', *dignitas*, the author presented figures of thought, including 'refining', *expolitio* (4.43.54). There one finds one form of *expolitio*, 'declaiming on a theme', which consisted of this seven-part arrangement: (1) the statement of a theme, (2) the reason, (3) the paraphrase, (4) the opposite, (5) an analogy, (6) a comparison and an example and (7) a conclusion (4.43.56–44.57). The author illustrated this *expolitio* using the *sententia*, 'The wise man will, on the republic's behalf, shun no peril' (4.44.57).[100] In this illustration, part

99. Bonner (*Education in Ancient Rome*, pp. 259-60) is the first to draw attention to this parallel.

100. Note that in a footnote (*Rhetorica ad Herennium* [LCL], p. 371 n. e), Harry Caplan (ed.) incorrectly called this *sententia* a χρεία. It is not an attributed saying.

six contains both a comparison and the example of Decius, the latter being an argument from authority. Except for the lack of an opening encomium, the pattern of this *expolitio* is very similar to that of the χρεία-elaboration found in Hermogenes. It is a simple step to attribute a *sententia* to a character and produce a *chria*. The seven-part arrangement of Hermogenes's χρεία-elaboration, except for the encomium, is produced by focusing on the saying and not on the speaker. Given the existence of the *expolitio* in the *Rhetorica ad Herennium*, therefore, one can argue that an exercise like the ἐργασία was probably in use with the χρεία in the first century CE.

Moreover, just as the grammarians Theon and Nicolaus were to emphasize that the practice of the προγυμνάσματα, including the ἐργασία, was preparation for composing various parts of a speech, the author of *Rhetorica ad Herennium* urged the practice of *expolitio* to develop skill in style. One is urged to practice the exercise first 'divorced from a real cause'; then it should be used in an actual speech within the 'embellishment of an argument', *cum exornabimus argumentationem* (4.44.58) which had been dealt with previously by the author.

Book 1 of *Rhetorica ad Herennium* is concerned with 'invention' (*inventio*), 'the devising of matter, true or plausible, that would make a case convincing' (1.2.3). The author was concerned primarily with *inventio* in each of the six parts of the forensic speech, namely: (1) 'introduction', *exordium*, (2) 'statement of facts', *narrationem*, (3) 'division', *divisionem*, (4) 'proof', *confirmationem*, (5) 'refutation', *confutationem* and (6) 'conclusion', *conclusionem* (1.3.4). Book 2 covers *inventio* in the *confirmationem* of the speech. There, after discussing which arguments to use in different types of legal issues, the author considered how 'to deliberate or carry on a discussion' (*tractare*) using the appropriate arguments.[101] In 2.18.28–19.30 one finds what the author has termed 'the most complete and most perfect argument', *absolutissima et perfectissima argumentatio*. This 'complete argument' consists of five parts: (1) 'the proposition', *propositio*, (2) 'the reason', *ratio*, (3) 'the proof of the reason', *confirmation*, (4) 'the embellishment', *exornatio* and (5) 'the resume', *complexio*. The author illustrated this arrangement using the proposition that 'Ulysses had a motive in killing Ajax'. In the embellishment of this proposition, one finds an analogy, examples and amplification. These are all characteristics of embellishment that the author discusses

101. See the *The Oxford Latin Dictionary* (ed. P.G.W. Glare; Oxford: Clarendon Press, 1982), p. 1955, col. 2, for this translation of *tractare*.

later in 2.29.46. In that section one also finds the argument from authority as a type of embellishment. With these considerations of embellishment, one pattern of the 'complete argument' could be: (a) the proposition, (b) the reason, (c) the proof of the reason, (d) the embellishment, that is, analogy, example, argument from authority, and (e) the resume.

This possible pattern resembles the author's *expolitio* in his Book 4 as well as the pattern of argumentation in the ἐργασία of Hermogenes; however, the three patterns differ somewhat from one another. Additionally, the 'complete argument' deals with a proposition, while the *expolitio* is worked out on a *sententia*, and the ἐργασία on an attributed *sententia*, a *chria.* Nonetheless, it can be concluded that the *expolitio* and the χρεία-elaboration did indeed provide the future rhetor with practice in patterns of argumentation that would be useful for the *inventio* necessary to produce the proof in a persuasive speech.[102]

In summary, one recognizable form of the anecdote in the Greek and Latin orators and authors is the χρεία. This unit was clearly defined and extensively treated in the προγυμνάσματα of the grammarians. Additionally, I have shown that in one rhetorical handbook dated immediately before the dawn of the common era, one figure of thought, the *expolitio*, might take the form of a pattern of argumentation and that practice with *expolitio* was useful for the technique of invention employed in constructing the proof of a forensic speech. This *expolitio* resembled the argumentative pattern of the χρεία exercise of ἐργασία, and thus both the *expolitio* and the ἐργασία were, in a sense, 'practice in argumentation'.

Burton Mack and Vernon Robbins have shown that some of the elements of argumentation in the χρεία-elaboration are present in the anecdotes of the New Testament. Before studying the form, function and contents of the anecdotes of Mark's Gospel, discussing their genre and looking for evidence of an argumentative pattern in them, an investigation of the use of anecdotes in another Greek literary work of the same time period would be useful as a basis of comparison. In the final section of this chapter, therefore, I will analyze the anecdotes of Lucian's *Demonax.*

4. *Anecdotes in the* ΔΗΜΩΝΑΚΤΟΣ ΒΙΟΣ *of Lucian of Samosata*

The choice of Lucian's *Demonax* for this study is motivated by two 1984 essays of Hubert Cancik that addressed the issue of the Greek βίος and

102. These results counter some of the conclusions of Vernon Robbins and Burton Mack. See section a, pp. 175-80.

the genre of Mark's Gospel.[103] In his 'Die Gattung Evangelium', Cancik asserted that Greek and Roman readers of Mark would have considered the gospel to be a βίος of Jesus, while Hellenistic Jews who read the Hebrew Bible in Greek or Latin would have treated Mark as a prophetic book.[104] In his second essay, 'Bios and Logos', Cancik argued that Lucian's Δημώνακτος Βίος, the *Demonax*, is a Greek βίος, in fact a 'Cynic Bios', and that Mark's Gospel can be compared with the *Demonax*.[105] Cancik's claims, both that Mark's Gospel is a Greek βίος and that the Gospel is similar to Lucian's *Demonax*, need further investigation, beyond the scope of this book. However, one contribution to such an investigation is the following study of the form and function of the anecdotes contained in the *Demonax*. Since Chapter 5 of this monograph will examine Mark's use of anecdotes, the results of the study on anecdotes in the *Demonax* can be compared with the results in Chapter 5. This will offer one element in a comparison of the genres of the *Demonax* and Mark's Gospel. Additionally, the results of the present chapter will provide a basis for comparing the function of Markan anecdotes with the function of anecdotes in another Greek work.

a. *Lucian of Samosata*

Over 80 works are attributed to Lucian, and all information about him is gleaned from these works.[106] Born in Samosata on the middle Euphrates c. 120 CE, he was trained in rhetoric and traveled throughout the empire as a Sophist, declaiming and lecturing in public. Around the age of 40, Lucian turned from this role to the study of 'philosophy', and began writing and performing satiric dialogues for the educated class. He died sometime after 180 CE. There is disagreement among contemporary scholars on the

103. Hubert Cancik, 'Die Gattung Evangelium: Markus im Rahmen der antiken Historiographie', in *Markus-Philologie: Historische, literargeschichtliche und stilistische Untersuchungen zum zweiten Evangelium* (WUNT, 33; Tübingen: J.C.B. Mohr, 1984), pp. 85-113, and *idem*, 'Bios and Logos: Formengeschichtliche Untersuchungen zu Lukians "Demonax"', in *Markus-Philologie*, pp. 115-30.

104. Cancik, 'Die Gattung Evangelium', pp. 94-98, 110.

105. Cancik, 'Bios and Logos', pp. 115-18.

106. See the historical-critical account of Lucian's life by C.P. Jones (*Culture and Society in Lucian* [Cambridge, MA: Harvard University Press, 1986], pp. 6-23) and his chronology of Lucian's life with documentation from Lucian's works (p. 167). See also Walter M. Edwards and Robert Browning, 'Lucian', *OCD*, p. 621, cols. 1-2; and R. Helm, 'Lukianos', PW, XIII, cols. 1725-77.

authenticity of many of the works attributed to Lucian, but the majority agree that the *Demonax* is genuine.[107]

b. *The* ΔΗΜΩΝΑΚΤΟΣ ΒΙΟΣ *of Lucian of Samosata*

Δημώνακτος Βίος, written c. 174–77 CE,[108] concerns one Δημῶναξ whom Lucian identified as a philosopher and with whom he had studied for a long period of time (1.8-9). Demonax is known principally from this text, although some 30 other quotations attributed to him exist in medieval collections, some of which may be genuine.[109] The purpose of Lucian's work is to ensure that Demonax is remembered and that young persons have a contemporary example, παράδειγμα, on which to base their lives rather than having to look only to ancient models (2.2-7).

Demonax was born c. 70–80 CE in Cyprus of wealthy parents. The account Lucian gave of Demonax's studies indicates that he followed the academic curriculum of the ancient world (3.1–4.9). Living at Athens, Demonax was an eclectic philosopher whose teachers included the Cynics Agathobulus and Demetrius, the Stoic Epictetus and the Sophist Timocrates of Heraclia (3.5-8).[110] Demonax was put on trial at Athens on charges of failing both to offer sacrifices to the gods and to be initiated into the Eleusinian mysteries (11.7-10); however, his defense won him acquittal. Despite these charges Demonax was well liked by the Athenian people. He had a reputation as a witty, calm and friendly person who worked as a reconciler (9.1-6). At the age of one hundred,[111] when he could no longer function independently, Demonax took his own life (4.10-

107. Donald Dudley (*A History of Cynicism from Diogenes to the 6th Century A.D.* [Cambridge: Cambridge University Press, 1937], p. 158 [repr. Chicago: Ares Publishers, 1980]) presents the arguments and accepts Lucian's authorship of *Demonax*. See also the list of disputed works in Jones, *Culture and Society*, pp. 170-71.

108. On the difficulty of dating *Demonax* and for these approximate dates see C.P. Jones, *Culture and Society*, p. 91 n. 5. For the Greek text of Lucian's *Demonax* see Harmon's *Lucian*, LCL edition. All translations of passages from the *Demonax* are mine unless otherwise noted.

109. See the discussion of these fragments by Jones, *Culture and Society*, p. 91.

110. For Agathobulus see H. v. Arnim, 'Agathobulos', PW, I, col. 745. Agathobulus is also mentioned as a teacher of Peregrinus by Lucian in his '*The Passing of Peregrinus*'. For Demetrius see Miriam T. Griffin, 'Demetrius (19)', *OCD*, p. 450, col. 2; for Epictetus see: Brad Imwood, 'Epictetus', *OCD*, p. 532, col. 2; and for Timocrates of Heraclia see W. Capelle, 'Timocrates (14)', PW, VI.A, cols. 1266-67.

111. From this statement Jones (*Culture and Society*, p. 92) calculates that Demonax was born c. 70–80 CE.

12, 65.1-10). This 'noblest of all the philosophers' (2.7-8) was given a 'magnificent public funeral' and attendant honors (67.1-10).

The *Demonax* itself consists of a prose account of Demonax's earlier life, a series of anecdotes placed one after the other, and a closing prose section that narrates Demonax's last years. The formal structure of the text can be outlined as follows:

The Formal Structure of the Demonax

A.	Introduction	1–2
B.	Prose narrative of training and way of life	3–11
C.	Anecdotes involving Demonax	12–62
D.	Prose narrative of old age, death and burial	63–67.10
E.	Epilogue	67.11

The *Demonax* conforms with what Friedrich Leo identified as the Suetonian literary type of a biography, that is, one that contains a chronological narrative with a characterization of the person and his or her achievements.[112] The two narrative sections, 3–11 and 63–67.10, function as a chronological framework for Lucian's collection of sayings and actions that further illustrated the 'sort of man' Demonax was (67.13). Leo himself included remarks on the *Demonax* as a supplement to his discussion of Diogenes Laertius's *Lives of Eminent Philosophers*. Leo saw in Diogenes Laertius's collection a subtype of the Suetonian literary βίος, namely the βίοι φιλοσόφων.[113] Commenting on the *Demonax*, Leo sketched out a structure for the work similar to the one presented above, and presented this structure as the form of a βίος φιλοσόφου. He held that such a form 'shines through everywhere' in Diogenes Laertius's collection.[114]

Cancik began his discussion of the genre of the *Demonax* by citing Leo's reference to Diogenes Laertius. Cancik was even more specific, saying that the *Demonax* is an 'exemplar' of a type of ancient biography that existed before Lucian's time, remnants of which can be found in Diogenes Laertius's *Lives of Eminent Philosophers* Book 6, on the Cynics.

112. Friedrich Leo, *Die griechisch-römische Biographie nach ihrer litterarischen Form* (Leipzig: Teubner, 1901), pp. 11-16.

113. Leo, *Die griechisch-römische Biographie*, pp. 35-82.

114. Leo, *Die griechisch-römische Biographie*, p. 83. Leo also conjectured that the form of the βίος found in *Demonax* was what Diogenes Laertius sought to emulate (p. 84).

With no further explanation Cancik concluded that the *Demonax* was a representative of a 'branch of Hellenistic biography, the βίος κυνικός'.[115] Unfortunately, Cancik did not present the form of such a 'Cynic Bios'; instead, he posited the existence of this genre because of the similarity of the content of Demonax's sayings with those of the cynic Diogenes from his life as recorded by Diogenes Laertius. It should be noted also that Cancik appealed to this similarity despite Lucian's statement that Demonax followed no particular philosophy and resembled Diogenes only in dress (5.1–6.2).

Cancik also viewed the genre of the *Demonax* under what he termed 'genre categories': that of βίος, ἀπομνημόνευμα and παράδειγμα.[116] These categories come from the form, source (Lucian's reminiscences), and a function of the *Demonax*, respectively. In regard to the latter Cancik asserted that, since for many philosophers their way of life was part of their philosophical teaching, the βίοι φιλοσόφων, which contain accounts of the philosophers' sayings and deeds, functioned as both a παράδειγμα and a διδαχή.[117] Because of these functions, Cancik stated that the *Demonax*, and all other βίοι φιλοσόφων, do not fall under the category of Leo's Suetonian βίος but constitute a separate genre.

The text of the *Demonax* does confirm Cancik's observation on the paradigmatic function of the biography. As noted above, one of Lucian's stated purposes was to present the life of Demonax as a model (2.2-7). However, there is no need to reject Leo's subtype of Suetonian βίος, the βίοι φιλοσόφων, for the *Demonax*. If one defines a genre as a complex of form, content and function, then Cancik's argument that each work belonging to the genre βίος φιλοσόφου was a παράδειγμα and a διδαχή adds the necessary element of a genre definition, namely that of function, to the discussion of the *Demonax*. Furthermore, Adela Yarbro Collins has argued that another Suetonian βίος, Suetonius's 'Life of Julius Caesar', has the structure of a chronological account interrupted by a section containing descriptions of various aspects of Caesar's person and character.[118]

115. Cancik, 'Bios and Logos', p. 118.

116. Cancik, 'Bios and Logos', p. 120.

117. Cancik, 'Bios and Logos', p. 124.

118. Adela Yarbro Collins, 'Is Mark's Gospel a Life of Jesus?', pp. 16-17. See also David Aune's discussion of Leo's classification of ancient biographies where Aune comments that chronological and topical tendencies are often found together in these works ('Greco-Roman Biography', in David Aune [ed.], *Greco-Roman Literature and the New Testament: Selected Forms and Genres* [SBLSBS, 21; Atlanta: Scholars Press, 1988], pp. 107-26 [107-109]).

The structure of this Suetonian biography is very similar to the structure of the *Demonax.* Hence, using Leo's categories, the *Demonax* is a βίος of the Suetonian subtype βίοι φιλοσόφων, two of whose functions are those of παράδειγμα and διδαχή.

Lucian also sought to preserve the memory of Demonax (2.1-2) and referred to him, along with Sostratus, as a noteworthy and memorable person (1.4-7). The structure of the *Demonax* indicates that Lucian followed the directions given in the rhetorical handbooks for an ἐγκώμιον, *encomium.* Burton Mack has given an outline of the structure of a speech of encomium based on the ancient handbooks.[119] While the *Demonax* is not a speech, the prose work can be outlined, nonetheless, according to Mack's structure as follows:

The Biographical Contents of the Demonax—*An Encomium*

A. Introduction	1–2
B. Birth and Genealogy	3.1-2
C. Achievements	
1. Education/Pursuits	3.3–4.9
2. Virtues	5–10
3. Deeds [and sayings]	11–62
4. Blessings/Endowments	63–64
D. Conclusion	
Honor/Memorial	65–67

In place of a prose description of the deeds of Demonax, Lucian has given us the series of anecdotes involving Demonax. One may conclude, therefore, that another important function of the *Demonax*, and perhaps for the genre subtype βίοι φιλοσόφων, was that of encomium. In summary, Lucian's *Demonax* was a Greek βίος of the Suetonian subtype βίοι φιλοσόφων that functioned as an encomium, as a παράδειγμα and as διδαχή.

c. *The Anecdotes of the* ΔΗΜΩΝΑΚΤΟΣ ΒΙΟΣ

All but two of Lucian's anecdotes about Demonax are contained in one long section of his work, 12–62. Lucian had had a personal acquaintance

119. Burton L. Mack, *Rhetoric and the New Testament* (Guides to Biblical Scholarship, NT Series; Philadelphia: Fortress Press, 1990), p. 48. See the discussion of an encomium in Theon, Προγυμνάσματα, Ch. 9; *Rhet. Alex.* 35.1440b-1441b.13; Quintilian, *Inst.* 3.7.15-16; and *Rhet. Her.* 3.10-15.

with Demonax for a period of time, and had been one of his students. Thus, Lucian may have written the series of anecdotes from memory, given the ancient practice of memorizing anecdotes and sayings. It is also possible that Lucian had at hand his own and/or another's collection(s) of anecdotes involving Demonax. Such collections of anecdotes did exist in the ancient world and writers made use of them. Seneca, although opposed to it, recorded the practice of reading summaries of the words of famous persons for the purpose of learning wisdom (*Ep.* 33.5-6). Plutarch recounted how he collected and studied those παραδείγματα of philosophers, kings and tyrants that indicated how one handled anger in a controlled manner (*Cohib. ira* 457D). Samples of these παραδείγματα offered by Plutarch included anecdotes.[120] Diogenes Laertius referred to many collections of χρεῖαι, including that of the fourth century BCE Demetrius of Phalerum (*Lives Phil.* 5.81).[121] Valerius Maximus's first century CE *Factorum et dictorum memorabilium* is one witness to such collections. Given Lucian's acquaintance with Demonax, it is possible that, if Lucian used an earlier collection of anecdotes about Demonax, it may have been Lucian's own work; or, if not, Lucian would have been able either to edit another's collection or to add to any such collection.

1. *Form and Content.* Lucian introduced the anecdotes about Demonax by saying that he wished to cite a few of his 'apt and witty sayings' (12.1–2). The series does not exhibit any coherent organization; rather, one anecdote merely follows another. Given Lucian's purpose no other order to the collection would have been necessary.[122]

There are 52 anecdotes in the *Demonax*, 50 in the anecdotal section and two embedded in the narrative of Demonax's death.[123] One also finds three

120. See also Plutarch's references to 'notebooks', ὑπομνήματα, in *Tranq. an.* 464F, and to those who collect anecdotes and stories but produce nothing else, *Virt. prof.* 78F.

121. See Hock, 'General Introduction', pp. 8-9, for further references to these collections in Diogenes Laertius's work.

122. This point is in keeping with the conclusion of Martha Turner's study of ancient literary collections (*The Gospel According to Philip: The Sources and Coherence of an Early Christian Collection* [NHS, 38; Leiden: E.J. Brill, 1996], pp. 60-79). Given the diversity of such collections, Turner determines that, rather than attempt to develop a classification for ancient collections, 'it is better to think in terms of the relation of the apparent purposes of the collection to its individual organizing strategies' (p. 78).

123. The two embedded anecdotes are found in 64.1-5 and 66.1-7.

aphorisms in the anecdotal section. All but two of these units can be classified as χρεῖαι.[124] Using Theon's general three-part classification, the following is a typology of the χρεῖαι in the *Demonax* according to their content:

χρεία[125]

A. Saying-χρεία		
1. Statement		22
a. unprompted[126]	[3]	
b. from a specific situation	22	
2. Response-χρεία		22
a. to a simple question	0	
b. to an inquiry	9	
c. to a question calling for an explanatory response	1	
d. to a remark	12	
3. Double χρεία		2
B. Action-χρεία		2
1. active	2	
2. passive	0	
C. Mixed-χρεία		2

In this classification one finds two anecdotes of the mixed-χρεία type, 22.1-4 and 41.1-5. Theon had commented that this type makes its point through the action. The first of the two mixed-χρεία, 22.1-4, does just that:

> Now when a natural philosopher was discussing the antipodes,[127] [Demonax] made him stand up and led him to a well. He pointed to the reflection in the water and asked: 'Are you speaking about antipodes such as these?'

Clearly the action, pointing to the reflection, is essential in this anecdote; the question (saying) is incomprehensible without the action. In the second mixed-χρεία, 41.1-5, it is not immediately clear that the action is essential to the χρεία. It reads:

124. That is, 13.1-8 and 19.4–20.7.

125. Using the paragraphs of the Loeb text, the anecdotes of the *Demonax* are classified as follows: A.1.a: (aphorisms in 59, 60, 61); A.1.b: 17, 23, 25, 26, 28, 29, 30, 31, 33, 34, 37, 42, 44, 46, 47, 48, 49, 53, 54, 56, 57, 58 ; A.2.b: 15.1-5a, 24, 39, 43, 45, 50, 51, 52, 62; A.2.c: 32; A.2.d: 12.4-10a, 12.10b-13, 14, 16, 18, 21, 27, 35, 36, 38, 40, 55; A.3: 15.5b-9, 66.1-7; B.1: 19, 64.1-5; and C: 22, 41.

126. These are aphorisms, not anecdotes.

127. I.e., persons dwelling at a directly opposite point on the globe of the earth (*Webster's New Collegiate Dictionary*, p. 50).

> When he saw a certain pompous person who prided himself on the width of the purple stripe on his garment, [Demonax] leaned over to his ear and, taking hold of his garment, pointed out to him, 'A sheep wore this before you and he was nevertheless (just) a sheep.'

Taking hold of the person's garment specifies the 'this' of Demonax's comment and hence is needed for understanding the saying. The action and the saying together make the point in this χρεία. Moreover, if one considers that Demonax 'leaned over to his ear', that is, privately admonished him, then the anecdote adds to the portrait of Demonax as a gentle person (9.7-8).

The collection of anecdotes in the *Demonax* contains all but two of the items in Theon's typology. Lucian did not include a χρεία that was a response to a simple question (A.2.a) nor a passive action-χρεία (B.2). Nonetheless, because of the diversity of their forms, the anecdotes of the *Demonax* provide an excellent starting point to glean illustrations for Theon's typology.

As already noted, two anecdotes of the *Demonax* cannot easily be classified as χρεῖαι using Theon's typology. The first, 13.1-8, deals with a question posed by the Sophist Favorinus[128] about Demonax's philosophical leanings.

> At another time the same man [Favorinus] approached and asked Demonax what philosophical school he favored the most. He replied: 'Why, who told you that I am a philosopher?' After he was away from him [Demonax] laughed very heartily. When [Favorinus] asked, 'What are you laughing at?' he replied: 'It seemed laughable to me that you think philosophers can be determined by a beard when you yourself do not have a beard.'

This anecdote describes a dialogue between Favorinus and Demonax, consisting of a question, a responsive saying, an action, a question and a responsive saying. One may assume from Demonax's second response that he wore a beard, while Favorinus had none. Favorinus's lack of a beard is the key to understanding Demonax's laugh. In his *Eunuch*, Lucian relates the story of two philosophers, Diocles and Bagoas, competing for a chair of philosophy in Athens.[129] Diocles accused Bagoas of being a eunuch and thus excluded from philosophical pursuits. In his defense Bagoas alluded to Favorinus as one eunuch who practiced philosophy.

128. On Favorinus see Michael B. Trapp, 'Favorinus', *OCD*, p. 590, col. 1.

129. The two philosophers Diocles and Bagoas are probably fictitious; the composition probably reflected Lucian's disapproval of Favorinus.

Diocles rejected Favorinus as a model and made sport of him (7). Moreover, one of the judges mentioned that a philosopher should have a long beard (8). A third person described Bagoas as beardless and effeminate (10). In his *Lives of the Sophists*, Philostratus also referred to Favorinus as a eunuch, saying that 'even when he was old [Favorinus] had no beard' (1.489). Thus, Demonax's reference to Favorinus's lack of a beard indicates that the laugh is actually directed at Favorinus's being a eunuch.

With this background information on Favorinus, the anecdote appears as a cleverly constructed brief, but complex, story. However, as the anecdote stands in Lucian's work, it does not fit exactly any entry in Theon's typology. It probably should be considered to be a more complicated mixed-χρεία, consisting of an action amidst a short dialogue.

The second anecdote, 19.4–20.7, is also structured as a dialogue:

> When someone inquired what he [Demonax] considered to be a definition of happiness, he replied that only the free person was happy. When the other person asserted that free persons were numerous, [Demonax said], 'But I am thinking of that person who neither hopes for nor fears anything.' But the other said, 'And how can anyone possibly achieve this, since, for the most part, we are all slaves to these things?' 'But see', [Demonax said], 'if you should observe human affairs you would find them worthy of neither hope nor fear, since, at any rate, both painful things and pleasures will cease to be.'

This anecdote consists of a series of three interchanges: (1) a question and a response, (2) a counter-statement and a response, and (3) a counter-question and a response. The three interchanges lead the questioner to Demonax's definition of happiness, namely 'Happiness is freedom from hope and fears.' The present form of the dialogue may be an expansion of a condensed χρεία that read: 'When a person asked Demonax for his definition of happiness, he replied: "Happiness is freedom from hopes and fears."' As the present anecdote reads, however, it does not fit any of the categories in Theon's typology.

The contents of the dialogue do resemble the process in the Socratic method of dialectic, διαλεκτική, especially if the questioner's counter-statement is recast as a question. The Socratic method was 'the process of eliciting the truth by means of questions aimed at opening out whatever is implicitly known'.[130] Examples of this method can be found in some of the

130. Simon Blackburn, 'dialectic', in *The Oxford Dictionary of Philosophy* (Oxford: Oxford University Press, 1994), p. 104, cols. 1-2. See also George A. Kennedy, *A New History of Classical Rhetoric* (Princeton, NJ: Princeton University Press, 1994), p. 52.

early dialogues of Socrates among Plato's works, for example, *Protagoras*.[131] In his section on the proof in a judicial case, Quintilian spoke of examining witnesses and also gave as a model the method in 'the dialogues of Socrates' (*Inst.* 5.7.28). Quintilian described the posing of shrewd questions by which 'the questioner reaches the conclusion at which he is aiming'.[132]

There are two important differences between the Socratic dialogues and the dialogue in the anecdote of Demonax under discussion. First, the Socratic dialogues were longer compositions, and, secondly, in the Socratic method the master usually asked the questions and the pupil came to knowledge through answering them.[133] The anecdote of 19.4-20 is a short composition in which the master, Demonax, answered rather than asked the questions. Thus, there is no clear parallel between the dialogue of the Demonax anecdote and the actual Socratic dialogue. Nonetheless, the method is similar: through a series of questions and answers, even a short series, the questioner is led to Demonax's definition of happiness. Perhaps it is best to say that the form of this anecdote is a brief dialogue embodying a philosophical teaching.

Given the discussions of the nine exercises with the χρεία that are found in the various προγυμνάσματα, it is appropriate to ask here whether any of the χρεῖαι of the *Demonax* display evidence of these exercises. None of the anecdotes illustrate seven of the exercises, that is, recitation, inflection, approving, objecting, refuting, confirming or elaborating. However, one can argue that expanded and condensed χρεῖαι are found in the *Demonax* collection. For example, 14.1-4 might contain an expansion in its descriptive introduction. The anecdote reads:

> Once the Sidonian sophist was distinguishing himself in Athens and voicing his own praise to the effect that he had examined all philosophy—but it is well to cite the very words he used: 'If ever Aristotle calls me to the Lyceum, I shall attend; if Plato calls me to the Academy, I shall arrive; if Zeno calls, I shall spend my time in the Poecile [great hall]; if Pythagoras calls, I shall keep silence.' Demonax arose in the midst of the audience and said, calling him by name, 'Pythagoras is calling you.'

131. For a recent study on the Early Dialogues of Socrates see Terry Penner, 'Socrates and the Early Dialogues', in Richard Kraut (ed.), *The Cambridge Companion to Plato* (New York: Cambridge University Press, 1993), pp. 121-69.

132. See Aristotle (*Rhet.* 3.18.2) who described such questioning in his comments on 'interrogation' as employed in the proof of a speech.

133. Blackburn, 'dialectic', p. 356, col. 1.

The χρεία could have been understood and made its point in the condensed form:

> The Sidonian sophist once bragged: 'If ever Aristotle calls me to the Lyceum, I shall attend; if Plato calls me to the Academy, I shall arrive; if Zeno calls, I shall spend my time in the Poecile [great hall]; if Pythagoras calls, I shall keep silence.' Demonax arose in the midst of the audience and said: 'Pythagoras is calling you.'

The phrases 'was distinguishing himself in Athens and voicing his own praise to the effect that he had examined all philosophy—but it is well to cite the very words he used', could have been Lucian's expansion of a shorter χρεία.

On the other hand, the anecdote of 46.1-3 is a good example of a condensed χρεία; it is as brief as possible: 'When he saw a Spartan whipping his house slave, [Demonax] said: "Stop making the slave your equal."'

This is the only 'evidence' of the χρεία exercises one finds in the *Demonax*.

2. *Function of the Anecdotes in the* ΔΗΜΩΝΑΚΤΟΣ ΒΙΟΣ. Since a genre involves form, content and function, an investigation of the function of the anecdotes within the *Demonax* is necessary for this study. In the concluding sentence of the *Demonax* Lucian himself spoke to the general function of the anecdotes about Demonax: 'they suffice to give my readers a notion of the sort of man [ὁποῖος ἀνὴρ] [Demonax] was' (67.12-13). The understanding that sayings and humorous incidents reveal the character, ἦθος, of the person involved is found also in Plutarch's introduction to his 'Life of Alexander' (1.1). There Plutarch insisted that anecdotal incidents often yielded 'a greater revelation of character [ἦθος] than battles where thousands fall, or the greatest armaments, or sieges of cities'. Plutarch looked to anecdotes for the 'signs of the soul in a person' and used these units to 'portray the life of each person'.[134] Likewise, the anecdotes Lucian employed revealed the character, ἦθος, of Demonax and thus offered a 'life' of this man.

The anecdotes of the *Demonax* also functioned in several more specific ways. There are two anecdotes embedded in the narrative of Demonax's death. The first of these, 64.1-5, is as follows:

134. While Plutarch does not restrict himself to anecdotes in the writing of his *Lives*, he does employ a sufficient number of them to justify his statements. See the discussion on this point in Alan Wardman, *Plutarch's Lives* (Berkeley: University of California Press, 1974), pp. 7-8.

> Once when party discord occurred in Athens, [Demonax] went into the assembly and just by showing himself caused them to be silent. Then, when he saw that they had already changed their minds, he said nothing and departed.

This narrative is the fourth illustration Lucian used to justify his assertion that 'all Greece' had affection for Demonax and that 'when he entered, the chief magistrates arose and made room for him and everyone was silent' (63.4-7). Thus the anecdote is a παράδειγμα that functioned as 'proof' of Lucian's assertion.

The second embedded anecdote, 66.1-7, reads:

> A short time before his death he was asked: 'What orders are you giving about your burial?' He replied: 'Don't be meddlesome! The stench will get me buried.' But the man asserted, 'How so? Isn't it shameful that the body of such a man should be exposed as food for birds and dogs?' [Demonax] replied: 'I see nothing unusual in this, if even in death I am going to be useful to some living things.'

This incident followed Lucian's statement that Demonax ended his life 'in the same cheerful humor that people whom he met always saw him in' (65.7-8). In its immediate narrative context, then, the anecdote served as an example, παράδειγμα, of Lucian's preceding description of Demonax's cheerfulness. The anecdote also portrays a certain simplicity and humility on the part of Demonax. This portrayal served to heighten, by contrast, the honor the mourners gave Demonax, which Lucian described in the very next sentence: 'The Athenians gave him a magnificent public funeral and mourned him over a long period of time' (67.1-3). Additionally, this anecdote illustrates that Demonax practiced what he taught. Verses 19.4–20.7 portray Demonax teaching that happiness was freedom from fear. Here, in 66.1-7, he shows that he has no fear, not even fear of death.[135]

Finally, Demonax's last remark about being 'of service to living things' was in harmony with a similar sentiment expressed in a prior humorous anecdote. In 35.1-6, someone asked Demonax if he wasn't afraid that his boat might capsize and that he would then be eaten by fish. He replied: 'I would be hard-hearted if I shrank from being devoured by fish, when I have eaten so many fish!' The later remark in 66.5-7 brought a certain harmony to Lucian's portrait of Demonax. This anecdote (66.1-7), then,

135. The anecdotes in 35.1-6 and 45.1-3 also illustrate Demonax's lack of fear of death.

has multiple functions in the narrative: as a παράδειγμα it functions as 'proof' of a prior assertion about the character of Demonax; by depicting a humble Demonax it heightens the effect on the reader of the high honors accorded him upon his death; and finally, it strengthens the consistency of Lucian's portrait of Demonax.

The remainder of the anecdotes in the *Demonax* occur in the collection found in 11–62. Lucian introduced the anecdotes saying that he wished to present some of Demonax's 'shrewd and witty remarks', τῶν εὐστόχως τε ἅμα καὶ ἀστείως ὑπ' αὐτοῦ λελεγμένων (12.1-2).[136] These qualities of Demonax's sayings are evident throughout the collection; they can be seen readily in those anecdotes cited above, particularly those involving the Antipodes, Favorinus and the Sidonian Sophist. A further anecdote that clearly demonstrates Demonax's humor is that of 54.1-4, which reads:

> When he noticed that Rufinus the Cypriote (I am speaking of the lame man of the school of Aristotle) was spending much time in the walkways [of the Lyceum], he remarked: 'Isn't it pretty impudent—a lame Peripatetic!'[137]

As the outline of the *Demonax* presented above indicates, the collection of anecdotes follows immediately upon Lucian's description of the education and the virtues of Demonax. In the overall narrative, these anecdotes served as παραδείγματα, illustrating certain aspects of Demonax's life and character as found in Lucian's description.

In his education Demonax had followed the curriculum of the schools, having been 'brought up on the poets' and showing that he was a 'practiced speaker' (4.3-4). His knowledge of poetry is illustrated in the anecdote of 31.1-5 in which Demonax's comment on his contemporary Apollonius ('There goes Apollonius and his Argonauts!') alludes to Apollonius Rhodius, the third century BCE poet who wrote the epic *Argonautica*.[138] In the aphorism in 60.1-2, Demonax cited Homer's *Iliad*; and Demonax recited poetry just prior to his death (65.1-6). In 47.1-3, where Demonax

136. See also 10.1-2.

137. This anecdote contains a play on the words ἐκ του' περιπάτου, 'of the school of Aristotle', τοῖς περιπάτοις, 'the walkways', and Περιπατητικοῦ, 'a Peripatetic'. Aristotle taught in the walkways of a gymnasium, the Lyceum, built at the sanctuary of Apollo outside the city walls of Athens. Hence, his followers were called 'Peripatetics'. See David J. Farley, 'Peripatetics', *OCD*, p. 1141, cols. 1-2.

138. It is possible that the Apollonius who was Demonax's contemporary was Apollonius of Tyana, the Neopythagorean who lived in the first century CE. See Herbert J. Ross and Antony Spawforth, 'Apollonius', *OCD*, p. 128, col. 1. On Apollonius of Rhodes, see Herbert J. Ross, 'Apollonius Rhodius', *OCD*, pp. 124-26.

tells Danae that she should sue her brother for she is not 'the daughter of Acrisius', Demonax demonstrated an acquaintance with mythology, a subject learned along with poetry.[139] The allusion to Apollonius and the Argonauts (31.1-5), just mentioned, also confirms Demonax's familiarity with mythology.

Demonax himself followed no single philosophy (5.1-2). This is shown by the varied background of his teachers, whom Lucian listed, that is, the Cynics Agathobulus and Demetrius, the Stoic Epictetus and the Sophist Timocrates of Heraclia (3.5-9). This is also reinforced by the anecdote in 62.1-4 in which Demonax stated his admiration for Socrates, his wonder at Diogenes the Cynic, and his love of Aristippus the Cyrenaic.[140] According to Lucian, one clear teaching of Demonax was his reminder against basing one's happiness on blessings and his caution about worrying over misfortunes (8.1-9). The anecdote in 19.4–20.7, discussed above, laid out this teaching in the form of a brief philosophical dialogue.[141]

Lucian recounted the charges leveled against Demonax concerning his not practicing religion (11.1-32). The anecdotes in 27.1-5 and 34.1-5 present Demonax's critical attitude toward religious practices. The attitudes shown in the two anecdotes, while not illustrating the charges against him, add to the portrait of Demonax as a person detached from the religious practice of his time.

Among the aspects of his character noted in the introduction, one reads that Demonax was not prone to anger (7.2), cheerful and witty (10.1-2; 12.1-2), and clever and cutting (50.1-2). The narrative in 16.1-8 illustrated Demonax's own lack of anger when he had been injured and that of 51.1-4 chronicled his advice against anger. Demonax's cheerfulness and wit are evident throughout the anecdotes but especially in 35.1-6, 45.1-3 and 54.1-4, anecdotes that are just plain amusing. His cheerfulness is displayed in the double anecdote, 66.1-7, connected with his death. In 39.1-2a, Lucian indicated that Demonax even had 'pointed' or 'apt' remarks for unanswerable questions. In the anecdote that followed, 39.2b-6, concerning the weight of the smoke from the burning of a thousand pounds of wood, Demonax humorously replied, 'Weigh the ashes and the rest will be

139. In mythology, Acrisius, whose name means 'lawless,' was the father of Danae. See Herbert J. Ross, 'Acrisius', *OCD*, p. 9, col. 2.

140. On Aristippus see Christopher C.W. Taylor, 'Aristippus (1)', *OCD*, p. 161, col. 1.

141. One may speculate that Lucian's description of Demonax's advice to his friends in 8.1-9 was composed on the basis of the contents of this anecdote.

smoke.' Wit is also evident in his response to another unanswerable question about what it was like in Hades; he replied, 'Wait and I'll write a letter to you from there' (43.1-2).

The introduction to 50.1-14 demonstrated Lucian's own narrative skill. In 50.1-2 he referred to Demonax's clever and 'biting' or 'stinging' (δηκτικός) remark to a proconsul. Lucian's introductory statement follows immediately upon the anecdote in 49.1-5, which had described athletes engaging in foul play by 'biting', δάκνοντας, one another instead of boxing. Moreover, the narrative in 50.3-14 deals with a proconsul who had used hot pitch to remove hair from his legs and body, an action that itself can be considered 'stinging'. The proconsul was about to jail a Cynic who had criticized the proconsul as effeminate. Demonax urged the proconsul to release the Cynic, saying that if the Cynic should repeat his insult, the proconsul could have the Cynic's own hair removed with hot pitch as punishment! Thus, Lucian's remark that Demonax's saying was clever and δηκτικός was a segue from one anecdote to the next, using a play on the two related meanings of the word δηκτικός. The two anecdotes and the connecting statement form a small 'motif cluster' within the larger collection of anecdotes on Demonax.[142] Other clever and cutting remarks of Demonax are found in 18.1-5, 21.1-4, 28.1-6 and 44.1-8.

Finally, Demonax is described as an 'ordinary person', πεζός, who was not subject to vanity, τύφος, and who did not put on false airs (literally, 'falsify his mode of life', οὐ παραχαράττων τὸ εἰς τὴν δίαιταν) in order to attract attention and admiration (5.6-9). Introducing an anecdote about a Cynic, 48.1-7, Lucian said that Demonax 'above all else' fought against those who practiced philosophy not with sincerity but with vainglory (ἐπίδειξις), or to show (themselves) off. In the anecdote that followed, Demonax attacked a Cynic who carried a cudgel (ὕπερον) as a staff and who claimed to be a follower of the Cynics Antisthenes, Crates and Diogenes. Demonax remarked: 'Don't lie, for you happen to be a disciple of Hyperides!'[143]

The lack of vanity and sham in his own life was perhaps manifest most

142. M. Turner has shown that within works that are collections, one organizing principle of smaller groupings of the material was the 'clustering of material by motif or image' or by catchword association (*The Gospel According to Philip*, pp. 115-16, 246-50). Wilson also comments on small, linked clusters of χρεῖαι within larger collections ('The Ancient Genres of Gnomic Wisdom', p. 17).

143. Hyperides in Greek reads Ὑπερείδος; hence Lucian probably meant this as a pun on ὕπερον, 'cudgel', and not the name of a real person.

in the attacks Demonax made on these vices in others, the most predominant speech-act displayed in the anecdotes.[144] Demonax spared no one, including prominent persons, especially philosophers. He attacked pretense in the Stoic Epictetus, 55.1-6;[145] the Pythagorean Apollonius, 31.1-5; the Cynics Peregrinus, 21.1-4, and Honoratus, 19.1-3, and an anonymous Cynic, 48.1-7; the Peripatetics Agathocles, 29.1-4, and Herminus, 56.1-6; and two anonymous philosophers, 28.1-6. Sophists were also included: Herodes Atticus, 33.1-4; the Sidonian Sophist, 14.1-10; the rhetor, 36.1-4; and the person using 'ancient and unusual words', 26.1-6.[146] Other prominent persons under attack for vanity and false airs included Roman officials, 18.1-5, 30.2-6, 38.1-5, aristocrats, 15.19, 41.1-5, and a poet, 44.1-8.

Within the *Demonax*, then, the anecdotes functioned as 'revelations' of the character, ἦθος, of Demonax by presenting Demonax himself to the reader. They also served as παραδείγματα, illustrating the facts about or character traits of Demonax that Lucian had asserted. As such, the anecdotes advanced the encomiastic function of the *Demonax*, that is, Lucian's desire that Demonax be remembered as the 'noblest of all philosophers' (2.6-7). Furthermore, they aided Lucian's didactic purpose, to present Demonax as a model, παράδειγμα, for youth of Lucian's day. When an anecdote presented Demonax teaching, admonishing or praising a person, the hearer or reader of the *Demonax* was in turn taught, admonished or praised. Thus, the anecdotes taught youth how they should think, speak and behave. Even the χρεία form, with its 'usefulness for life', adds to this function.

The humor present in many of the anecdotes entertained the reader and served to hold the reader's interest, an authorial purpose. Moreover, contemporary scholars demonstrate that the anecdotes about Demonax also served Lucian's personal purposes. Noting the similarity in the

144. On this point see also R. Bracht Branham, 'Authorizing Humor: Lucian's *Demonax* and Cynic Rhetoric', in Vernon K. Robbins (ed.), *The Rhetoric of Pronouncement* (Semeia, 64; Atlanta: Scholars Press, 1993), pp. 45-46.

145. In this anecdote, Epictetus rebukes Demonax for failing to marry and leave behind children as a substitute for 'his nature'. Demonax is probably attacking the fact that Epictetus himself remained unmarried until he was much older. He then married a woman merely to help him raise a child whose parents were friends of his and who were about to dispose of the child by exposing it. See W.A. Oldfather, 'Introduction', *Epictetus* (LCL), I, p. x n. 1.

146. The use of Atticisms was a characteristic of the Sophists.

portrait of Demonax with that which Lucian paints of himself in his *Dream* and *Double Indictment*, C.P. Jones asserts that *Demonax* is a 'kind of indirect autobiography'.[147] Moreover, Barry Baldwin holds that, in fact, *Demonax* is 'essentially a cover for ventilating typical Lucianic criticisms of Favorinus, Herodes, Peregrinus, and assorted grammarians and archaists'.[148] Several themes in the anecdotes are also found in Lucian's other works, namely: the well as a mirror (22.1-4) in '*A True History*' 1.26; money as a sorcerer (23.1-9) in '*The Lover of Lies*' (15); gods hearing prayers from a sanctuary (27.15) in *Icaromenippus* or '*The Sky-man*' (25); barbarians excluded from the mysteries (34.1-5) in '*The Mistaken Critic*' (5); and a person visiting Hades (43.1-2) in '*Dialogues of the Dead*' (1).[149]

For the scholar interested in life in Athens in the second century, the background details in the *Demonax* yield valuable information.[150] Lucian mentioned the civic assembly in 11.10-32, quarrels among the citizens in 9.4-6 and 64.1-4, religious practices in 11.5-32, 27.1-5 and 34.1-5, honorific statuary in 53.1-3 and 58.1-5, burial practices and honors in 67.1-10, and the cosmopolitan makeup of the citizenry (see the list of those who put on false airs, above). Since many of these details are found in the anecdotes, these narratives also functioned as vehicles for background information of the life and times of Demonax.

The function of the anecdotes within the *Demonax*, then, was primarily to reveal the character of Demonax. They did this either by presenting him directly to the reader or by serving as παραδείγματα to illustrate data about the life and the character traits of Demonax as Lucian had portrayed them. The anecdotes furthered the encomiastic and didactic functions of the work as a whole. Additionally, the anecdotes entertained, were a vehicle for Lucian's own purposes, and they provided the reader with background details of ancient Athens.

147. Jones, *Culture and Society*, p. 98.

148. Barry Baldwin, *Studies in Lucian* (Toronto: Hakkert, 1973), p. 29. See my previous remarks in this chapter, section c, pp. 95-96, for comments on the unfavorable allusion Lucian made to Favorinus in the *Eunuch*.

149. See further comments in Graham Anderson, *Lucian: Theme and Variation in the Second Sophistic* (Mnemosyne Sup., 41; Leiden: E.J. Brill, 1976), pp. 64-65.

150. Here the same caution against naively attributing historicity to these anecdotes must be given as was mentioned above. Anderson warns of this in his chapter entitled, 'Storytelling', in *Lucian*, pp. 41-66.

d. *Conclusions on the Anecdotes of the* ΔΗΜΩΝΑΚΤΟΣ ΒΙΟΣ

This study of the anecdotes in the *Demonax* has shown that there are 52 anecdotes in the work and that all but two of them occur in a collection of anecdotes that appear in a series from 12–62. Two anecdotes are embedded in the narrative of Demonax's death. Additionally, there are three aphorisms within the series of anecdotes.

Except for two of the anecdotes, they take the form of the χρεία, and these 50 χρεῖαι can be classified according to Theon's typology of the χρεία. The two exceptions are 13.1-8 and 19.4–20.7; these may be classified, respectively, as a more complicated mixed-χρεία containing a short dialogue along with an action and as a brief dialogue embodying philosophical content. There is little evidence of the nine χρεία-exercises of the προγυμνάσματα in the *Demonax*; however, one does find examples of expanded and condensed χρεῖαι.

The anecdotes functioned primarily as παραδείγματα to establish the character, ἦθος, of Demonax and thus assist the encomiastic and didactic aims of the work as a whole. The chief trait of Demonax portrayed is his lack of vanity and sham; this is particularly seen in his interactions with persons of prestige. The anecdotes, and the work as a whole, also served the agenda of the author, Lucian. Finally, they provided glimpses into the social and cultural background of the times.

5. *Conclusions*

Through a study of grammarians' προγυμνάσματα and the rhetorical handbooks, as well as literary works themselves, this chapter has clarified the ancient terms used both for sayings and for anecdotes. For the purpose of this book, that is, an analysis of the anecdotes in the Gospel of Mark, an anecdote was defined as a brief narrative unit that contains a saying, an action, or both, as well as a description of a situation. The conclusion I reached is that the ancient anecdote was referred to either as a type of an ἀπόφθεγμα or a χρεία. The subtype of these units that fits the definition of an anecdote is that of an ἀπόφθεγμα or a χρεία that contains a brief narration of a situation. I chose the χρεία rather than the ἀπόφθεγμα as the ancient name for an anecdote because the χρεία is more clearly defined in the handbooks. Sayings without situations, yet attributed to a person, I refer to as aphorisms.

The χρεία was discussed in regard to its definition, types, and the grammatical exercises with it found in the προγυμνάσματα from the ancient world. I presented sufficient examples of the χρεία to show that this form was indeed used by ancient writers. My literary study of the anecdotes in Lucian's *Demonax* likewise confirmed the use of the χρεία in a literary work of the second century CE. Furthermore, the study yielded the major function of the χρεία, or anecdote, in the *Demonax*: that of establishing the ἦθος of the main character in the anecdote(s). The anecdote could also function as a vehicle of the author's own interests and as a carrier of background information about the life and times of the focal person of the anecdote.

Chapter 3

The Anecdote in Rabbinic Writings

This chapter investigates the assertion of Vernon Robbins that brief stories were 'a powerful and natural form of communication in Mediterranean culture'[1] as this claim pertains to that culture of early rabbinic Judaism that is reflected in the *Mishnah*. Beginning with the pioneering form critics of this century, Rudolf Bultmann, Martin Albertz and Martin Dibelius, New Testament scholars have drawn attention to rabbinic narratives in their search for analogies to Gospel anecdotes.[2] This interest in anecdotes from both literary worlds continues today, as shown by an article on early rabbinic stories in a recent issue of *Semeia* devoted to the significance of the presentations on the χρεία in the ancient προγυμνάσματα for the study of the anecdotes in the ancient world, particularly those of the New Testament.[3]

The following investigation follows the methodology employed in Chapter 2 on Greek and Roman anecdotes. Thus, the general definition of an anecdote, developed in the first chapter of this book, is used to examine the brief stories found in the *Mishnah*. Any similarities between rabbinic and Gospel anecdotes will be discussed later in Chapter 5, the study of the anecdotes in Mark's Gospel.

1. *Introduction*

The *Mishnah* (*M*), a compilation of legal rulings, edited about the year 200 CE, has been selected for study since it is the earliest extant work of the

1. Robbins, 'The Chreia', p. 22.
2. Bultmann, *Geschichte der synoptischen Tradition*; Albertz, *Die synoptischen Streitgespräche*; and Dibelius, *Formgeschichte*.
3. Alan J. Avery-Peck, 'Rhetorical Argumentation in Early Rabbinic Pronouncement Stories', in Vernon K. Robbins (ed.), *The Rhetoric of Pronouncement* (Semeia, 64; Atlanta: Scholars Press, 1993), pp. 49-71.

rabbinic corpus.[4] There are no early narrative writings in the rabbinic corpus; rabbinic midrashim, which contain a greater number of narrative units than *M*, are later compilations whose dating is problematic.[5] Despite its legal focus, anecdotes do exist in *M*, and these brief narratives can be analyzed for their form, content and function. Additionally, while there is no one work of rabbinic literature devoted to an individual personage that is comparable to either Lucian's *Demonax* or Mark's Gospel, numerous rabbis are cited in the legal arguments of *M* and it is possible to isolate halakhic and haggadic traditions associated with several of these sages.[6] Problems exist in extracting historically reliable biographical information about any one sage; nonetheless, *M* presents 'images' of many of the important early rabbis. Thus, for example, Joel Gereboff is able to speak of 'the Tarfon of the *Mishnah*'.[7] Using the necessary precautions, it is possible to investigate whether and, if so, how the anecdotes about a particular sage contribute to the presentation of that person in the *Mishnah*.

This chapter examines the anecdotes of one division of *M*, מועד קטן *Mo'ed Qaṭan*, or 'Appointed Times'. All of the anecdotes in *Mo'ed Qaṭan* were chosen so that a manageable number of anecdotes are studied within

4. For introductory material on the *Mishnah* and rabbinic literature see: Chanoch Albeck, *Einführung in die Mischna* (Berlin: W. de Gruyter, 1971); Herbert Danby, *The Mishnah: Translated from the Hebrew with Introduction and Brief Explanatory Notes* (London: Oxford University Press, 1933), pp. xiii-xxxii; Abraham Goldberg, 'The Mishna—A Study Book of Halakha', in Shmuel Safrai (ed.), *The Literature of the Sages, First Part. Oral Tora, Halakha, Mishna, Tosefta, Talmud, External Tractates* (CRINT, 3.1; Philadelphia: Fortress Press, 1987), pp. 211-62; Jacob Neusner, *Introduction to Rabbinic Literature* (Anchor Bible Reference Library; New York: Doubleday, 1994); Anthony J. Saldarini, 'Reconstructions of Rabbinic Judaism', in Robert A. Kraft and George W.E. Nickelsburg (eds.), *Early Judaism and its Modern Interpreters* (The Bible and its Modern Interpreters, 2; Atlanta: Scholars Press, 1986), pp. 437-77; and H.L. Strack and G. Stemberger, *Introduction to the Talmud and Midrash* (trans. Markus Bockmuehl; Edinburgh: T. & T. Clark, 1991; German original, 1982).

5. See Strack and Stemberger, *Introduction to the Talmud and Midrash*, pp. 259-62.

6. For example, Joel Gereboff, *Rabbi Tarfon: The Tradition, the Man, and Early Rabbinic Judaism* (BJS, 7; Missoula, MT: Scholars Press, 1979); Shamai Kanter, *Rabban Gamaliel II: The Legal Traditions* (BJS, 8; Chico, CA: Scholars Press, 1980); Diane Levine, 'Eleazar Ḥisma', in William S. Green (ed.), *Persons and Institutions in Early Rabbinic Judaism* (BJS, 3; Missoula, MT: Scholars Press, 1977), pp. 149-205; Jacob Neusner, *Development of a Legend: Studies in the Traditions Concerning Yohanan ben Zakkai* (SPB, 16; Leiden: E.J. Brill, 1970); *idem*, *Eliezer ben Hyrcanus: The Tradition and the Man* (SJLA, 3–4; 2 vols.; Leiden: E.J. Brill, 1973).

7. Gereboff, *Rabbi Tarfon*, p. 438.

a single literary unit, a division. The chapter also investigates the brief stories pertaining to a single Mishnaic authority, namely Rabbi Gamaliel II. I chose Rabbi Gamaliel II because Kanter demonstrates that almost one-half (47.9 per cent) of the tannaitic traditions about him are in narrative form.[8] A study of the Mishnaic anecdotes pertaining to Gamaliel II is useful in evaluating further results of Kanter's study.

Before proceeding to these anecdotes, some comments are in order on genre criticism of literary units in rabbinic literature as well as on what can be said concerning the educational system in early rabbinic Judaism. The study of literary genres in early rabbinic literature is more difficult than such a study in Greek and Roman writings. There are no extant early rabbinic writings analogous to *progymnasmata* or rhetorical handbooks. Furthermore, it is only within the last 30 years that scholars have attempted a type of 'form criticism' of early rabbinic works.[9] Much of this contemporary discussion of 'forms' in early rabbinic literature, including Neusner's work, deals with larger units of material within a particular work. The 'narrative units' that have been identified are described in general terms with almost no discussion of their individual form, content or function. The exceptions to this are the studies on the 'pronouncement stories', legends, the parables or *mashalim*, citations of Scripture, and the narrative unit commonly named the מעשׂה, *ma'aśeh*. This last unit, the מעשׂה, is of particular interest to this chapter and will be discussed below.[10]

In writing on the subject of the Jewish educational system in Israel prior to the time of *M*, some scholars use later rabbinic texts uncritically to present a homogenized picture of such a system.[11] Even the later rabbinic

8. Kanter, *Rabban Gamaliel II*, pp. 246-51.

9. See the discussion of this point in Strack and Stemberger, *Introduction to the Talmud and Midrash*, pp. 56-58. Their discussion refers to the works of Jacob Neusner and his students, in particular, the 'forms' and types developed by Neusner in 'Types and Forms in Ancient Jewish Literature: Some Comparisons', *HR* 11 (1972), pp. 354-90.

10. See section c, pp. 115-18.

11. For example; Eliezer Ebner, *Elementary Education in Ancient Israel (During the Tannaitic Period 10–220 CE)* (New York: Bloch, 1956); Nathan Morris, *The Jewish School: An Introduction to the History of Jewish education* (London: Eyre & Spottiswoode, 1937); Rainer Riesner, *Jesus als Lehrer: Eine Untersuchung zum Ursprung der Evangelien-Überlieferung* (WUNT, 2.1; Tübingen: J.C.B. Mohr, 1981), pp. 182-86; and Shmuel Safrai, 'Education and the Study of the Torah', in Shmuel Safrai *et al.* (eds.), *The Jewish People in the First Century: Historical Geography, Political History, Social, Cutural and Religious Life and Institutions* (CRINT, 1.2; Philadelphia:

texts do not describe an actual process of learning or a curriculum. The discussion here follows the more cautious approach, which takes a rabbinic text as evidence for its own time.[12]

Deuteronomy 11.19 enjoins adult Jews to teach 'these words of mine' to their children, and Josephus (*Apion* 2.26) gives testimony that this indeed took place in the first century CE. Prior to this there is mention of a *bet ha-midrash* in Sirach (c. 180 BCE), but nothing is known about whether this meant a circle of disciples or some more formal educational endeavor. *Jubilees* records that Abraham was taught to write by his father (11.16) and that Jacob also learned writing (19.14), a possible indication of what may have been happening at the time *Jubilees* was written (161–140 BCE). The argument for the existence of a widespread elementary school system in Israel in the last century BCE and the first century CE is based on either *y. Ket.* 8.11, 32c, where the system is attributed to Simeon ben Shetahi, or *b. B. Bat. 31a*, where Joshua ben Gamla is credited with its institution. These later traditions are of dubious historicity.[13]

The *Mishnah* again enjoins the study of the Torah (*Pe'ah* 1.1), however, it is not to be taught to one's daughters (*Soṭ.* 3.4). A *bet ha-seper* is mentioned in *Ket.* 2.10 in relation to a minor; thus, this term probably denotes a place where elementary instruction was given. The *bet ha-midrash* is also mentioned, for example, in *Beṣ.* 3.5 and *Šab.* 16.1, but there is, once again, no description of such an entity. Children evidently were taught to read, since it is noted that supervision of their reading on the Sabbath by an adult does not constitute work (*Šab.* 1.3). Teachers are mentioned in *Qid.* 4.13, where it is forbidden for an unmarried man or for a woman to teach students. In *Mak.* 2.2 the ruling is given that teachers may strike students. Finally, in *Ab.* 5.21, a later addition to *M*, where the stages of a person's life are presented, it is recorded that at 5 one learns Scripture, at 10 the *Mishnah*, at 13 religious duties, and at 15 the *Talmud*. Thus, for the time immediately preceding *M*, one can conclude that elementary education, probably reading and writing, took place in the *bet ha-seper* and

Fortress Press, 1976), pp. 945-70. James L. Crenshaw, using a critical approach to the sources, argues that even in ancient Israel 'considerable diversity characterized education' ('Education in Ancient Israel', *JBL* 104 [1985], pp. 601-615 [615]).

12. For example, Lee I. Levine, *The Rabbinic Class of Roman Palestine in Late Antiquity* (New York: Jewish Theological Seminary of America, 1985), pp. 23-42; Schürer, *The History of the Jewish People*, II.417-22; and Strack and Stemberger, *Introduction to the Talmud and Midrash*, pp. 9-16, 42-49.

13. See Strack and Stemberger, *Introduction to the Talmud and Midrash*, p. 10.

'higher' education took place at a *bet ha-midrash*. How widespread this education was and what classes of people were thus taught is not known.

Moreover, *b. Sanh.* 32b tells of the existence of 'schools' associated with certain sages at Lydda, Beror Ḥayil, Peqiin, Yavneh, Bene Beraq, Sikhnin, Sepphoris and Beth Shearim. Since other rabbinic citations refer to these schools, this text is probably historically reliable.[14] These schools, each called either a *bet ha-midrash* or a *bet ha-talmud*, appear to have conducted advanced training in Scripture and in early rabbinic legal rulings. Judah the Patriarch moved from Bet Shearim to Sepphoris and then to Tiberias, and these latter two cities are known to have had a *bet ha-midrash* (*y. Šab.* 6, 8a; 12, 13c).[15]

Moreover, Sepphoris and Tiberias were Hellenized cities, both having served as the capital for Herod Antipas. Tiberias, with a Hellenized city council, was an important commercial center and was also the site of several pagan temples.[16] It is possible that in the third century some rabbinic sages of both Sepphoris and Tiberias were literate in Greek. *M* records a ruling of Yoḥanan b. Zakkai that the 'books of Homer' do not impart uncleanness (*Yad.* 4.6). Hence, at least some Jews, possibly sages, were reading Greek texts. *Soṭah* 9.14 D reads, 'And [they said] a man should not teach Greek to his son.' This, in fact, may indicate that Greek was being taught. There is a later statement in the *Tosefta*, *Soṭ.* 15.8, that the household of Rabbi Gamaliel II was permitted to teach Greek to their sons because they were involved with the government. This may reflect the fact that those in the patriarchal families and circles were literate in Greek. Recent scholarship on the languages of Palestine in the first centuries of the common era has led some scholars to posit that Greek was widely used by Jews in Palestine at the time of the compilation of *M*.[17]

In summary, we know little of the actual education of the rabbinic sages or other Jewish students. We can assume that some men were provided

14. See Strack and Stemberger, *Introduction to the Talmud and Midrash*, p. 12, and Martin Goodman, *State and Society in Roman Galilee, A.D. 132 to 212* (Totowa, NJ: Rowman & Allanheld, 1983), pp. 32-33, 75-81.

15. Levine, *The Rabbinic Class of Roman Palestine*, pp. 28-29.

16. Schürer, *The History of the Jewish People*, II, pp. 178-82.

17. For example, Joseph Fitzmyer, 'The Languages of Palestine in the First Century A.D.', in *A Wandering Aramean: Collected Aramaic Essays* (SBLMS, 25; Missoula, MT: Scholars Press, 1979), pp. 29-56 (repr. as *The Semitic Background of the New Testament: Combined Edition of Essays on the Semitic Background of the New Testament and A Wandering Aramean: Collected Aramaic Essays* [Biblical Resource Series; Grand Rapids, MI: Eerdmans, 1997]), p. 38.

with an elementary education, that is, reading, at least of the Torah, and writing. Students or disciples of the sages received further instruction in the legal opinions of their masters. However, it cannot be shown that there was a rabbinical instructional system that communicated the techniques demonstrated in the *Mishnah* in a manner similar to the way in which the Greek and Roman grammarians taught the exercises of the *progymnasmata*. It remains a possibility, but with no hard evidence to prove it, that some of the sages at the time of the *Mishnah*'s compilation were literate in Greek. It cannot be shown, however, that Greek genres like the χρεία influenced rabbinic genres, since it is not clear how much Greek education was available to such figures as Gamaliel II.

The following investigation of rabbinic anecdotes comprises four sections. The first section begins with general comments on the *Mishnah* itself and then covers the forms of the anecdotes appearing in *M* as well as their various functions. This is followed by sections on the anecdotes of *Mo'ed Qaṭan* and on the stories that pertain to Gamaliel II. The chapter closes with a presentation of general conclusions.

2. *Anecdotes in the* Mishnah

a. *The* Mishnah

The word *Mishnah* (משנה) means 'repetition' or 'verbal teaching by repeated recitation' and is derived from the verb *šanah* (שנה), 'to repeat'.[18] The term '*mishnah*' is used to designate the legal rulings collected about 200 CE, that is, 'the *mishnah*', or a collection of teachings by an individual teacher of this period such as the '*mishnah* of Rabbi Aqiba', or an individual paragraph in the collections. The *Mishnah*, as we know it today, is comprised of six 'Divisions' or 'Orders', *Sedarim* (סדרים), as follows: *Zera'im* (זרעים), 'Seeds'; *Mo'ed Qaṭan* (מועד קטן), 'Appointed Times'; *Našim* (נשים), 'Women'; *Neziqin* (נזיקין), 'Damages'; *Qodašim* (קדשים), Holy Things'; and *Ṭoharot* (טהרות), 'Purities'. Each *Seder* is divided into *massekhtot* (מסכתות), 'tractates', which are further subdivided into *peraqim* (פרקים), 'chapters', each of which consists of paragraphs. An individual paragraph is a *mishnah*.

The *Mishnah* itself does not relate how it came into existence. It is traditionally held to be a code of laws promulgated by Rabbi Yehuda ha-

18. Marcus Jastrow, *A Dictionary of the Targumim, the Talmud Babli and Yerushalmi, and the Midrashic Literature* (2 vols.; London: Luzac, 1886–1903), pp. 857 a (מִשְׁנָה) and 1605 a (שׁנה) (repr. NY: Pardes Publishing House, 1950).

Nasi, Rabbi Judah the Patriarch, about 200 CE. The earliest extant evidence of this tradition is in the letter of Gaon Sherira dated to 987 CE.[19] The letter asserts that Judah collected past legal rulings particularly those of Rabbi Meir, who in turn based his rulings on the teachings of Rabbi Aqiba. A non-Jewish source for the activity of Judah and Aqiba exists in a reference from Epiphanius: 'Among the Jews the traditions of the elders are called *Deuteroseis*. These are four: one is in the name of Moses, the second is according to the so-called R. Aqiba, the third according to Adda or Judah, the fourth according to the sons of the Hasmonaeans' (*Panarion* 33.9).[20]

Contemporary scholars accept the original role that Rabbi Judah played in assembling the *Mishnah*; however, they do not agree on the genre of *M.* Four opinions as to its genre prevail today, namely that it is a collection of legal rulings,[21] a definitive law code,[22] a textbook for teaching possible legal interpretations,[23] or a 'philosophical law code'.[24] Each of these proposed genres for *M* is directly related to its legal content. Since the Mishnaic anecdotes are all brief narratives that function within legal arguments of a paragraph of *M*, a decision on the exact definition of this host genre, the *Mishnah*, does not affect the form and function of the anecdotes.

Jacob Neusner has undertaken a 'documentary' study of the texts of early rabbinic Judaism. His approach treats each of the documents of early rabbinic literature individually to determine what it says 'in *its* own setting, within the limits of *its* own redactional framework, upon the subjects chosen by *it*, and for purposes defined within the mind of those specific people, *its* authors, who flourished in one concrete setting'.[25] With respect to *M*, Neusner investigated the text to see how its authors presented a Judaism that made sense in the wake of the destruction of the Temple (70 CE) and the failure of the Bar Kokhba revolt (132–35 CE). He

19. See Strack and Stemberger, *Introduction to the Talmud and Midrash*, pp. 138-41.

20. See Strack and Stemberger, *Introduction to the Talmud and Midrash*, p. 141.

21. For example, Albeck, *Einführung*, pp. 106-107, 270-83, and Danby, *The Mishnah*, p. xxii.

22. For example, J.N. Epstein, *Introduction to Tannaitic Literature: Mishna, Tosephta and Halakhic Midrashim* (ed. E. Z. Melam; Jerusalem: Magnes Press, 1957; Hebrew), pp. 255-56; cited in Abraham Goldberg, 'The Mishna', p. 214.

23. Goldberg, 'The Mishna', p. 214.

24. Neusner, *Introduction to Rabbinic Literature*, p. 97.

25. Jacob Neusner, 'The Modern Study of the *Mishnah*', in *The Study of Ancient Judaism*. I. *Mishnah, Midrash Siddur* (New York: Ktav, 1981), pp. 3-26 (21).

concludes that the emphases on the priestly caste and the Temple cult, as well as everyday life, which one finds in *M* all point to the document's principal concern, the continuation of sanctification after the end of the Temple rituals. Sanctification is understood as 'the correct arrangement of all things...just as with the cult itself as set forth in Leviticus'.[26] To achieve this sanctification, the compilers of *M* strove to distinguish Israel from the world and then to establish stability, order and regularity in Israel's life.[27]

Neusner developed a history of the legal traditions of *M* by separating its rulings into three strata, representing the time period before 70 CE, between 70 and 135 CE, and from 135 to 200 CE. It is especially difficult to arrive at reliable conclusions in dating the materials of *M*, since, although it contains many attributions, the document has been extensively edited. Claims concerning the historicity of any attributions as the exact words of the named sage or even the content of his teaching are difficult to maintain.[28] Neusner, however, attempts to separate out traditions attributed to certain sages, following what he calls 'attestations'. He distinguishes between a legal ruling 'attributed' to a named authority and the 'attestation' to such an attribution by another named sage. Thus 'Rabbi Gamaliel II said...' is an attribution, while 'Rabbi Aqiba testified that Rabbi Gamaliel II said...' is an attestation. The second sage attests to the existence of the teaching of the first sage; thus, the teaching of the first sage can be reliably dated to the time of the second sage as its latest starting point.[29] Neusner also finds thematic consistencies among the attestations

26. Neusner, *Introduction to Rabbinic Literature*, p. 99. See also Neusner's *Judaism: The Evidence of the Mishnah* (BJS, 129; Atlanta: Scholars Press, 2nd edn, 1988), pp. 230-56.

27. Neusner, *Introduction to Rabbinic Literature*, p. 100. Alan Avery-Peck remarks that this sanctification process is intended to demonstrate that the disastrous events of 70 and 135 CE are not the end of God's covenant with Israel nor of 'the sacred circle once established by the presence, in the nation's midst, of the holy Temple and its cult... Israelites assume the role of priests, and their villages take on the aspect of the Temple. This is meant to lead to the reestablishment of a world whose order and sense are informed by the nature of God's original creation' ('Judaism without the Temple: The *Mishnah*', in Harold W. Attridge and Gohei Hata (eds.), *Eusebius, Christianity, and Judaism* [Detroit: Wayne State University Press, 1992], pp. 409-31).

28. See the discussion in Strack and Stemberger, *Introduction to the Talmud and Midrash*, pp. 62-68.

29. J. Neusner, *Eliezer Ben Hyrcanus*, II, pp. 92-94. See also Neusner's 'The Dating of Sayings in Rabbinic Literature', in *Formative Judaism: Religious, Historical, and*

of contemporary rabbinic authorities; such consistencies, in turn, allow him to posit historical layers within *M*.[30]

This theory of attestations proves useful for Neusner in his construction of the history of various legal traditions within *M*. While this book is not directly concerned with such a history, Neusner's understanding of attestations is of assistance in deciding which anecdotes in *M* pertain to Gamaliel II. Additionally, the attestation or testimony of a rabbinic authority to the ruling or actions of another sage adds an 'argument from authority' to the rhetoric of a passage.

b. *Mishnaic Anecdotes*

This investigation of the anecdotes in the *Mishnah* begins with the definition of an anecdote given in Chapter 1, above, that is:

> a brief narrative, either oral or written, describing an incident, including its setting, which involves one or more persons and which focuses on an action, saying, or dialogue; the function of an anecdote is to entertain, instruct, relate an historical incident, characterize a person, or authoritatively legitimate a specific opinion, a specific practice, or a broader view of reality.

According to this definition there is a maximum of 180 anecdotes in *M*. There are 41 anecdotes in *Mo'ed Qaṭan* and those anecdotes in the whole of *M* that pertain to Gamaliel II[31] total 36. Given that 13 anecdotes about Gamaliel occur in *Mo'ed Qaṭan*, the total number of rabbinic anecdotes that are studied in detail in this book is 64.

c. *Form of the Anecdotes*

The great majority of these Mishnaic anecdotes are very brief stories, although there are a few expanded narratives. Among the brief narratives two groups are distinguished by the use of either the term מעשׂה, *ma'aśeh*,

Literary Studies, Seventh Series: The Formation of Judaism, Intentionality, Feminization of Judaism, and Other Current Results (South Florida Studies in the History of Judaism, 94; Atlanta: Scholars Press, 1993), pp. 99-119; *idem*, *A History of the Mishnaic Law of Damages. Part Five. The Mishnaic System of Damages* (SJLA, 35; 5 vols.; Leiden: E.J. Brill, 1985), V, pp. 190-91 (succinctly stated); and *idem*, *The Rabbinic Traditions about the Pharisees before 70. Part III. Conclusions* (Leiden: E.J. Brill, 1971), pp. 180-84.

30. Anthony Saldarini ('"Form Criticism" of Rabbinic Literature', *JBL* 96 [1977], pp. 257-74 [264]) cautions that even these attestations 'may have been revised or harmonized [by the redactors of *M*] to form a useful structure'. See also Saldarini's 'Reconstructions of Rabbinic Judaism', pp. 443-44.

31. For the remainder of this book, the name 'Gamaliel' identifies Gamaliel II. For any other sage named Gamaliel a specific identification is given.

or the phrase פעם אחת, *p'm 'ḥt*, 'one time', in their opening words or as an introductory 'formula'.

The מעשים, *ma'asîm*, comprise by far the larger group, there being 28 in *Mo'ed Qaṭan* and 101 in the whole of *M.*[32] Derived from the verb עשׂה, 'to do', 'to make', 'to prepare', מעשׂה developed in meaning from 'deed' or 'work' in the Hebrew Bible[33] to 'act', 'incident' or 'event' in tannaitic literature, and then to 'case' in ammoraic writings.[34] In the anecdotes under discussion, the term מעשׂה most often occurs at the outset of the story. For example, *Pes.* 7.2 A occurs within an argument, 7.2 A-B, which reads: '7.2 A. They do not roast the Passover offering either on a spit or on a grill. B. R. Zadoq said: "מעשׂה Rabbi Gamaliel said to Tabi, his servant, 'Go and roast for us the Passover offering on a grill.'"'[35] I have left מעשׂה, untranslated to make clear that the term מעשׂה appears in the wording of the Hebrew text.[36] In this pericope, Zadoq is citing an 'incident' from the life of Gamaliel that contradicts the legal ruling of the preceding statement. Zadoq does not give the contrary statement, merely the incident from Gamaliel's life. The anecdote is an attestation, as defined by Neusner, and as such adds the argument from authority, that is, Gamaliel, to Zadoq's legal ruling.

The *ma'aśeh* has been studied as a literary genre, that is, its form, content and function, by Arnold Goldberg in his essay 'Form und Funk-

32. See the listing in Chayim Kasovsky, *Otsar lashon ha-Mishnah, Thesaurus Mishnae: Concordantiae verborum quae in sex Mishnae ordinibus reperiunter* (Jerusalem: Massadah Publishing, 1956-60), pp. 1426-27 under מעשׂה (2), and p. 1427 under ומעשׂה (2).

33. BDB, pp. 795 b-796 a (מעשׂה) and 793 b (עשׂה).

34. Jastrow, *Dictionary*, p. 819 b (מעשׂה) and p. 1124 b (עשׂה). See also M. Elon, 'Ma'aseh', *EncJud*, XI, cols. 641-49.

35. The numbering of the verses in each *mishnah* of a chapter follows that used by Neusner in *The Mishnah: A New Translation*. Neusner's translation is based on the standard Hebrew text published by Ch. Albeck and H. Yalon (*Shishah Sidre Mishnah* [6 vols.; Jerusalem: Bialik Institute; Tel Aviv: Dvir, 1952–59]) and conforms to ms. Kaufman A 50. The translation used here also follows Albeck and Yalon, *Shishah Sidre Mishnah*.

36. In English translations מעשׂה is sometimes rendered as 'it happened once' or 'once'. These are the translations given for מעשׂה in *Ber.* 1.1 by Philip Blackman (*Mishnayoth*. II. *Order Zeraim* [Gateshead: Judaica Press, 2nd edn, 1973], p. 33) and Herbert Danby (*The Mishnah*, p. 2), respectively. In *'Erub.* 4.2, פעם אחת is translated as 'on one occasion' by Blackman (II, p. 119) and as 'once' by Danby (p. 126). Thus, it is not clear in these English translations whether or not the term מעשׂה occurs in the Hebrew of the passage.

tion des Ma'ase in der Mischna'.[37] According to Goldberg, the *ma'aśeh* is a narrative relating 'an event which turned into a legally relevant datum'.[38] The form of the *ma'aśeh* consists of three elements, namely a case, a question and a verdict. The 'case' is a situation or an event that is stated as briefly as possible with only as much detail 'as is of significance for the verdict'. The question may be stated or it may be implicit in the description of the case.[39] Since the verdict in the *ma'aśeh* always involves a named authority or group of sages, Joel Gereboff adds 'a subject' as an element of the form of the unit.[40] The study of the *ma'aśim* in the collection of rabbinic anecdotes used in this study further reveals that the 'verdict' may be a statement or an action, sometimes given without comment. Thus the *ma'aśeh* is defined as a short narrative consisting of a person(s), a setting, with an implicit or explicit question, and a verbal ruling or an action.

In a much smaller group, the anecdotes are introduced with the formula פעם אחת, 'one time'. There are six of these narratives in the entire *Mishnah*, namely *'Erub.* 4.2 A-C, *Yom.* 3.2 B, *Suk.* 4.9 N-O, *Roš Haš.* 4.4 B-D, *Bek.* 5.3 K-L, and *Mid.* 1.2 G.[41] All six of these narratives have the same form as that of the *ma'aśeh*. It will be shown below that these אחת פעם units also function in the same manner as the *ma'aśim*.

There are other brief narratives of the very same form as the מעשה that lack any introductory word or words that function as a formula. For example, *Suk.* 3.9 D: 'Rabbi Aqiba said, "I was watching Rabban Gamaliel

37. Arnold Goldberg, 'Form und Funktion des Ma'ase in der Mischna', *Frankfurter Judaistische Beiträge* 2 (1974), pp. 1-38. Goldberg's is the only study that analyzes the מעשה as a genre. Gereboff (*Rabbi Tarfon*, pp. 337-42) pursues a brief study of those narratives concerning Rabbi Tarfon that are of the 'מעשה type'; however, his work is admittedly dependent on Goldberg.

38. Goldberg, 'Form und Funktion des Ma'ase', p. 3.

39. Goldberg, 'Form und Funktion des Ma'ase', p. 8.

40. Gereboff, *Rabbi Tarfon*, pp. 337, 355 n. 18.

41. See the listing in Kasovsky, *Otsar lashon ha-Mishnah*, under פעם אחת and שפעם אחת, p. 1485. Another brief story, *Ab.* 6.9, is also given in the listing under פעם אחת. The tractate *Abot* is dated approximately a century later than the other tractates of the *Mishnah* and the sixth chapter of *Abot*, often entitled *Kinyan Tora*, was added even later during the Geonic period. See Alexander Guttman, 'Tractate Abot—Its Place in Rabbinic Judaism', *JQR* 41 (1950), pp. 181-93, and M.B. Lerner, 'The Tractate Avot', in Shmuel Safrai (ed.), *The Literature of the Sages, First Part: Oral Tora, Halakha, Mishna, Tosefta, Talmud, External Tractates* (CRINT, 3.1; Philadelphia: Fortress Press, 1987), pp. 263-81.

and Rabbi Joshua when all the people waved their palm branches but they waved them [palm branches] only at 'We beseech you, O Lord, save us now'"' (Ps. 118.25). Goldberg has suggested that these brief narratives be considered '*ma'aśim* without a formula'.[42] The fact that these stories are identical to the *ma'aśim* except for the formula might indicate a stage in the use of מעשׂה when this term was developing into the meaning 'case', but was not yet used consistently. The forms of the actual anecdotes, whether they contain מעשׂה, פעם אחת or neither are all similar.[43]

Applying the definition of an anecdote used in this book, the brief stories can be further divided into those that contain a 'saying', an 'action', or those that are 'mixed', that is, those that contain both a saying and an action. Furthermore, there is a difference in form between an anecdote that is recorded by the redactors of *M* and one that is given as an attestation, that is, reported by a named authority. As seen in both *Pes.* 7.2 B and *Suk.* 3.9 D, cited above, an attested anecdote has the additional function of a testimony or argument from authority.

Most of the anecdotes in *M* can be classified as narratives that contain a recorded saying, an attested saying, a recorded action, an attested action, a recorded mixed story or an attested mixed story.[44] *Pesaḥim* 7.2 B, above, is an example of an anecdote with an attested saying while *Suk.* 3.9 D contains an attested action. Examples of the other types are presented here. An anecdote with a recorded saying is found in *'Erub.* 4.2 A-C:

4.2 A. פעם אחת they did not enter the harbor until it had gotten dark [on a Sabbath night].

B. They said to Rabban Gamaliel, 'May we disembark?'

C. He said to them, 'It is all right, for beforehand I was watching, and we were within the [Sabbath] limit before it got dark.'

An anecdote with a recorded action is found in *Suk.* 4.9 N-O:

M. And to the one who pours out the water libation, they say, 'Lift up your hand!'

N. פעם אחת one [priest] poured out the water on his feet,

O. And all the people stoned him with their citrons.

42. Goldberg, 'Form und Funktion des Ma'ase', pp. 7-8.

43. Additionally, the anecdotes that contain מעשׂה or פעם אחת, all function in the same way as the other anecdotes. See the typologies for the מעשׂה in Appendix C and the discussion of the פעם אחת units in n. 92, below.

44. While this study did not find any 'attested mixed stories', nonetheless the category remains a logical possibility.

A recorded mixed anecdote is found in *Suk.* 2.5 A-C:

2.5 A. מעשׂה They brought Rabban Yoḥanan ben Zakkai some cooked food to taste, and to Rabban Gamaliel two dates and a bucket of water.

B. And they said, 'Bring them up to the *sukkah*.'

C. And when they gave R. Ṣadoq food less than an egg's bulk, he took it in a cloth and ate it outside of the *sukkah* and said no blessing after it.

While the most common form of the Mishnaic anecdote is the brief narrative of a saying or an action, there are three types of other narratives in the collection under discussion. These take the form of a dialogue as in *Beṣ.* 2.6 E-G and *Yad.* 3.1 K-N, or a debate as in *Yad.* 4.4 A-L. Both *Beṣ.* 2.6 E-G and *Yad.* 4.4 A-L are straightforward in their form, that is, one or more verbal interchanges between two parties. The narrative of *Beṣ.* 2.6 E-G has one interchange while *Yad.* 4.4 A-L records three exchanges. The anecdote of *Yad.* 3.1 K-N requires a brief comment. Within its immediate context, *Yad.* 3.1 I-O, the anecdote reads:

I. 'Food and vessels which have been made unclean by liquids impart uncleanness to the hands so that they are in the second degree of uncleanness', the words of R. Joshua.

J. And the sages say, 'That which is made unclean by a primary source [literally, "father"] of uncleanness imparts uncleanness to the hands. By a derivative source [literally, "offspring"] of uncleanness [it] does not impart uncleanness to the hands.'

K. Said Rabban Simeon ben Gamaliel, 'מעשׂה A certain woman came before father [Gamaliel II].

L. She said to him, "My hands entered the contained airspace of a clay vessel."

M. He said to her, "My daughter, by what had it been made unclean?"

N. But I did not hear what she said to him.'

O. Said the sages, 'The matter is clear. That which has been made unclean by a primary source [literally, "father"] of uncleanness imparts uncleanness to the hands. By a derivative source [literally, "offspring" of uncleanness] [it] does not impart uncleanness to the hands.'

Simeon's statement in N indicates that he does not know the remainder of the dialogue, which undoubtedly included Gamaliel's ruling. Thus, in form, this anecdote is an incomplete dialogue. It does function, however, as a proof for the sages' ruling in J, since Gamaliel's very question indicated that the degree of uncleanness of the vessel would have made a difference in his ruling.[45] This anecdote is an attestation and thus also functions as an argument from authority.

There are two remaining anecdotes that do not fit the categories discussed above, namely *Roš Haš.* 2.8-9 and *Yeb.* 16.7 A-G. They are classified as 'other'. The first will be discussed below in the section on the anecdotes of *Mo'ed Qaṭan*, and the second in the section on the anecdotes of Gamaliel.

This discussion of the form of the anecdotes yields the following typology of rabbinic anecdotes based on their form:

Typology of Rabbinic Anecdotes Based on Form

A. Narrative with a Saying
   1. Recorded
   2. Attested

B. Narrative with an Action
   1. Recorded
   2. Attested

C. Narrative with both a Saying and an Action
   1. Recorded
   2. Attested

D. Narrative with a Dialogue or a Debate
   1. Recorded
   2. Attested

E. Other

d. *Function of the Anecdotes*

Arnold Goldberg's discussion of the function of the *ma'aśim* is a good starting point in the investigation of the function of all the Mishnaic anecdotes. In his essay, Goldberg presents three typologies for the *ma'aśim* of *M.* The first typology is based on the content of the *ma'aśeh*, that is, whether it records a legal decision, the conduct of a particular rabbinic authority, a fact within a larger argument, the origin of a particular practice or a personal characteristic of a sage.[46]

Goldberg assumes that the מעשים existed in oral or written form as

45. See Kanter, *Rabban Gamaliel II*, pp. 212-13.

46. Goldberg, 'Form und Funktion des Ma'ase', pp. 13-20.

independent literary units before they were incorporated into *M*. He gives a typology for the function of such an independent מעשׂה, that is, it served to fix, either orally or in writing, the circumstances of a legal case and the authoritative decision regarding the case, to incorporate these matters into the larger legal tradition, and, finally, to hand on this ruling. Not only did the cases provide the contents of the legal questions, but the backgrounds of the rulings also served as an aid in the accurate transmission of a legal decision.[47] If, in fact, it can be shown that a מעשׂה or an anecdote existed as an independent entity, then these three functions are possible for such an independent unit.

This investigation, however, deals with anecdotes that are incorporated into the argumentation of the *Mishnah* in its present, written form. Goldberg's third typology deals with just that, the function of the מעשׂה within the individual chapters or sentences of a Mishnaic tractate. He delineates four such purposes, that is, to serve as the source of or proof for a lemma, to record a contrary opinion to that expressed in the preceding lemma, to operate as a 'narrative lemma', that is, to act in place of an actual statement of a legal decision, or to clarify a 'fragmentary *mishnah*'.[48] The first three of Goldberg's categories in this third typology were found to be functions for the anecdotes of *Mo'ed Qaṭan* and those of Gamaliel investigated in this chapter. Goldberg's fourth function of the מעשׂה, to clarify a fragmentary *mishnah*, was not present as a function of the anecdotes analyzed in this chapter.

A distinction can be made, however, between an anecdote serving as the source of a legal lemma and one that serves as a 'proof' for a law. In this chapter, the first is treated as a 'precedent', that is, 'an anecdote which functions as a basis or source for the stated law which follows it'. The second is called a 'proof from authority' or an 'example', that is, 'an anecdote which functions as evidence for the stated law which precedes it'. First presenting another sage's opinion and then stating one's agreement with it places the cited authority's ruling in the primary position. On the other hand, when an author first states a legal opinion and then provides an example from an authority figure who also holds to this opinion, the author's ruling is presented as the primary one. Furthermore, Goldberg's definition of a 'narrative lemma' can be further clarified as 'a legal opinion or action in the place of a statement of a law'.

Anecdotes in this study also serve two other functions: that of an

47. Goldberg, 'Form und Funktion des Ma'ase', p. 27.

48. Goldberg, 'Form und Funktion des Ma'ase', pp. 27-38.

'etiology' that 'relates the origin of a practice or belief', and that of an *'aggadah'*, which 'transmits a biographical reference to or highlights a personal characteristic of a sage'. These two functions were viewed by Goldberg as categories of the content of a מעשׂה in his first typology. In this study, these are also evident as the way certain anecdotes function. Hence, five functions, that is, precedent, proof, narrative law, etiology and *aggadah*, were found to be the primary functions of the anecdotes under investigation.

Many of the anecdotes also served additional functions. The attested anecdote is used as a 'testimony'; it lends the authority of one or more sages to another sage's ruling. Other anecdotes serve as 'contrary opinions', that is, as Goldberg noted, an anecdote may present a contrary legal opinion to a stated law. However, no anecdote in the collection studied functions just as a testimony or just as a contrary law. An anecdote that displays either of these two additional functions always serves one of the five primary functions of the anecdote discussed above. In the present study, therefore, 'testimony' and 'contrary opinion' are considered secondary functions of the anecdotes.

Examples of Mishnaic anecdotes that serve each of these functions are given here. *Šabbat* 24.5 E functions both as a precedent and as a proof. The entire *mishnah* reads:

24.5 A. They abrogate vows on the Sabbath.

B. And they receive questions concerning matters which are required for the Sabbath.

C. They stop up a light hole.

D. And they measure a piece of stuff and an immersion pool.

E. מעצה In the time of the father of R. Ṣadoq and of Abba Saul ben Botnit, they stopped up the light hole with a pitcher and tied a pot with reed grass [to a stick] to know whether or not there was in the roofing an opening of a handbreath square.

F. And from their deed we learned that they stop up, measure, and tie up on the Sabbath.

The action מעשׂה in E occurs in a discussion of what works are allowed on the Sabbath. Since two of the actions described in E, stopping up a light hole and measuring, are actions ruled as permissible in lemmas C and D, the מעשׂה functions as a proof for lemma C and part of lemma D. The מעשׂה also mentions that a 'pot was tied with reed grass'. The lemma allowing that action follows in F, and thus this anecdote also functions as a precedent for that last lemma.

Pesaḥim 7.2 B, cited above, functions as a narrative law. In *Pes.* 7.2 B, the anecdote of Gamaliel's order to use a grill to roast the Passover offering is not followed by a statement of a lemma to that effect, therefore, the story itself serves as the lemma. Moreover, the lemma is both a contrary ruling to that of 7.2 A and is attested to by R. Zadoq. Hence, *Pes.* 7.2 B has the primary function of a narrative law with the secondary functions of testimony and a contrary law.

Sukkah 4.9 N-O, cited above, serves as an etiology for the practice in 4.9 M. The priest who performs the libation is told to lift up his hand, since a former priest did not and suffered dire consequences.

Finally, *Beṣ.* 3.2 D is an example of an anecdote that carries aggadic information. The entire *mishnah* is given here:

3.2 A. Nets for trapping a wild beast, fowl, or fish, which one set on the eve of a festival day

B. one should not take out of them on the festival day

C. unless one knows for certain that [they] were trapped on the eve of the festival day.

D. מעשׂה A gentile brought fish to Rabban Gamaliel, and he said, 'They are permitted. But I do not want to accept them from him.'

This paragraph applies the ruling of *Šab.* 1.6 E, that is, game trapped prior to the Sabbath is permitted for use on the Sabbath, and applies this to the game trapped prior to festival days. C rules that one must be certain that the game was trapped prior to the festival day. The anecdote in D is placed here to present a contrary ruling. It is assumed that since a Gentile brought the fish, that person may not have known of the 'prior day' restriction and therefore Gamaliel could not be certain that the restriction had been followed. His 'permitting' the fish contradicts lemma C but no legal statement of this contradiction follows the anecdote. Hence, *Beṣ.* 3.2 D also functions as a narrative law. The anecdote portrays Gamaliel's choice not to accept the fish. This displays a mark of extra piety on the part of Gamaliel that is also portrayed in other Mishnaic anecdotes.[49] *Beṣah* 3.2 D, then, highlights a personal characteristic of a sage and, consequently, also functions as *aggadah*. Here we have an anecdote that fits two of the primary types of the functions of Mishnaic anecdotes, narrative law and

49. See the comments on this passage by Kanter, *Rabban Gamaliel II*, p. 104.

aggadah, and one of the secondary types, a contrary opinion.

The following is the typology for the function of Mishnaic anecdotes based on the collection analyzed in this investigation:[50]

Typology of Rabbinic Anecdotes Based on Function

A. Primary Functions
   1. Precedent
   2. Proof from Authority
   3. Narrative Law
   4. Etiology
   5. *Aggadah*

B. Secondary Functions
   1. Testimony
   2. Contrary Opinion

The typologies of the forms and the functions of the rabbinic anecdotes were developed after studying the anecdotes that are found in Division *Mo'ed Qaṭan* and those stories involving Rabbi Gamaliel II. The next two sections of this chapter furnish the details of that study.

3. *Anecdotes of Division* Mo'ed Qaṭan

The *Mishnah*'s second division, *Mo'ed Qaṭan*, 'Appointed Times', comprises laws that deal with the sacred times of early rabbinic Judaism. The overarching concern of *Mo'ed Qaṭan*, according to the studies of Jacob Neusner, is the sanctification of the village and the home during a recurring cycle of sacred times, either in consort with the Temple or as its replacement.[51]

Mo'ed Qaṭan contains 12 tractates which are listed here along with the subject of their rulings: (1) *Šabbat*, the Sabbath; (2) *'Erubin* 'mixtures', that is, how the law forbidding certain movements on the Sabbath can be

50. Jacob Neusner presented a typology of 'forms and types' of Mishnaic pericopae (*Rabbinic Traditions. Part III. Conclusions*, pp. 64-66; also in 'Types and Forms in Ancient Jewish Literature', pp. 354-90). These 'forms' are not discussed as genres and may be described more accurately as 'literary patterns' (Donald Stevens, 'Rabbi Yose the Galilean: A Representative Selection of his Legal Traditions' [PhD dissertation, Duke University, 1978], p. 7) or, as Neusner himself admits, 'techniques of story-telling' ('Types and Forms in Ancient Jewish Literature', p. 386).

51. Jacob Neusner, *A History of the Mishnaic Law of Appointed Times.* V. *The Mishnaic System of Appointed Times* (SJLA, 34; 5 vols.; Leiden: E.J. Brill, 1981), V, p. 15.

by-passed; (3) *Pesaḥim*, the Feast of Passover; (4) *Šeqalim*, the half-shekel tax to the Temple; (5)*Yoma*, the Day of Atonement; (6) *Sukkah*, the Feast of Booths; (7) *Beṣah*, 'egg', (from the first word) on work during the festival days; (8) *Roš haš-Šanah*, the New Year's Feast; (9) *Ta'anit*, fast days; (10) *Megillah*, the Feast of Purim; (11) *Mo'ed Qaṭan*, minor festival days; and (12) *Ḥagigah*, festival sacrifices and pilgrimages.

a. *Form of the Anecdotes*

In the whole of division *Mo'ed Qaṭan* there are 41 anecdotes. There is at least one example of every classification of narrative in the typologies of the forms and functions of rabbinic anecdotes given above with the exception of the form of an attested dialogue or debate, D.2. Moreover, there is one unit, *Roš Haš*. 2.8-9, which does not fit any classification in the typology and thus is designated 'Other'.

Roš haš-Šanah 2.8-9 reads as follows:

2.8 A. Rabban Gamaliel had a picture of the shapes of the moon on a tablet and on the wall of his upper room, which he would show untrained people, saying, 'Did you see it like this or like that?'

B. מעשׂה Two people came and said, 'We saw it in the east in the morning and in the west in the evening.'

C. R. Yoḥanan b. Nuri said, 'They are false witnesses.'

D. Now when they came to Yabneh, Rabban Gamaliel accepted [their testimony].

E. And again two came and said, 'We saw it at its proper time, but on the night of the added day it did not appear.'

F. Then Rabban Gamaliel accepted [their testimony].

G. Said R. Dosa b. Harkinas, 'They are false witnesses.

H. How can they testify that a woman has given birth if the next day, her stomach is still up there between her teeth [that is, she is still pregnant]?'

I. R. Joshua said to him, 'I approve of your words.'

2.9 A. Rabban Gamaliel sent to him [saying], 'I decree that you come to me with your staff and purse on the Day of Atonement which is determined in accord with your reckoning.'

B. R. Aqiba went and found him [R. Joshua] troubled.

C. He [Aqiba] said to him, 'I can demonstrate that everything that Rabban Gamaliel has done is validly done, since it says, "These are the appointed feasts of the Lord, even holy convocations, which you shall proclaim (Lev. 23.4)." Whether they are in their proper time or not in their proper time, I have no appointed feasts but these.'

D. He [R. Joshua] came along to R. Dosa b. Harkinas.

E. He [Dosa] said to him, 'Now if we are going to take issue with the court of Rabban Gamaliel, we have to take issue with every court which has come into being from the days of Moses until now,

F. since it says, "Then went up Moses and Aaron, Nadab and Abihu, and seventy of the elders of Israel (Exod. 24.9)."

G. Now why have the names of the elders not been given? Only to teach that every group of three who came into being as a court of Israel is equivalent to the court of Moses.'

H. He [Joshua] took his staff and his purse in his hand and went along to Yabneh, to Rabban Gamaliel, on the day which fell as the Day of Atonement determined in accord with his [Joshua's] reckoning.

I. Rabban Gamaliel stood up and kissed him on his head and said to him, 'Come in peace, my master and my disciple—

J. My master in wisdom and my disciple since you accepted my rulings.'

Together these two paragraphs of *Roš haš-Šanah* form a carefully crafted passage, the longest narrative in *M*, which begins and ends with Gamaliel. It is treated as one story in this study since it is clearly meant to be a unity. The narrative, as it now stands in *M*, consists of four parts: 2.8 A, 2.8 B-D, 2.9 B-C, and the remainder, 2.8 E–2.9 A and 2.9 D-J.[52]

The core of the passage, 2.8 E–2.9 A and 2.9 D-J, is a story involving three personages, Gamaliel, Dosa and Joshua. Gamaliel accepts the testimony of false witnesses to proclaim a festival. Dosa opposes the witnesses and Joshua agrees with Dosa. Gamaliel then orders Joshua to travel to visit him on the Day of Atonement as Joshua would calculate it. Dosa, who had opposed the testimony given to Gamaliel, advises Joshua not to disagree with the court of Gamaliel. Joshua obeys Gamaliel and earns his praise.

The other three parts, 2.8 A, 2.8 B-D, 2.9 B-C, are independent units that appear to be additions. Verse 2.8 A, a description of the method Gamaliel used to examine the witnesses who came to him, connects the passage to

52. See Kanter (*Rabban Gamaliel II*, pp. 108-11) for a discussion of the pre-history of this narrative; also W.S. Green, *The Traditions of Joshua Ben Hananiah*. I. *The Early Legal Traditions* (SJLA, 29; Leiden: E.J. Brill, 1981), pp. 116-20.

Roš Haš. 2.6, on examining witnesses. It also indicates Gamaliel's knowledge of the phases of the moon.

The מעשה in 2.8 B-D, while concerned with the subject matter of the passage, refers to R. Yoḥanan b. Nuri, a rabbi of a younger generation than Gamaliel, Dosa and Joshua.[53] This story may well have been an independent unit that was placed here to produce two examples, 'witnesses', of the miscalculation of Gamaliel. The unit 2.9 B-C, describing Aqiba's opinion, is also an addition. Aqiba, like Yoḥanan, is from a younger generation of authorities. His support of Gamaliel's decision is a confirmation of the ruling already given in 2.7. Since Dosa's support for Gamaliel's court is indicated in the next verses, Aqiba's support for Gamaliel is not essential to the story. However, the combination of Aqiba and Dosa again provides two 'witnesses', this time to the primacy of Gamaliel's ruling.

In 2.9 C Aqiba cites Lev. 23.4, already utilized in 1.9 E. There the verse is interpreted literally to emphasize the importance of overcoming obstacles and even violating the prohibition of Sabbath travel in order to report the new moon, thereby insuring that the festival is *proclaimed*. Aqiba also interprets the verse literally, but with a different emphasis, that is, 'these are the feasts...*you* shall proclaim'. Thus the court's proclamation makes the day holy whether it is calculated correctly or not. Both these interpretations take Lev. 23.4 out of context. The writer of 1.9 E extends the 'festivals of the Lord' to include the new moon, which is not mentioned in the Leviticus text. Aqiba omits the closing words of the verse, that is, 'at the time appointed for them', and, thus, he is able to emphasize the court's role in setting the dates of the feasts.[54]

Dosa also cites Scripture in his arguments in 2.9 E-G. There he uses Exod. 24.9 and picks up on an element of the text, namely the mention of specific leaders followed by an anonymous group of 70 elders. Dosa builds his interpretative argument on the anonymity of the elders in order to arrive at support for the decisions of the court of Gamaliel.[55] In both instances, Aqiba's and Dosa's use of a Scripture verse adds the authority of the Torah to their arguments and, therefore, to the decision of Gamaliel's court.

Verse 2.9 H-J records Joshua's obedience to Gamaliel's order. Joshua's action wins the praise of Gamaliel, since Joshua had both traveled and

53. See the lists of Rabbi's according to generations in Strack and Stemberger, *Introduction to the Talmud and Midrash*, pp. 76-83.

54. Peter A. Pettit, 'Shene'emar: The Place of Scripture Citation in the Mishna' (PhD dissertation, Claremont Graduate School, 1993), pp.196-97.

55. Pettit, 'Shene'emar', p. 197.

carried a burden on what he himself would have considered to be the Day of Atonement. If it was indeed the feast, Joshua would have violated the law (Lev. 23.26-32; *Yom.* 8.1 A). Since he went to Yabneh with staff and purse, Joshua acknowledged that Gamaliel's set date for the feast was the legitimate day for its observance.

Gamaliel's closing words, 'my master in wisdom and my disciple since you accepted my rulings', are meant not only for Joshua but for Aqiba and Dosa as well. Not only does this narrative speak to the authority of Gamaliel, but Gamaliel's closing words of praise add his own testimony to the authority of Joshua, Aqiba and Dosa.

As a single narrative 2.8-9 functions as a proof for the argument in 2.7 A-C that when the head of the court declares 'sanctified time', that is, an appointed feast, it is sanctified whether or not it is properly calculated according to the new moon. Kanter notes, 'Indeed, the remarkable claim of this pericope…is that Gamaliel's action shows astronomical facts to be secondary to the power of the court to *decree* the sacred time.'[56] God, in effect, accepts the rulings of the head of the court. The passage also emphasizes the knowledge and authority of Gamaliel and hence functions as *aggadah*. Finally, the entire narrative, with its careful development, portrays the skill of the redactor(s) of the *Mishnah*.

The following is the typology of the anecdotes in *Mo'ed Qaṭan* according to form:

Typology of the Anecdotes of Mo'ed Qaṭan *Based on Form*

A. Narrative with a Saying		9
1. Recorded	5	
2. Attested	4	
B. Narrative with an Action		27
1. Recorded	14	
2. Attested	13	
C. Narrative with both a Saying and an Action		2
1. Recorded	1	
2. Attested	1	
D. Narrative with a Dialogue or a Debate		2
1. Recorded	2	
2. Attested	0	
E. Other		1
Total		41

56. Kanter, *Rabban Gamaliel II*, p. 110.

b. *Function of the Anecdotes*

The functions of the anecdotes in *Mo'ed Qaṭan* are discussed below under the conclusions. The following is the typology based on their functions:

Typology of the Anecdotes of Mo'ed Qaṭan *Based on Function*[57]

A. Primary Functions	
1. Precedent	1
2. Proof from Authority	21
3. Narrative Law	11
4. Etiology	6
5. *Aggadah*	6
B. Secondary Functions	
1. Testimony	22
2. Contrary Opinion	6

c. *Conclusions*

The first conclusion from this study is that anecdotes do indeed exist in the *Mishnah*. All but one of the 41 anecdotes in *Mo'ed Qaṭan* are very brief narratives.[58] The exception is *Roš Haš.* 2.8-9, a long, intricately crafted narrative composed of four parts, three of which could stand as independent anecdotes. The statistic that is most striking from the typology of the forms of the anecdotes of *Mo'ed Qaṭan* is that brief narratives involving an action (B.1 and B.2) occur three times as often as those involving a saying (A.1 and A.2).

As can be seen from the typology of the functions of the anecdotes in *Mo'ed Qaṭan*, the proof from authority, which occurs 21 times, is the primary function of these anecdotes. Closely related to this function are those of precedent and narrative law. As one would expect in a legal document, one observes that most of the anecdotes function to state or strengthen a legal opinion. The secondary function of testimony also occurs for 22 of the anecdotes. These results attest to the prominent role of the sages in the establishment of legal rulings. Not only were anecdotes about rabbis used as precedents, proofs and narrative laws, but other sages added their authority to that of another, thus heightening the influence of

57. Since several of the anecdotes have more than one function, a sum total of functions for the anecdotes would have little statistical meaning and so is not given here.

58. A summary listing of the anecdotes of *Mo'ed Qaṭan*, along with their forms and functions, may be found in Appendix A.

the rabbis as a class. Moreover, often these anecdotes pointed out the behavior of the sage. Thus the life of the rabbi served a didactic function.

All the anecdotes that functioned as contrary opinions had the primary function of a narrative law. No anecdote served as a precedent for or a proof of a stated contrary ruling. The anecdote alone was narrated as sufficient to record a contrary legal opinion. While beyond the scope of this book, it would prove interesting to study all the anecdotes of the *Mishnah* that function as contrary opinions to observe whether throughout the work as a whole such anecdotes always, or most often, function primarily as narrative laws, as is the case in *Mo'ed Qaṭan*.

Finally, it is of interest to the next section of this chapter to note that of the six anecdotes of *Mo'ed Qaṭan* that function as *aggadah*, three deal directly with Gamaliel, namely *Beṣ*. 3.2 D, and *Roš Haš*. 1.6 A-C and 2.8-9, while two others, *Beṣ*. 2.6 E-G and *Šeq*. 3.3 A, deal with Gamaliel's father. The remaining anecdote that serves as *aggadah* is *'Erub*. 1.2 E-J, which highlights the authority of Aqiba. All of the anecdotes of Rabbi Gamaliel are studied in the next section.

4. *Anecdotes Concerning Gamaliel II*

Any presentation on the personage of Gamaliel II must take into account the lack of historically reliable data on early rabbinic sages. There are no systematic or coherent biographies of prominent tannaitic rabbis extant in the corpus of rabbinic literature. Our information comes from rabbinic literature itself and Geonic texts. The two most important Geonic texts in this regard are *Seder Tannaim we-Amoraim*, c. 884 CE, and the *Letter of Sherira Gaon*, 987 CE.[59] Over and above their late dates, there are problems of inconsistency among the various recensions of these texts.[60]

Actual dates, moreover, are never transmitted in the rabbinic texts. Dates for the life of individual rabbis are relative, that is, they are 'determined by a rabbi's relationship to another as his teacher, conversation partner, student, or tradent (always assuming that the nomenclature is clear and the name is correctly preserved)'.[61] Additionally, as has been noted above, all the extant rabbinic literature has been highly edited and each

59. See Strack and Stemberger, *Introduction to the Talmud and Midrash*, pp. 6-7. See also their remarks on the difficulties of gathering reliable data on the rabbis, pp. 62-68.

60. Strack and Stemberger, *Introduction to the Talmud and Midrash*, p. 62.

61. Strack and Stemberger, *Introduction to the Talmud and Midrash*, p. 63.

text reflects the interests of its own redactor. William Green has pointed out that it is a mistake to assume that 'the words ascribed to a rabbinic master were really said by him and that the narrative accounts accurately reflect events which actually occurred'.[62]

In addition to the problem of limited or no chronological data on the tannaitic rabbis, there are also no written records of the teachings of any one authority that exist as individual texts. Inasmuch as the texts we do have are edited, they block access to the growth and development of any master's thought over a period of time. Therefore, since each autonomous document has its own legal and theological agenda, one should not gather the traditions about or attributed to one rabbi from all of these autonomous texts, consider them as a whole and then claim to have either the complete or consistent teaching of that rabbi or even to have a schema of the development in that rabbi's teaching.[63] In this investigation, therefore, there is a distinction made between Gamaliel II of history and 'the Gamaliel II of the *Mishnah*', that is, the portrait of Gamaliel II as he appears in that work as a whole.

Studies of Gamaliel II are further complicated by the need to determine, in several passages, which Gamaliel is meant, Gamaliel I (the Elder) or Gamaliel II. When the term 'the elder' is present, this usually indicates Gamaliel I. Kanter has developed four other criteria to aid in deciding that a passage refers to Gamaliel II: (1) mention in the same pericope of Gamaliel's Yavnean contemporaries; (2) citation of Gamaliel's words by a contemporary or a later authority in the line of transmission of Gamaliel's views; (3) consistency with the views of Gamaliel or conflict with the views of Gamaliel the Elder; and (4) the historical context (for example, a Gamaliel of Yabneh is Gamaliel II while a Gamaliel at the Temple in Jerusalem is Gamaliel I).[64] The following investigation follows Kanter's determinations.

Critical scholars generally agree that the historical Gamaliel II was the grandson of Gamaliel the Elder, the son of Simeon ben Gamaliel I, the

62. William S. Green, 'What's in a Name?—The Problematic of Rabbinic "Biography"', in *idem* (ed.), *Approaches to Ancient Judaism*. I. *Theory and Practice* (BJS, 1; Missoula, MT: Scholars Press, 1978), pp. 77-97. Green (p. 94 n. 53) faults biographies of rabbis written 20 years ago that make this mistake, for example, Judah Goldin, 'Toward a Profile of the Tanna, Aqiba ben Joseph', *JAOS* 96 (1976), pp. 38-56.

63. See William S. Green, 'Context and Meaning in Rabbinic "Biography"', in *idem* (ed.), *Approaches to Ancient Judaism*, II (BJS, 9; Chico, CA: Scholars Press, 1980), pp. 81-99.

64. Kanter, *Rabban Gamaliel II*, pp. ix-x.

father of Simeon ben Gamaliel II, and the grandfather of Yehuda ha-Nasi.[65] Gamaliel succeeded R. Yoḥanan ben Zakkai[66] as leader in Yavneh, functioning from c. 80 or 90 to 110 CE. Mishnaic passages indicate that Gamaliel was married (*Ber.* 2.5), widowed (*Ber.* 2.6), had sons (*Ber.* 1.1), and had a servant, Tabi (*Pes.* 7.2 B). Both Talmudim (*b. Ber.* 27b-28b; *y. Ber.* 4.17c-d) recount a time when Gamaliel was temporarily unseated as the leader in Yavneh by R. Eleazar ben Azariah. The historicity of this event can be established, although the reasons behind it remain uncertain.[67] Finally, according to *M*, Gamaliel may have traveled by sea to Rome with Joshua, Aqiba and Eleazer ben Azariah (*'Erub.* 4.1-2; *Ma'as. Š.* 5.9; *Šab.* 16.8). The 'Gamaliel II of the *Mishnah*' is discussed below after the presentation of the form and function of the anecdotes about him in the *Mishnah*.

a. *Form of the Anecdotes*

There are 35 anecdotes involving Rabban Gamaliel in the whole of the *Mishnah*. There is at least one example of every classification of narrative in the typologies of the forms and functions of rabbinic anecdotes, given above, with the exception of the form of a recorded narrative that contains both a saying and an action (C.1). Moreover, there is one unit that is classified 'Other', *Yeb.* 16.7 A-G, which reads as follows:

16.7 A. a. Rabbi Aqiba said,
b. 'When I went down to Nehardea to intercalate the year, Neḥemiah of Bet Deli came to me. He said to me, "I heard that only R. Judah b. Baba permits a wife in the Land of Israel to remarry on the evidence of a single witness."

B. I stated to him, "That is indeed so."

C. He said to me, "Tell them in my name—

D. you know that the country is alive with ravaging bands—

E. I have a tradition from Rabban Gamaliel the Elder that

F. they permit a wife to remarry on the testimony of a single witness."

65. Strack and Stemberger, *Introduction to the Talmud and Midrash*, pp. 76, 85; Kanter, *Rabban Gamaliel II*, passim; and Aryeh Carmell, *Aiding Talmud Study* (Jerusalem: Feldheim, 1988), p. 89.

66. Strack and Stemberger, *Introduction to the Talmud and Midrash*, p. 76.

67. See the study of this occurrence by R. Goldenberg, 'The Deposition of Rabban Gamaliel II: An Examination of the Sources', *JJS* 22 (1972), pp. 167-90.

G. And when I came and recounted the matter before Rabban Gamaliel, he was overjoyed at my report and said, "We now have found a pair for R. Judah b. Baba." '

In this passage 16.7 A. (a) and G are a frame narrative whose form is an attested story with a saying. Aqiba narrates a statement of Gamaliel in response to Aqiba's report of another incident. The report, 16.7 A.b to F, is in the form of a narrative account of a dialogue between Aqiba and Neḥemiah. The closing statement by Neḥemiah in the dialogue, C and E-F, is a testimony to a statement of Rabban Gamaliel the Elder. Thus, 16.7 A-G is a narrative of a saying occasioned by a report; the report, in turn, is a narrative of a dialogue; and the final response in the dialogue is a testimony to a legal ruling of yet another sage. Hence, this unit has a composite form; it is classified 'Other'.

Within the *Mishnah* this passage is a narrative report of the circumstances of two previously stated legal lemmas. *'Eduyyot* 6.1 C states the lemma by Judah b. Baba found here in 16.7 A and *'Ed.* 8.5 A records only an attestation of Aqiba to a ruling, attributed to Neḥemiah, that a woman was allowed to remarry on the evidence of one witness.[68] Within *Yebamot* the composite narrative 16.7 A-G serves two primary functions and one secondary. It is a precedent for the legal lemma that follows it in 16.7 I (1) that allows a woman to remarry on the strength of one witness. The passage also serves as a proof for the ruling of Judah b. Baba as told in 16.7 A. Finally, the composite narrative offers the testimony of Aqiba to the rulings of Judah b. Baba and Rabban Gamaliel the Elder as well as to the statement by Gamaliel.

The next sentence in *Yeb.* 16.7, that is, H, reads: 'And in the same discourse Rabban Gamaliel remembered that men were slain at Tel Arza, and Rabban Gamaliel the Elder allowed their wives to remarry on the evidence of a single witness.' In this study, 16.7 H is treated as a separate anecdote because it is not integral to the first passage. It is connected to what precedes it by the words 'And in the same discourse'. Taken together with *Yeb.* 16.7 A-G, however, 16.7 H presents Gamaliel as having forgotten his grandfather's ruling and in need of Aqiba's report to refresh his memory. Verse 16.7 H gives an image of Aqiba as the instructor of Gamaliel and thus functions as *aggadah* for Aqiba's authority.

A group of three anecdotes all have the same form, namely *Ker.* 3.7 A-E, 3.8 A-G and 3.9 A-F. The setting for all three is given in 3.7 A: 'R.

68. See Kanter, *Rabban Gamaliel II*, p. 133.

Aqiba said, "I asked Rabban Gamaliel and R. Joshua in the meat market of Emmaus, where they had gone to buy a beast for the banquet of Rabban Gamaliel's son…"' The remainder of 3.1, B-E, and all of the other two anecdotes take the form of a question from Aqiba to Gamaliel and R. Joshua, followed by their response. In each case the response begins, 'We have not heard, but…' A law based on another case is then cited and a response to Aqiba's questions is arrived at by extrapolation from the law for this other case. In each anecdote the extrapolation is stated as deriving from the rule קל וחמר, *qal waḥomer*, that is, from the lesser to the greater. This rule involves 'learning the more stringent from the more lenient, based on the logical assumption that if the less stringent has a certain חמרא [element of severity], then the more stringent law will certainly have it'.[69] *Keritot* 3.7 B-E is given here as an example:

> 3.7 B. [Aqiba asked,] 'He who has sexual relations with his sister, with his father's sister, and with his mother's sister, in a single act of forgetting, what is the rule?
>
> C. Is he liable [for a sin offering] once for all of them, or once for each and every action?
>
> D. They said to me, "We have not heard, but we have heard the rule that he who has sexual relations with his five wives when they are menstruating, in a single act of forgetting, that he is liable for each and every act.
>
> E. And we regard the matter as subject to a proof by an argument of *qal waḥomer.*"'

Keritot 3.9 E contains one deviation from the above form, namely instead of both Gamaliel and Joshua providing the response only Joshua answers. This may indicate that this third anecdote circulated independently of the other two.

The fact that R. Aqiba attests to these rulings adds his authority for the decisions to that of Gamaliel and Joshua. Nonetheless, since Aqiba asked the opinion of the other two authorities, the group of anecdotes adds to the prestige of both Gamaliel and Joshua as they are portrayed in *M.* Furthermore, as Kanter points out, Joshua's presence alongside Gamaliel in this anecdote is significant. Joshua had a reputation for asceticism, particularly abstention from meat and wine as a sign of mourning for the loss of the Temple (*b. B. Bat.* 60b). Gamaliel's opponents would have taken issue

69. Eliyahu Krupnick, שערי למקד: *The Gateway to Learning: A Systematic Introduction to the Study of the Talmud* (Jerusalem: Feldheim, 1981), p. 56.

with his wedding celebration as a violation of the national mourning. 'They would be eager to use such a charge to discredit the Patriarch [Gamaliel], vulnerable through his close dealings with the Roman authorities. Joshua's appearance in the story would demonstrate that Gamaliel's celebration was within the bounds of propriety.'[70] Thus, the anecdotes function as *aggadah*, supporting Gamaliel's person and authority, as well as the authority of the office of the Patriarch.

Three other anecdotes also have the same form, that is, *Ber.* 2.5 C-F, 2.6 A-C and 2.7 A-C. These three stories present important characteristics of Gamaliel and are discussed in the section on the portrait of Gamaliel in the *Mishnah*. The following, then, is the typology of the anecdotes involving Rabbi Gamaliel II according to their form:

Typology of Anecdotes of Gamaliel II Based on Form

A.	Narrative with a Saying		17
	1. Recorded	10	
	2. Attested	7	
B.	Narrative with an Action		13
	1. Recorded	6	
	2. Attested	7	
C.	Narrative with both a Saying and an Action		1
	1. Recorded	0	
	2. Attested	1	
D.	Narrative with a Dialogue or a Debate		2
	1. Recorded	1	
	2. Attested	1	
E.	Other		2
Total			35

b. *Function of the Anecdotes*

The opening passage of the *Mishnah*, *Ber.* 1.1, contains an anecdote of Gamaliel, 1.1 G-I. The passage deals with the conclusion of the evening time period during which one is obligated to recite the *Shema'* and reads as follows:

1.1 A From what hour do they recite the *Shema'* in the evening?

B. From the hour that priests enter to eat their heave offerings.

C. 'Until the end of the first watch',

D. the words of R. Eliezer.

70. Kanter, *Rabban Gamaliel II*, p. 189.

E. But sages say, 'Until midnight.'

F. Rabban Gamaliel says, 'Until the rise of dawn.'

G. מעשה His [Gamaliel's] sons returned from a banquet hall [after midnight].

H. They said to him, 'We did not yet recite the *Shema'*.'

I. He said to them, 'If the dawn has not yet risen, you are obligated to recite [the *Shema'*].

J. And not only in this matter. Rather all which the sages said "until midnight", the obligation remains until the rise of dawn.'

K. The offering of fats and entrails, the obligation until rise of dawn [see Lev. 1.9, 3.3-5].

L. And all [sacrifices] which must be eaten within one day, the obligation until rise of dawn.

M. If so why did sages say until midnight?

N. In order to protect man from transgression.

Here the anecdote of I-J serves as a proof for Gamaliel's opinion in the debate with Eliezer (ben Hyrcanus)[71] and the sages. That Gamaliel's opinion became the accepted ruling is shown by J-N, which harmonizes the opinion of the sages with his ruling.

This opening passage of *M* has been discussed recently by Alan Avery-Peck, who notes that in *Ber.* 1.1 the rabbis use their understanding of the Temple practices to formulate their rulings.[72] In effect, then, Temple practice, even though the Temple had been destroyed, 'forms the model for common Israelites' liturgical activities'. The rabbis, however, do more than just legislate non-Temple liturgical practice; 'they appropriate to themselves responsibilities traditionally held by priests'.[73] Thus, the rabbinic authorities constitute themselves as the new leaders of what remains of the liturgical cult.

The named authority for the legislation that actualizes this position is Rabban Gamaliel since his is the ruling and the example that decide the matter under debate. Therefore, not only does *Berakot* 1.1 support the leadership and authority of the rabbinate as a whole, the passage also spotlights Gamaliel's role in establishing this authoritative position. The

71. See Neusner, *Eliezer Ben Hyrcanus*, pp. 18-20, for this identification of Eliezer.
72. Avery-Peck, 'Judaism without the Temple', pp. 416-17.
73. Avery-Peck, 'Judaism without the Temple', p. 417.

opening words of *M*, then, acknowledge Gamaliel's authoritative role in legal decisions and accord him a prominent role in the rise of the rabbinate.

The functions of other anecdotes in the collection of Gamaliel stories, particularly those which serve as *aggadah*, will be discussed below in the section on the portrait of Gamaliel in the *Mishnah*. The following is the typology of the anecdotes about Gamaliel based on their function:

Typology of the Anecdotes of Gamaliel II Based on Function

A. Primary Functions	
1. Precedent	4
2. Proof from Authority	25
3. Narrative Law	9
4. Etiology	1
5. *Aggadah*	11
B. Secondary Functions	
1. Testimony	17
2. Contrary Opinion	2

c. *Gamaliel II of the Mishnaic Anecdotes*

Gamaliel II emerges from the *Mishnah* as a figure of authority. His leading role in establishing the rabbinate, as presented in *Ber.* 1.1, was noted above. Additionally, like the function of the anecdotes in *Mo'ed Qaṭan*, the majority, 25, of the stories on Gamaliel function as 'proof from authority'. Of these 25, 3 anecdotes, *Ber.* 1.1 G-I, 2.5 C-E and *Yeb.* 16.7 A-G, also serve as precedents. If one combines the anecdotes that act as precedents, proofs or narrative laws,[74] they total 35, or the total number of anecdotes about Gamaliel. No anecdote functions solely as an etiology or an aggadic statement. All the anecdotes about Gamaliel therefore serve an overtly 'legal' function in their respective passages of *M*. Once again, this data highlights Gamaliel's position as a legal authority.

In his *Rabban Gamaliel: The Legal Traditions*, Shamai Kanter analyzed the corpus of the legal traditions of Gamaliel. Kanter concentrated on the traditions found in the *Mishnah* and *Tosefta* but also included tannaitic midrashim, the talmudim and later collections. His investigation was not limited to anecdotes and included non-narrative dispute forms, exegeses and lemmas. Using his form categories, Kanter analyzed 169 passages and

74. The definition of narrative law precludes that an anecdote that functions as a narrative law would also function as a precedent or as a proof from authority.

found that 81, or 47.9 per cent, were in narrative form. He further noted that this number was a significant increase over the number of narratives associated with pre-70 Pharisees, as well as a greater number than those told about the rabbis in the generation following Gamaliel. That is, only 29 per cent of the legal traditions of the pre-70 Pharisees and 4 per cent of the legal traditions of the post-Gamaliel generation rabbis were in narrative form.[75] With respect to the high number of narrative traditions about Gamaliel, similar results are found if one combines Kanter's study with the one in this book. Kanter notes 24 legal traditions on Gamaliel in the division *Mo'ed Qaṭan*.[76] My investigation identifies 12 anecdotes about Gamaliel in *Mo'ed Qaṭan*, all of which appear in Kanter's list. Hence, 50 per cent of the legal traditions about Gamaliel in *Mo'ed Qaṭan* are, in fact, in narrative form. This sampling from one division of *M* supports Kanter's research, at least on Gamaliel.

From his statistics, Kanter concluded that the 'paradigmatic action, through use of the narrative is especially important *only* to Gamaliel'.[77] That Christians at the same time were transmitting narratives about 'a master' is used as a point of comparison by Kanter. For Christians, he asserted, 'the narratives revealed the nature of [Jesus'] divinity, and provided the basis for the authority of the Church and its faith'.[78] Noting the lack of such theological purposes in *M*, Kanter posited a similar political purpose for the narratives about Gamaliel as follows:

> The patriarchate was a new institution, linked with a religious movement, the emergent rabbinical group, itself relatively new… The marked increase in frequency [of the narrative form] to 47.9% within the Gamaliel traditions, records establishing the legitimacy of the new figure of authority.[79]

A proper evaluation of this intriguing claim by Kanter would entail a full investigation of the narratives about the pre-70 Pharisees as well as the traditions about R. Simeon ben Gamaliel II. However, 47.9 per cent of the traditions about Gamaliel are, in fact, in narrative form. This in itself is

75. Kanter, *Rabban Gamaliel II*, pp. 246-51. Kanter used the figure 29 per cent for narratives of the pre-70 Pharisees without citing a source. Kanter himself (p. 248) listed the breakdown of the traditions about Gamaliel's son, R. Simeon b. Gamaliel II, without discussion and arrived at the figure of 4.3 per cent for the post-Gamaliel generation.

76. Kanter, *Rabban Gamaliel II*, pp. 259-61.

77. Kanter, *Rabban Gamaliel II*, p. 248.

78. Kanter, *Rabban Gamaliel II*, p. 248.

79. Kanter, *Rabban Gamaliel II*, p. 248.

significant. Furthermore, since the anecdotes of Gamaliel do portray him as an early, prominent authoritative figure, one has some concrete support for Kanter's assertion.

The piety of Gamaliel has been noted already in the presentation on *Beṣ.* 3.2 D. There, in a discussion on eating game properly trapped before a festival day, Gamaliel refused to accept a fish from a Gentile even though it was permitted to do so. Gamaliel held himself to a stricter interpretation.[80] His piety is indicated more strikingly in *Ber.* 2.5. All of *Berakot* 2 is concerned with the necessary 'intention' or 'devotion', כוונה, which is required for the proper recitation of the *Shema'*. *Berakot* 2.1 B rules that one must have 'directed his heart', כיון לבו, in order to fulfill his obligation; 2.1 C–2.5 B discusses various distractions that break this required level of concentration. Basically, these are fear (2.1 F), emotion (2.5 A-B) and grief (3.1–3.2).[81]

The circumstance of emotional distraction described is a wedding night. *Berakot* 2.5 A-B reads: 'A. A bridegroom is exempt from the recitation of the *Shema'* on the first night [of the wedding] until after the Sabbath B. if he did not consummate [the marriage.]' There follows this anecdote of Gamaliel:

> C. מעשה Rabban Gamaliel recited [the *Shema'*] on the first night of his marriage.
>
> D. They [his students] said to him, 'Did our master not teach us that a bridegroom is exempt from the recitation of the *Shema'* [on the first night]?'
>
> E. He said to them, 'I cannot heed you and suspend from myself the kingdom of heaven for one hour.'

Berakot 2.5 C-E indicates that Gamaliel considered himself to have the requisite devotion to recite the *Shema'* even on his wedding night.

Two additional anecdotes of Gamaliel, *Ber.* 2.6 A-C and 2.7 A-C, follow immediately. These are of the same form as 2.5 B-E, that is,

80. Kanter (*Rabban Gamaliel II*, p. 104) notes other pericopae in the later *Tosefta* where Gamaliel declares things permitted but practices a stricter interpretation, that is, *t. Ter.* 2.13 and *t. M. Qaṭ.* 2.14.

81. See Tzvee Zahavy, '*Kannanah* for Prayer in the Mishnah and Talmud', in Jacob Neusner *et al.* (eds.), *New Perspectives on Ancient Judaism*. I. *Religion, Literature, and Society in Ancient Israel, Formative Christianity and Judaism* (BJS, 206; Atlanta: Scholars Press, 1990), pp. 35-48 (47), and 'The Psychology of Early Rabbinic Prayer', in *Studies in Jewish Prayer* (New York: University Press of America, 1990), pp. 111-19.

Gamaliel's students question him when his practice does not follow his own rulings. These anecdotes do not deal with the recitation of the *Shema'* and probably were placed here because of the similarity of their form.[82]

Berakot 2.8 A-C continues the topic of the devotion needed to recite the *Shema'* properly. It rules that it is possible for a bridegroom to recite the prayer on his wedding night, but cautions, in a statement attributed to Rabban Simeon b. Gamaliel, that, in these circumstances, 'Not all who wish to take the name of God [recite the *Shema'*] may do so.' Gamaliel's action in the preceding anecdote of 2.5 C-E functions as a precedent for the ruling here in 2.8 A-C. The anecdote is also a proof of 2.5 A-B since Gamaliel's students testify that the exemption for a bridegroom was, in fact, the ruling of Gamaliel. Moreover, given the caution expressed by Simeon b. Gamaliel and since Gamaliel is presented previously as an example of a person who had been able to recite the *Shema'* on his wedding night, *Berakot* 2.8 A-C also highlights the piety and devotion of Gamaliel.

Berakot 2.7 A-C gives further indication of Gamaliel's devoutness. There Gamaliel is questioned by his disciples because he accepted condolences upon the death of his servant Tabi. Evidently, based on their question, Gamaliel had ruled that this was not permitted.[83] Gamaliel answers his students' question by indicating that Tabi was not like other servants because he was כשר, that is, 'ritually pure', 'pleasing' or 'worthy'. In *Suk.* 2.1 C-D, Gamaliel praises Tabi as knowing the law. Hence, Gamaliel had such high regard for the law that he apparently taught it to his slave or at least taught Tabi some of the proper observances.

Finally, *B. Meṣ.* 5.8 C-H speaks of Gamaliel's 'stricter observance' of a law. This passage discusses the repayment for loans of wheat in the face of fluctuating prices. Gamaliel always took repayment for loans from his tenants at the cheaper price since 'he wished to impose a strict rule on himself' (5.8 H). On the other hand, *M* also records that Gamaliel did not overindulge in austere practices. *Berakot* 2.6 A-C records that he washed on the first night of the death of his wife. When his students questioned him, Gamaliel excused himself from the observance of his own ruling, saying that he was 'of feeble health', איסטנים.[84] In this anecdote Gamaliel

82. See Kanter, *Rabban Gamaliel II*, p. 7. Kanter holds that it is possible that the three anecdotes circulated as a unit prior to their incorporation into the *Mishnah*.

83. Kanter (*Rabban Gamaliel II*, p. 6) gives a later ruling on this prohibition recorded in *b. Ber.* 16b.

84. Jastrow, *Dictionary*, p. 58 a. Kanter (*Rabban Gamaliel II*, p. 6) gives a later ruling on this prohibition recorded in *b. M. Qaṭ.* 15b.

indicated his willingness to allow for those who were unable to observe legal observance due to weakness. Thus, Gamaliel is presented as a man of deep devotion, given to some austere practices, but one who also maintained a balance in this matter.

A master–disciple relationship is evident in *Ber.* 2.5, 2.6 and 2.7. Gamaliel is approached by his students and asked to clarify his actions. Evidently Gamaliel's way of life was closely followed by his students. In all three passages, Gamaliel is addressed by the title רבינו, 'our teacher'. *Keritot* 3.7 and 3.8, moreover, depict R. Aqiba asking Gamaliel and R. Joshua for their teachings. Gamaliel's individual role as a teacher of Aqiba is most evident in *Roš Haš.* 1.6 A-C, which reads:

1.6 A. מעשה More than forty pairs of witnesses came forward.

B. But R. Aqiba detained them at Lud.

C. Rabban Gamaliel sent [a message] to him, 'If you hold back the people, you will cause them to err in the future.'

This anecdote occurs in the context of a discussion on the obligation of those who see the new moon to travel to the place of the patriarch in order to testify to that fact. Such testimony was necessary in order to set the dates of the appointed festivals. Aqiba evidently did not see the necessity of all 40 pairs traveling to testify to the new moon. Since *Roš Haš.* 1.5 speaks of the exemption from the prohibition of Sabbath travel in order to give this testimony, it is assumed that Aqiba's action in 1.6 is done out of concern for the Sabbath. Gamaliel sends word to Aqiba that Sabbath observance is not as important as the need to set the calendar properly. Gamaliel is concerned that if the witnesses are prevented from traveling to testify, such witnesses may not accept their obligation to do so in the future. Here Gamaliel assumes his role as teacher of Aqiba without being asked a question by Aqiba. No debate is recorded in *M*, hence, at least as far as *M* is concerned, Aqiba accepted the advice of Gamaliel.

The last aspect of the *Mishnah*'s portrayal of Gamaliel to be considered here is his relationship with Gentiles as seen in the anecdotes. Six stories record Gamaliel dealing with Gentiles, that is, *Šab.* 1.9 A and 16.8 H, *Beṣ.* 3.2 D, *Ma'as. Š.* 5.9 C-E, *'Ed.* 7.7 I -K, and *'Abod. Zar.* 3.4. The anecdote in *Beṣ.* 3.2 D has been discussed above. It depicts Gamaliel exercising caution in that he did not accept a fish from a Gentile on a festival day. *Šabbat* 1.9 A records that Gamaliel gave white clothes to a Gentile laundry man but did so three days before the Sabbath. This time frame was necessary to ensure that the work would be finished before the Sabbath. In other words, Gamaliel's dealings with the Gentile did not cause Gamaliel to break the Sabbath. Again, he exercised cautious concern for the law in dealings with a Gentile.

Šabbat 16.8 H and *Ma'aser Šeni* 5.9 C-E both narrate anecdotes involving Gamaliel and other authorities on a boat trip. They are among the passages in rabbinic literature that speak of Gamaliel traveling by sea to Rome. In *Šab.* 16.8 H a story is told to illustrate the ruling that a Jewish person could benefit, but only indirectly, from an action performed by a Gentile on the Sabbath if that action was done by the Gentile purely for his or her own sake (16.8 A-G); 16.8 H reads: 'מעשה Rabban Gamaliel and the elders were traveling by boat, and a gentile made a gangway by which to come down off the ship, and Rabban Gamaliel and the sages went down by it.' It can be assumed from the passage that the Gentile made the gangway for her or his own use. Gamaliel's action is a proof for 16.8 F-G, but also indicates that in dealings with Gentiles Gamaliel was careful to observe the law. *Ma'aser Šeni* 5.9 C-E finds Gamaliel, R. Joshua and R. Aqiba traveling on a ship and observing the laws concerning agricultural tithes. Hence, Gamaliel observed the law even while out at sea and far from his home.

'Abodah Zarah 3.4 A-F is by far the most entertaining of all the anecdotes on Gamaliel in *M.* This passage was partially cited in the Introduction, above. It is given here in its entirety:

3.4 A. Peroqlos b. Pelosopos asked Rabban Gamaliel in Akko when he was washing in the bathhouse of Aphrodite, saying to him, 'It is written in your Torah, "And there shall cleave nothing of a devoted thing to your hand" [Deut. 13.18]. Why do you wash in Aphrodite's bathhouse?'

B. He said to him, 'They do not give answers in a bath.'

C. a. When he came out, he said to him, 'I never came into her domain; she came into mine.

b. They do not say, "Let us make Aphrodite a bath for an ornament." But they say, "Let us make Aphrodite as an ornament for the bath."

D. Another explanation: even if someone gave you a great deal of money, you would not come into your temple of idolatry naked, or having an emission, nor would you urinate in her presence.

E. Yet this thing is standing there at the mouth of the gutter and everyone urinates in her presence.

F. a. It is said only, "[Cut down images of] their gods" [Deut. 12.3].
b. That which one treats as a god is prohibited, but that which one does not treat as a god is permitted.'

This story could easily have circulated in a much shorter form, namely 'When someone in Akko asked Rabban Gamaliel why he was washing in a bathhouse which contained a statue of Aphrodite, he replied, "I never came into her domain; she came into mine."' The brevity of this version of the story and the pithy quality of Gamaliel's response are reminiscent of the anecdotes about Demonax studied in Chapter 2. Kanter has shown that the remaining verses of *'Abod. Zar.* 3.4 A-F can all be viewed as additions.[85] 3.4 B once again demonstrates Gamaliel's respect for the law even though he allows himself the use of the bath. C. (b) is an addition, perhaps of a popular saying, that further explains the statement in C. (a). Finally, D-F is yet another justification for Gamaliel's behavior. D-E indicate that the statue of Aphrodite is not treated with the respect due to a goddess. F. (a) serves as testimony from authority and also allows Gamaliel to demonstrate his own skill with the use of Scripture to argue his legal position. *'Abodah Zarah* 3.4 A-F, then, presents Gamaliel as a person who enjoyed Gentile amenities, uttered 'pithy sayings', was skilled at the use of Scripture, and, yet again, cautious about the legalities of his dealings with Gentiles. In this respect Kanter notes: 'As one in frequent contact with the Romans, and permitted greater familiarity with their religion and culture... he [Gamaliel] was fair game for questions about his personal piety.'[86] This pericope would be an answer to such questions.

Finally, in a discussion on how to rule on calendar concerns in the absence of the patriarch, *'Ed.* 7.7 I-K relates a time when Gamaliel 'traveled to Syria to receive authority' from the Roman governor of Syria. Thus, Gamaliel probably had some civil authority in Palestine, as well as religious authority.[87] This supports the image of Gamaliel as partaking of the Gentile culture. Taken together these six anecdotes on Gamaliel's interchanges with Gentiles present him as having the freedom to participate in aspects of their culture, all the while being an observant Jew.

85. Kanter, *Rabban Gamaliel II*, pp. 176-77.

86. Kanter, *Rabban Gamaliel II*, p. 177.

87. Lee I. Levine ('The Jewish Patriarch [Nasi] in Third Century Palestine', *ANRW*, II.19, pp. 649-88 [683]) cautions that the support and recognition of the patriarchate by Rome evident in the late second century with Judah may not have been in place at the time of Gamaliel.

d. *Conclusions*

There are 35 anecdotes in the *Mishnah* that involve Rabban Gamaliel II.[88] All but two of these stories (*Roš Haš*. 2.8-9; *Yeb*. 16.7) exhibit one of the common forms of the Mishnaic anecdotes. The major function of the anecdotes is 'overtly legal', that is, they all serve as precedents, proofs or narrative laws. This fact highlights Gamaliel's position as a legal authority. Moreover, *Ber*. 1.1, the opening passage of *M*, cites Gamaliel as the authority for its legislation. Thus, the anecdotes depict Gamaliel not only as a legal master, but as a prominent one who played a major role in establishing the authoritative position of the rabbinate as a whole.

Moreover, the anecdotes reveal aspects of the *Mishnah*'s portrait of Rabbi Gamaliel II, the person. He is shown as a person of at least moderate economic means. He has a servant, Tabi (*Suk*. 2.5), is able to procure meat for a banquet for his son (*Ker*. 3.7), has tenant farmers with whom he can afford to be generous (*B. Meṣ*. 5.8), and has the leisure to travel (*Šab*. 16.8; *Ma'as. Š*. 5.9 C-E) and to attend a Gentile bath (*'Abod. Zar*. 3.4). Gamaliel of the *Mishnah* has the knowledge to chart distances (*'Erub*. 4.2) and to produce astronomical charts (*Roš Haš*. 2.8).

Rabban Gamaliel is a master whose disciples follow and imitate his behavior. His actions are often cited as proofs or narrative laws. His disciples are attentive to his behavior and question his actions if they contradict his rulings (*Ber*. 2.5; 2.6; 2.7), while other sages seek out his opinions (*Ker*. 3.7; 3.8). Gamaliel is also portrayed as correcting a younger, future prominent master, R. Aqiba (*Roš Haš*. 1.6).

Above all, the aspect of Gamaliel's character most emphasized in the anecdotes of *M* is his piety or sanctity of life. This is accomplished by highlighting his devotion at prayer, even on his wedding night (*Ber*. 2.5), his sometimes stricter than necessary observance of the laws (*B. Meṣ*. 5.8), his teaching the law to his servant, Tabi (*Ber*. 2.7), his proper religious observances (*Ker*. 3.7), even in his dealings with Gentiles (*Šab*. 1.9), and his ability to cite Scripture (*'Abod. Zar*. 3.4).

In the figure of Rabbi Gamaliel II, then, the Mishnaic anecdotes present the reader with a respected personage, a religious authority and a pious man worthy of imitation.

88. A summary listing of the anecdotes of the *Mishnah* that involve Gamaliel, along with their forms and functions, is given in Appendix B.

5. *Conclusions*

In this chapter, 64 of the many anecdotes in the *Mishnah* have been identified and studied. Forty-one of these anecdotes are found in Division *Mo'ed Qaṭan* and another 23 are anecdotes of Rabbi Gamaliel II outside of *Mo'ed Qaṭan*. In form, the majority of these anecdotes are brief narratives of sayings or actions. Three anecdotes relate both sayings and actions while another four narrate dialogues or debates. Two longer, composite narratives, *Roš Haš.* 2.8-9 and *Yeb.* 16.7 A-G, are found in the collection. The following typology summarizes the data on the forms of the anecdotes studied:[89]

Typology of Rabbinic Anecdotes Based on Form

A. Narrative with a Saying		22
1. Recorded	12	
2. Attested	10	
B. Narrative with an Action		33
1. Recorded	18	
2. Attested	15	
C. Narrative with both a Saying and an Action		3
1. Recorded	1	
2. Attested	2	
D. Narrative with a Dialogue or a Debate		4
1. Recorded	3	
2. Attested	1	
E. Other		2
Total		64

It is noteworthy that the narratives of actions outnumber the narratives of sayings. The fact that the actions of the rabbis are reported indicates the didactic function of their way of life. This data also reinforces the conclusion reached about Rabbi Gamaliel above, that is, that his behavior is imitated by his disciples. Not only is at least one rabbi, Gamaliel II, put forth as someone to be imitated, but the Mishnaic anecdotes portray the rabbis in general as examples to be followed.

All but eight of the anecdotes in this research had overtly legal functions within the *Mishnah*; they were precedents, proofs or narrative laws. Six

89. The data in this typology was compiled using the anecdotes of *M. Qaṭ.* and those of Gamaliel outside of *M. Qaṭ.*

anecdotes served only to give the etiology of a practice, while the remaining two stories provided only aggadic information.[90] Furthermore, there were 34 stories that were attested, that is, another sage reported the incident, thereby lending his own authority to the legal ruling, etiology or aggadic statement. These results affirm the prominent role of the sages in the establishment of legal rulings. The added testimony of one or more sages also served to heighten the portrait of the rabbis as knowledgeable and authoritative leaders.

The following typology summarizes the data on the functions of the anecdotes studied:

Typology of Rabbinic Anecdotes Based on Function

A. Primary Functions	
1. Precedent	5
2. Proof from Authority	38
3. Narrative Law	16
4. Etiology	7
5. *Aggadah*	15
B. Secondary Functions	
1. Testimony	34
2. Contrary Opinion	6

Those anecdotes introduced with the formulas מעשׂה or פעם אחת were no different in form and function than were those without an introductory formula. Typologies of the מעשׂים based on form and function are given in Appendix C. The six anecdotes that contain the phrase פעם אחת are also similar in form and function to the other anecdotes.[91]

The Mishnaic anecdotes function within the purpose of the redactor(s) of the *Mishnah*. In other words, within the legal text that is the *Mishnah* the anecdotes functioned in support of the legal rulings favored by the redactor(s). Overall, the anecdotes provided the redactor(s) of *M* with arguments from authority, that is, exempla of past rabbinic authorities.

While there is no apparent attempt on the part of the redactor(s) of *M* to present the life and teachings of any particular sage, the study of the 35

90. The six anecdotes that function only as an etiology are: *Šab.* 12.3 G-H, *Šeq.* 6.2 A-D, *Yom.* 2.2 A-D, *Yom.* 3.2 B, *Suk.* 4.9 N-O and *Roš Haš.* 4 B-D. The two anecdotes that function only as *aggadah* are *'Erub.* 1.2 E-J and *Šeq.* 3.3 A.

91. These six anecdotes with their forms and functions are: *'Erub.* 4.2 A-C, form A.1, function A.3; *Yom.* 3.2 B, form B.1, function A.4; *Suk.* 4.9 N-O, form B.1, function A.4; *Roš Haš.* 4.4 B-D, form B.1, function A.4; *Bek.* 5.3 K-L, form A.1, function A.2; and *Mid.* 1.2 G, form B.2, function A.2, B.2.

anecdotes about Gamaliel reveal that these compilers intended to portray him as a leading authority. His is the example that opens the *Mishnah*. It is also clear from the above investigation that Gamaliel was an authority to be obeyed and imitated. However, as with other aspects of this rabbinic text, *M* does not state that Rabban Gamaliel was a teacher and an example. One learns this by a careful reading of the text.

In the previous chapter of this book, the function of the anecdotes in Lucian's *Demonax* was studied. Lucian stated the purpose of his text, that is, he wished both to assure that Demonax would be remembered and to provide the youth of his, Lucian's, day with a near contemporary as an example on which to base their lives. The anecdotes in the *Demonax* functioned primarily to establish the character of Demonax. Secondarily, they provided glimpses into the social and cultural background of the times.

Just the reverse is the case with the Mishnaic anecdotes. The rabbinic stories function first and foremost to establish legal aspects of early rabbinic culture and only secondarily do they reveal aspects of a rabbi's, Gamaliel's, character. The primary function of the anecdotes in each text reflects the purpose of the host genre. Thus, the anecdotes in both works serve similar functions with the predominant function determined by the author's or redactor's objective.

Finally, the emergence of the מעשׂה as a formula to introduce an anecdote in the *Mishnah* gives rise to the question whether the term מעשׂה can be used to designate the 'rabbinic anecdote'. The lack of any true distinguishing features between Mishnaic anecdotes that do or do not contain the introductory term מעשׂה can justify the usage of the term for the rabbinic anecdote. While מעשׂה is found in rabbinic writings, the term is used there as an introductory formula; it is not employed to designate a literary genre. The term מעשׂה is adopted in this study to designate the type of anecdote (involving form, content and function) that occurs in *M*.

A further, tantalizing question arises, which is, is there a relationship between the rabbinic anecdote, now designated by the term מעשׂה, and the Greek and Roman literary genre, the χρεία? Certainly from a consideration of form and content, the מעשׂה and the χρεία are similar. In Chapter 2 above, Theon's definition of the χρεία was employed, that is, 'the χρεία is a concise statement or action which is attributed with aptness to some specified character or to something analogous to a character'. This closely resembles the definition of the מעשׂה used in this chapter, which is, 'a short narrative consisting of a person(s), a setting, with or without an implicit or explicit question, and a verbal ruling or an action'. It was shown that all but two of the rabbinic anecdotes selected for analysis in this study fit this definition of the מעשׂה. Furthermore, the מעשׂה and the χρεία have similar functions. The מעשׂה functions principally as an argument from authority, an exemplum of the action or saying of a past sage. Similarly, several functions of the χρεια were to instruct, to persuade and to influence behavior. Hence, generically, that is, with respect to form, content and function, the מעשׂה and the χρεία are very similar.

However, these two types of anecdotes are differentiated in two ways. First, the subject matter of the sayings for both the מעשׂה and the χρεία is peculiar to each of their respective cultural settings. The sayings, and for that matter the actions, in the χρεία pertain to valued and esteemed aspects of the Greek or Roman culture. For example, the anecdotes in Lucian's *Demonax* depict actions and sayings of Demonax in which he demonstrates the values of the philosophical life as he attacked the vices of vanity and sham in others. Rabbinic anecdotes, on the other hand, present the sages' concerns about the proper observance of the Torah and their own legal rulings.

The other difference between the מעשׂה and the χρεία is related to the length of the anecdotes. The Mishnaic anecdotes are almost all very brief stories. The χρεία, on the other hand, is found in 'expanded' or 'elaborated' form in Greek and Roman texts. The 'expansion' and the 'elaboration' of a χρεία were discussed in Chapter 2, in the presentation on the progymnasmatic exercises with the χρεία. An expansion consisted of adding descriptive remarks to each member of a concise χρεία. An elaboration was a preliminary exercise in argumentation; it included adding both a statement to the χρεία that served as a rationale for the χρεία-saying and statements that presented analogies and opposites to the χρεία-saying.

Among those studied in this chapter, the only rabbinic anecdote that can be compared to either an expanded or an elaborated χρεια is *'Abodah Zarah* 3.4 A-F. It was suggested above that this story may have circulated in a shorter version, namely 'When someone in 'Akko asked Rabban Gamaliel why he was washing in a bathhouse which contained a statue of Aphrodite, he replied, "I never came into her domain; she came into mine."' The verse 3.4 B, 'He said to him, "They do not give answers in a bath,"' can be viewed as an insertion into the story to show Gamaliel's piety. 3.4 C (b), 'They do not say, "Let us make Aphrodite a bath for an ornament." But they say, "Let us make Aphrodite as an ornament for the bath,"' may have been a rationale for the saying of 3.4 C (a), 'He said to him, "I never came into her domain; she came into mine."' The format of 3.4 A and C (a-b), a saying with a rationale, is the beginning of the pattern of an ἐργασία, 'elaboration', as presented by Hermogenes. *'Abodah*

Zarah 3.4 A-F is the only anecdote studied in this chapter that can be analyzed in a way that is comparable to the elaboration of a χρεία.

Is it possible, then, to assert that the Greek and Roman χρεία influenced the literary form of the rabbinic anecdote, particularly the מעשׂה? This investigation has dealt only with anecdotes in the *Mishnah*. The one example of a *possible*, short elaboration in '*Abodah Zarah* 3.4 A-F cannot be used to support such an assertion. Even the additional argument that the sages responsible for the redaction of *M* may have been literate in Greek is insufficient to warrant the conclusion that the χρεία influenced the genre of the Mishnaic anecdotes.[92]

This chapter has shown that anecdotes are present in the *Mishnah* and has investigated the form and function of a representative sampling of these anecdotes. The results indicate that the anecdotes functioned primarily as arguments within the legal framework of *M*. Secondarily, the anecdotes presented the personage involved as an authority figure. In the case of those anecdotes about Rabbi Gamaliel II, the stories portray him as a leading, early authority and a pious observer of the law. Many actions of the rabbis are recorded in the anecdotes. This indicates the interest of the redactor(s) of *M* in enhancing the position of the rabbis. Jacob Neusner has remarked that rabbinic literature presents the rabbi as a 'law giver in the model of Moses'. This is accomplished in two ways:

> First of all, tales about the rabbis' behavior on specific occasions immediately were translated into rules for the entire community to keep... Second, and far more common, are instances in which the deed of a rabbi is adduced as an authoritative precedent for the law under discussion.[93]

Neusner was referring to later midrashic texts. The present study has shown Neusner's observation to be true for the *Mishnah* in general and for Rabbi Gamaliel II in particular.

92. Other scholars have made this assertion for early rabbinic texts; however, the examples of rabbinic passages they used in their studies were all from later texts. See Raphael Edelman, 'Some Remarks on a Certain Literary Genre in Talmud and Midrash and Its Relation to the Hellenistic Culture', in *Third World Congress of Jewish Studies [Jerusalem, 1961] Report* (Hebrew; Jerusalem: World Union of Jewish Studies, 1965), pp. 108-10; Henry A. Fischel, 'A *Chria* on Absentmindedness', in *Rabbinic Literature and Greco-Roman Philosophy: A Study of Epicuria and Rhetorica in Early Midrashic Writings* (SPB, 21; Leiden: E.J. Brill, 1973), pp. 78-89; and Hezser, 'Die Verwendung der hellenistischen Gattung Chrie', pp. 371-439.

93. Jacob Neusner, *Midrash in Context: Exegesis in Formative Judaism* (BJS, 141; Philadelphia: Fortress Press, 1983), pp. 133-34.

Chapter 4

The Gospel Anecdote in New Testament Scholarship

As one would suspect, the history of the scholarship on Gospel anecdotes parallels the history of developments within New Testament 'form criticism' itself.[1] Early or traditional form criticism focused on identifying the 'forms', that is, the genres, of those Gospel units believed to have been transmitted orally in the early church. The pioneer critics sought to establish the original contents of the Gospel units, to identify the genres of Gospel and pre-Gospel traditions, and to ascertain the function(s) for those genres within a discernible *Sitz im Leben* of the early Christian community.

Contemporary form criticism incorporates the insights of the study of Greek and Roman rhetorical practice and in that sense may be called 'rhetorical form criticism'. Building on the work of earlier form critics, rhetorical form criticism deals with narrative units of the Gospels and Acts, the letters of Paul, and the other New Testament letters as examples of Greek or Roman rhetorical genres. In the case of the Gospels, these critics are much less concerned with the oral traditions that predate a particular unit than with the written text before them. Recognizing the rhetorical function of genres in different social locations and for different social purposes, they apply these insights to the persuasive function of a unit within the larger host genre of a Gospel.[2]

There has been a great deal of study of the Gospel anecdotes from a form critical approach, and, presently, rhetorical-critical studies are grow-

1. For a summary of the history of New Testament 'form criticism' see: Berger, *Formgeschichte des Neuen Testaments*; McKnight, *What Is Form Criticism?*, pp. 1-16; *idem*, 'Form and Redaction Criticism', pp. 148-74; and Vernon Robbins, 'Form Criticism, New Testament', *ABD*, II, pp. 841-44. See section 1, pp. 7-19, for a discussion of the terms 'form' and 'genre'. In this summary, to avoid confusion, I adopt the common usage in past scholarship of the term 'form criticism' for what I have argued to be, in fact, the study of genres.

2. See Robbins's discussion of rhetorical form criticism in 'Form Criticism, New Testament', p. 844.

ing in number. In order to focus my review of scholarship, I concentrate on those scholars who have made major contributions to both approaches. Additionally, I present an evaluation of the comparisons of Gospel anecdotes with similar units within rabbinic literature. I approach these critical summaries with an eye to evaluating the scholars' definitions of anecdotal units and comparing any definition to what I have developed in Chapter 1. I also look for a genre presentation, that is, a discussion of the form, content and function of the narrative units. Finally, I critique the typologies that are developed; for instance, are they based on form, on content, or on function?

1. *Form-critical Approaches*

As mentioned above, form critics attempted to identify Gospel and pre-Gospel forms, including oral forms, and their respective *Sitze im Leben* in the early Christian community. The difficulties of pinpointing the original story-telling situation of an independent anecdote were noted in Chapter 1, as were the problems one encounters when attempting to move from a Gospel text to a pre-Gospel oral or written source. Despite these cautions, the work of form critics on identifying and defining Gospel anecdotal units is to be admired.

The three years following the close of World War I saw the publication of the first major form-critical studies of Gospel narrative units. In 1919, Martin Dibelius published the first work entirely devoted to the study of these 'individual stories', the first edition of his *Formgeschichte des Evangeliums*. Two years later both the first edition of Rudolf Bultmann's *Geschichte der synoptischen Tradition* and Martin Albertz's *Die synoptischen Streitgespräche* were published. The work of these pioneer scholars will be presented at the outset, followed by that of other form critics who have moved the discussion forward.

a. *Martin Dibelius*

In *Formgeschichte des Evangeliums*, Martin Dibelius employed a method that began with suppositions about 'the conditions and activities of the life of the first Christian Churches'.[3] Hence, he assumed a certain *Sitz im Leben* for many of the Gospel narrative units and then considered the

3. Dibelius, *From Tradition to Gospel*, p. 10. This translation of the German original (*Die Formgeschichte des Evangeliums*) is generally accepted as well done. I cite this as *Tradition*. When I cite the German, I cite it as *Formgeschichte*.

function of these units within that assumed setting. He believed that the setting of many Gospel units was the early preaching of the community; within this category he included missionary work, community worship and catechetical instruction.[4] Dibelius studied three narrative genres, the paradigm, the tale and the legend, as well as the genre of 'isolated saying of Jesus'. His work on the paradigm, or anecdote, is the most highly developed in terms of his premises and stated method.

In the course of the community's preaching, Dibelius believed that their message needed to be supported or illustrated by means of brief 'example-narratives' from the deeds of Jesus; he named this type of narrative unit a 'paradigm'. In his second edition (1933), he offered this description of a paradigm: it is a narrative unit of 'technical brevity, and with [a]... concentration upon conceptions of a definite character which can be used in preaching'.[5] This narrative genre, he believed, corresponded to the missionary aim of preaching. He claimed an historical trustworthiness for the paradigms, believing there to be a continuity 'from the time of the first reports of the eye witnesses to the formation of the narrative type'.[6] However, he noted that this historical trustworthiness was not equivalent to 'literal authenticity in the sense of a judiciary pronouncement or a police report'.[7] Rather, the paradigms presented an authentic picture of the 'person and work of Jesus'.[8]

Since Dibelius considered the focus of those paradigms that contained a dialogue to be the climactic word of Jesus, he rejected the notion that these dialogues arose within the discussions of the early Church rather than with the historical Jesus.[9] Furthermore, he denied the existence of the separate genre 'controversy dialogues', saying: 'A genre *Streitgespräche* is not perceptible.'[10]

Dibelius identified 18 Gospel units that suited his concept of a para-

4. Dibelius, *Tradition*, p. 15.

5. Dibelius, *Tradition*, p. 133. In the first edition of his work, Dibelius gave no clear definition of the paradigm. The introductory material to the 1966 English edition, contained a definition of paradigm as follows: 'A short illustrative notice or story of an event, not more descriptive than is necessary to make the point for the sake of which it is introduced' (p. vi). This does not appear in the German edition and is not Dibelius's definition but probably that of the translator, Woolf.

6. Dibelius, *Tradition*, p. 40. See also pp. 59-69.

7. Dibelius, *Tradition*, p. 62.

8. Dibelius, *Tradition*, p. 63.

9. Dibelius, *Tradition*, p. 68.

10. Dibelius, *Formgeschichte*, p. 222.

digm: 8 of a 'substantially pure type' and 10 of a 'type of lesser purity'.[11] While he did not comment on what constituted each type, his discussions of individual paradigms indicated that the 'less pure' type were those narratives that showed signs of a later 'development'.[12] Thus, his typology appeared to be based on aspects of form; this is not clearly explicated, however.

Next, Dibelius laid out five characteristics of the paradigm: 'an external rounding off' that points to the unit's originally isolated, independent existence; a brevity and simplicity, necessitated by its use in sermons; a religious coloring; a climax in and conclusion with a word or deed of Jesus; and an ending that contains a thought useful for preaching.[13] Since he considered the paradigm as a unit in the pre-literary stage of the Jesus tradition, he spoke of the paradigm's function only in its original setting; he never addressed its function within the written Gospel texts.

In the second edition of his book, Dibelius sought analogies to the Gospel paradigms from within rabbinic literature, Greek literature and patristic apophthegms.[14] Within rabbinic literature, Dibelius identified short narrative units that he referred to variously as 'rabbinic anecdotes', 'cases', 'stories about a Rabbi' or 'Halakhic stories', and he discussed examples of these units from the *Talmud*.[15] The closest Dibelius came to a definition of these units is that they were 'short' narratives, often introduced with the word מעשׂה, which present an historical case used to confirm a legal decision of a rabbi.[16]

Dibelius admitted that the rabbinic anecdotes were similar to several of his Gospel paradigms in which a question of a halakhic nature was posed to Jesus. He maintained, however, that there were significant differences: (a) the primary function of the rabbinic anecdote was to confirm a rabbi's decision and not, as in the case of the paradigm, to record an historical

11. See Appendix D for the units under each type.

12. See Dibelius's comments on Lk. 9.51-56 (*Tradition*, pp. 47-48).

13. Dibelius, *Tradition*, pp. 45-56.

14. For my purposes, I will comment only on the first two areas. Dibelius briefly discussed the collection entitled 'Apophthegmata Patrum', a collection of sayings of desert fathers compiled from 460–500 CE. His comments, in the main, focused on the process of collecting these traditions and are not relevant to this study.

15. Dibelius, *Tradition*, pp. 133, 134, 136 and 142, respectively. He justified the use of this late compilation because he believed it contained historically reliable tannaitic stories and because he sought 'only analogies, not dependence' (p. 133). He did discuss one Mishnaic story, *Ber.* 2.5.

16. Dibelius, *Tradition*, p. 134.

event; (b) the rabbis presented a correct interpretation of the Law, whereas Jesus was 'far beyond the Law'; (c) the rabbis often gave an interpretation of a passage of Scripture, while Jesus spoke as one who had his own authority; (d) rabbinic literature is a collection of normative opinions based on 'agreement of voices', whereas the Gospels present the decisions of one man based on the worth of that man; and (e) rabbinic stories were gathered over a period of centuries for the purpose of creating a new legality, while 'paradigms' emerged in 'a few decades and were used to illustrate preaching and to call to repentance'.[17] These distinctions are not based on the genres of the rabbinic anecdote and the paradigm themselves; rather they flow from Dibelius's suppositions about the nature of the literature involved. Moreover, my study of rabbinic anecdotes in Chapter 3 puts into question several of his distinctions.

In the popular narratives of Greek literature Dibelius identified analogies to the Gospel paradigms in the 'tale' and the 'legend', as well as in a third unit, which he defined as 'traditions containing sayings of famous men, especially of well known and popular philosophers, useful and edificatory for succeeding ages'.[18] He rejected the name 'apophthegm' for such units, saying, correctly, that it was an imprecise term since it was used both of isolated sayings and of sayings found within an anecdote. Instead he opted for the rhetorical term χρεία. However, rather than employing a definition of the χρεία from a Greek or Roman source, he gave his own: 'It is the reproduction of a short pointed saying of general significance, originating in a definite person and arising out of a definite situation.'[19] He stated that its terse style may be expanded somewhat, even to the inclusion of a dialogue and that the χρεία functioned 'to honor some well known man or to keep alive some joke or foible of his'.[20] Unfortunately, Dibelius limited his understanding of the χρεία, since he did not accurately follow the rhetorical definitions for the χρεία. For example, according to the grammarian Theon, the χρεία records either a saying or an action, and furthermore the saying may be either a general statement, or a specific one (3.2-14).[21]

Pursuing a comparison of the paradigm and the χρεία, Dibelius found a

17. Dibelius, *Tradition*, pp. 131-44.

18. Dibelius, *Tradition*, p. 151.

19. Dibelius, *Tradition*, p. 152. Dibelius cited Theon's definition of the χρεία in a footnote (p. 152 n. 1).

20. Dibelius, *Tradition*, p. 156.

21. See Butts, 'The "Progymnasmata" of Theon'.

similarity of origins, but a difference in both content and form. He believed that both the paradigm and the χρεία originated in 'unliterary circles' that were interested in preserving the memory of a hero. The content of the χρεία, however, displayed an essential side of Greek intellectual life in its clever play on words, conceptions and thoughts. The paradigm, on the other hand, originated among uneducated persons who had no share in the Greek and Roman culture, and for whom 'elegant speech' was foreign.[22] Moreover, according to Dibelius, the content of the Jesus tradition, with its somber references to a divine judgment at the end of the world, was ill-suited to 'wit, punning, or an elegant and brilliant manner of speech'.[23] Finally, he found an 'essential' difference in form between the paradigm and the χρεία; in the former the situation is really described, whereas in the latter only those elements essential for understanding the saying are narrated.[24] Here, Dibelius contradicted his earlier statement that the 'terse style of the "Chria" tolerates many entensions without spoiling the form'.[25] Such an essential difference also displayed a lack of knowledge of the full discussion of the χρεία in the *progymnasmata*, which included a description of the expansion and condensation of a χρεία.

Despite these differences in content and form Dibelius admitted that there was a strong relationship between the two literary expressions. Acknowledging the existence of a number of χρεῖαι in the Gospels,[26] he accounted for them by assuming a development within the tradition of Jesus' sayings. He believed that when the early Christians had become authors it would have been easy 'to dress the sayings of Jesus in the form of "Chriae," when they would become more striking and impressive'. [27] For Dibelius, the paradigm existed in the *Kleinliteratur* stage of the Jesus tradition, that is, in a stratum of literary works that accords 'no place to artistic devices and tendencies of literary and polished writing'.[28] The pre-Gospel *Kleinliteratur* included oral units and written collections of early Jesus traditions; Mark's Gospel was also considered *Kleinliteratur*. For

22. Dibelius, *Tradition*, pp. 156-57.

23. Dibelius, *Tradition*, p. 157.

24. Dibelius, *Tradition*, p. 158.

25. Dibelius, *Tradition*, p. 155.

26. He considered the following units to be χρεῖαι: Mt. 23.35-40; Lk. 3.21-22; 8.19-21; 9.61-62; 11.1-4, 27-28; 13.23-24, 31-33; 16.14-15; 17.20-21; 19.39-40, 45-46; and 22.24-27.

27. Dibelius, *Tradition*, p. 160.

28. Dibelius, *Tradition*, p. 1.

example, Dibelius presented Mt. 22.35-40 as a χρεία developed from the paradigm of Mk 12.28-34 by shortening the description of the setting in Mark. Thus, even though this particular example reflected his thinking on the necessity of a terse style for a χρεία, it supported his classification of Mark as *Kleinliteratur*. In fact, Dibelius considered both Mark and Matthew to be collectors or editors of pre-Gospel traditions and authors only in a 'lowly degree'.[29]

On the other hand, Dibelius considered the use of the χρεία to be 'indicative of the secular style into which the gospel tradition was entering'.[30] Except for the Matthean unit mentioned above, all the Synoptic χρεῖαι Dibelius identified were from Luke. He asserted that Luke 'constantly reached out toward literature as such', showing himself to be a true author in Acts, although his Gospel displayed a strong literary character.[31] Dibelius's discussion of Lukan Gospel χρεῖαι demonstrated his belief in the movement from paradigm to χρεία. He presented examples in which he claimed that Luke abbreviated a framework to highlight the saying, for example, 3.21-22, or formed a single, striking sentence out of several in his source, 8.19-21. Given that the *progymnasmata* contained exercises on the expansion and on the condensation of a χρεία, Dibelius's theory on a movement from oral and written paradigms to the χρεῖαι cannot be accepted. Moreover, it can be shown that Mark's Gospel itself contains χρεῖαι.[32] Dibelius's presupposition concerning the historical trustworthiness of the paradigms seems to have prevented him from fully studying the units as examples of the Greek or Roman χρεία. However, he was correct to note that Luke did place individual Jesus sayings within a χρεία-form, for example, 11.1-4 and 13.23-24.

Although his work had limitations, Dibelius made an initial and lasting contribution to the study of Gospel anecdotes. His attempts to clarify the genre of the Gospel anecdotes, his inclusion of a discussion of the χρεία, and to some extent the rabbinic anecdote, faulty though they were, indicated a direction for subsequent scholars.

b. *Rudolf Bultmann*

The first edition of Rudolf Bultmann's influential *Geschichte der synoptischen Tradition* was published in 1921. The second edition (1931), was a

29. Dibelius, *Tradition*, pp. 3-4.
30. Dibelius, *Tradition*, p. 163.
31. Dibelius, *Tradition*, pp. 161 and 3-4.
32. See my study in Chapter 5.

significant revision of the original; it is this second edition that is considered here.[33] Unlike Dibelius, Bultmann began with an analysis of the Gospel units themselves and worked back to their pre-literary shapes and *Sitze im Leben*. Seeking to categorize all of the Synoptic tradition, he divided the material into two major categories, the 'Sayings Material' and the 'Narrative Material', and began his study with the former.

The Gospel anecdotes appeared not among the narratives but within the 'Sayings Material' as 'Apophthegms'.[34] Admitting that apophthegms might be considered stories, Bultmann defined them as a 'genre [*Gattung*] of traditional material...namely such units whose focus is a saying of Jesus set in a brief framework'.[35] Since he considered the framework of many apophthegms to be a secondary accretion, these units could be reduced to their sayings alone and then studied with the 'Sayings Material'.

Bultmann presented the following typology for the apophthegms:

Apophthegms

I. Controversy Dialogues
 1. Occasioned by Jesus' healings
 2. Occasioned by other conduct of Jesus or of his disciples
 3. An unbelieving person lays claim on Jesus

II. Scholastic Dialogues
 1. Jesus is questioned by friends
 2. Jesus is questioned by opponents

III. Biographical Apophthegms[36]

This typology was based partially on form and partially on the contents of the apophthegms: on form, where he distinguished those with dialogues from those without; on contents, where he further divided the dialogues based on the tenor of the dialogue, an attack or a friendly question.

Bultmann's study comprised a detailed analysis of each unit of the three subgenres followed by conclusions on each of the subgenres. From these

33. The English translation of Bultmann's *Die Geschichte der synoptischen Tradition*, that is, *The History of the Synoptic Tradition* (trans. J. Marsh; New York: Harper & Row, 3rd rev. edn, 1963), is considered an inadequate work. All citations are my translations of the German.

34. Bultmann, *Geschichte der synoptischen Tradition*, pp. 8-346. The other subgenre of the 'Sayings Material' was 'Dominical Sayings'. The 'Narrative Material' included 'Miracle Stories', 'Historical Stories' and 'Legends'.

35. Bultmann, *Geschichte der synoptischen Tradition*, p. 8.

36. See Appendix D for the units under each type.

conclusions he presented the following characteristics of the apophthegm in general: (a) a focus on the saying, which is as brief as possible; (b) a saying is occasioned by something happening to Jesus; (c) an 'economy' in the description of the situation; (d) a lack of attention to personal characteristics; and (e) an 'awkward' appearance of secondary characters.[37] He argued that the apophthegms served an apologetic function in the early Church. Finally, Bultmann believed that the apophthegms developed within the tradition 'when independent sayings were joined to a scene' or when a context was composed 'out of a saying'.[38]

With regard to the subgenre 'controversy dialogue', Bultmann concluded, that they followed this form: (a) a starting point in an action or an attitude of Jesus, or one of his disciples, (b) which was seized upon by the opponent and used in an attack by accusation or question, and (c) the reply of Jesus often appeared as a counter-question, a metaphor, or a scripture citation. Additionally, their *Sitz im Leben* was the discussions of the early Church with its opponents. Finally, they do not record historical happenings in the life of Jesus; rather the controversy dialogues are all 'ideal scenes' developed in the early Palestinian tradition and represent the 'outlook of the early church'.[39]

The 'scholastic dialogues' received a shorter treatment by Bultmann. The distinguishing feature of the scholastic dialogue was its starting point: a situation in which Jesus was questioned, not attacked, by someone seeking knowledge. The *Sitz im Leben* and historicity of the scholastic dialogue matched that of the controversy dialogue.

The 'biographical apophthegms' also received a brief treatment, perhaps because, as Bultmann admitted, their formal structure was 'more varied than the others'.[40] The only characteristic given for this subgenre was that the saying usually appeared at the end. While he rejected Dibelius's theory that preaching formed the background for all the narrative genres of the gospels, Bultmann did accept the sermon as the *Sitz im Leben* for the biographical apophthegms. He concluded that their purpose was twofold: to present the 'living realization of the Master' and to 'serve as a comfort and an admonition to the Church as it hoped'.[41]

Bultmann drew attention to rabbinic units as analogies to the Synoptic

37. Bultmann, *Geschichte der synoptischen Tradition*, pp. 66-70.
38. Bultmann, *Geschichte der synoptischen Tradition*, p. 65.
39. Bultmann, *Geschichte der synoptischen Tradition*, pp. 39-42, 57, 393.
40. Bultmann, *Geschichte der synoptischen Tradition*, p. 58.
41. Bultmann, *Geschichte der synoptischen Tradition*, p. 64.

dialogues, stating that 'to carry on disputes in this way is typically rabbinic'.[42] He gave 20 illustrations of rabbinic dialogues, 10 of which were treated in more detail. Among these examples only 3, none treated in detail, were from the tannaitic stratum.[43] Bultmann's study determined that the rabbinic dialogue began with some particular event, sometimes an action of a rabbi, about which a question was raised. The reply was given by a counter-question, a metaphor, a parable, a Scripture citation, or a symbolic action.[44] Thus their form was: event, question, reply. The function of these dialogues was to illustrate propositions of the law.[45] Further, he asserted that the dialogues grew out of 'the question and answer form' in the rabbinic schools, which in turn was 'clearly' influenced both by the oriental way of thinking and discussing and by primitive art forms, particularly the fairy tale.[46] Bultmann offered no evidence for the existence of 'the question and answer form' nor for rabbinic schools in the first century CE. The influence of the fairy tale was not given detailed discussion; he merely listed examples from various bodies of literature.

His comparison of the Synoptic and rabbinic dialogues led Bultmann to conclude that the Gospels preserved a 'more pure form' of the dialogue genre, while the rabbinic examples were more 'self-conscious' and 'artificial'.[47] Furthermore, he posited that, given their parallelism with rabbinic units, both the controversy and the scholastic dialogues were formulated in the Palestinian Christian tradition: '[T]he Church did not create new literary genres but took over traditional forms that had long been used in Judaism.'[48] Unfortunately, there is no evidence that a 'rabbinic dialogue form' predates the Gospels.

Greek analogies to the dialogues received only a brief mention by Bultmann. When discussing the beginning of the controversy dialogue of Lk. 17.20-21, he mentioned that its opening followed the pattern of a 'genre of Greek philosophical apophthegms' which took 'the form (ἐπ)επωτηθεὶς

42. Bultmann, *Geschichte der synoptischen Tradition*, p. 42. Bultmann admitted that the studies of the rabbinic dialogues were inadequate in his time (42-43 n. 2). He presented the rabbinic examples as analogies to both the controversy and the scholastic dialogues.

43. The three examples are *m. 'Abod. Zar.* 3.4 and *m. Ber.* 2.5 and 2.6.

44. Bultmann, *Geschichte der synoptischen Tradition*, p. 43.

45. Bultmann, *Geschichte der synoptischen Tradition*, p. 52.

46. Bultmann, *Geschichte der synoptischen Tradition*, p. 48.

47. Bultmann, *Geschichte der synoptischen Tradition*, p. 42.

48. Bultmann, *Geschichte der synoptischen Tradition*, p. 393.

ὑπο...εἶπεν'. He referred to examples found in Wartensleben's work on the χρεία and Gemoll's study of apophthegms.[49] Bultmann, however, gave no examples to illustrate his point. He also mentioned the variant reading found at Lk. 6.5 in Codex D, observing that its 'Hellenistic form' contained an introduction 'formulated according to the Greek philosophical apophthegm'.[50] Unfortunately, since he again gave no example of such an apophthegm, it is not clear whether Bultmann was referring in both instances to the same Greek unit. Finally, Bultmann held that there is a 'general historical analogy' to the Synoptic controversy dialogues in the Greek literature dealing with 'sages and teachers who did not engage in literary activities' but who were known 'for their personal way of life, for example, Socrates and Diogenes' as well as in the tradition of the Delphic oracle.[51]

For the biographical apophthegms, Bultmann also presented rabbinic analogies. He cited, usually without discussion, 16 rabbinic examples, of which only *m. 'Abodah Zarah* 4.7 is a tannaitic pericope. On their structure and function, Bultmann commented in a general way that the rabbinic biographical 'apophthegms' were highly stylized constructions that give 'a metaphorical presentation of life'.[52] Once again Bultmann spoke, although tentatively, of the Palestinian origins of the Synoptic biographical apophthegms. He admitted, however, that there were parallels to these units in Greek literature and that these needed more study before origins of the biographical apophthegms could be positively stated.[53]

Bultmann employed the name 'apophthegm' for the anecdotes; however, as noted in Chapter 2, there is no clear definition of ἀπόφθεγμα in the ancient rhetorical handbooks and the term often refers to a saying alone.[54] His attention to the sayings in the apophthegms probably influenced

49. Bultmann, *Geschichte der synoptischen Tradition*, p. 24. Bultmann cited G. von Wartensleben's *Begriff der griechischen Chreia und Beiträge zur Geschichte ihrer Form* (Heidelberg: Carl Winter, 1901) and Gemoll's *Das Apophthegma*.

50. Bultmann, *Geschichte der synoptischen Tradition*, p. 24.

51. Bultmann, *Geschichte der synoptischen Tradition*, p. 53.

52. Bultmann, *Geschichte der synoptischen Tradition*, p. 60.

53. Bultmann, *Geschichte der synoptischen Tradition*, p. 63.

54. However, see my study of the ἀπόφθεγμα in section e, pp. 66-68, where I conclude that this term included units that I define as anecdotes. Vernon Robbins ('Chreia and Pronouncement Story in Synoptic Studies', in Burton L. Mack and Vernon K. Robbins, *Patterns of Persuasion in the Gospels* [Sonoma, CA: Polebridge, 1989], pp. 1-29 [7]) implies that Bultmann deliberately chose an obscure term so that 'he was free to analyze the apophthegms in the synoptic tradition without reference to classical rhetorical theory'. This assertion is not at all clear from Bultmann's work itself.

his choice of the term. This, however, excluded units that closed with an action of Jesus from his designation apophthegm.

Bultmann's discussion of analogies for his apophthegms was one-sided, with the rabbinic units given extensive study whereas he only referred to a genre of Greek philosophical apophthegm. The rabbinic stories that he used as analogies for the biographical apophthegms of the Gospels were neither fully discussed nor analyzed. The lack of a full study of rabbinic anecdotes in general is one criticism of his work. Further criticisms are that he did not limit himself to the earliest stratum of the rabbinic writings, that is, the tannaitic stratum, that closest to the time of the Gospels, nor did he take into consideration the relationships among the rabbinic writings.[55] These criticisms aside, Bultmann's pursuit of analogies within rabbinic literature was an important contribution to the early discussion of Gospel anecdotes.

The most serious criticism of Bultmann's study is his lack of attention to Greek or Roman analogies, despite the fact that he acknowledged their existence. This lack is undoubtedly due to his concern to discover the preliterary traditions and his conviction that the earliest formulation of the apophthegms, particularly the dialogues, took place within the early Palestinian church. Such a conviction would have led him to focus on rabbinic analogies. Thus, while Bultmann presented his opinion about the Palestinian origins of the apophthegms as a result of his study, that belief appears to have influenced the materials he considered for analogies, and hence skewed his work.

Despite these criticisms, Bultmann's major, full-scale study of Gospel genres remains an influential piece of scholarship today. His analysis of the individual synoptic apophthegms continues as a starting point for analyses of the Gospel anecdotes. Indeed, his differentiation of primary units from their secondary additions is helpful for contemporary scholars who discuss the elements in an 'elaborated χρεία'. The starting point of his analytic method, that is, with the text itself, rather than with a supposed *Sitz im Leben* is the preferred approach today.

c. *Martin Albertz*

Martin Albertz's *Die synoptischen Streitgespräche* was the first work devoted exclusively to one Gospel narrative type, the controversy dialogue.

55. See the critique of Bultmann on this point by Gary G. Porton ('The Pronouncement Story in Tannaitic Literature: A Review of Bultmann's Theory', in Robert C. Tannehill [ed.], *Pronouncement Stories* [Semeia, 20; Chico, CA: Scholars Press, 1981], pp. 81-100).

Like Dibelius and Bultmann, Albertz concerned himself with the historicity and the *Sitz im Leben* of the units. Albertz, as did Bultmann, began with the Gospel units themselves; however, Albertz took issue with Bultmann's attempt to determine primary and secondary elements in the narratives. Instead, Albertz asserted that the Gospel units contained historically accurate accounts of the dialogues of the 'living Jesus'.[56] On this point he moved beyond the 'historical trustworthiness' Dibelius would accord his paradigms to the position of their 'literal authenticity' rejected by Dibelius.

Albertz defined the 'controversy dialogue' as a narrative unit consisting of at least two parts: the 'description of the situation', which he termed 'exposition', and the 'dialogue'. Sometimes a third element appears, namely the 'closing remarks'. The exposition introduces both the opponent or questioner and the question. The dialogue, which may contain several interchanges, is the focus of the narrative and its major interest is the saying of Jesus.[57] The purest form of the dialogue is the simple question and answer.[58] Those controversies in which the final element is not a saying of Jesus but a healing action contain closing remarks, for example, Mk 2.1-12. Hence, Albertz would include as a controversy dialogue a unit containing a dialogue but which ended in an action of Jesus.

From a comparison with other Synoptic dialogues, Albertz determined three characteristics that distinguished the controversy dialogues, namely their emphasis is on conflict; they raise a controversial question; and they describe the struggle of Jesus with his earthly opponents.[59] Moreover, the controversy dialogues functioned in an apologetic and a catechetical manner in the early Church.[60]

The main categories of Albertz's typology for the controversy dialogues were based on content, namely whether or not the question is meant to put Jesus on trial (a *versucherische* or *nichtversucherische* controversy). The typology is as follows:

56. Albertz, *Streitgespräche*, pp. v-vi. Albertz admitted to a 'process of development' for the units from the original dialogue of Jesus, through the oral narration and the writing down of the story, to collections of some of these units. Although an abbreviation or slight expansion of the narrative may have taken place during the process, he held that these did not affect the historicity of the dialogue (pp. 57-58).

57. Albertz, *Streitgespräche*, pp. 91-96.

58. Albertz, *Streitgespräche*, p. 86.

59. Albertz, *Streitgespräche*, pp. 133-37.

60. Albertz, *Streitgespräche*, pp. 98-101.

Controversy Dialogues

I. 'Trial' Controversy Dialogues[61]

- A. The Galilean collection
- B. The Jerusalem collection
- C. On the obligations of rabbinic tradition
- D. On divorce
- E. The three-fold dialogue of Jesus with Satan

II. 'Non-trial' Controversy Dialogues

- A. Accusations of demonic origins of Jesus' holiness
- B. The demand for a messianic sign
- C. The conditions of salvation
- D. The person of the 'One to Come'[62]

Unfortunately, Albertz did not distinguish further between a 'trial dialogue' and a 'non-trial dialogue'. One might expect that Albertz's trial dialogues and non-trial dialogues matched, for the most part, Bultmann's controversy dialogues and scholastic dialogues, respectively; this was not the case. Only 7 of Albertz's trial dialogues are among Bultmann's 13 controversy dialogues. Mark 3.22-30 appeared as a non-trial dialogue according to Albertz; Bultmann considered this a controversy dialogue. Furthermore, one of Albertz's non-trial dialogues, Mk 8.11-13, was not even identified as an apophthegm by Bultmann.

Influenced by his belief in the historicity of the controversy dialogues, Albertz searched for the origins of this genre in the Hebrew Bible, particularly the prophetic books. He investigated the forms of expression employed by the prophets and also discussed the disputes of Satan with God in the book of Job. However, Albertz merely asserted a relationship between his controversy dialogues and these 'disputational' genres without defining the latter or describing the latter's characteristics.[63] Moreover, the prophetic 'dialogues' he cited are not dialogues, as such, but oracles containing the prophet's interpretation of the opponents' words as well as the prophet's citation of God's response.[64]

Albertz, like Bultmann, sought analogies for the controversy dialogue in

61. The first two elements under the 'Trial' dialogues are what Albertz had identified as pre-Markan collections.

62. See Appendix D for the units under each type.

63. Albertz, *Streitgespräche*, pp. 156-61.

64. For example, Isa. 28.14-22. See the critical remarks on Albertz's point by Arland J. Hultgren (*Jesus and his Adversaries: The Form and Function of the Conflict Stories in the Synoptic Tradition* [Minneapolis: Augsburg, 1979], pp. 31-32).

early rabbinic writings, but presented only four examples from 'The Sayings of the Fathers'. He referred to these disputes as 'teaching discussions' and spoke of their narrowness of interest, covering only matters of the Torah. Albertz thought that such a degree of narrowness was not found in the Gospel tradition. A final distinction he made was that in the rabbinic teaching-discussions the dialogue is between equals, whereas Jesus disputed with the leaders.[65] For Albertz, the Gospel controversy dialogues were not based on rabbinic disputes. Instead, from his search of 'Israelite-Jewish' writings, Albertz concluded that Jesus appeared as a 'continuer', *Fortsetzer*, of the great prophets, since he too struggled against the false leaders of the people.[66] Albertz's sampling of rabbinic texts was so limited that, along with the criticism of his use of Hebrew Bible texts, this conclusion cannot be accepted.

Of further interest to my investigation are Albertz's remarks on the 'devices used in the conflict', that is, what the rhetorical units employed in the argument. Albertz identified the following devices: comparison, antithesis, proof from reason and proof from Scripture.[67] While he did not refer to any Greek or Roman analogies for his controversy dialogues, these 'devices' he identified can be compared to the elements used in the Greek and Roman ἐργασία, 'elaboration', of the χρεία. Among the steps of an elaborated χρεία, one finds analogy, opposite, rationale and statement from authority.[68] The relationship of the argumentative 'devices' in the controversy dialogues to the χρεία was not to be noted by scholars for another 25 years.[69]

Albertz's work is greatly limited by his assumption of the historicity of the controversy dialogues. His contribution lies more in the two 'hints' he gave for future study of the χρεία, namely the fact that an action of Jesus rather than a saying might conclude a dialogue unit and his listing of the 'devices used in the conflict'.

d. *Vincent Taylor*

The first English work on the Gospel anecdotes was published by Vincent Taylor in 1933.[70] He considered the anecdotes to be a genre of oral narra-

65. Albertz, *Streitgespräche*, pp. 162-64.

66. Albertz, *Streitgespräche*, p. 163.

67. Albertz, *Streitgespräche*, pp. 65-74.

68. See the discussion of this in section d, pp. 82-87.

69. See R.O.P. Taylor's 'Greek Forms of Instruction' (1946).

70. Vincent Taylor, *The Formation of the Gospel Tradition* (London: Macmillan, 2nd edn, 1953).

tive present in the cultural world of the early Christians.[71] He criticized both 'disintegrating' the anecdotes by an attempt to distinguish early and secondary elements as well as searching for particular *Sitze im Leben* for the units. He cautioned that at best these were studies in 'historical probability'; he himself held to the historicity of many of the traditions contained in the anecdotes.[72]

Taylor rejected both Dibelius's term 'paradigm' as too general and too closely associated with sermons and Bultmann's term 'apophthegm' as too literal and with an emphasis on the saying to the detriment of the context.[73] Since, according to Taylor, the anecdotes climaxed in a saying of Jesus, he preferred the designation 'pronouncement story'.[74] He defined 'pronouncement stories' as short narratives whose 'chief characteristic is that they culminate in a saying of Jesus which expresses some ethical or religious precept', a definition close to Bultmann's for the apophthegm. Taylor included Mk 3.1-5 among the pronouncement stories, allowing that in this case 'the pronouncement is expressed in the action of Jesus more than in His words'.[75] Finally, he maintained that the function of these stories was to give 'guidance to the first Christians'.[76]

Taylor's essay did not include a typology for the pronouncement stories. Instead, he examined the units already identified in the work of Dibelius, Bultmann and Albertz. Taylor accepted 34 of these units as pronouncement stories and identified two of his own, namely Mk 4.1-10 and the addition in later manuscripts of John at 7.53–8.11. Of these units, he considered Mk 12.13-17 to be the best example of a pronouncement story.[77]

In his later commentary on Mark's Gospel, Taylor mentioned, without definition, a group of narratives he designated 'Markan constructions' and

71. Taylor, *The Formation of the Gospel Tradition*, pp. 29-30, 175. See his *The Gospel According to St. Mark*, where he remarked that a 'distinctive feature of these stories is that they are popular in origin' (p. 78).

72. Taylor, *The Formation of the Gospel Tradition,* pp. 85-87.

73. Taylor, *The Formation of the Gospel Tradition*, p. 30. Taylor also rejected Fascher's suggestion of the term 'anecdote', holding that this term is too 'ill-defined' (p. 71). See Erich Fascher, *Die formgeschichtliche Methode* (BZNW, 2; Geissen: Alfred Töpelmann, 1924), p. 203, where he suggested that the name 'anecdote' be used for ἀπόφθεγμα.

74. Taylor, *The Formation of the Gospel Tradition*, p. 23.

75. Taylor, *The Formation of the Gospel Tradition*, p. 65.

76. Taylor, *The Formation of the Gospel Tradition*, p. 63.

77. Taylor, *The Formation of the Gospel Tradition*, p. 64. See below, Appendix D, for the list of Taylor's 'Pronouncement Story' units.

remarked on their similarity to the Greek χρεῖαι. However, he distinguished these Gospel units from the χρεῖαι, saying that the former 'record, not wise or witty maxims, but sayings with a narrative interest and a religious purpose'.[78] Unfortunately, he did not pursue a comparison of his pronouncement story with the Greek and Roman χρεία.

Taylor's work added nothing new to the discussion of Gospel anecdotes. In his earlier volume he followed Bultmann's schema and definitions, while giving little attention to the rabbinic and Greek analogies found in the works of Bultmann, Dibelius or Albertz.[79] Taylor's main contribution was that he introduced the work of the German scholars into English-speaking form-critical studies. His designation 'pronouncement story' influenced later English-speaking scholars.[80]

e. *Arland Hultgren*

Arland Hultgren published, in 1979, a 'fresh attempt' to ascertain the 'form and function' of the Synoptic controversy dialogues, units he named 'conflict stories'.[81] He identified 18 Synoptic conflict stories.[82] From these units he determined the 'form' of the conflict story as (a) an introductory narrative, preparing for a conflict, (b) an opponent's question or attack and (c) a closing dominical saying which dominates the story.[83] This schema followed Bultmann's for his controversy dialogues and was close to Albertz's, differing only in that Hultgren separated Albertz's second element, the dialogue, into two parts, (b) and (c). Albertz's third component, the occasional closing remarks, was used by Hultgren to justify his terminology conflict 'story' versus conflict 'dialogue', since he preferred to speak of 'the narrative' of a conflict that could include closing remarks.

78. Taylor, *The Gospel According to St. Mark*, p. 82.

79. In his Appendix B, 'Tendencies of Oral Transmission' (*The Formation of the Gospel Tradition*, pp. 202-209) Taylor cited six rabbinic anecdotes to illustrate his 'chain of oral transmission' but he gave no citation for the sources of these narratives nor did he refer to the gospel units.

80. See the discussion of Robert Tannehill's work, section g, pp. 172-75.

81. Hultgren, *Jesus and his Adversaries*.

82. Hultgren's list agreed neither with Bultmann's units nor with Albertz's units. In his 'Appendix A' (*Jesus and his Adversaries*, pp. 203-205), Hultgren provided a comparison of his units with those of Bultmann, Albertz, Dibelius and V. Taylor.

83. Hultgren, *Jesus and his Adversaries*, pp. 52-58. See Joanna Dewey (*Markan Public Debate: Literary Techniques, Concentric Structure and Theology in Mark 2:1–3:6* [SBLDS, 48; Chico, CA: Scholars Press, 1979], p. 29) who closely followed the schema of Hultgren.

Hultgren also noted three features found in some of the stories: the presence of a counter-question, of a Scripture citation, or Jesus' remarks presented in parallelism.[84]

Hultgren commented on the function of the conflict story within pre-Gospel traditions and within the Synoptic Gospels. He separated the pre-Gospel units into a Palestinian collection that used the stories as apologetic responses to Jewish criticism, and a Hellenistic collection, where the units functioned catechetically in the teaching of converts and the regulating of the life of the community.[85] In Mark's Gospel some of the conflict stories functioned as preludes to the passion of Jesus, while others showed that the verbal victories of Jesus were a continuation of his victory over 'supernatural hostile powers'.[86] Matthew employed the stories to present Jesus as a teacher who departed from the Pharisaic position on details of the law.[87] Finally, Luke highlighted his redemptive-historical outlook with conflict stories, also using them to demonstrate that the separation of the early Christians from Judaism was anticipated in the life of Jesus.[88] Thus, both pre-Gospel and Synoptic stories had an apologetic as well as a catechetical function.

Based on his study of the formation of the units, Hultgren established a typology for the conflict stories, that is, 'unitary' and 'non-unitary' conflict stories.[89] 'Unitary' conflict stories were those in which the 'saying is comprehensible only in terms of its contextual situation' and which circulated as a unit, while a 'non-unitary' story was 'composed to create a conflict story out of an originally independent saying'.[90] Hultgren listed 7 stories as unitary and 11 as non-unitary.[91] Given the tenuous nature of decisions about pre-literary sources, a typology based on the process of the formation

84. Hultgren, *Jesus and his Adversaries*, p. 58.

85. Hultgren, *Jesus and his Adversaries*, pp. 175-80. Hultgren's Palestinian collection contained all but one unit of Albertz's Galilean and Jerusalem collections, combined. The additional unit, Mk 11.15-17, is in Albertz's Jerusalem collection. See Dewey's *Markan Public Debate* for a critique of the existence of a pre-Markan collection in 2.1–3.6.

86. Hultgren, *Jesus and his Adversaries*, pp. 182-84.

87. Hultgren, *Jesus and his Adversaries*, p. 198.

88. Hultgren, *Jesus and his Adversaries*, p. 192.

89. For this Hultgren (*Jesus and his Adversaries*, p. 20 n. 3) acknowledged his debt to Bultmann's work (*Geschichte der synoptischen Tradition*, pp. 47-48) on units that he had named 'unitary compositons' and 'secondary constructions', respectively.

90. Hultgren, *Jesus and his Adversaries*, p. 67.

91. See my Appendix D for the units under each type.

of pre-Gospel units is too hypothetical to be accepted.

Hultgren rejected both rabbinic and Hellenistic analogies to the conflict stories. First, without discussing a single rabbinic text,[92] and without explanation, he asserted four differences between Gospel conflict stories and rabbinic controversy dialogues. Since Hultgren presented no evidence, the differences cannot be accepted. Hultgren also rejected Hellenistic analogies to the conflict stories. Citing the definitions of a χρεία given by Hermogenes and Quintilian,[93] Hultgren stated that there were few similarities between conflict stories and χρεῖαι, while there were differences, namely: conflict stories gave specific situations while χρεῖαι had 'the character of "once upon a time"'; χρεῖαι need not contain sayings, let alone a dialogue; and χρεῖαι could lack either the narrated scene or the discourse in direct speech, both found in Synoptic conflict stories.[94] Again, Hultgren gave neither examples of a Greek or Roman χρεία or of a Synoptic conflict story, nor arguments for his conclusions.[95] His statements revealed a lack of familiarity with the full discussion of the χρεία in the grammatical handbooks. Furthermore, he failed to mention the essay of R.O.P. Taylor on the Gospel χρεῖαι.

His cursory investigation of rabbinic and Hellenistic analogies led Hultgren to conclude that the synoptic conflict stories were 'as new in form as they are in content' having been 'composed' to meet the needs of the early Christian community.[96] After discussing four conflict stories, he posited a process of their formation from the initial report of a conflict situation to a full-fledged dialogue.

In the final analysis, Hultgren's most valuable contribution to the study of Gospel anecdotes, limited to conflict stories, was the modest attempt he made to recognize the rhetorical use of a narrative unit within each Gospel.

f. *Wolfgang Weiss*

With the 1989 publication of his *'Eine neue Lehre in Vollmacht': Die Streit- und Schulgespräche des Markus-Evangeliums*, on the controversy

92. In his 'Appendix B' (*Jesus and his Adversaries*, pp. 206-12), Hultgren cited without comment 12 rabbinic units. Only one, *m. 'Abod. Zar.* 4.7, is from the tannaitic writings.

93. Hermogenes, *Progymnasmata* 6.4-6 and Quintilian, *Inst.* 1.9.3-6.

94. Hultgren, *Jesus and his Adversaries*, p. 35.

95. In his 'Appendix C' (*Jesus and his Adversaries*, pp. 213-14), Hultgren cited, without comment, the six χρεῖαι used by Dibelius.

96. *Jesus and his Adversaries*, pp. 19 and 39.

and scholastic dialogues of Mark's Gospel, Wolfgang Weiss sought to fill a need for a critical study of these units within German scholarship, where Bultmann's treatment prevailed and Hultgren's study had gone almost unnoticed.[97]

Weiss noted, as had Bultmann and Albertz, that both literary forms consisted of a dialogue setting and a saying and that the framework concentrated on the saying of Jesus, the climax of the unit. Hence, the purpose of the units was to frame the saying of Jesus. Weiss then developed a working hypothesis whereby he distinguished the controversy dialogues from the scholastic dialogues according to each of their 'constitutive form-elements'.[98]

Weiss asserted that the essential elements of a controversy dialogue were the components of attack or reproach and a clearly contrasting reply. With these criteria, Weiss accepted eight of Bultmann's Markan controversy dialogues and eliminated three that were free of polemics. Furthermore, he considered both the depiction of the dialogue partners as known opponents of Jesus and the 'characterization of the intention of the question' to be Markan additions. Hence, he correctly argued that the classification of dialogues as controversies should be made solely on the polemical contrast between the attack or reproach and the reply.[99]

Weiss further distinguished among the controversy dialogues based on whether the dialogue began with a reproach or an attack. He noted that those containing an attack concerned the activities of Jesus and functioned to legitimate Jesus; these he designated 'dialogues on the activity of Jesus'. The other controversies contained a reproach of the behavior of Jesus' disciples; hence, Weiss named these 'dialogues on Christian life praxis'. This second type functioned to legitimate a specific Christian behavior that had been opposed by other Jews.[100]

In the scholastic dialogues, on the other hand, the contemporaries raised a 'genuine question', and thus they were descriptive of a teaching

97. Wolfgang Weiss, *'Eine neue Lehre in Vollmacht': Die Streit- und Schulgespräche des Markus-Evangeliums* (BZNW, 52; Berlin: W. de Gruyter, 1989). E.g., see Jean-Gaspard Mundiso Mbâ Mundla (*Jesus und die Führer Israels: Studien zu den sog. Jerusalemer Streitgesprächen* [NTAbh, NS, 17; Münster: Aschendoff, 1984]) who, although commenting on Hultgren, follows Bultmann closely.

98. Weiss, *'Eine neue Lehre in Vollmacht'*, pp. 33-34.

99. Weiss, *'Eine neue Lehre in Vollmacht'*, pp. 34-35.

100. Weiss, *'Eine neue Lehre in Vollmacht'*, pp. 36-37.

situation.[101] Once again, Weiss began with Bultmann's group of five Markan scholastic dialogues and rejected three since they are not based on a question.[102] Weiss did include, however, the three units mentioned above that Bultmann had incorrectly, according to Weiss, identified as controversy dialogues. Thus Weiss presented five scholastic dialogues in Mark, four containing a specific question. He considered Mk 10.17-21 as a separate type of dialogue because of the tenor of the question, regarding it an 'instructional dialogue'. Hence, Weiss employed the following typology:

I. Controversy Dialogues
   A. On Christian life praxis
   B. On the activity of Jesus

II. Scholastic Dialogues
   A. On general religious questions
   B. On legal questions

III. Instructional Dialogue

After a detailed analysis of each of these units,[103] Weiss presented his conclusions beginning with the controversy dialogues on Christian life practice. He went beyond the work of Bultmann, Dibelius and Hultgren by distinguishing between the 'framing scene' and the 'dialogue scene' of the units. He argued that the framing scene was a secondary Markan addition to the dialogue scene since the reply of Jesus is not absolutely derived from the scene. Indeed, the framing scene is intelligible in terms of the response of Jesus, but not necessarily vice versa. The dialogue scene itself, with its constitutive elements of reproach and answer, represented the 'basic form' of these controversy dialogues. These dialogue scenes originated in debates between Christian communities and Jewish groups and their *Sitze im Leben* would have been in Hellenistic–Jewish communities, possibly in Syria.[104]

Weiss's conclusions on the dialogues involving the activity of Jesus and on the scholastic dialogues received a briefer treatment. He gave no 'basic form' for the controversies on the activity of Jesus but reiterated that their schema comprised attack and answer. He concluded that these dialogues

101. Weiss, *'Eine neue Lehre in Vollmacht'*, p. 34.

102. Weiss, *'Eine neue Lehre in Vollmacht'*, p. 39.

103. In his analysis, Weiss sought to ascertain the original form, the pre-Markan transmission, and the Markan redactional elements of each unit, an approach similar to Bultmann's.

104. Weiss, *'Eine neue Lehre in Vollmacht'*, pp. 267-84.

were apologetic in nature and probably functioned within an unspecified Jewish Christian community. Finally, without elucidation, he remarked that the scholastic dialogues had a composition 'similar to the basic form' of the controversy dialogues on Christian life praxis. The scholastic dialogues originated within internal debates over the concerns of the early community and reflected the influence of a Hellenistic Jewish point of view.[105]

Weiss concluded his remarks on the 'form' of these dialogues with an excursus entitled 'Zum Problem der Formanalogie in der Umwelt'. Here Weiss disposed of rabbinic analogies to Gospel dialogues by asserting that if the Synoptic units did indeed originate from the same *Sitz im Leben* as the rabbinic dialogues, as Bultmann claimed, then 'for the transmission of the controversy and scholastic dialogues one would have to assume an intact teaching and educational profession, respectively'.[106] Weiss correctly stated that there was no indication of either profession found in pre-Markan traditions. In regard to Greek and Roman analogies, Weiss noted that Bultmann's categorization of the Synoptic dialogues as ἀποφθέγματα had remained largely unchallenged. However, he observed that both Dibelius and Hultgren had mentioned the χρεία and he asserted, incorrectly, that Klaus Berger had classified the controversy dialogue and the scholastic dialogue as ἀπόφθεγμα and χρεία, respectively.[107]

Weiss began his own search for Greek and Roman analogies by admitting that the ἀπόφθεγμα and the χρεία were closely related and then attempting to differentiate them. Like Berger, Weiss noted that the ἀπόφθεγμα took the form of question and answer.[108] He also took up Berger's two assertions, namely that a χρεία was tied more closely to its setting than an ἀπόφθεγμα and that the ἀπόφθεγμα and the χρεία were subgenres of the ἀπομνημόνευμα. Furthermore, Weiss adopted Berger's belief in a development in genre from the γνώμη to the ἀπόφθεγμα to the

105. Weiss, *'Eine neue Lehre in Vollmacht'*, pp. 308-15.

106. Weiss, *'Eine neue Lehre in Vollmacht'*, p. 317.

107. Weiss (*'Eine neue Lehre in Vollmacht'*, p. 317) cited Berger ('Hellenistische Gattungen', p. 1305, and *Formgeschichte des Neuen Testaments*, pp. 80-93) for this statement. In fact, Berger did not comment on the scholastic dialogues in either work. Under 'Streitgespräche', in 'Hellenistische Gattungen' (pp. 1305-10), Berger classified the controversy dialogues as a combination of the χρεία and the ἀγών, while in *Formgeschichte des Neuen Testaments* (pp. 88-89) he classified them simply as χρεῖαι.

108. Weiss (*'Eine neue Lehre in Vollmacht'*, pp. 321-22) cited Gemoll's remark on the 'classic form' of the ἀπόφθεγμα and said that it was found in Xenophon.

χρεία.[109] Thus, according to Weiss, 'at a later time', which he did not designate, the χρεία came to include the ἀπόφθεγμα; here again Weiss followed Berger.[110] Weiss contradicted himself and apparently did so in order to affirm Bultmann's position. Weiss stated: 'With respect to the controversy and scholastic dialogues (and the biographical apophthegms) Bultmann's designation of these materials as apophthegmata can thus be confirmed.' Without proof or argument of any kind, Weiss went on to assert that while the 'basic form' of the dialogues is based on the schema of an apophthegm, the expanded form of the controversy dialogue and the literary structure of such a dialogue correspond to the χρεία. Yet Weiss again contradicted himself in the conclusion of his excursus by stating that neither the 'form' of the controversy dialogue nor that of the scholastic dialogue was identical to the χρεία or the ἀπόφθεγμα.[111]

Given his 'basic form' of the controversy dialogues, that is, question and answer, one can accept Weiss's contention that this 'basic form' appears as an ἀπόφθεγμα and that the 'expanded' synoptic units follow the pattern of a χρεία. However, Weiss's arguments as to the distinction between these two genres cannot be accepted.[112] He did not engage the ancient sources adequately enough to have reached his conclusions; indeed, his work depended too heavily on the scholarship of Bultmann and Berger.

g. *Robert C. Tannehill*

The Pronouncement Story Group of the Society of Biblical Literature published the results of the first phase of its work, 1975–1981, in a *Semeia* issue entitled *Pronouncement Stories*.[113] The group sought to explore

109. Weiss, *'Eine neue Lehre in Vollmacht'*, pp. 320-22.

110. Weiss, *'Eine neue Lehre in Vollmacht'*, pp. 324-25. See Berger, *Formgeschichte des Neuen Testaments*, p. 82.

111. Weiss, *'Eine neue Lehre in Vollmacht'*, p. 325.

112. One finds a further objection to Weiss's work in that earlier in the excursus (*'Eine neue Lehre in Vollmacht'*, p. 318) he rejected Mundla's assertion (*Jesus und die Führer Israels*, p. 306) that Christian authors would have been influenced by existing literary 'forms' or categories, modifying the contents according to their faith. Later on, Weiss (p. 324) posited that in the formation of the early stages of the Jesus tradition, the Christians consciously sought to imitate Hellenistic genres. I would contend that this held true not only for the early stages but also for the written works.

113. Robert C. Tannehill (ed.), *Pronouncement Stories* (Semeia, 20; Chico, CA: Scholars Press, 1981). The essays in this publication pertinent to my investigation are: Tannehill, 'Introduction: The Pronouncement Story and Its Types', pp. 1-13; *idem*, 'Varieties of Synoptic Pronouncement Stories', pp. 101-19; Vernon Robbins,

further Bultmann's work on the form and function of Synoptic apophthegms; however, they moved beyond a concern for pre-literary traditions to a study of the function of the units within their present setting. Vincent Taylor's term, 'pronouncement story', was used for the literary genre represented by Bultmann's 'apophthegm', Dibelius's 'paradigm', and the χρεία.[114] The work of Robert Tannehill will be taken as representative of the conclusions of the first phase of this group's work.[115]

Tannehill defined a pronouncement story as 'a brief narrative in which the climactic (and usually final) element is an utterance, often expressed in a succinct and striking way, by which someone responds to something said or observed on a particular occasion'.[116] Additionally, he presented three criteria for this genre: (1) the narrative is meaningful in itself and able to stand alone; (2) the saying is the dominant element in the story; and (3) the parties in the story are not given an equal hearing.[117] The Gospel stories undoubtedly influenced these criteria; thus, Tannehill's method is somewhat circular. When Tannehill presented the criteria, however, he did not indicate that he was limiting the genre 'pronouncement story' to the Gospels. In fact, he pointed to the presence of this genre in Greek and Latin works of the period.[118]

Tannehill saw a close relationship in the stories between the situation

'Classifying Pronouncement Stories in Plutarch's *Parallel Lives*', pp. 29-52; and Gary Porton, 'The Pronouncement Story in Tannaitic Literature: A Review of Bultmann's Theory', pp. 81-99. See also John Painter, 'Quest and Rejection Stories in John', *JSNT* 36 (1987), pp. 17-46.

114. Tannehill, 'Introduction', p. 1. While the term χρεία is mentioned here and in Tannehill's 'Types and Functions of Apophthegms in the Synoptic Gospels' (*ANRW*, II.25.2, p. 1792 n. 1), the χρεία is not discussed further in the 'pronouncement story' phase of the group's work.

115. In addition to Tannehill's three essays cited in nn. 113 and 114 above, see his *The Sword of his Mouth: Forceful and Imaginative Language in Synoptic Sayings* (Philadelphia: Fortress Press, 1975); 'Attitudinal Shift in Synoptic Pronouncement Stories', in R.A. Spencer (ed.), *Orientation by Disorientation: Studies in Literary Criticism and Biblical Literary Criticism Presented in Honor of William A. Beardslee* (Pittsburgh: Pickwick Press, 1980), pp. 183-97; 'Synoptic Pronouncement Stories: Form and Function', in Paul J. Achtemeier (ed.), *SBLSP 1980* (SBLSP, 19; Chico, CA: Scholars Press, 1980), pp. 51-56; and 'Tension in Synoptic Sayings and Stories', *Int* 34 (1980), pp. 138-50. 'Types and Functions of Apophthegms' contained the more highly developed presentation of his definition and typology.

116. Tannehill, 'Types and Functions of Apophthegms', pp. 1-2.

117. Tannehill, 'Introduction', p. 3.

118. Tannehill, 'Introduction', p. 3. See also the articles cited in n. 115 above.

and the saying, referring to these elements as 'stimulus' and 'response'.[119] He noted the differing 'movements' from the stimulus to the response and these movements formed the basis for his typology:

Pronouncement Stories[120]

I. Corrections

II. Commendations

III. Objections

IV. Quests

V. Inquiries
 A. Testing
 B. Request for Instruction

VI. Descriptions

The six types of stories were defined as follows: corrections, 'the response corrects the views or conduct of the person or group occasioning the response'; commendations, 'the primary character commends something said or done by a secondary character'; objections, 'an objection is raised against the words or actions of the primary character or his close associates, and a response is given by the primary character'; quests, 'someone approaches the primary character in quest of something very important to the well-being of the questor'; and inquiries, which 'contain a question or a request for instruction' and a response. Testing inquiries depict a hostile or skeptical group, while request inquiries contain a request for additional instruction or clarification.[121]

The first four types of pronouncement stories functioned, according to Tannehill, to influence the hearer's or reader's attitudes.[122] The inquiry stories, on the other hand, served to present Jesus as a teacher with insight and authority.[123] Finally, Tannehill held that a number of pronouncement stories were 'hybrids', that is, they fall under more than one category. Thus, for example, Mk 3.31-35, concerning the mother and brothers of

119. Tannehill, 'Introduction', p. 5.

120. See Appendix D for the units under each type.

121. 'Types and Functions of Apophthegms', pp.1803-21. Tannehill's typology in 'Introduction', pp. 10-11, contained a sixth category, 'Description stories'. However, he found no examples of these stories in the Gospels.

122. On this point see Tannehill's 'Attitudinal Shifts in Synoptic Pronouncement Stories' and 'Tension in Synoptic Sayings and Stories'.

123. Tannehill, 'Types and Functions of Apophthegms', p. 1822.

Jesus, is both a correction and a commendation story. The existence of these hybrids points out a weakness of the typology since it was difficult to apply with precision. Tannehill's work did move the scholarship of Gospel anecdotes from the pioneering form critics' definitions and typologies toward more precise definitions and the recognition of rhetorical features within the stories. The major criticism of Tannehill's and the group's work remains that they did not use Greek and Roman rhetorical genres in their study. They began with a definition and a typology developed from Gospel units and applied these to other bodies of literature. There is no evidence that the types of stories in Tannehill's typology were conscious story-types in other cultural worlds of antiquity. On the other hand, the gospels, as we have them, are Greek works and there is evidence that at least Mark employed the χρεία, a Greek and Latin story-type in his Gospel.[124] Those scholars whose approach begins in Greek and Roman rhetorical education are discussed in the following section.

2. *Rhetorical Approaches*

In the United States, detailed application of Greek and Roman rhetorical definitions and methods of argumentation to Gospel anecdotes resulted from the cooperation of two working groups: the Society of Biblical Literature's Pronouncement Story Work Group and the Chreia in Greco-Roman Literature and Education Project of the Institute for Antiquity and Christianity at Claremont.[125] Two scholars from these groups have published important studies on the Gospel anecdotes as χρεῖαι.

a. *Burton Mack and Vernon Robbins*

In 1989, Burton Mack, a member of the Chreia Project at Claremont, and Vernon Robbins, chair of the second phase of the SBL's Pronouncement Story Group, co-authored *Patterns of Persuasion in the Gospels*. This work contained essays by each scholar representing the fruit of their individual studies on the χρεία and on Gospel anecdotes up to that time. Their hypothesis throughout this book was that 'the pronouncement stories

124. See Chapter 5.

125. For an account of the history of these two groups see: Mack, 'Anecdote and Arguments', pp. 1-3; Robbins, 'Pronouncement Stories from a Rhetorical Perspective', pp. 4, 9; *idem*, 'Introduction: Using Rhetorical Discussions of the Chreia to Interpret Pronouncement Stories', p. vii; *idem*, 'Chreia and Pronouncement Story in Synoptic Studies', pp. 26-27; and Mack and Robbins, *Patterns of Persuasion*, pp. viii-ix.

in the gospels could be defined as *chreiai* in keeping with Hellenistic practice'.[126] Their studies on the χρεία presented Theon's definition of the genre, his three-part typology and the exercises with a χρεία found in the handbooks, especially the exercises of ἐπέκατᾰσις, 'expansion', and ἐργασία, 'elaboration'. The work of these two scholars is presented here as representative of those who are engaged in the χρεία studies.

Prior to this joint publication, Burton Mack had used a discussion of the χρεία in his work on anecdotes in Philo of Alexandria.[127] Then, in 1987, Mack applied the theory of the χρεία and the exercise of 'elaboration', ἐργασία, to the anecdotes of the Gospels.[128] *A Myth of Innocence*, Mack's 1988 study of Mark's Gospel in pursuit of the origins of Christianity, contained a section, 'The Pronouncement Stories', in which he concentrated on the χρεία in relation to some of the anecdotes of Mark.[129] Since *Patterns of Persuasion*, Mack has published brief comments on the χρεία and the Q source,[130] and his *Rhetoric and the New Testament*. This latter work presents more fully his understanding of the rhetorical methods of the Greek and Roman orators.

Vernon Robbins began his studies in 1978 with an analysis of anecdotes in Plutarch's *Parallel Lives.*[131] Robbins moved on to study Gospel anecdotes in 1983 with his 'Pronouncement Stories and Jesus' Blessing of Children'.[132] Robbins emphasized the argumentation in the pronouncement stories and, in 1988, decided that these narratives can be understood best if analyzed according to the exercises with χρεῖαι and Greek and Roman rhetorical theory.[133] His essays in *Patterns of Persuasion* were the

126. Mack and Robbins, *Patterns of Persuasion*, p. 196.

127. Mack, 'Decoding the Scriptures'.

128. Mack, 'Anecdote and Arguments'.

129. Burton L. Mack, *A Myth of Innocence: Mark and Christian Origins* (Philadelphia: Fortress Press, 1988).

130. Burton L. Mack, *The Lost Gospel: The Book of Q and Christian Origins* (San Francisco: Harper Collins, 1990), pp. 193-200.

131. Vernon K. Robbins, 'Pronouncement Stories in Plutarch's Lives of Alexander and Julius Caesar', in Paul J. Achtemeier (ed.), *SBLSP 1978* (SBLSP, 13-14; 2 vols.; Missoula, MT: Scholars Press, 1978), I, pp. 21-38. This was updated in his 'Classifying Pronouncement Stories in Plutarch's *Parallel Lives*'.

132. Vernon K. Robbins, 'Pronouncement Stories and Jesus' Blessing of Children: A Rhetorical Approach', in Daniel Patte (ed.), *Kingdom and Children* (Semeia, 29; Chico, CA: Scholars Press, 1983), pp. 42-74 (reprint of 'Pronouncement Stories and Jesus' Blessing of Children: A Rhetorical Approach', in Kent H. Richards (ed.), *SBLSP 1982* [SBLSP, 21; Chico, CA: Scholars Press, 1982], pp. 407-30).

133. Robbins, 'Pronouncement Stories from a Rhetorical Perspective'.

culmination of over ten years of study on the Gospel anecdotes.[134] Robbins's opening essay in *Patterns of Persuasion* contains, in addition to a review of scholarship, a general presentation on the χρεία, including Theon's definition, his exercise of the χρεία-expansion, ἐπεκατἄσις, as well as Greek, Roman and Synoptic Gospel examples of each.[135]

The second chapter, 'Elaboration of the Chreia in the Hellenistic School', contains Burton Mack's work on the elaboration of a χρεία and its relation to the form of a complete argument as found in rhetorical handbooks.[136] He first explains that the exercises contained in the *progymnasmata* were a series of guided lessons that served as an introduction to rhetorical theory and practice. He gives Theon's list of eight exercises in four sets of complementary pairs. He further divides the sets into two groups: the first concerned style and delivery, that is, recitation and inflection as well as expansion and abbreviation; the second dealt with analysis and argumentation, that is, commentary and critique as well as refutation and confirmation. The second set of exercises was especially helpful in preparation for rhetorical debate. Mack notes that Theon also suggested, without explanation, that more advanced students might take up the 'arrangement of topics' in relation to a 'thesis'.[137] However, in his *progymnasmata*, Hermogenes did explicate such an 'arrangement of topics' under what he called the exercise of 'elaboration', ἐργασία.

Mack moves beyond the presentation of Hermogenes' χρεία elaboration, however, and argues that such an elaboration followed the pattern of what he termed a 'complete argument'. Mack begins with Hermogenes' eight-step elaboration exercise, namely praise of the χρεία's subject, then the χρεία, followed by: the rationale, a statement of the opposite, an analogy, an example, a statement from authority and an exhortation. Mack

134. One can trace the development of Robbins's interest in both rhetorical techniques and the χρεία in his essays: 'A Rhetorical Typology for Classifying and Analyzing Pronouncement Stories', in Kent H. Richards (ed.), *SBLSP 1984* (SBLSP, 23; Chico, CA: Scholars Press, 1984), pp. 93-122; 'The Chreia'; 'Writing as a Rhetorical Act in Plutarch and the Gospels', in Duane F. Watson (ed.), *Persuasive Artistry: Studies in New Testament Rhetoric in Honor of George A. Kennedy* (JSNTSup, 50; Sheffield: JSOT Press, 1991), pp. 142-68; and his *Ancient Quotes and Anecdotes*.

135. Robbins, 'Chreia and Pronouncement Story in Synoptic Studies'. Robbins gives a more succinct presentation of the χρεία exercises in his 'Introduction: Using Rhetorical Discussions of the Chreia to Interpret Pronouncement Stories'.

136. Mack, 'Elaboration of the Chreia'. His presentation is also given in *Rhetoric and the New Testament*, pp. 41-47, 50-56.

137. Mack, 'Elaboration of the Chreia', pp. 34-41.

also cites Hermogenes' example of an elaboration of a χρεία concerning Isocrates.[138]

A comparison of this elaboration with three passages from the first century BCE text, *Rhetorica ad Herennium*, is then presented by Mack. The first describes a 'complete argument', that is, (a) *propositio*, (b) *ratio*, (c) *confirmatio*, (d) *exornatio* and (e) *complexio* (*Rhet. Her*. 2.18.28). Mack asserts that the *ratio* of the complete argument corresponded to the 'rationale' of Hermogenes' elaboration. Next, Mack presented the list of arguments used in the *exornatio* of this 'complete argument', namely *simile, exemplum, amplification* and *res iudicata* (*Rhet. Her*. 2.39.46). This list was viewed by Mack to be very close to the elaboration outline. Finally, Mack cited a passage dealing with the development of a thesis: (a) *res* or statement of the theme; (b) rationale; (c) paraphrase; (d) statement of contrary; (e) analogy; (f) example; and (g) conclusion (*Rhet. Her*. 4.43.56). From these passages, he concluded, that the steps of Hermogenes' elaboration corresponded very closely, but not completely, to these three patterns of argumentation. Mack is to be credited with pointing out the similarities in these patterns of argumentation, that is, Hermogenes' χρεία-elaboration, the 'complete argument' of *Rhet. Her*. 2.18.28, and the development of a thesis in *Rhet. Her*. 4.43.56. However, in Chapter 2 I pointed out the differences among these three patterns and concluded only that the χρεία-elaboration and the development of a thesis provide a student with practice for the rhetorical speech. The distinction between 'complete argument' of *Rhet. Her*. 2.18.28 and a complete rhetorical speech is not presented by Mack, nor does he emphasize that a χρεία-elaboration is a 'preparatory exercise'.

In Chapters 3–7 of *Patterns of Persuasion*, Mack and Robbins applied their rhetorical analyses to various Synoptic passages. Robbins compared Mt. 8.19-22 with the parallel Lk. 9.57-60 in 'Foxes, Birds, Burials and Furrows'. There his analysis dealt not only with a comparison of the units but also with the rhetorical features of each passage within its host Gospel. In 'Plucking Grain on the Sabbath', Robbins discussed this Synoptic tradition, specifically considering the rhetorical situation within each Gospel. Finally, Robbins studied four Synoptic units that depicted Jesus as casting out demons in Chapter 7, 'Rhetorical Composition and the Beelzebul Controversy'.[139] Once again he analyzed each unit within its host Gospel.[140]

138. Mack, 'Elaboration of the Chreia', pp. 51-52.

139. See Vernon Robbins, 'Foxes, Birds, Burials and Furrows', 'Plucking Grain on the Sabbath' and 'Rhetorical Composition and the Beelzebul Controversy', in Burton

Burton Mack's further contributions to the volume consisted in discussions of a Gospel tradition about a woman anointing Jesus and of a long collection of parables in Mark as an elaboration. In 'The Anointing of Jesus: Elaboration within a Chreia', Mack examined the four Gospel units dealing with a woman's anointing of Jesus with perfumed oil.[141] Mack showed that Mk 14.3-9 and Lk. 7.36-50 are presented by the evangelists in the form of elaborated χρεῖαι. These rhetorical arrangements of the material led Mack to assert that 'the elaboration pattern provides a way of analyzing the rhetorical design of clusters and blocks of sayings-material'.[142] He then remarks that 'one trained in the tradition of Bultmann' needed to re-think the assumption that sayings attracted scenes in the development of Gospel anecdotes or that one saying attracted others of similar content.[143] Finally, in Chapter 6, Mack breaks down Mk 4.1-34, a section of parables, according to the pattern of an elaboration.[144] Unfortunately, his pattern appears 'forced', as for example when he presents the parable of 4.2b-9 as the χρεία-element in an elaboration of a χρεία. Mack could still have made his point if he had referred to one of the patterns of argumentation he had cited from *Rhetorica ad Herennium.*

Their examination of Gospel anecdotes as χρεῖαι led Mack and Robbins to the following conclusions for the study of the Jesus traditions. In the first place, 'The integrity of the χρεία means that interpreters should not separate saying and scene, and that behavior as well as statements belong to the primary form…'[145] Secondly, while a 'thematic selection' is an aspect of the cluster of sayings found in Gospel anecdotes, it is equally apparent that 'the underlying principle of selection was undoubtedly rhetorical'.[146] This rhetorical principle of selection implies that sayings of Jesus were attached to the anecdotes for the sake of argumen-

L. Mack and Vernon K. Robbins, *Patterns of Persuasion in the Gospels* (Sonoma, CA: Polebridge Press, 1989), pp. 69-84, 107-41 and 161-93, respectively.

140. The units are Mt. 9.32-34; 12.22-37; Mk 3.19a-30; and Lk. 11.18-28.

141. Burton L. Mack, 'The Anointing of Jesus: Elaboration within a Chreia', in Burton L. Mack and Vernon K. Robbins, *Patterns of Persuasion in the Gospels* (Sonoma, CA: Polebridge Press, 1989), pp. 85-106. The units are Mk 14.3-9, Mt. 26.6-13, Lk. 7.36-50 and Jn 12.1-8.

142. Mack, 'The Anointing of Jesus', p. 105.

143. Mack, 'The Anointing of Jesus', p. 106.

144. Burton L. Mack, 'Teaching in Parables: Elaboration in Mark 4.1-34', in Burton L. Mack and Vernon K. Robbins, *Patterns of Persuasion in the Gospels* (Sonoma, CA: Polebridge Press, 1989), pp. 143-93.

145. Mack and Robbins, *Patterns of Persuasion*, p. 201.

146. Mack and Robbins, *Patterns of Persuasion*, p. 203.

tation and may not have been associated with the original setting. Such a principle of selection allows for 'the wide-ranging authorial activity of those involved in portraying Jesus as a powerful speaker'.[147] The analysis of the anecdotes in Mk 8.27–10.45 in Chapter 5 shows these conclusions to be valid in many cases. However, Mk 9.43-50 is shown to be a collection of sayings added to the sayings of 9.41-42 by association of 'catchwords', not for a pattern of argumentation.[148] Finally, after arguing that within the Hellenistic culture any evaluation of a speaker's authority involved an assessment of his or her rhetoric, Mack and Robbins contend that presenting elaborated χρεῖαι in the Gospels not only served the rhetorical argument of the evangelist, but enhanced the authority of Jesus, since he was seen as skilled in argumentation. 'The Jesus of the unelaborated chreia does not speak with the same kind of authority as the Jesus who goes on to argue for its principle.'[149] Chapter 5 demonstrates that the argumentation patterns present in the χρεία-like anecdotes of Mk 8.27–10.45 do indeed provide the hearer and reader of Mark with a portrait of Jesus as a persuasive teacher. The methods presented by Mack and Robbins in *Patterns of Persuasion in the Gospels* have set an agenda for future analysis of Gospel anecdotes.

3. *Rabbinic Analogies to Gospel Anecdotes*

In his discussions of rabbinic dialogues, Bultmann admitted that in his day the scholarship on such dialogues was inadequate. Very little critical study of rabbinic narratives in comparison with Gospel units has been undertaken to date; however, the work of three scholars who have made contributions toward such a study will be discussed here.[150]

a. *David Daube*

David Daube's *The New Testament and Rabbinic Judaism* contained three essays dealing with 'forms' common to the Gospels and rabbinic litera-

147. Mack and Robbins, *Patterns of Persuasion*, p. 203.

148. See section e, pp. 214-21.

149. Mack and Robbins, *Patterns of Persuasion*, p. 207.

150. Philip Alexander's classification of rabbinic anecdotes ('Rabbinic Biography and the Biography of Jesus', in Christopher Tuckett [ed.], *Synoptic Studies: The Ampleforth Conference of 1982 and 1983* [JSNTSup, 7; Sheffield: JSOT Press, 1984], pp. 19-50) is not discussed here since he used only two tannaitic units for his typology. Furthermore, he cited no Gospel units and only made general references to earlier form critics' assertions regarding Gospel anecdotes.

ture.[151] In 'Public Retort and Private Explanation', Daube noted that two Gospel units resembled a form found in rabbinic literature. He named the form: 'public-retort-private-explanation' and gave it a four-part structure: (1) a question by an opponent; (2) public retort, mysterious but sufficient; (3) a private request by followers for explanation; and (4) full explanation in private.[152] Daube offered four rabbinic examples: *Pesiqta deRab Kahana* 40a, *y. Berakot* 12d, *Leviticus Rabbah* on Lev. 4.1, and *Pesiqta Rabbati* 21.[153]

In 'Socratic Interrogation', Daube commented further on parts (1) and (2) of the 'public-retort-private-explanation' form.[154] He noted the existence of a short form consisting of four parts: (1) hostile question; (2) counter-question; (3) opponent's answer; and (4) refutation. He pointed out that, in reference to Socrates, Aristotle commented on a similar method of argumentation in *Rhet.* 3.18.2; hence, Daube named the form 'Socratic interrogation'.[155] He studied the form in three Gospel units and in one talmudic passage.

Finally, in his essay, 'Two Tripartite Forms', Daube presented two genres related to the 'Socratic interrogation'. The first consisted of (a) a revolutionary action by Jesus or his disciples, (b) a protest from Jewish leaders and (c) a silencing pronouncement. He listed seven gospel units that fit this genre, but only one rabbinic passage, *b. Ḥullin* 6b.[156] These units functioned to demonstrate the newness of Jesus' message as well as to vindicate some particular 'revolutionary' conduct.[157] The second, similar, genre was composed of (a) a provoking gesture, (b) a question and (c) a pronouncement. Both of these forms were similar to Bultmann's controversy dialogue, although Daube nowhere referred to Bultmann's work. For his second genre Daube referred to only one Gospel unit and

151. David Daube, *The New Testament and Rabbinic Judaism* (London: Athlone Press, 1956). See also his earlier 'Public Pronouncement and Private Explanation in the Gospels', *ExpTim* 57 (1945–46), pp. 175-77.

152. David Daube, 'Public Retort and Private Explanation', in *The New Testament and Rabbinic Judaism*, pp. 141-50 (141-42).

153. Daube, 'Public Retort and Private Explanation', pp. 141-45.

154. David Daube, 'Socratic Interrogation', in *The New Testament and Rabbinic Judaism*, pp. 151-57.

155. Daube also mentioned that Quintilian discussed this form ('Socratic Interrogation', pp. 153-54).

156. Daube, 'Socratic Interrogation', p. 170.

157. David Daube, 'Two Tripartite Forms', in *The New Testament and Rabbinic Judaism*, pp. 170-75.

two talmudic passages; he saw the function of these units as didactic.[158] In this regard, Daube pointed out that Xenophon (*Mem.* 1.2.17) had reported that students learn through the example of a master's life followed by an explanation. For the remainder of his essay, Daube argued, using highly questionable datings, that the entire Passover Seder service was arranged in this particular tripartite form, a point irrelevant to the study of individual passages.

In all three essays, none of the rabbinic texts Daube cited are considered to be from the tannaitic stratum of rabbinic literature. Daube's conclusion that when a passage dealt with rabbis from the tannaitic age, the actual units themselves could be considered from this era is highly questionable. The author also held that Hellenism had so thoroughly influenced the Mediterranean world in antiquity that it is possible that Gospel units in the Socratic-interrogation form reflected Jewish sources or at least a Jewish milieu that had already adopted the Greek and Roman form.[159] This argument is difficult to accept given the late date of the text of Daube's one rabbinic example. Daube's essays do call attention to the fact that some similar genres existed in the Gospel and in rabbinic literature; however, the conclusions he drew from this observation were not warranted.

b. *Gary G. Porton*

As part of the first phase of the SBL Pronouncement Story Group, Gary Porton published an essay on the pronouncement story in tannaitic literature, in which he reviewed Bultmann's use of rabbinic examples as analogies for Gospel 'apophthegms'.[160] The major criticism Porton offered, correctly, on Bultmann's work was that he had failed to confine his search for parallels to those rabbinic documents edited before the middle of the third century CE, that is, the tannaitic literature.[161] Hence, Porton proceeded to conduct his own search of the tannaitic literature for such parallels. While he used the term 'pronouncement story', Porton did not follow Tannehill's definition of the term. Instead, Porton used the term for a narrative form in which: (a) specific information is given about a setting; (b) the principal saying is attributed to a named sage; (c) the saying responds to a question, statement or phenomenon encountered by the sage;

158. Daube, 'Two Tripartite Forms', pp. 175-83.

159. Daube, 'Socratic Interrogation', pp. 156-57.

160. Porton, 'Pronouncement Story', pp. 81-100.

161. Porton, 'Pronouncement Story', p. 83. Tannaitic literature, according to Porton, consisted of the *Mishnah*, *Tosefta*, *Sifra*, *Sifre* and the *Mekhilta deRabbi Ishmael*.

and (d) the principal pronouncement is not part of a dialogue between equals.[162] Porton found only 15 units that fit his definition. However, he does list 11 more passages, two that lack a setting, 3 that involve rabbis of equal status, and 6 in which the pronouncement is attributed to several people or to a single person, all of whom are anonymous.[163]

From his study Porton concluded that there were relatively few good parallels to the Gospel pronouncement stories in early rabbinic literature. He reasoned that since the main interest of pronouncement stories was the 'pronouncer', the scarcity of this form within the rabbinic writings was due to that literature's lack of focus on the 'personality of a single individual or of select groups of individuals'.[164]

Porton's work is open to several criticisms. First, he used the term 'pronouncement story' in a more restrictive sense than did those who worked on Gospel units. Secondly, two criteria Porton used are clearly based on the pronouncement story as it appears in the context of the Gospels, that is, that such a unit always had as its main interest a 'pronouncer', and that the principal pronouncement should be assigned to only one sage.[165] If the context shifted to a rabbinic halakhic discussion such as one finds in the *Mishnah*, the same criteria do not necessarily hold. The third point of argument with Porton lies in his assertion that tannaitic literature is unconcerned with the personalities of individuals or groups of individuals. While no biographies of early rabbinic masters are preserved,[166] nonetheless, rabbinic literature in general, including the tannaitic stratum, is interested in the 'office' of the rabbi. Jacob Neusner has referred to rabbinic literature's presentation of the rabbi as 'a lawgiver in the model of Moses'.[167] This is done, he noted, in two ways:

> First of all, tales told about rabbis' behavior on specific occasions immediately were translated into rules for the entire community to keep... Second, and far more common, are instances in which the deed of a rabbi is adduced as an authoritative precedent for the law under discussion.[168]

162. Porton, 'Pronouncement Story', p. 84.
163. Porton, 'Pronouncement Story', pp. 89-93.
164. Porton, 'Pronouncement Story', p. 94.
165. These two criteria do not appear in Tannehill's discussion of pronouncement stories. The pronouncement was the focus of Tannehill's units.
166. On this point see Green, 'What's in a Name?'
167. Neusner, *Midrash in Context*, p. 133.
168. Neusner, *Midrash in Context*, pp. 133-34.

Thus, the pronouncement stories confirmed the status of a particular group, the rabbis, even if these anecdotes did not develop individual personalities.[169]

Finally, I take issue with Porton's claim that there are only 24 'pronouncement stories' in tannaitic literature. Chapter 3 shows that within the *Mishnah* alone many more rabbinic anecdotes do indeed exist.

c. *Alan Avery-Peck*

He has written three essays on rabbinic 'pronouncement stories', each of which reflect developments within the scholarship of Vernon Robbins. In his first essay, Avery-Peck accepted Porton's definition of a rabbinic 'pronouncement story' as well as his 24 rabbinic units and classified them according to the typology for pronouncement stories developed by Robbins in his study of Plutarch's *Lives*.[170] Thus the categories he used were 'aphoristic', 'adversative' and 'affirmative' stories. He then studied the type of rhetoric present in each anecdote, employing the Greek and Roman categories of forensic, deliberative or epideictic. Having done so, he affirmed Porton's conclusion that the Gospel anecdotes were not influenced by rabbinic pronouncement stories and added that additional study of rabbinic pronouncement stories is not apt to lead to 'fruitful conclusions regarding either the rabbinic literature or the pronouncement story form in general'.[171]

In 'Rhetorical Analysis of Early Rabbinic Pronouncement Stories', Avery-Peck reconsidered the methods and conclusions of his first essay.[172] He justified this further analysis of rabbinic stories by saying that his prior research was an 'incomplete analysis' since it was based on a typology attentive to only 'a single rhetorical phenomenon in each story'.[173] This time, while he continued to use Porton's 24 rabbinic units, he moved to Tannehill's definition of a pronouncement story and employed Robbins's second typology for Gospel pronouncement stories, which was attentive to

169. On the function of rabbinic anecdotes to underscore the authority of the rabbis, see Alexander, 'Rabbinic Biography and the Biography of Jesus', p. 37.

170. Alan J. Avery-Peck, 'Classifying Early Rabbinic Pronouncement Stories', in Kent H. Richards (ed.), *SBLSP 1983* (SBLSP, 22; Chico, CA: Scholars Press, 1983), pp. 223-44, using Robbins, 'Classifying Pronouncement Stories in Plutarch's *Parallel Lives*'.

171. Avery-Peck, 'Classifying Early Rabbinic Pronouncement Stories', p. 242.

172. Alan J. Avery-Peck, 'Rhetorical Analysis of Early Rabbinic Pronouncement Stories', *HAR* 13 (1991), pp. 1-24.

173. Avery-Peck, 'Rhetorical Analysis', p. 3.

internal rhetorical features of the genre as well as the function of that genre in a larger literary context. Avery-Peck proceeded to classify the rabbinic stories as display, thesis, defense, praise or censure stories. While he found no display stories, the other categories were all represented with most rabbinic units, 19, being either defense, praise or censure stories.[174]

This second analysis led Avery-Peck to conclude that the rabbinic stories (a) contained settings or focused on a particular rabbi only when these matters shed light upon a certain aspect of the legal system, (b) were concerned with the specific ability of a rabbi to 'manipulate and implement' the law, and (c) presented dialogues among persons of equal stature, thereby building up the rabbinic movement itself.[175] This last conclusion directly contradicted his previous contention that the principal pronouncement in the rabbinic story was not part of a dialogue between equals. The weaknesses of this essay are that Avery-Peck continued to use Porton's small sampling of rabbinic units and that he used a typology developed from Greek and Roman literature, and thus his starting point was not within rabbinic argumentation itself.

In his third publication on the topic, Avery-Peck studied the rabbinic anecdotes, the same 24 units, in light of the recent emphasis on the Greek and Roman χρεία among Gospel form critics. In 'Rhetorical Argumentation in Rabbinic Pronouncement Stories', he made mention of the steps in an elaboration of a χρεία as given by Hermogenes. Referring to these steps as a 'taxonomy', apparently of different types of χρεῖαι, he proceeded to classify the rabbinic stories according to these types.[176] While he used the term χρεία, nowhere did he define this term; instead, the author used Tannehill's definition of a pronouncement story for the rabbinic units. Throughout his essay he interchanged the terms χρεία, pronouncement story and anecdote. Furthermore, he never clarified what he meant by the 'expansion' or the 'elaboration' of a χρεία. In fact, he incorrectly referred to the long 'expansion' of a unit, namely *t. Pisha* 4.13, as 'clear elaboration'.[177] In speaking of the Greek and Roman χρεία in a comparison limited to his small sampling of rabbinic units, Avery-Peck did draw a

174. Avery-Peck, 'Rhetorical Analysis', pp. 20-21.

175. Avery-Peck, 'Rhetorical Analysis', pp. 22-23.

176. Alan Avery-Peck, 'Rhetorical Argumentation in Rabbinic Pronouncement Stories', in Vernon K. Robbins (ed.), *The Rhetoric of Pronouncement* (Semeia, 64; Atlanta: Scholars Press, 1993), pp. 49-71 (67).

177. Avery-Peck, 'Rhetorical Argumentation', p. 68. See his analysis of this unit on p. 65.

correct conclusion: 'We find no evidence of significant procedural overlap in the use of the rhetorical form or in the application of a rhetorical method.'[178] However, his own scholarship revealed inadequate knowledge of the Greek and Roman handbook presentations on the χρεία, and this, coupled with his limited number of stories, resulted in the fact that his conclusion did not follow from his presentation.

The work of Porton and Avery-Peck serves to illustrate the contention that the definition of a literary genre taken exclusively from one cultural world, such as that of the Synoptic Gospels, cannot be imposed on narrative units of another cultural world. Instead, there must be a recognition of the movement from one world to another and an adequate cognizance of how literary genres might develop or find expression within separate cultural worlds. The early rabbinic anecdotes need to be investigated as a genre within their own literary world, that is, the form, content and function of the rabbinic anecdote need to be determined within the categories of thought and argumentation of early rabbinic Judaism. Then one can compare the genre 'anecdote' in rabbinic literature with that same genre in the Synoptic Gospels and in a Hellenistic work.

Confirmation of this methodology can be found in the work of Henry Fischel on a comparison of rabbinic, Greek and Christian anecdotes. Unfortunately, in his studies, Fischel, like Bultmann and Daube, used examples from later rabbinic works rather than confining himself to the early tannaitic literature.[179] Due to the late editing of the material Fischel studied, it cannot be assumed that examples of the χρεία-like stories Fischel found in later rabbinic literature actually existed in the tannaitic era. Additionally, Fischel gave no detailed study of an actual tannaitic passage; his only references to the units are in lists of citations. On the other hand, Fischel's work did present elements of a sound methodology that would be helpful if applied to earlier material. He noted that 'the field is wide open' for a study of literary genres in tannaitic literature.[180] Prior to the comparative study of a literary genre as it exists in differing literary

178. Avery-Peck, 'Rhetorical Argumentation', p. 69.

179. Henry A. Fischel, 'A *Chria* on Absentmindedness', pp. 78-89; *idem*, 'Story and History: Observations on Greco-Roman Rhetoric and Pharisaism', in *Essays in Greco-Roman and Related Talmudic Literature* (New York: Ktav, 1977), pp. 443-72; and *idem*, 'Studies in Cynicism and the Ancient Near East: The Transformation of a *Chria*', in J. Neusner (ed.), *Religions in Antiquity: Essays in Memory of Erwin Ramsdell Goodenough* (Leiden: E.J. Brill, 1970), pp. 372-411.

180. Fischel, 'Story and History', p. 73.

worlds, Fischel insisted upon an analysis of that genre within each of the cultural worlds under consideration; moreover, these analyses should be accompanied by an appreciation of what it might mean for one cultural world to adopt a literary genre from a differing cultural world.[181]

Fischel's recommended methodology has been adopted in this book. Chapter 3 undertook an investigation of a literary genre, the anecdote, in a work of tannaitic literature, the *Mishnah*. Chapter 2 studied the anecdote as it is expressed in a Greek work, Lucian's *Demonax*. An examination of the function of anecdotes in a Christian writing, Mark's Gospel, follows in Chapter 5. Having completed the work on the Markan anecdotes, the Conclusion of this book presents the results of a comparative study of the anecdote as it exists in these three differing cultural worlds.

181. Fischel, 'Story and History', pp. 79-85.

Chapter 5

THE ANECDOTE IN THE GOSPEL OF MARK 8.27–10.45: 'ON THE WAY'

'The detachable little stories of which so much of Mark consists'[1] are the focus of this chapter. In the preceding chapters the literary genre 'anecdote' has been defined, its form and function has been studied in both a Greek and a rabbinic text, and the scholarship on the anecdotes of the Synoptic Gospels has been reviewed. The present chapter investigates the anecdote as it appears in Mark's Gospel, particularly in the section from 8.27 to 10.45. The results of the previous chapters are brought to bear on the analyses of both the form and function(s) of these anecdotes and on the comparisons of Markan anecdotes with those of both the *Demonax* and the *Mishnah*.

The methodology of this chapter follows the pattern employed in the study of the anecdotes of both the *Demonax* and the *Mishnah*. First, introductory remarks are presented on the Gospel of Mark, its author, setting and structure. Next the definition of an anecdote used throughout this book is employed to identify the anecdotes in Mk 8.27 to 10.45. Then, since Mark's Gospel is written in Greek, the presentations on the Greek χρεία in the ancient προγυμνάσματα are utilized to investigate the genre of the Gospel anecdotes, as to their form and structural content, for example, whether a Markan anecdote takes the form of a saying-χρεία.

This chapter engages in a formal analysis of the building blocks of discourse, hence 'form' criticism, with attention to the literary context in which those blocks appear, that is, the present text of Mark.[2] Those questions of traditional form criticism (*Formgeschichte*) related to the form, content, function and *Sitz im Leben* of any oral traditions or written

1. R.O.P. Taylor, 'Form-Criticism in the First Centuries', p. 218.

2. See Mark Alan Powell, 'Literary Criticism and Historical Criticism', in *What Is Narrative Criticism?* (Guides to Biblical Scholarship New Testament Series; Minneapolis: Augsburg–Fortress Press, 1990), pp. 6-10.

sources that stand behind the Markan anecdotes are treated only when such questions are relevant to the purposes of this chapter.

The previous studies on the anecdotes of the *Demonax* and those concerning Rabbi Gamaliel II in the *Mishnah* demonstrate that these stories function in various ways. The stories demonstrate how both Demonax and Gamaliel embodied his own teaching; they also provide glimpses of the human characteristics of both Demonax and Gamaliel, at least as far as each was portrayed by Lucian and the compilers of the *Mishnah*, respectively. The anecdotes also fulfill other purposes of the author or compiler(s) of their host works. For example, all of the anecdotes about Rabbi Gamaliel II in the *Mishnah* functioned in some manner as legal arguments. The individual Markan anecdotes likewise express aspects of Mark's portrait of Jesus and the stories are examined for this function. The anecdotes function within the host that is Mark's Gospel, thus the genre of this narrative greatly influences the function of the individual anecdotes. As this chapter argues below, the host genre of Mark's Gospel is taken to be 'an apocalyptic historical monograph'[3] and the anecdotes are investigated within this genre.

Additionally, within the host narrative of the Gospel, several functions of the anecdote relate to the Gospel's having been written to be read aloud to an audience. The section 'From Orality to Literacy' (section 4, pp. 38-50), discussed some aspects of the oral communication process and elements of 'residual orality' present in Mark's Gospel. There it was noted that, according to Eric Havelock, the oral process communicates knowledge in the context of happenings presented and remembered in 'separate, disjunct episodes each complete and satisfying in itself, in a series which is joined together paratactically'.[4] In other words, in an oral culture or a culture of high 'residual orality' traditional information is often transmitted through the narrative of a situation or an event. Joanna Dewey, in her study on the structure of his Gospel, remarks that such 'embedding of teaching in event is characteristic of Mark'.[5] Moreover, as Havelock indicates, the arrangement of an oral narrative contains paratactic structures that set events side by side, rather than structures that subordinate

3. See Collins, 'Is Mark's Gospel a Life of Jesus?', p. 27.

4. Havelock, *Preface to Plato*, p. 180.

5. Joanna Dewey, 'Oral Methods of Structuring Narrative in Mark', p. 35. See also the remarks of Christopher Bryan on 'Orality and Narrative', in *A Preface to Mark: Notes on the Gospel in its Literary and Cultural Settings* (Oxford: Oxford University Press, 1993), pp. 72-73.

one event to another as in a cause and effect relationship. Some chronology as well as cause and effect relationships are found in the arrangements of oral narratives, however, simply because they are narratives.[6] Parataxis, chronology and cause and effect relationships are all present in the arrangement of the Markan narrative, with parataxis appearing as a predominant feature of the Gospel.[7] In an effort to demonstrate an aspect of residual orality in Mark, the translations of the anecdotes below do not seek to smooth out the καὶ-parataxis.

Since an oral performance is such that the hearer cannot go back and review what has gone before, the repetition of significant themes is another important aspect of an oral narrative.[8] One repetitive feature is what Havelock refers to as the 'acoustic echo principle':

> [T]he basic method for assisting the memory to retain a series of distinct meanings is to frame the first of them in a way which will suggest or forecast a later meaning which will recall the first without being identical with it. What is to be said and remembered later is cast in the form of an echo of something said already; the future is encoded in the present. All oral narrative is in structure continually both prophetic and retrospective...[9]

In her work on the structure of Mark's Gospel, Joanna Dewey refers to Havelock's 'prophetic anticipations and retrospective summations'[10] as 'forecasts and echoes'.[11] Forecasts and echoes, as well as other features of residual orality in the anecdotes of Mk 8.27–10.45, are studied when these features are pertinent to the discussion.

6. Bryan, *A Preface to Mark*, p. 74.

7. See BDF, §§458, p. 47, and Nigel Turner, *A Grammar of New Testament Greek*. IV. *Style* (ed. J.H. Moulton and F.W. Howard; 4 vols.; Edinburgh: T. & T. Clark, 1949–76), IV, p. 19. In Mk 8.27–10.52, 21 of the 25 pericopes delineated in NA begin with καὶ-paratactic.

8. Ernest Best, 'Mark's Narrative Technique', *JSNT* 37 (1989), pp. 43-50 (50).

9. Eric A. Havelock, 'Oral Composition in the *Oedipus Tyrannus* of Sophocles', p. 183.

10. Havelock, 'Oral Composition in the *Oedipus Tyrannus* of Sophocles', p. 187.

11. Joanna Dewey, 'Mark as Interwoven Tapestry: Forecasts and Echoes for a Listening Audience'; *idem*, 'Mark as Aural Narrative: Structure as Clues to Understanding', *Sewanee Theological Review* 36 (1992), pp. 45-56; and *idem*, 'The Gospel of Mark as an Oral-Aural Event: Implications for Interpretation', in Elizabeth Struthers Malbon and Edgar V. McKnight (eds.), *The New Literary Criticism and the New Testament* (JSNTSup, 109; Sheffield: Sheffield Academic Press, 1994), pp. 145-63. See also Charles H. Lohr ('Oral Techniques in the Gospel of Matthew', *CBQ* 23 [1961], pp. 403-35), who writes of foreshadowing and retrospection in Matthew (pp. 411-16).

1. *The Gospel of Mark*

The 'Gospel According to Mark', the shortest of the four canonical Gospels, is generally considered to be the earliest Gospel and a source for both Matthew and Luke.[12] Mark's narrative provides no information concerning the identity of its author, nor the place of origin and date of the work; as yet, contemporary New Testament scholars have not reached a consensus on these matters.

Earlier this century there was a general agreement that the Gospel was composed at Rome after the persecution of Christians under Nero in 64 CE but before the destruction of the Temple in 70 CE. Many held that the Gospel was written by the early Christian disciple (John) Mark referred to in Acts (12.12, 25; 15.37) and 1 Pet. 5.13 and that the composition contained the memoirs of the apostle Peter.[13] To a considerable extent, this traditional postion is based on the material contained in the 'Papias fragment' found in Eusebius's *History of the Church*. There Eusebius cited Papias who in turn quoted a 'presbyter' (John) as having said that Mark, while not a disciple of Jesus, was a follower of Peter and his 'translator' or 'interpreter'.[14] Today scholars debate the historical value of the Papias fragment; some hold that it cannot be considered reliable, while others argue for its historicity.[15]

12. In regard to the synoptic problem, this book follows the Two-Source Theory with Markan priority. See Frans Neirynck, 'Synoptic Problem', in R.E. Brown, J.A. Fitzmyer and R.E. Murphy (eds.), *The New Jerome Biblical Commentary* (Englewood Cliffs, NJ: Prentice Hall, 1990), pp. 587-95.

13. See the summary of this position in John R. Donahue, 'The Quest for the Community of Mark's Gospel', in F. Van Segbroeck *et al.* (eds.), *The Four Gospels 1992* (Festschrift Frans Neirynck; BETL, 100; 3 vols.; Leuven: Leuven University Press, 1992), II, pp. 817-18, and Raymond E. Brown, *An Introduction to the New Testament* (Anchor Bible Reference Library; New York: Doubleday, 1997), pp. 158-64.

14. Eusebius, *Hist. Eccl.* 3.39.14-16. See the comments on the growth of the tradition of the identity of Mark and the background of his Gospel in Frank J. Matera, *What Are They Saying about Mark?* (New York: Paulist Press, 1987), pp. 3-5.

15. Among those who dispute the historicity of the Papias fragment are Werner G. Kümmel, *Introduction to the New Testament* (trans. H.C. Kee; Nashville: Abingdon Press, 17th rev. edn, 1975; German, 17th edn, 1973), pp. 95-97, and Kurt Niederwimmer, 'Johannes Markus und die Frage nach dem Verfasser des zweiten Evangeliums', *ZNW* 58 (1967), pp. 172-88. Those who support the historical value of the fragment include Martin Hengel, 'Literary, Theological and Historical Problems in

Given the difficulties with the reliability of the information contained in the Papias fragment as well as the fact that 'Mark' was a common Greek (Μάρκος) and Latin (*Marcus*) name in the ancient world, some scholars conclude that the author was an otherwise unknown early Christian named 'Mark'.[16] Others dispute that 'Mark' was the name of the author and hold rather that the Gospel was originally anonymous and that the name of the actual author is irrecoverable.[17] While acknowledging the disagreement on the identity of the author of the Gospel, I nonetheless employ the name 'Mark' for this author for the sake of expediency. From the Gospel one can assume that Mark was literate in Greek, having had at least the education offered by a grammarian,[18] and that he knew Aramaic, since he cites Aramaic phrases and translates them for his audience or readers (e.g. 5.41).

Contemporary scholars look to the text of Mark's Gospel for internal evidence of its date, place of composition and intended audience. An overview of scholarly opinions is presented here. Among the general features of the Gospel employed to ascertain a date and place for the composition of Mark are the fact that the author was writing for Christians who expected the imminent parousia (13.24-31), had experienced or knew of persecution (4.17; 9.1; 10.38; 13.9), were acquainted with Christians who had failed during a time of trial (4.16-17; 8.38; 14.27), and needed to be warned of false messiahs (13.6, 21-22). These features of the narrative,

the Gospel of Mark', in *Studies in the Gospel of Mark* (trans. John Bowden; Philadelphia: Fortress Press, 1985; German original, 1983), pp. 45-53, and Robert Gundry, *Mark: A Commentary on his Apology for the Cross* (Grand Rapids, MI: Eerdmans, 1993), pp. 1026-45. A summary of the arguments is found in C. Clifton Black, *Mark: Images of an Apostolic Interpreter* (ed. D. Moody Smith; Studies in Personalities of the New Testament; Columbia, SC: University of South Carolina Press, 1994), pp. 82-94, and John R. Donahue, 'The Quest for the Community of Mark's Gospel', pp. 817-19, along with the works cited there. See also Donahue's 'Windows and Mirrors: The Setting of Mark's Gospel', *CBQ* 57 (1995), pp. 1-26. Pieter J.J. Botha ('The Historical Setting of Mark's Gospel: Problems and Possibilities', *JSNT* 51 [1993], pp. 35-37) adds a further caution in regard to the use of Papias, i.e., one must be aware that 'Papias says only what Eusebius wants him to say' (p. 36).

16. See, for example, Martin Hengel ('The Gospel of Mark: Time of Origin and Situation', in *Studies in the Gospel of Mark*, pp. 28-30) who argues for the reliability of the name 'Mark' for the actual author of the gospel.

17. For the argument concerning anonymity, see, for example, Kümmel, *Introduction to the New Testament*, pp. 95-97, and Philipp Vielhauer, *Geschichte der urchristlichen Literatur: Einleitung in das Neue Testament, die Apokryphen und die Apostolischen Väter* (Berlin: W. de Gruyter, 1975), pp. 346-47.

18. See the remarks, in this chapter below, on Mark's use of the χρεία.

along with historical allusions in ch. 13, lead scholars to conclude that Mark's Gospel was written to address a situation during the Jewish War in the late sixties or immediately after the destruction of the Jerusalem Temple in 70 CE.

The context in which the Gospel was written and Mark's intended audience need not be identical. While Mark may have been a member of a particular Christian community and hence his work may reflect, to a certain degree, the experiences of that community, this does not imply that Mark's intended audience was necessarily limited to that community. Mary Ann Tolbert writes that Mark's Gospel was written for a wider audience of individual Christians who were experiencing persecution and for interested outsiders and their persuasion.[19] Pieter Botha, arguing from the perspective of studies on oral literature, also would not necessarily limit Mark's Gospel to one intended audience. He notes the residual orality of the Markan text and contends that the Gospel should be viewed as 'oral traditional literature...performed in many contexts'.[20]

Richard Bauckham has argued recently that each evangelist 'expected his work to circulate widely among the churches, had no particular Christian audience in view, but envisaged as his audience any church (or any church in which Greek was understood) to which his work might find its way'.[21] Bauckham gives the following arguments for his thesis: the early Christian movement was a network of communities in close and constant contact with each other; early Christians had a strong sense of participation in a worldwide movement; early Christian leaders traveled widely and worked in more than one community; early Christian literature did in fact circulate broadly; there is concrete evidence for close contact between churches in the time period during which the Gospels were written; and that conflict and rivalry between early Christians leaders took place across the network of Christian communication.[22]

There are weaknesses in Bauckham's arguments.[23] First, he too easily equates the four evangelists with the traveling preachers, teachers and

19. Mary Ann Tolbert, *Sowing the Gospel*, p. 304.

20. Botha, 'The Historical Setting of Mark's Gospel', p. 54.

21. Richard Bauckham, 'For Whom Were Gospels Written?', in *The Gospels for All Christians: Rethinking the Gospel Audiences* (Grand Rapids, MI: Eerdmans, 1998), pp. 9-48 (11).

22. Bauckham, 'For Whom Were Gospels Written?', pp. 3, 32-44.

23. Space in this book does not allow for a full critique of Bauckham's thesis. Four weaknesses are discussed here.

leaders of the early Christian communities; Bauckham presents no evidence that any of the four Gospel writers did, in fact, travel.[24] Secondly, Bauckham compares the Gospels with the letters of Paul and argues that since the evangelists were resident teachers of a community, 'An evangelist writing his Gospel (for his community) is like Paul writing 1 Corinthians while permanently resident in Corinth.'[25] Nonetheless, Bauckham uses the broad circulation of these same letters of Paul (and those of Ignatius of Antioch)[26] throughout the churches as an argument for his thesis that the Gospels were intended for a wide audience. Thirdly, Bauckham does not allow for the possibility that an evangelist, while being aware that his work could or would circulate throughout all the churches of the late first century CE, nonetheless intended his Gospel primarily for a specific Christian community or group of communities of a particular geographic area. Likewise, Bauckham's thesis does not allow the additional possibility that while an evangelist intended his message for a wide audience, his expectations of that audience may well have been formed by his own immediate context. While not proving that any of the evangelists wrote for a broad audience, Bauckham has nonetheless raised this important possibility.

General features of the Gospel that would support a broad audience include the fact that the Gospel was written in Greek, a common tongue throughout the world of the early Christians. Moreover, Mark translates Aramaic phrases and does not assume that his hearers know that language. While Mark assumed that his hearers knew of the Scriptures and understood terms coming from Judaism, for example, 'Gehenna' and 'rabbi', yet he explained some Pharasaic customs, such as the purification of hands (7.3-4). Hence, the Gospel would be intelligible to Greek-speaking, Gentile or Jewish Christians anywhere in the Roman empire who had been evangelized by Christians somewhat familiar with Jewish Scripture and traditions. These features alone, however, do not necessarily imply the broad audience for Mark's Gospel that is claimed by Bauckham. It seems best to distinguish between a specific context or place for the composition of the Gospel and its intended audience, whether this audience was specific or more broadly conceived.

There is no general agreement on a place, or context, of composition for

24. Bauckham, 'For Whom Were Gospels Written?', pp. 33-38, esp. pp. 37-38.
25. Bauckham, 'For Whom Were Gospels Written?', p. 29.
26. Bauckham, 'For Whom Were Gospels Written?', pp. 38 and 40-42, respectively.

Mark's Gospel.[27] Those who argue for a geographical origin other than Rome generally place the Gospel's origin in the region of Syria or Palestine.[28] For example, Willi Marxsen, asserting the theological importance of Galilee in the Gospel, would see Mark as having been composed in Galilee between 67 and 69 CE,[29] while Howard Kee uses Mark's imprecise geographical references to argue for the Gospel's composition in a rural region of Syria between 66 and 70 CE.[30] On the other hand, Gerd Theissen places Mark in southern Syria after 70 CE[31] and Joel Marcus traces the work to a Transjordanian, Hellenistic city shortly after the destruction of the Temple in 70 CE.[32] Adela Y. Collins argues from historical allusions to messianic pretenders and false prophets in Mk 13.6, 21-22 for a setting in the general area of Syria Palestine after the time of the messianic leader Menahem, that is, between 66 and 70 CE.[33]

Meanwhile, contemporary scholars have not ruled out Rome as the place of composition of Mark's narrative. For example, Donald Senior, emphasizing Mark's rejection of Rome's use of abusive power, accepts the Roman origin of Mark.[34] C. Clifton Black discusses a reconstruction of

27. Not all of the scholars mentioned in the following discussion distinguish between the gospel's place of origin and its intended audience.

28. See the summaries of the arguments for the different geographical locations of Mark's Gospel in W.R. Telford, *Mark* (New Testament Guides; Sheffield: Sheffield Academic Press, 1995), pp. 23-26, and Matera, *What Are They Saying about Mark?*, pp. 7-15.

29. Willi Marxsen, *Mark the Evangelist: Studies on the Redaction History of the Gospel* (trans. James Boyce; Philadelphia: Fortress Press, 1969; German 2nd edn, 1959), pp. 54-116, esp. 92-95.

30. Howard C. Kee, *Community of the New Age: Studies in Mark's Gospel* (Philadelphia: Westminster Press, 1977), pp. 101-105 (repr. Macon, GA: Mercer Press, 1983).

31. Gerd Theissen, *The Gospels in Context: Social and Political History in the Synoptic Tradition* (trans. Linda M. Maloney; Philadelphia: Fortress Press, 1991; German original, 1989), pp. 236-71.

32. Joel Marcus, 'The Jewish War and the Sitz im Leben of Mark', *JBL* 111 (1992), pp. 441-62.

33. Adela Yarbro Collins, 'The Apocalyptic Rhetoric of Mark 13 in Historical Context', *BR* 41 (1996), pp. 5-36, and 'Mark 13: An Apocalyptic Discourse', in *The Beginning of the Gospel: Probings of Mark in Context* (Philadelphia: Fortress Press, 1992), pp. 73-91 (repr. of 'The Eschatological Discourse of Mark 13', in F. Van Segbroeck *et al.* [eds.], *The Four Gospels 1992* [Festschrift Frans Neirynck; BETL, 100; 3 vols.; Leuven: University Press, 1992], II, pp. 1125-40).

34. Donald Senior, '"With Swords and Clubs...": The Setting of Mark's Community and His Critique of Abusive Power', *BTB* 17 (1987), pp. 10-20.

first-century Roman Christianity and concludes that there existed 'an appreciable social, religious, and theological congruence' between the community addressed by Mark's Gospel and the Christian community at Rome.[35] For Black, a Roman provenance for Mark is, 'if not proven, then at least not improbable'.[36]

One concludes, therefore, that Mark was written sometime between 66 CE and the early seventies either in Rome or in the region of Syria Palestine and was intended for a specific Christian community or group of communities, or, possibly, for all Christians of that time. While not adding to this scholarly discussion on the date, place of origin and intended audience of Mark's Gospel, the present study reinforces aspects of Mark's concept of Christian discipleship, especially the experience or expectation of persecution and the recognition of Jesus as the true Messiah.

The function of an oral or literary genre as 'a principle of meaning' was discussed in Chapter 1. There it was pointed out that an understanding of the genre of a text provides readers or hearers with an interpretive context within which to evaluate the functions of the various elements of that text and thereby arrive at the meaning of the text. Until recently, many New Testament scholars theorized that the term 'Gospel', when used in reference to one of the four canonical Gospels, describes a unique literary genre that developed out of the oral kerygma of the Christian community. The Gospels were viewed as an expanded, written form of this kerygma.[37]

More recently, scholars investigate literature contemporary with the written Gospels for generic parallels to them.[38] Several Greek and Roman literary genres have been proposed as the ancient model followed by Mark;[39] the one most often suggested is the Greco-Roman biography.[40]

35. C. Clifton Black, 'Was Mark a Roman Gospel?', *ExpTim* 105 (1993), pp. 36-40 (39).

36. Black, 'Was Mark a Roman Gospel?', p. 40.

37. For example, Bultmann, *The History of the Synoptic Tradition*, pp. 347-48, and Kümmel, *Introduction to the New Testament*, p. 37. For a summary of this theory see David E. Aune, *The New Testament in its Literary Environment*, pp. 23-25, and A.Y. Collins, 'Is Mark's Gospel a Life of Jesus?', pp. 6-10.

38. Much earlier, C.W. Votaw had argued that the Gospels were a form of Greek and Roman popular biography ('The Gospels and Contemporary Biographies', *AJT* 19 [1915], pp. 45-73, 217-49 [reprinted as *The Gospels and Contemporary Biographies in the Greco-Roman World* (Facet Book; Philadelphia: Fortress Press, 1970)]). As Ralph Martin notes, 'Votaw's plea went largely ignored' (*Mark: Evangelist and Theologian* [Grand Rapids, MI: Zondervan, 1972], p. 20).

39. For a summary of these proposals see Telford, *Mark*, pp. 94-100.

One scholar who pursues this model is David Aune.[41] He asserts that the genre 'Greco-Roman biography', while a single genre, exhibits variety in its content, form and function; this variety accounts for the genre's various expressions.[42] The contents of Greco-Roman biographies differ since they present 'an account of the stylized career and significance of a variety of public types of personalities'.[43] With regard to form, Aune maintains that the biographies do not display a set form but rather a 'spectrum' of options for form, that is, from continuous narrative to episodic narrative, chronological narration to topical exposition,[44] elevated to popular diction, and periodic style to paratactic style.[45] Finally, these biographies served as powerful tools of propaganda since their function included 'the historical legitimation (or discrediting) of a social belief/value system personified in the subject of the biography'.[46] To this end, many Greco-Roman biographies were encomiastic and presented the subject as a paradigm of virtue, thus serving a didactic function. One such encomiastic and didactic biography is Lucian's *Demonax*, studied in Chapter 2.

Applying this understanding of Greco-Roman biographies to Mark's Gospel, Aune classifies the Gospel under a subtype of these biographies, a subtype determined by its content, that is, its Judeo-Christian assump-

40. For example, R. Burridge, *What Are the Gospels?*; Bryan, *A Preface to Mark*, pp. 9-64; and Cancik, 'Die Gattung Evangelium' and 'Bios und Logos'. Cancik did conclude that a decision on the genre of Mark was influenced by the background of the hearer, that is, those well-versed in Jewish literature would have considered it to be a prophetic book, while those familiar with Greco-Roman biographies would have perceived it as such a work ('Die Gattung Evangelium', pp. 94-98, 110).

41. David Aune, *The New Testament in its Literary Environment*, pp. 17-76, and 'Greco-Roman Biography', pp. 107-26. In his studies, Aune concentrates on Mark as a Greco-Roman biography but also classifies Matthew and John as examples of this genre (*The New Testament in its Literary Environment*, p. 77, and 'Greco-Roman Biography', p. 122). At times Aune refers to the Gospel of Luke as an ancient biography ('Greco-Roman Biography', p. 122), but he also argues that the Gospel must be considered along with Acts as constituting a single two-volume historical work. Hence, Luke's Gospel is a history and 'does not belong to a type of ancient biography for it belongs with Acts, and Acts cannot be forced into a biographical mold' (*The New Testament in its Literary Environment*, p. 77).

42. Aune, *The New Testament in its Literary Environment*, p. 32.

43. Aune, *The New Testament in its Literary Environment*, pp. 32-33.

44. Aune's 'chronological narration' and 'topical exposition' match Friedrich Leo's (*Die griechisch-römische Biographie*) two types of ancient biographies.

45. Aune, *The New Testament in its Literary Environment*, p. 35.

46. Aune, *The New Testament in its Literary Environment*, p. 35.

tions.[47] Such content, with its focus on Jesus of Nazareth, differentiated Mark from other Greco-Roman biographies. In form and function, however, Aune claims that these biographies and the Gospel are similar.[48] The form of Mark, for Aune, is a chronologically ordered biography in a popular literary style.[49] The Gospels, in general, functioned to legitimate 'the present beliefs and practices of Christians by appealing to the paradigmatic role of the founder, just as the cultural values of the Hellenistic world were exemplified by the subjects of the Greco-Roman biographies'.[50] Elsewhere, Aune asserted that the primary function of Mark's Gospel was 'the *historical legitimation* of the saving significance of Jesus'.[51] Unfortunately, Aune did not discuss the relationship between this primary function of Mark and the function of the Gospels in general.

In her essay, 'Is Mark's Gospel a Life of Jesus? The Question of Genre', Adela Yarbro Collins refers to Mark's 'vision of the significance of God's activity in Jesus for history and for the world'.[52] Collins allows that while major themes or biographical interests, such as the 'identity of Jesus and the proper understanding of that identity' and Jesus' role as a model for his followers, are present in the Gospel, Mark is not intended primarily as a life of Jesus modeled on Greek and Roman biographies. Rather, for Collins, Mark's Gospel is 'an apocalyptic historical monograph'.[53]

After noting many of the differences between Mark and Greek and Roman biographies,[54] Collins turns to the relationship of history and biography in the ancient world. She refers to Charles Talbert's discussion of those literary works in which history and biography are closely related.[55] Sallust's *Catiline* is such a work. The aim of this work is to recount political events associated with Catiline; thus, *Catiline* 'belongs to the genre "history" even though it concentrates on an individual'.[56]

47. Aune, *The New Testament in its Literary Environment*, pp. 46-47.

48. Aune, 'Greco-Roman Biography', p. 122.

49. Aune, *The New Testament in its Literary Environment*, p. 47.

50. Aune, 'Greco-Roman Biography', p. 122.

51. Aune, *The New Testament in its Literary Environment*, p. 25.

52. Collins, 'Is Mark's Gospel a Life of Jesus?', p. 37.

53. Collins, 'Is Mark's Gospel a Life of Jesus?', pp. 25-27.

54. See Collins's critique of many aspects of Aune's argument for Mark as a Greco-Roman biography in 'Is Mark's Gospel a Life of Jesus?', pp. 17-27.

55. Charles Talbert, 'Once Again: Gospel Genre', in Mary Gerhart and James G. Williams (eds.), *Genre, Narrativity and Theology* (Semeia, 43; Atlanta: Scholars Press, 1988), pp. 53-73.

56. Collins, 'Is Mark's Gospel a Life of Jesus?', p. 27.

Arguing that Mark is analogous to *Catiline*, Collins states:

> Mark focuses on Jesus and his identity not in the interest of establishing his character or essence but in order to write a particular kind of history. This type of history may be defined as a narration of the course of the eschatological events. These events began with the appearance of John the Baptist, continued with the baptism of Jesus and with his activity of teaching, healing, and exorcising, came to a climax with his arrest and crucifixion, continued with his resurrection, and at the time of writing are not yet complete.[57]

Moreover, at the outset of the Gospel, 1.1-3, 14-15, Mark recounts the beginning of the fulfillment of promises; hence, the evangelist 'implies that the life of Jesus is a key part of the history of salvation'.[58] As Collins further argues, Mark was not the first in the Israelite literary tradition to treat history from an apocalyptic point of view. Portions of *1 Enoch*, *The Apocalypse of Weeks* and *The Animal Apocalypse*, as well as the book of Daniel also do so in massive and obvious ways.[59] Mark's historical monograph on Jesus adopts an analogous perspective. The arguments that Adela Collins puts forth are convincing. My investigation therefore takes the genre of Mark to be an historical monograph in the apocalyptic mode and such a genre is the interpretive context within which Mk 8.27–10.45 is studied in the discussion below.

Finally, the delineation of Mk 8.27–10.45 as a discernible section of the gospel requires some comment. A survey of Markan studies yields a variety of different schemas for the structure of Mark, to cite Robert Gundry, 'Modern outlines of Mark are legion...'[60] For example, in *The End of Mark's Story*, Paul Danove demonstrates how different criteria yield different outlines of Mark.[61] Danove provides six examples of different schemata each of which is based on a different set of criteria, that is, geographic,[62] theological,[63] thematic,[64] geographical and literary,[65] and

57. Collins, 'Is Mark's Gospel a Life of Jesus?', p. 27.

58. Collins, 'Is Mark's Gospel a Life of Jesus?', pp. 21, 36-37.

59. Collins, 'Is Mark's Gospel a Life of Jesus?', pp. 27-34.

60. Gundry, *Mark*, p. 1046.

61. Paul L. Danove, *The End of Mark's Story: A Methodological Study* (Biblical Interpretation Series, 3; Leiden: E.J. Brill, 1993), pp. 90-93.

62. Taylor, *The Gospel According to St. Mark*, pp. 107-11.

63. Walter Grundmann, *Das Evangelium nach Markus* (Berlin: Evangelische Verlagsanstalt, 1959), pp. 12-15.

64. Hugh Anderson, *The Gospel of Mark* (London: Marshall, Morgan & Scott, 1976), pp. 56-58.

theological, thematic and geographic.[66] One of these schemata contains 8.27–10.45 as a discrete section,[67] four have 8.27–10.52,[68] and the remaining schema has 8.27–13.37.[69] Joanna Dewey also notes the many outlines of Mark and observes that of the 17 outlines she compared, 14 delineated a distinct section in the middle of the Gospel beginning at either 8.22 or 8.27 and ending with 10.45 or 10.52.[70]

Dewey's work on the residual orality of the Markan narrative provides a plausible reason for the variety of proposals for the structure of Mark. She argues that the Gospel has a nonlinear, recursive compositional style, characteristic of 'aural' narrative, and that the gospel therefore 'does not have a single structure made up of discrete sequential units but rather is…made up of multiple overlapping structures and sequences, forecasts of what is to come and echoes of what has already been said'.[71] Dewey notes, however, that Mark contains interconnections that remind a hearer of other parts of the Gospel, for example, setting, geography, form-critical types, key words, inclusions and frames. These means of interconnection can form '*congruent* patterns of repetition [so that] the structure of the episode, section, or Gospel will be clearly defined, delimited, and recognized by the hearer/reader'.[72]

From this perspective, the two healings of the blind in Mk 8.22-26 and 10.46-52, since they are of the same 'form-critical type', the miracle story, as well as the only two cures of blindness in Mark, form a frame around 8.27–10.45. The two pericopes also echo and foreshadow other Markan material. For example, the cure of 8.22-26 in portraying Jesus' use of spittle (8.23) recalls Jesus' act of spitting during the healing of the deaf and speech-impaired man found in 7.31-37. On the other hand, the cure of blind Bartimaeus in 10.46-52 reminds one of the previous two-stage

65. Bas van Iersel, *Reading Mark* (trans. W.H. Bisscheroux; Collegeville, MN: Liturgical Press, 1988; Dutch original, 1986), p. 20, and Augustine Stock, *The Method and Message of Mark* (Wilmington, DE: Michael Glazier, 1989), p. 28.

66. Eduard Schweizer, *The Good News According to Mark* (trans. Donald H. Madvig; Richmond, VA: John Knox Press, 1962), pp. 226, 284, 384-85.

67. That is, von Iersel, *Reading Mark*.

68. That is, Taylor, *The Gospel According to St. Mark*; Anderson, *The Gospel of Mark*; Stock, *The Method and Message of Mark*; and Schweizer, *The Good News According to Mark*.

69. Grundmann, *Das Evangelium nach Markus*.

70. Dewey, 'Mark as Interwoven Tapestry', p. 221.

71. Dewey, 'Mark as Interwoven Tapestry', p. 224.

72. Dewey, 'Mark as Interwoven Tapestry', p. 225.

healing of the blind man in 8.22-26. Dewey herself remarks that one of the overlapping structures in which these two passages participate is the opening and closing of a frame around the section 8.27–10.45.[73]

Another means of interconnection for 8.27–10.45 is the keyword ὁδός, which occurs throughout the section (8.27; 9.33, 34; 10.32). Danove studies the 'narrative emplotment' or 'frames' of ὁδός in the Markan narrative and concludes that the use of this term in the Gospel prior to 8.27 establishes the term ὁδός as an 'appropriate vehicle' for the developments within the story found in 8.27–10.52. For example, the use of ὁδός in the parable of the sower in 4.4 and 4.15 indicates the potential for failure among those who hear the words of Jesus. The use of ἐν τῇ ὁδῷ in 8.3 again indicates that 'on the way' is a potential 'place of fainting' or failure.[74] This foreshadows the disciples' failure to understand after each passion prediction within 8.27–10.45. A failure on the part of disciples is also alluded to in 8.35, 'the one who would save one's life, will lose it', and in 8.38, 'whoever is ashamed of me and of my words'. Secondly, in 6.8, the twelve are told to take only a staff, sandals and one tunic for their journey (ὁδός). This lack of worldly goods is echoed in 10.17-22. There, as Jesus starts out 'on (his) way', a potential disciple of Jesus asks what he must do to gain eternal life. He is told to sell all before following Jesus. Finally, ὁδός appears early in the Gospel in the story of the disciples' picking grain on the Sabbath (2.23-28). This narrative opens with the disciples 'making their way', ὁδὸν ποιεῖν, through the grainfields and ends with Jesus' use of the title 'Son of Man'. Within the section 8.27–10.45 this title appears seven times (8.31, 38; 9.9, 12, 31; 10.33, 45). The third passion prediction (10.32-34) occurs ἐν τῇ ὁδῷ ἀναβαίνοντες εἰς Ἱεροσόλυμα, 'on the way, going up to Jerusalem', and in this passage Jesus once more refers to himself as the 'Son of Man' (10.33). Thus, prior to 8.27, the word ὁδός is connected with the Markan themes of discipleship failure, voluntary lack of worldly possessions and the 'Son of Man'. All three of these themes are developed in close association with the key word ὁδός within 8.27–10.45.

The presence of ἐν τῇ ὁδῷ at the conclusion of the Bartimaeus narrative accounts for the pericope's inclusion within a delineated section (8.27–10.52) in many outlines of Mark. This passage (10.46-52) is an excellent example of a unit that functions in 'overlapping structures'. In the pericope Mark presents a disciple who recovers his sight and who follows

73. Dewey, 'Mark as Interwoven Tapestry', pp. 230-31.

74. Danove, *The End of Mark's Story*, pp. 94-97.

Jesus 'on the way'. Metaphorically this cure of blindness is connected to the theme of the lack of understanding on the part of the disciples that begins with the parable of the sower in 4.3-9. After the parable, the disciples ask Jesus for a private explanation of its meaning. (Twice within 8.27–10.45 the disciples also ask for private explanations, that is, in 9.28-29 when they were unable to perform an exorcism and at 10.10-12 when they inquire about Jesus' teaching on divorce.) In his response, 4.10-20, Jesus first refers to 'outsiders' and, in a paraphrase of Isa. 6.9, connects seeing (βλέπωσιν) and not perceiving (ἴδωσιν) and hearing (ἀκούωσιν) and not understanding (συνιῶσιν) (4.12). Jesus then asks his disciples, 'Do you not understand [οἴδατε] this parable?' (4.13). Jesus explains that the 'seed' in the parable of the sower symbolizes 'the word' (4.14). Thus, for Mark seeing and hearing are metaphors for knowing and understanding the word. As already noted, the two healings of blindness in 8.22-26 and 10.46-52 frame the section of Mark under discussion. Just before the two-stage cure of the blind man at Bethsaida, Jesus had asked his disciples, 'Do you not yet understand [συνίετε]?' (8.21) in reference to their lack of bread and the previous feeding of four thousand people. Thus, Bartimaeus, who recovers his sight in the second healing story, symbolizes a disciple who sees and understands 'the word'. This is true not only of all that precedes this section of the gospel, but especially of 'the word' that is taught between the two healings of blindness, including the self-denial and acceptance of the cross (8.27) that Jesus demands of a follower who is not ashamed of him and of 'his words' (8.38).

The phrase ἐν τῇ ὁδῷ in 10.52 also echoes its last occurrence in the opening of 10.32. The ἐν τῇ ὁδῷ of 10.52 ends the verse forming an *inclusio* with 10.32; thus, the use of this phrase emphasizes that following 'on the way' involves both the recognition of Jesus as the suffering Son of Man and servant discipleship, the content of 10.32-52. Moreover, in 10.32, 'on the way' is further specified as 'going up to Jerusalem'. After the use of the phrase in 10.52, one hears that Jesus and the disciples are now 'near Jerusalem' (11.1). Hence, the phrase ἐν τῇ ὁδῷ in 10.52 connects the preceding material with the remainder of the Gospel narrative that takes place in or near Jerusalem. The use of ἐν τῇ ὁδῷ of 10.52 therefore need not signal the conclusion of the section. Since 10.46-52 is involved in many overlapping structures it is better seen as both a frame around 8.27–10.45 and as a transitional passage.[75]

75. For example, see the outline of Mark's structure by von Iersel (*Reading Mark*, p. 20).

Finally, if one considers the mechanics of an oral performance of Mark's Gospel, one can hear a natural break before 8.27 and another after 10.45. The pericope that precedes 8.27, that is, 8.22-26, closes with the command of Jesus, 'Do not even enter the village!' In 8.27, on the other hand, the narrator begins a new scene with, 'And Jesus went out with his disciples…' In a similar way, 10.45 closes with the Markan Jesus' comment on the meaning of his approaching death, 'For the Son of Man also came not to be served but to serve and to give his life as a ransom for many.' The next pericope switches the scene with the narrative comment, 'And they came to Jericho…' To be effective in his or her reading for an audience, a narrator would have to pause, at least momentarily, and alter her or his voice in some manner to change from speaking the words of Jesus to the words of a narrator. While this pause and voice change would occur also between other verses in the material from 8.27 to 10.45, for example, between 9.1 and 9.2, the presence of this vocal mechanic both before 8.27 and after 10.45 adds weight to the previous arguments that 8.27–10.45 can be considered a section of the Markan Gospel.[76] Moreover, a further argument that 10.52 is not the conclusion of a section of Mark can be made from the fact that no such voice change is necessary between 10.52 and 11.1.

Mark 8.27–10.45 opens with the identification of Jesus as Messiah by Peter (8.27-30) and the remainder of the section follows with Jesus' first prediction of his passion, death and resurrection (8.31-33). Two other such predictions by Jesus occur in 9.30-32 and 10.32-34. Moreover, each passion prediction by Jesus is followed by a misunderstanding by the disciples (8.32b-34; 9.33-34; 10.35-41) and a resulting teaching on discipleship from Jesus (8.34–9.1; 9.35-50; 10.42-44). The repetition of this threefold pattern gives a recognizable structure to and links all of the material in 8.31–10.45. Furthermore, the teaching in 8.31 that 'the Son of Man must suffer many things' is echoed in 'the Son of Man came…to give his life as a ransom for many' in 10.45. The two references to the suffering Son of Man form an inclusion further linking the material between 8.31–10.45.

Following these introductory comments on the Gospel of Mark, its setting and genre, as well as the section from 8.27 to 10.45, the focus of this chapter turns to an investigation of the anecdotes in this Markan section.

76. See the comments by Ernest Best on the devices open to speakers in order to delineate sections of narrative material ('Mark's Narrative Technique', p. 47).

2. *Anecdotes in Mark 8.27–10.45*

The identification of the anecdotes within Mk 8.27–10.45 makes use of the definition of an anecdote developed in Chapter 1, that is, an anecdote is

> a brief narrative, either oral or written, describing an incident, including its setting, which involves one or more persons and which focuses on an action, saying, or dialogue; the function of an anecdote is to entertain, instruct, relate an historical incident, characterize a person, or authoritatively legitimate a specific opinion, a specific practice, or a broader view of reality.

Since Mark's Gospel is written in Greek, the analysis of the anecdotes also utilizes the definition of the Greek χρεία as stated by Theon, that is, 'a concise statement or action which is attributed with aptness to some specified character or to something analogous to a character (3.2-3)'.[77] In his Προγυμνάσματα, Theon presented two typologies for the χρεία. His first typology was useful in the study of the anecdotes in the *Demonax*; the Markan anecdotes can also be categorized according to the same classification. The typology is as follows:

χρειαι

- A. Saying-χρεία
  - 1. Statement
    - a. unprompted
    - b. from a specific situation
  - 2. Response
    - a. to a simple question
    - b. to an inquiry
    - c. to a question calling for an explanatory response
    - d. to a remark
  - 3. Double χρεία
- B. Action-χρεία
  - 1. active
  - 2. passive
- C. Mixed-χρεία

The Markan anecdotes in the following study are identified using the definition of an anecdote and then the form of each anecdote is analyzed in relationship to the genre χρεία. Thus, Mk 8.27–10.45 contains the follow-

77. Citations of Theon are from Butts, 'The "Progymnasmata" of Theon'.

ing 14 anecdotes: (1) 8.27-30, Peter's confession; (2) 8.31-33, the first passion prediction and misunderstanding; (3) 8.34–9.1, the teaching on discipleship; (4) 9.28-29, a private explanation; (5) 9.33-42, 50d, teaching on discipleship; (6) 9.38-40, forbidding the other exorcist; (7) 10.2-9, the teaching on divorce; (8) 10.10-12, a private teaching; (9) 10.13-16, the blessing of children; (10) 10.17-22, the rich man; (11) 10.23-30, riches and the kingdom; (12) 10.32-34, the third passion prediction; (13) 10.35-40, the request of James and John; and (14) 10.41-45, the reaction of the ten.

3. *Form of the Anecdotes in Mark 8.27–10.45*

A discussion of the form of each anecdote is presented here. Those anecdotes that are χρεῖαι are classified according to Theon's typology, if possible.

a. *8.27-30: Peter's Confession*

The section of Mark from 8.27 to 10.45 opens with a story containing a dialogue. This passage, 8.27-30, often referred to as 'Peter's Confession', is unique among the anecdotes of this section in that it is the only story in which the central statement is made by a character other than Jesus. It is Peter's statement, 'You are the Messiah', that climaxes the dialogue in the anecdote. Jesus elicits this response with his questions and accepts the identification as the Messiah since he does not correct Peter as he does the rich man who calls him 'Good' in 10.18. Moreover, Jesus instructs the disciples not to speak to anyone about him which presumes that he accepts the designation.

The elements of the dialogue in this anecdote are that of a general question posed by Jesus to the disciples (v. 27c), their response (v. 28), a specific question from Jesus (v. 29a) and a response by Peter (v. 29b). The disciples' response to the general question (v. 28) is a summary of Mark's comments in 6.14-16. There, in his introduction to the story of Herod's execution of John the Baptist, Mark notes that Herod had heard of Jesus, since people were saying that Jesus was John raised from the dead or Elijah or a prophet.[78] The repetition of this material in 8.28 raises the question whether the author of Mark has expanded an originally briefer dialogue. Such a brief dialogue may have been a saying-χρεία about Peter and might

78. For comments on Jesus' association with John the Baptist and the social role of Jesus as 'popular prophet' within an eschatological framework, see Adela Yarbro Collins, 'Jesus the Prophet', *BibRes* 36 (1991), pp. 30-34.

have read: 'When Jesus asked the disciples, "Who do you say that I am?" Peter answered, "You are the Messiah."' The existence prior to Mark of such a brief dialogue is speculative;[79] however, considering the possibility enables one to see how Mark may have included 'echoes' of past material, particularily echoes of the fate of John the Baptist, in the present text.

Verse 30, 'And he sternly ordered them to tell no one about him', recounts an after-effect of Peter's statement and reveals the form of the story to be that of a διήγημα. In his Προγυμνάσματα, Theon devoted his fifth chapter to the διήγημα. There he defined the διήγημα as 'an explanatory account of matters which have occurred or as if they occurred' (5.2-3).[80] James Butts translates διήγημα as 'narrative'. However, I use the term 'narrative' to refer to both Mark's Gospel as a whole and to individual anecdotes. In Chapter 1, a 'narrative' was defined as an 'account of events'. A distinction was made between a 'simple narrative', which describes events chronologically, and 'narratives with a plot', whose development is based on some element of the plot. I noted that an anecdote, a 'simple narrative', is an account of a single incident and lacks a plot. As will be shown below the διήγημα has a plot, that is, an outline of events. Thus, since the term 'narrative' does not describe a precise entity, the Greek term διήγημα is employed, without English translation, in my study to clarify that a reference is being made to Theon's 'explanatory account'.

Theon presented ten exercises with the διήγημα, one being that of 'changing the order of the principal events' (5.229). His discussion of this exercise clearly indicates that the διήγημα is composed of three elements, that is, the beginning, middle and final portions (5.237-39). An example of a διήγημα from the writings of Herodotus (*Hist.* 3.1) was included by Theon, which he paraphrased as follows: the king of the Persians had an eye-problem and

79. Throughout the analyses of the Markan anecdotes, briefer forms of the anecdotes will be suggested. These suggestions are not meant to imply that such shorter versions actually existed; rather, the procedure is a heuristic technique intended to aid in the analyses of particular anecdotes.

80. Theon uses διήγημα and διήγησις interchangeably (5.2, 4) and in an earlier chapter (1.26-29) he indicated that he did not accept a distinction between the two terms. However, the term διήγησις was used by others to designate the 'statement of facts' section of a rhetorical speech (LSJ, p. 427, col. 1). Cicero's definition of the *narratio* (διήγησις) of a speech reads: 'The narrative is an exposition of events that have occurred or are supposed to have occurred' (*Inv.* 1.29.27). Theon intended his elementary exercise with the διήγημα to prepare students to produce the 'statement of facts' section of the rhetorical speech (1.26-28).

> he sent to Egypt and requested an eye-doctor from the one who was king there. [And] the king of Egypt sent an Egyptian man [doctor]. The doctor, angry at being deprived of his wife and children, avenged himself on the one who had sent him away by advising the king of the Persians to request a daughter from the king of the Egyptians 'so that if he gave her he would be aggrieved, and if he did not give her he would be hated' (5.256-64).

From this example and the exercise itself James Butts correctly concludes that, for Theon, a διήγημα must always recount 'the information that leads up to the central incident...as well as those things which happen after this central incident'.[81] Moreover, the διήγημα differs from the χρεία since the latter 'does not need and never includes any narrational explication of the after-effects of its climactic statement or action'.[82]

Mark 8.27-30, I argue, is in the form of a διήγημα. The beginning portion includes 8.27-28, the setting and the first interchange of the dialogue. Since Mark's audience has already heard the information of the disciples' report of others' response to Jesus (6.14-16), 8.28 is included in the beginning portion of the διήγημα. The middle portion contains the central incident, the dialogue in v. 29. Finally, 8.30 recounts an after-effect of the designation of Jesus as 'Messiah'. Jesus 'sternly ordered' his disciples to keep secret his identity as Messiah. Thus, the unit 8.27-30 is a διήγημα. Within this διήγημα, 8.27-29 is an anecdote that contains a dialogue.[83]

b. *8.31-33: The First Passion Prediction and Misunderstanding*

The first passion prediction by Jesus, Mk 8.31-33, is a mixed-χρεία, according to Theon's typology. Verse 33 of the anecdote contains both an an action and a saying of Jesus. For the sake of analysis, the anecdote can be condensed to a saying-χρεία that would read, 'When Peter rebuked Jesus for predicting his suffering and death, Jesus turned to the disciples and said: "Get behind me, Satan, for you are setting your mind not on divine things but on human things!"' The details of the suffering and death

81. James R. Butts, 'The Voyage of Discipleship: Narrative, Chreia, and Call Story', in C.A. Evans and W.F. Stinespring (eds.), *Early Jewish and Christian Exegesis: Studies in Memory of William Hugh Brownlee* (Atlanta, GA: Scholars Press, 1987), pp. 199-219 (216).

82. James R. Butts, 'Passion Apologetic, the Chreia, and the Narrative', *Foundations and Facets Forum* 3 (1987), pp. 96-127 (105).

83. In the listing of anecdotes of Mk 8.27–10.45 above, the entire passage of 8.27-30 is listed as an anecdote for the sake of identifying the pericope.

of Jesus and his rising, the title 'Son of Man' and the note that Jesus spoke plainly, can all be viewed as items added in the expansion of a χρεία. Such a condensation is speculative; these observations, however, aid the classification of the Markan unit as a mixed-χρεία focusing on Jesus' reaction to Peter.

In the text as it stands, in response to Peter's 'rebuke' Mark records that Jesus first turns away from Peter. It is then that Jesus rebukes Peter with the strong statement, 'Get behind me, Satan!' Theon's definition of a mixed-χρεία includes the observation that a mixed-χρεία makes its point with the action (3.105-107). Mark probably intended that his hearers picture Jesus with his back toward Peter; then the statement of Jesus explains his action. At the same time, Jesus' reference to Peter as 'Satan', which would not be implied in the action, adds force not only to Jesus' words but to his action. The point of this anecdote is made through both the action and the words.

The statement of Jesus, 'for [ὅτι] you are setting your mind not on divine things but on human things', gives an explanation for his rebuke of Peter. Theon's second typology for χρεῖαι was based on how the saying-χρεῖαι were expressed (3.85-138). One of the types Theon identified was a χρεία expressed 'in the manner of an explanation [ἀποδεικτικῶς]'.[84] Theon's example of such a χρεία reads, 'Isocrates the rhetor used to advise his students to honor their teachers before their parents, because [ὅτι] the latter are the cause only of living, while teachers are the cause of living nobly' (3.93-97). The saying in 8.33 follows this same pattern. Thus, the anecdote of Mk 8.31-33 is in the form of a mixed-χρεία and the saying within the χρεία contains an explanation.

In the passion prediction of 8.31 Jesus refers to himself as the 'Son of Man'. This 'Son of Man' saying, as well as the sayings in the other two passion predictions (9.31; 10.33) that use the title, have been shown to have originated among the followers of Jesus after the resurrection.[85] The

84. See LSJ, p. 195, col. 2. There it is noted that while the adjective ἀποδεικτικός can mean 'affording proof', with respect to history or a διήγησις, the adjective describes facts that are 'set forth and explained'. Hence, in the narrative context of a χρεία, the adverb can be translated 'in the manner of an explanation' rather than 'in the manner of a proof'.

85. Adela Yarbro Collins, 'The Origin of the Designation of Jesus as "Son of Man"', *HTR* 80 (1987), pp. 391-407 (reprinted in Adela Yarbro Collins, *Cosmology and Eschatology in Jewish and Christian Apocalypticism* [JSJSup, 50; Leiden: E.J. Brill, 1996], pp. 139-58). For a summary of recent scholarship on the title 'Son of

narrative of 8.31-33 is linked with the preceding passage, 8.27-30, by the presence of the character of Peter in both pericopes. The Markan Jesus' use of the title 'Son of Man' therefore associates the title 'Messiah' (8.29) and 'Son of Man' (8.31) and clarifies that the Messiah must suffer.

c. *8.34–9.1: The Teaching on Discipleship*

The pericope that follows Jesus' rebuke of Peter is an anecdote in which Jesus teaches requirements for those who wish to be his followers. Taken as an anecdote out of its context in Mark, the teaching of Jesus begins with an 'unprompted saying' (v. 34b).[86] However, if the context in Mark is considered, then the saying in v. 34b can be classified as 'from a specific situation', that is, in response to Peter's rebuke of Jesus recorded in the previous pericope. The initial saying of Jesus is followed by six additional statements. These additional statements are not merely a collection of related sayings 'bound together by catchwords, similarities of grammatical structure, and connections of thought'.[87] Rather, the first five of these verses, 8.35-38, compose an argument for the elaboration (ἐργασία) of the initial saying of Jesus (v. 34b).

Mark 9.1, the sixth of the additional verses, is an independent saying added to 8.38. Bultmann classified this verse as an 'admonition', a subtype of prophetic and apocalyptic sayings of Jesus. He commented that Mk 9.1, 'a formula of consolation', was 'an isolated saying joined to its context by the formula καὶ ἔλεγεν'.[88] Paul Achtemeier has pointed out that in oral

Man', see A.Y. Collins, 'The Influence of Daniel on the New Testament: The Son of Man Tradition', in John J. Collins, *Daniel: A Commentary on the Book of Daniel* (Hermeneia; Philadelphia: Fortress Press, 1993), pp. 90-105, and John R. Donahue, 'Recent Studies on the Origin of "Son of Man" in the Gospels', *CBQ* 48 (1986), pp. 484-98.

86. This is a category in Theon's typology for the saying-χρεία.

87. Gundry, *Mark*, p. 434. On Mk 8.34–9.1 as a collection of isolated sayings gathered together because of their common theme see: Morna D. Hooker, *The Gospel According to Saint Mark* (BNTC; London: A. & C. Black, 1991), pp. 207-209; William L. Lane, *The Gospel According to Mark: The English Text with Introduction, Exposition and Notes* (NICNT, 2; Grand Rapids: Eerdmans, 1974), pp. 305-306; and Taylor, *The Gospel According to St. Mark*, p. 380.

88. Bultmann, *The History of the Synoptic Tradition*, p. 121. For Mk 9.1 as an addition of an independent saying see, e.g., Hooker, *The Gospel According to Saint Mark*, pp. 211-12, and Taylor, *The Gospel According to St. Mark*, pp. 384-86. Taylor notes that 'Mark introduces the saying at this point because he sees at least a partial fulfillment in the Transfiguration (ix.2-8)' (p. 385).

literature, particularly in speeches, 'the anaphoric phrase καὶ ἔλεγεν αὐτοῖς or a variation on it helps the listener understand that what follows the phrase continues that particular narrative scene'.[89] The use of καὶ ἔλεγεν αὐτοῖς as the opening phrase of 9.1, then, is a signal that the author intends that the saying that follows should be heard as a continuation of the speech of Jesus in 8.34-38. In other words, it is not necessarily clear to a listener that such is the case. It is shown below that 8.34-38 is in fact an argumentative unit. In this analysis, then, 9.1 is considered part of the anecdote, but a saying added to the elaboration present in 8.34-38.

One pattern of argumentation for an elaboration of a χρεία is found in the Προγυμνάσματα of Hermogenes.[90] The pattern he gives contains these elements: praise of the speaker, the χρεία and a rationale. In his example of an elaboration, Hermogenes adds the following arguments after the rationale: a statement from the opposite, an analogy, an example, an exhortation and, if one wished, an argument from authority. It is important to note that Hermogenes' schema of arguments for an elaboration is not the only possible pattern. Theon, when he speaks of 'providing arguments' for the χρεία states that 'it is impossible in the case of every χρεία to argue from every [topic (τόπος)]' (3.278-80).

Before the discussion of Mk 8.34-38, it is important to note that both Theon's advanced confirmation (κατασκευή) of a χρεία and Hermogenes' elaboration of a χρεία are referring to argumentation created by a person other than the one to whom the saying of the χρεία is attributed.[91] I argue below that the Markan Jesus elaborated his own saying. Such a situation occurs elsewhere in Roman literature. As was pointed out in Chapter 2, *Rhetorica ad Herrenium* presented the rhetorical figure of thought *expolitio*, 'refining', one form of which was declaiming on a theme (4.44.57). The example given there was an argument worked out on an unattributed *sententia* with no indication that the one arguing was other than the speaker of the *sententia*. Except for 'the praise of the speaker', the pattern of this *expolitio* followed Hermogenes' arrangement for the elaboration of a χρεία. There is then a precedent in other ancient literature for a speaker providing an argumentation without a 'praise of the speaker' for his own statement.[92]

89. Achtemeier, '*Omne Verbum Sonat*', p. 21.

90. For a discussion of this exercise, including Hermogenes' treatment of it, see section d, pp. 82-87.

91. See Theon, Προγυμνάσματα 3.241-91, and Hermogenes' 'Περὶ Χρείας', 7.30-64 in Mack and O'Neil, 'Hermogenes of Tarsus'.

92. See also the example of the 'complete argument' (*Rhet. Her.* 2.18.28–19.30), which follows many of the steps in the pattern for the elaboration of a χρεία-saying.

Thus, it is legitimate to consider Mk 8.34-38, which also lacks a 'praise of the speaker', as following the pattern for the elaboration of a χρεία-saying.

The verses of Mk 8.34-38 function in the following pattern of the elaboration of the saying: the setting (v. 34a); the saying (v. 34b); a rationale for the saying (v. 35a); a statement of the opposite of the rationale (v. 35b); an example for the rationale (v. 36); an argument from authority for the rationale (v. 37); and an analogy for the rationale (v. 38).

Jesus makes this statement (*saying*) to the crowd, including his disciples: 'If one wishes to follow after me, one must deny one's self and take up his or her cross, and follow me' (v. 34b).[93] Next Jesus presents a *rationale* for his saying, 'For [γὰρ] the one who wishes to save his or her life will lose it' (v. 35a). In other words, failure to deny one's self or to take up one's cross is an attempt to save one's 'life', which, however, will result in losing that 'life'. Jesus then argues the *opposite* of the rationale's 'saving-losing life' pattern when he says, 'And the one who loses his or her life for my sake, and for the sake of the gospel, will save it' (v. 35b). Here Jesus' reversed pattern, that is, 'losing-saving life', is meant to teach that denying one's self and taking up one's cross, that is, 'losing one's life', leads to 'saving one's life'. In the *example* (v. 36) the Markan Jesus contrasts 'the whole world', with 'life'. As noted above, this section of Mark is related to the parable of the sower in Mark 4 by the theme, 'on the way'. In 4.18-19, Jesus explained to the disciples that the 'seed that fell among thorns' represented 'those who hear the word but the cares of the world, and the delight in riches, and the desire for other things, enter in and choke the word'. Given Jesus' call for self-denial in v. 34b, the phrase 'the whole world' in 8.36 reflects the 'delight in riches and the desire for other things' of 4.19.[94]

93. Jesus' saying here takes the form of a conditional sentence with an imperative in the apodosis. While most χρεῖαι are declarative sentences, Theon does recount one χρεία that contains a command accompanied by an explanation, that is, 'Diogenes the Cynic philosopher, on seeing a youth who was the son of an adulterer throwing stones, said: "Stop, boy! You may unwittingly hit your father!"' (3.136-38). Moreover, according to Theon, the saying in a χρεία can be a general statement, such as a maxim or a specific statement (3.9-11). There is nothing in the ancient προγυμνάσματα to preclude the saying in a χρεία being a conditional sentence.

94. Since 8.34-38 is the first teaching on discipleship in the section of Mark from 8.27–10.45, it can be argued that this pericope introduces important teachings that are further elucidated, or echoed, throughout this section. Thus, denying one's self 'the whole world' foreshadows other material that teaches that following Jesus involves

Verse 37 is an *argument from authority*, that is, the testimony of Scripture. The verse is a conflation of allusions to two Jewish wisdom sayings. Psalm 48.7b-8 (LXX), which is directed against those who trust in their wealth, reads: 'There is no price one can give to God for one's self. Nor a price for the redemption of one's soul, though one labor for ever.' The Greek of 7b-8a reads: 'οὐ δώσει τῷ θεῷ ἐξίλασμα ἑαυτοῦ, καὶ τὴν τιμὴν τῆς λυτρώσεως τῆς ψυχῆς αὐτοῦ'. Sirach 26.14 reads: 'A silent wife is a gift of God; and there is nothing to be given in exchange for a well-instructed mind (or well-bred soul).' The Greek of 14b reads: 'καὶ οὐκ ἔστιν ἀντάλλαγμα πεπαιδευμένης ψυχῆς'. The Greek text of Mk 8.37 reads: 'τὶ γὰρ δοῖ ἄνθρωπος ἀντάλλαγμα τῆς ψυχῆς αὐτοῦ'; that is, 'Indeed, what can a person give in return for his or her life?' Thus, Mk 8.37 combines allusions to both Ps. 48.7-8 and Sir. 26.14.

Verse 38 is the first Son of Man saying in Mark's Gospel that contains a clear allusion to Dan. 7.13. That is, Mk 8.38b, 'of that one will the Son of Man be ashamed when he comes in the glory of his Father with the holy angels', alludes to Dan. 7.13, 'I watched in the visions of the night, and behold, one like a Son of Man came with the clouds of heaven, and he approached the Ancient of Days and was presented before him.' Mark 8.38 is an apocalyptic saying and may well express the teaching of Jesus concerning a heavenly 'Son of Man' figure who would play a role in impending eschatological events.[95] In the context of Mk 8.38, the hearer already knows that Jesus is identified as the Son of Man from the passion prediction of 8.31. Verse 38 points to a vindication, a 'coming in glory', of Jesus after his suffering, death and resurrection.

Within the argumentation of 8.34-38, verse 38 functions as an *analogy* to the rationale, v. 35a. Thus, 'being ashamed of Jesus and his words' (v. 38a) is analogous to 'saving one's life' (v. 35a), while 'the coming Son of Man will be ashamed of that person' (v. 38b) is equated with 'losing one's life' (v. 35a). The analogy makes it clear that throughout this argument Jesus is contrasting physical life with a form of eternal life, that is, a state of being that is the opposite of an experience of shame before God (Father) in the coming eschatological time.

How is one to interpret 'the one who is ashamed [ἐπαισχύθῃ] of Jesus

willingly foregoing possessions (10.17-25), status (9.34-36a) and power (10.35-45) on account of the gospel.

95. See also Mk 13.26 and 14.62. See the discussion, 'Daniel 7 and Jesus', by Adela Y. Collins, in 'The Influence of Daniel', pp. 92-96.

and of his words'?[96] Jesus' explanation of the parable of the sower indicates that some of those who hear 'the word' will fall away 'when tribulation or persecution arises on account of the word' (4.17). In 8.38, then, being 'ashamed of Jesus and of his words' alludes to some type of failure on the part of followers of Jesus in the face of persecution. Later in 10.30 Jesus promises his disciples 'persecutions'. In 10.39 Jesus indicates that James and John will suffer, and in 13.9-13 Jesus predicts sufferings and trials for his followers. Failure on the part of the disciples occurs in 14.50, when at Jesus' arrest they forsake him and flee, and in 14.66-72 with Peter's denial. Thus the mention of 'one who is ashamed of me and of my words' is Jesus' warning of potential failure on the part of his followers in the face of trials and persecution.

The following schema for Mk 8.34-38 illustrates this pattern of the elaboration of the saying of Jesus in v. 34b:

> *Setting*:
> He called the crowd with his disciples, and said to them (v. 34a):
>
> *Saying*:
> 'If one wishes to follow after me, one must deny one's self and take up his or her cross, and follow me' (v. 34b).
>
> *Rationale*:
> 'For the one who wishes to save his or her life will lose it' (v. 35a).
>
> *Opposite (of the rationale)*:
> 'And the one who loses his or her life for my sake, and for the sake of the gospel, will save it' (v. 35b).
>
> *Example (for the rationale)*:
> 'For what will it profit a person to gain the whole world and forfeit his or her life?' (v. 36).
>
> *Argument from authority (for the rationale)*:
> 'Indeed, what can a person give in return for his or her life?' (v. 37).
>
> *Analogy (to the rationale)*:
> 'For the one who is ashamed of me and of my words in this adulterous and sinful generation, of that one the Son of Man will also be ashamed when he comes in the glory of his Father with the holy angels' (v. 38).

The recognition of this pattern of elaboration identifies the form of the anecdote in Mk 8.34–9.1 as the elaboration of a saying-χρεία, this first

96. The Q variant to this verse (Lk. 12.8-9; Mt. 10.32) presupposes a forensic situation.

saying being the words of Jesus in v. 34b, with a final saying, 9.1, added to the elaboration. The saying of 8.34b is classified as 'from a specific situation', A.1.b according to Theon's typology. The pattern also makes it clear that of the seven statements by Jesus in the anecdote, the central message is found in v. 34b. To follow Jesus one must deny one's self and take up one's cross. Furthermore, the argumentation indicates that such self-denial, undertaken for the sake of Jesus and his gospel, includes forfeiting an attachment to 'the whole world'. Finally, both the phrases 'taking up one's cross' and 'being ashamed of the Son of Man' foreshadow suffering, or even death, which may be encountered on account of Jesus or his words.

d. *9.28-29: A Private Explanation*

The concise anecdote of Mk 9.28-29 is the first of two narratives in this section of the Gospel in which the disciples ask Jesus for a private explanation.[97] Verses 9.28-29 are the concluding scene for the account of Jesus casting out an unclean spirit from a boy (9.14-29). In the opening verses of the exorcism story, the boy's father relates that the disciples were unable to cast the spirit out of the boy. Afterward, the disciples ask Jesus to explain why they failed in their attempt to perform the exorcism. Jesus responds, 'This sort cannot come out except by prayer.'

The form of the anecdote in 9.28-29 is a saying-χρεία, and it can be classified as a response to an inquiry, A.2.b in Theon's typology. It also functions as the ending portion of the exorcism story since it relates an incident that follows the climactic or central events of the story, the exorcism and 'lifting up' of the boy. Thus, the entire pericope, 9.14-29, is a διήγημα; 9.28-29, a saying-χρεία, functions as the ending portion of this διήγημα.

e. *9.33-36a; 9.36b-42, 50d; and 9.38-40: Teaching on Discipleship and Forbidding the Other Exorcist*

The section of Mark from 9.33 to 9.50 is composed of three distinct units of material, that is, two closely related anecdotes (9.33-42, 50d; 9.38-40) and a collection of sayings (9.43-50c). The collection of sayings, based on patterned statements and catchwords, begins with v. 43 and is attracted to this pericope by affinity with the word σκανδαλίσῃ in v. 42. Verses 43, 45 and 47 record a series of three sayings all following the same pattern: 'If your (body part) should cause you to stumble [σκανδαλίζῃ]…it is better

97. The other anecdote requesting private teaching, 10.10-12, is treated below.

for you to enter life (or the kingdom of God)...than having two (body parts) to go to (or enter into) Gehenna.' A citation of Isa. 66.24 containing a reference to the fate of the wicked (v. 48) is added as a description of Gehenna, which is referred to in vv. 43, 45 and 47. Finally, vv. 49-50c are attracted by the catchwords 'fire' (v. 48) and 'salt' (v. 49). The collection of sayings is extraneous to the other material and is not discussed here. The other units, the two anecdotes, are meant to be taken together, since v. 50d, 'Be at peace with one another', refers back to both the disciples' argument (v. 34) and their action against the exorcist (v. 38).[98] The discussion of these two anecdotes begins with the incident of the 'other exorcist'.

The story of the exorcist is related in 9.38-40 and is incorporated into the Markan Jesus' teaching on receiving children. Nonetheless, it is a separable unit and is classified as a saying-χρεία. It is possible to express it in a concise form as follows: 'When Jesus heard that the disciples had tried to stop a stranger who was expelling demons in Jesus' name, he said, "Do not stop him. For there is no one who performs a powerful deed in my name who, soon after, will be able to speak evil of me."' From this concise form it is clear that the report placed on the lips of John, one of the twelve, and John's address of Jesus as 'Teacher', are probably Markan details intended to link the story with the setting of v. 35. In that verse Jesus is seated, hence teaching, while speaking to the twelve. It can be argued, therefore, that the anecdote of 9.38-40 is connected with the dispute on greatness (9.33) and that the 'we' of 9.38 refers to the twelve (9.35). Furthermore, the address of Jesus as 'Teacher' can be considered as 'praise of the speaker', an element in an elaboration of a saying-χρεία.

The exorcist is identified as one who 'is not following us'. The man is someone outside their circle and, even though he acts in Jesus' name, the twelve attempt to stop him. Earlier in 9.17-18 it was reported that some of Jesus' disciples were not able to cast out a demon. This, along with the context of vv. 33-35, implies that this outsider is a threat to the position of those with Jesus. The response of Jesus to John's report is the command 'Do not stop him'. Jesus provides an explanation for his instruction, that is, 'For [γὰρ] there is no one who performs a powerful deed in my name who, soon after, will be able also to speak evil of me' (v. 39).[99] Thus, the χρεία-

98. A similar technique is employed elsewhere in Mark; for example, v. 10.31 echoes 9.35 and serves to connect all the material from 9.33 to 10.31. See the comments on 10.31 below.

99. See the comments on 10.14 below, where the same pattern occurs, that is, a command 'Do not stop them!' followed by an explanation.

saying is the type Theon would classify as 'expressed in the manner of an explanation' (3.93-97). Finally, Jesus adds a proverbial statement as a rationale for his command, 'For the one that is not against us is for us'.[100] This rationale produces an elaboration (ἐργασία) of Jesus' instruction.[101] The anecdote can be presented in the following argumentative schema:

> *Setting*:
> 'John said to him, "Teacher, we saw a man driving out demons in your name, and we tried to stop him, because he was not following us"' (v. 38).
>
> [*Praise of the speaker*:
> 'Teacher' (v. 38)].
>
> *Saying*:
> 'Do not stop him! For there is no one who performs a powerful deed in my name who, soon after, will be able to speak evil of me' (v. 39).
>
> *Rationale*:
> 'For the one that is not against us is for us' (v. 40).[102]

The anecdote of 9.38-40 is classified, therefore, as an elaborated saying-χρεία. The saying (v. 39) is a response to a remark, A.2.d in Theon's typology. Further comments on this anecdote are found below since the unit plays a role in the argumentation found within the narrative 9.33-42, 50d.

Mark 9.33-50 is often referred to as a teaching on discipleship and 9.33-

100. This proverbial statement is attributed to Caesar Augustus by Cicero in his oration on behalf of Ligarius (46 BCE), that is, 'Let the maxim [*vox*] which won you victory hold good today. For we have often heard you assert that, while we held all men to be our opponents save those on our side, you counted all men your adherents who were not against you' (*Lig.* 11.33). The first part of Cicero's statement is found in the Q source as, 'He who is not with me is against me' (Mt. 12.30a; Lk. 11.23a) in a context of demon exorcism, the Beelzebul controversy. See John S. Kloppenborg, *Q Parallels: Synopsis, Critical Notes, and Concordance* (Sonoma, CA: Polebridge Press, 1988), pp. 90-93.

101. As noted above, Hermogenes only required that an elaboration include praise of the speaker, the χρεία-saying, and the rationale. John's address of Jesus as 'Teacher' may be considered 'praise of the speaker'.

102. This schema does not agree with that of Robbins ('The Chreia', pp. 20-21), who considers v. 39b to be the rationale for Jesus command and v. 40 to be a statement from the opposite for this rationale. Verse 39b as the rationale would leave just 'Do not stop him!' as the χρεία-saying. To be a 'useful' χρεία, the explanation must be included. Robbins also includes 9.41 as the conclusion of the anecdote. It is argued below that this verse is connected to 9.37.

37 is viewed as one pericope in that teaching.[103] I would argue, however, that 9.33-37 may be the combination of two anecdotes, that is, 9.33-36a and 9.36b-42, since there is a break in 9.33-37 after the first action of Jesus in 36a. In the preceding verse Jesus has said, 'If anyone would be first, that one must be last of all and servant of all.' Verse 36a records Jesus demonstrating his saying for the twelve by his action of taking a little child, παιδίον, one with low status, and placing it in their midst. On the other hand, the second action of taking the little child in his arms (v. 36b) is connected to his saying which follows in v. 37. The Greek text of v. 36b reads καὶ ἐναγκαλισάμενος αὐτὸ εἶπεν αὐτοῖς. The participle connects the action 'of taking in his arms' to the following verb, 'he said'. Moreover, the action of enfolding a little child in his arms is more appropriate to the teaching about 'the one who welcomes one such child' of v. 37.[104] The action of embracing the little child does not necessarily illustrate the saying, 'If anyone would be first, they shall be last of all and servant of all', of v. 35; likewise, placing a child in the midst of the twelve (v. 36b) is not necessarily 'welcoming' a little child. I maintain, therefore, that 9.33-36a and 9.36b-37 may have been separate anecdotes, yet they now appear as a whole. A possible analogy is found in Mk 2.16-20 where two call stories have been intricately woven together into one unit.[105]

Theon's discussion of the different types of saying-χρεῖαι included the 'double-χρεία' (διπλῆ). He defined this double-χρεία as 'one with statements of two characters, either one of which creates a χρεία of the other'. Theon's example of a double-χρεία reads: 'Alexander the Macedonian king stood over Diogenes as he slept and said: "To sleep all night ill suits a counselor" [*Iliad* 2.24], and Diogenes responded: "On whom the folk rely, whose cares are many"' (*Iliad* 2.25). Theon comments on this example saying, 'For even as it was, this was a χρεία without the addition of the response [by Diogenes]' (3.62-70). This comment leads one to ask

103. For example, Hooker, *The Gospel According to Saint Mark*, pp. 226-28; Lane, *The Gospel according to Mark*, pp. 338-41; D.E. Nineham, *The Gospel of St Mark* (Pelican New Testament Commentaries; New York: Seabury, 1963), pp. 251-53; and Taylor, *The Gospel According to St. Mark*, pp. 403-406.

104. See the comments on 10.16 and the act of taking a child in his arms as Jesus' illustration of how one receives the kingdom of God below.

105. James Butts ('The Voyage of Discipleship', p. 217) has drawn attention to Theon's discussion of an exercise with the διήγημα, that is, 'to combine [συμπλέκειν] a διήγημα with a διήγημα'. Theon explained that this 'combination' is an 'attempt to narrate, at the same time, two or even more διηγήματα' (5.427-39). Thus grammarians did acquaint their students with a process of combining stories.

whether Mk 9.33-37 is not also a double-χρεία? The anecdote of 9.33-36 would be a χρεία without the addition of the saying in v. 37. Theon, however, specifies that there should be two characters and that is clearly not the case with Mk 9.33-37. Thus, the anecdote of Mk 9.33-37 is probably best described as a 'combination of two mixed-χρεῖαι'. Verses 9.33-36a are treated here first.

Immediately following the second passion prediction Mark narrates the controversy among the disciples about which one of them was the greatest. The story in 9.33-36a is set within a house in Capernaum. Jesus reacts to the argument by sitting down, a position of teaching, and calling the twelve to himself. These two elements of the narrative are clearly meant to convey that what follows is an important teaching. Then Jesus says, 'If anyone would be first, he or she shall be last of all and servant of all.' This teaching is exemplified for the twelve when Jesus takes a little child, παιδίον, and places it in their midst. Since children are of low status, the little child illustrates what Jesus means by being 'last of all'. The παιδίον also demonstrates the meaning of the phrase 'servant of all'. τὸ παιδίον is a diminutive of ὁ or ἡ παῖς, male or female child. In addition to child, παῖς can mean a male or female servant or slave. Hence παιδίον can also indicate a child-servant or child-slave.[106] If παιδίον is understood as child-servant, then one is dealing with a person who is 'doubly marginalized', to use a modern phrase. Thus Jesus' placing of a παιδίον in the midst of the twelve can leave no doubt in their minds or in the minds of Mark's audience about the meaning of Jesus' teaching. To be 'first' one must assume the status of a little child, even a child-servant. The dramatic action of Jesus 'clinches' his message. As it now stands in the Markan text, 9.33-36a can be viewed as a mixed-χρεία; the story, moreover, follows Theon's observation that a mixed-χρεία makes its point with the action.

The anecdote in the present context of Mark continues in 9.36b-37 within the same setting as the previous verses, that is, within the context of the dispute on greatness among the twelve. In this part of the story Mark records another of Jesus' actions with the παιδίον and a further saying of Jesus about children. This time Jesus takes the little child or child-servant in his arms and says, 'Whoever welcomes one such παιδίον in my name welcomes me; and whoever welcomes me, welcomes not me but the One who sent me' (v. 37). The saying follows Jesus' own action of welcoming

106. For these translations of παῖς and παιδίον, see LSJ, pp. 1289, col. 1 and 1287, col. 2, respectively.

a παιδίον. Thus the action and the saying are intertwined; the form of the story is a mixed-χρεία.

Immediately after the teaching in v. 37, Mark narrates the anecdote about forbidding the other exorcist. The story concerns John's report that 'we' encountered an exorcist who is 'not following us'. John's group attempts to stop the man even though he was driving out demons in Jesus' name. As shown above, 9.38-40 is connected with the disciples' dispute on greatness since the man is an outsider and a threat to the position of those with Jesus. The anecdote of 9.38-40 therefore serves as a 'statement from the opposite' for the saying of Jesus in v. 35b. However, the unit also, and in fact, primarily functions as an example of the 'opposite' of welcoming a child/servant, the saying in 9.37. The schema for 9.38-40 presented above is based on its being a self-contained unit. That schema has v. 38 as the setting for Jesus' χρεία-saying, 'Do not stop him!' etc. When the anecdote is viewed as 'an argument from the opposite', then v. 38 contains a statement of the opposite behavior, behavior that Jesus corrects.[107]

Verses 41 and 42 are elements of argumentation for the saying in 9.37. Verse 41, 'For truly I say to you, whoever gives you a cup of water to drink because you bear the name of Christ, will certainly not lose her or his reward', is an analogy to v. 37. 'Giving a cup of water' is analogous to 'welcoming' and 'not losing one's reward' is a consequence of 'welcoming Jesus and the One who sent him'. On the other hand, v. 42 records a statement from the opposite of the analogy in v. 41 and hence of the χρεία-saying in v. 37. Verse 42 reads: 'Whoever causes one of these little ones who believe in me to stumble, it would be better for that one to have a large millstone hung around his or her neck and to be thrown into the sea.' Here 'causing a little one to stumble' is the opposite of 'welcoming the little child' or 'giving a cup of water', and 'being thrown into the sea' is the opposite of 'receiving (not losing) one's reward', hence of being able to 'welcome Jesus and the One who sent him'.

Finally, v. 50d, which follows the sayings-collection in 9.43-50c, is an exhortation, καὶ εἰρηνεύετε ἐν ἀλλήλοις, 'And be at peace with one another.' Since this exhortation concludes the entire section of 9.33-50, it also functions as a conclusion both for 9.33-36a[108] and for the elaboration in 9.38-40. The twelve are admonished to be at peace with one another and

107. See the schema for 9.33-50 below.

108. See Mk 9.34b, πρὸς ἀλλήλους γὰρ διελέχθησαν ἐν τῇ ὁδῷ τίς μείζων, 'for on the way they had discussed *with one another* who was the greatest'.

with those outside their group who also perform mighty deeds in the name of Jesus.

The following schema presents the whole of Mk 9.33-50 according to the patterns of argumentation just discussed:

Setting:
In the house at Capernaum, after an argument over who is the greatest, Jesus is seated and speaking to the twelve (vv. 33-35a).

Response 1 (9.35b-36a):
Saying 1:
'If any one would be first, let that one be last of all and servant of all' (v. 35b).

Paradigmatic action 1:
Jesus placed a παιδίον in their midst (v. 36a).

[*Exhortation*:
'Be at peace with one another' (v. 50d).]

Response 2 (9.36b-42):
Paradigmatic action 2:
Jesus took a child in his arms (v. 36b).

Saying 2:
'Whoever welcomes one such child in my name welcomes me; and whoever welcomes me, welcomes not me but the One who sent me' (v. 37).

Opposite of Saying 2 (and 1): 'The Other Exorcist' (9.38-40):
Opposite (Setting):
'John said to him, " Teacher, we saw a man driving out demons in your name, and we tried to stop him, because he was not following us"' (v. 38).
[*Praise of the Speaker*:
'Teacher' (v. 38).]
Saying:
'Do not stop him! For there is no one who performs a powerful deed in my name who, soon after, will be able to speak evil of me' (v. 39).
Rationale:
'For the one that is not against us is for us' (v. 40).
[*Exhortation*:
'Be at peace with one another' (v. 50d).]

Analogy for Saying 2:
'For truly I say to you, whoever gives you a cup of water to drink because you bear the name of Christ, that one will certainly not lose her or his reward' (v. 41).

Opposite of Analogy and Saying 2:
'Whoever causes one of these little ones who believe in me to stumble, it would be better for that one if a great millstone were hung around his or her neck and they were cast into the sea' (v. 42).

[Collection of Sayings]

Exhortation:
'Be at peace with one another' (v. 50d).

The argumentation for the narrative in 9.33-42, 50d is not an elaboration. However, the arguments do employ commonplace topics from those that Theon considered appropriate for an 'advanced confirmation of a χρεία'. Among the commonplace topics listed by Theon are opposite and analogy (11.60-65).What is apparent from the above discussion and the schema of the argumentation is, first, that 9.33-42, 50d contains a carefully crafted 'confirmation' of both χρεία-sayings. The first saying and accompanying action (9.35b-36a) are argued 'from the opposite' with the anecdote on the 'other exorcist' (9.38-40). The second action and its saying (9.36b-37) are again argued 'from the opposite' by the anecdote on the 'other exorcist'; they are also argued 'with an analogy' (9.41) and 'from the opposite' (9.42). The anecdote of Mk 9.33-42 and 50d is, therefore, a combination of two mixed-χρεῖαι, and an elaborated saying-χρεία within an advanced confirmation of the first two sayings.

Secondly, the discussion and the schema show that the saying in 9.37 and its analogy in 9.41 frame the story of 'The Other Exorcist', that is, welcoming a child in Jesus' name and offering a cup of water in his name frame the account of an 'outsider' driving out demons in his name. Thus, as Harry Fleddermann states, 'If the least service done in Christ's name [a cup of water] will be rewarded, how much more an exorcism done in his name.'[109] The Markan Jesus is concerned about the exclusiveness of the twelve; he teaches them to be more concerned that possessed people are exorcised and less concerned about who is 'following us'.

f. *10.2-9 and 10.10-12: The Teaching on Divorce and a Private Teaching*
The Markan Jesus' teaching on divorce is the concern of the debate in 10.2-9. The elements of this debate are a question posed by the Pharisees (v. 2), Jesus' counterquestion (v. 3), their statement in response (v. 4) and Jesus' counterstatements (vv. 5-8). This Markan narrative reflects a certain

109. Harry Fleddermann, 'The Discipleship Discourse (Mark 9.33-50)', *CBQ* 43 (1981), pp. 46-66 (66).

method of argumentation employing the authority of Scripture. Jesus' counterquestion in v. 3, 'What did Moses command you?' leads the Pharisees to a response that reflects the law on divorce found in Deut. 24.1-4. Jesus replies with a reason for this Mosaic ruling, that is, 'their hardness of heart'. He then notes that the law was different 'from the beginning of creation', hence before the Mosaic Law, and he gives two citations from Genesis to show the original intent of God in regard to marriage. The first is a citation of text common to Gen. 1.27 and 5.2, that is, 'male and female (God) made them', and the second is Gen. 2.24, 'For this reason a man shall leave his father and mother and be joined to his wife and the two shall become one flesh.' Following this scriptural argumentation the anecdote climaxes with Jesus' exhortation to heed the intent of God in creation, that is, 'What God has joined together let no human being separate.'

In the legal debate of 10.2-9 both parties present arguments for their differing legal opinions; they both argue from the 'authority' or 'testimony' of Scripture. Jesus appears to win the debate, at least as far as Mark is concerned, by his appeal to an historical time-frame in which the verses of the creation account in Genesis precede in time the record of the Mosaic Law in Deuteronomy. The arguments of both parties are interpretations of Scripture. The verse from Deuteronomy to which the Pharisees allude does not state an actual permission to divorce; rather Deut. 24.1-4 implies that divorce, initiated by the husband, occurred. Similarily, Jesus draws a prohibition of divorce as an inference from the verses of Genesis.

Moreover, unlike the χρεία exercises of confirmation, refutation and elaboration, Jesus' argumentation in Mk 10.2-9 preceded his saying in 10.9, a general statement precluding divorce; his specific legal ruling occurs in 10.11-12. A Mishnaic anecdote, however, involving Rabban Gamaliel and Rabbi Joshua, recorded in *Yad.* 4.4 A-L, contains a close parallel to the pattern of argumentation and use of Scripture found in Mk 10.2-9. In the rabbinic narrative an Ammonite proselyte, Judah, asks to enter the congregation. Gamaliel rules against this, while Joshua would allow it. Gamaliel and Joshua then engage in a debate, using their interpretations of four separate verses of Scripture. Gamaliel gives two different reasons, each with a different scriptural verse, and Joshua, in turn, counters each reason with a scriptural interpretation of his own. At the end of this debate, the ruling of the gathered assembly follows Joshua's position. The presence of expressions of this pattern of scriptural argumentation for legal rulings in both Mark's Gospel and the *Mishnah* is significant. The similarity allows one to argue for the probability that this method of debate on legal rulings was in use, if not at the time of Jesus, then at the time of the composition of the Gospel. This is arguing from the New Testament to early rabbinic literature and not vice versa; a Gospel pericope contains an earlier example of a pattern found in a later rabbinic text.[110] In other words, Mk 10.2-9 offers evidence for students of rabbinic literature that such a use of Scripture in argumentation existed in the first century CE.

The Markan anecdote in 10.2-9 is best described as a brief debate. It embodies a legal principle of Jesus arrived at by his interpretation of scriptural verses, that is, his use of an argument from authority, the authority being Scripture.

The anecdote of 10.10-12 is closely connected to the preceding pericope. Following Jesus' debate with the Pharisees on whether divorce was permitted, the disciples indicate their failure to understand by asking Jesus for a private explanation. This is the second narrative, along with 9.28-29, in this section of Mark where the disciples ask for such a private clarification. As with the anecdote of 9.28-29, the story in 10.10-12 takes the form of a saying-χρεία and can be classified as a response to an inquiry, A.2.b according to Theon's typology.

Additionally, 10.10-12 functions to record an after-effect of the preceding debate. The disciples require a further explanation of Jesus' teaching on divorce. Jesus responds with the specific ruling, 'Whoever divorces his wife and marries another, commits adultery against her; and if she divorces her husband and marries another, she commits adultery' (10.11-12). Thus, 10.10-12 is the closing portion of 10.2-12, while the anecdote relating the debate with the Pharisees records the beginning (vv. 2-5) and central (vv. 6-9) portions of the story. Thus, the entire pericope is a διήγημα. The anecdote of 10.2-9 is a debate within a διήγημα and the anecdote requesting the private explanation, 10.10-12, is a saying-χρεία within a διήγημα.

Miriam Dean-Otting and Vernon K. Robbins view 10.1-12 as a 'juxtaposition of expansion and elaboration' in a pronouncement story.[111] They

110. Employing a similar line of reasoning, David Daube pointed out that the New Testament is an early witness to rabbinic law in regard to the *lex talonis* passage in Mt. 5.38-42. Daube states: '[T]he Matthean text witnesses to a "pre-Talmudic" stage of Jewish private law, a stage far removed from the law of the Bible but less advanced that that of the Mishnah and Mekhilta' (*The New Testament and Rabbinic Judaism*, p. 258).

111. Miriam Dean-Otting and Vernon K. Robbins, 'Biblical Sources for Pronounce-

propose that 10.1-4 is an expansion that enlarges upon the initial question of the Pharisees in 10.2. Verses 5-12, they argue, are an elaboration in that 'instead of simply "enlarging" Jesus' response, the Markan version [of the story] features Jesus introducing a series of arguments'.[112] They see 10.5 as the 'rationale' for dismissing the Mosaic ruling referred to in 10.4 and 10.6 as a 'rationale' for a different law. In their prior discussions, the authors refer to the elaboration-pattern of Hermogenes wherein the rationale is intended for the saying in a χρεία. It cannot be argued that 10.5 functions as the rationale in an elaboration for 10.4, since 10.5 does not portray Jesus as supporting the position presented in 10.4. Moreover, Dean-Otting and Robbins do not demonstrate that 10.6 is a rationale for what they see as the different law recorded in 10.11-12. To do this they would have to argue that 10.11-12 is equivalent to the saying of a χρεία and that the verses from 10.6-9 form an argumentative pattern for the elaboration of 10.11-12 with 10.6 as the rationale. Not only do these authors fail to present this pattern, they consider the exhortation in 10.9 to be the conclusion of the elaboration and that this 'conclusion (10.9) is *elaborated* [emphasis added] by paraphrasing the conclusion in the form of a new law (10.11-12)'.[113] This last use of 'elaborating' is confusing; moreover, 10.11-12 cannot function as both the saying and the paraphrase in the elaboration of a saying-χρεία. On the whole these authors' arguments for the 'juxtaposition of expansion and elaboration' in 10.1-12 and their argumentative schema are not persuasive when evaluated in light of the ancient προγυμνάσματα.

g. *10.13-16: The Blessing of Children*

The incident where Jesus receives and blesses the children (10.13-16) is another mixed-χρεία. The anecdote narrates the story of Jesus' welcoming and blessing of children, recording both statements and actions of Jesus. The parallel to this story found in Lk. 18.15-17 is condensed to a saying-χρεία by dropping the actions of Jesus recorded in Mk 10.16 (Mt. 19.15).[114] Matthew, on the other hand, retains a closing action on the part

ment Stories in the Gospels', in Vernon K. Robbins (ed.), *The Rhetoric of Pronouncement* (Semeia, 64; Atlanta: Scholars Press, 1993), pp. 95-115 (105).

112. Dean-Otting and Robbins, 'Biblical Sources for Pronouncement Stories', p. 107.

113. Dean-Otting and Robbins, 'Biblical Sources for Pronouncement Stories', p. 110.

114. Based on the two-source theory of the relationships among the Synoptic

of Jesus,[115] but condenses the anecdote by eliminating the teaching of Jesus found in Mk 10.15 (Lk. 18.17). The 'core' of the Markan story preserved by both Matthew and Luke reads as a brief anecdote:

> And they were bringing children to him that he might touch them; and the disciples rebuked them. But when Jesus saw it, he said to them, 'Let the children come to me, do not hinder them; for to such belongs the kingdom of God.'

Such a brief anecdote would be a saying-χρεία.

Only Mark notes that Jesus was indignant. Moreover, it is most likely that the second imperative in Mk 10.14c, 'Do not stop them!' is present to emphasize Jesus' wishes and possibly his indignation. The words of 14d, 'for [γὰρ] to such as these belongs the kingdom of God', are Jesus' explanation for his commands. The pattern of a saying (command) followed by an explanation is the same here as the pattern in 8.33 discussed above. Thus, the saying of 10.14d is also expressed in the manner of an explanation.[116]

The next verse of the Markan anecdote, 10.15, poses two difficulties for the exegete: first, how does one understand the phrase ὡς παιδίον, and, secondly, based on such an understanding, how does v. 15 fit into the periocope?[117] The difficulties with the phrase ὡς παιδίον lie in determining the grammatical case of παιδίον, that is, whether it is the nominative or accusative singular. The choice of the case for παιδίον is intimately related to how one understands the ellipse in ὡς παιδίον. If παιδίον is taken as nominative, the phrase would mean 'as a child (welcomes it)', whereas παιδίον as an accusative would yield 'as (I welcome) a child'.

Those who read παιδίον as a nominative understand that a child is to be the model for those who would welcome the kingdom. This understanding

Gospels, it can be argued that Luke and Matthew probably condensed the Markan pericope. However, a full discussion of the relationships among the Synoptic versions of this anecdote is beyond the scope of this book. A discussion of this anecdote in each of its synoptic versions (see also Mt. 19.13-15) is found in Robbins, 'Pronouncement Stories and Jesus' Blessing of the Children', pp. 407-30.

115. Matthew (19.15) abbreviates the actions of Jesus to 'he laid his hands on them' and then adds 'and [Jesus] went away'.

116. The use of γὰρ in 10.14d instead of the ὅτι found both in 8.33 and Theon's example for this type of χρεία presents no difficulty. Theon's first typology contains the classification of a saying-χρεία as an 'explanatory response' and his example of such an explanation employs γὰρ (3.50-54).

117. Perhaps these difficulties were recognized already by Matthew, who omits this verse in his parallel in 19.13-15.

is further influenced by a verse in the Matthean parallel to Mk 9.32-37, that is, Mt. 18.3, which reads, 'Truly I tell you, unless you change and become as children you will never enter the kingdom of heaven.' The interpretation of Mk 10.15, then, necessitates positing the manner in which a child welcomes or receives a gift, such as, with littleness or helplessness,[118] or as undeserving,[119] or that a child is content to receive the kingdom as pure gift.[120] Thus, according to this interpretation, v. 15 teaches that those who do not welcome the kingdom the way a child receives a gift cannot enter 'upon its blessings and responsibilities'.[121]

Many scholars who hold such an interpretation of v. 15 consider the verse to be an insertion into the Markan anecdote.[122] Some point out that Mk 10.15 fits better after Mk 9.36 and that 9.37 is more appropriate to the setting here.[123] Nineham readily admits the verse's 'incongruity as the centre-piece of a story which deals with Jesus' attitude to children, and not with children as examples to be imitated'.[124] Gundry lists ten additional reasons to consider verse 10.15, with παιδίον interpreted as nominative, to be an intrusion. Among these he notes the following: the parallel anecdote in Mt. 19.13-15 omits the verse; Mk 10.14 would naturally conclude the anecdote; and if, however, v. 16 is part of the original, 13-14 and 16 are a complete story, and not only would v. 15 be superfluous, it interrupts the flow of the story.[125] Some scholars explain this 'insertion' by an appeal to the habit of collecting sayings according to catchwords, in this instance παιδίον. For example, Gundry states, 'Catchwords lead to twists and turns in original speaking as well as to secondary association in later redaction.'[126]

On the other hand, if one takes the case of παιδίον in 10.15 as accusative, παιδίον can be considered to be parallel to τὴν βασιλείαν τοῦ θεοῦ.[127] Verse 10.15 then implies, 'Truly I tell you, whoever does not

118. Lane, *The Gospel According to Mark*, p. 360.

119. Nineham, *The Gospel of St Mark*, p. 268.

120. Hooker, *The Gospel According to Saint Mark*, p. 239.

121. Taylor, *The Gospel According to St. Mark*, p. 424.

122. The interpretation that Mk 10.15 is an insertion is probably also influenced by the omission of this verse in the Matthean parallel (19.13-15).

123. For example, Hooker, *The Gospel According to Saint Mark*, p. 239.

124. Nineham, *The Gospel of St Mark*, p. 269.

125. Gundry, *Mark*, p. 548.

126. Gundry, *Mark*, p. 548.

127. Robbins, 'Pronouncement Stories and Jesus' Blessing', p. 419; W.K.L. Clarke, *New Testament Problems* (London: SPCK, 1929), pp. 36-38; and F.A. Schelling, 'What Means the Saying about Receiving the Kingdom of God as a Little Child (τὴν

welcome the kingdom of God as I welcome this child will never enter it.'[128] The verse is appropriate then to the Markan context; 10.13-14c refer to the disciples' hindering the children, while vv. 15 and 16 deal with Jesus' saying and actions about welcoming children. In v. 14d Jesus says that 'such as these', meaning children, possess the kingdom of God. It can be inferred, then, that since children possess the kingdom if one welcomes them one welcomes what they possess, that is, the kingdom of God. This understanding finds support in the prior saying of Mk 9.37 where Jesus states that whoever welcomes a child in his name welcomes him and the one who sent him.

Turning to v. 16, one notes that Jesus not only welcomes the children by 'touching' them, the original intent of those who brought them, but he also 'takes them in his arms' and 'blesses them'. Jesus' actions demonstrate how one welcomes children and, therefore, how one welcomes the kingdom of God. One lays hold of the kingdom, embraces it, and offers a blessing.

A final argument for this interpretation of ὡς παιδίον and of v. 15 is found in the fact that the next pericope, 10.17-22, describes a man who, because of his possessions, is unable to embrace the kingdom in the manner Jesus teaches. Additionally, the next mention of the kingdom of God after 10.15 occurs immediately after the story of the rich man in 10.23 which reads, 'How hard it will be for those who have riches to enter the kingdom of God!' Taken with the prior teaching in 10.13-16, the statement of Jesus in 10.23 may be understood to mean that riches can impede a person from 'welcoming the kingdom of God' as one would embrace a child. This interpretation stays within the context of the anecdote as it stands in the text of Mark.

Mark 10.13-16 is an anecdote that appears in the form of a mixed-χρεία. The saying contains an explanation for Jesus' desire to receive the children (v. 14d). Verse 15 is a teaching couched in a warning, and follows immediately from the context of Jesus' wish to welcome the children and his explanation that they possess the kingdom of God. Verse 16 is a dramatization of Jesus' teaching and serves as an example to the disciples of how one is to welcome the kingdom of God. This anecdote is

βασιλείαν τοῦ θεοῦ ὡς παιδίον)? Mk x.15, Lk. xvii.17', *ExpTim* 77 (1965–66), pp. 56-58.

128. This understanding of the ellipse in 10.15 was suggested by Adela Yarbro Collins.

an excellent example of Joanna Dewey's contention that the embedding of teaching in event is characteristic of Mark.

h. *10.17-22 and 10.23-31: The Rich Man and Riches and the Kingdom*
Another dialogue occurs in 10.17-22 in which an unnamed rich man asks Jesus what is necessary 'to inherit eternal life'. The form of this dialogue involves two verbal interchanges between the man and Jesus. In the first interchange the man both addresses Jesus as 'Good Teacher' and asks him a question (v. 17b). In response, Jesus first asks the man a question, 'Why do you call me good?' and then explains his question, 'No one is good but God' (v. 18). Then Jesus answers the man's question (v. 19). In the second interchange, the man replies to Jesus with a statement (v. 20) that Jesus, in turn, answers with an observation, a command, a promise and an invitation (v. 21). Finally, the narrator records that the man responds to Jesus with an action, 'going away' (v. 22a). I argue below that the saying of Jesus, 'Go, sell what you have, give to the poor, and you will have treasure in heaven, and come, follow me', is the focus of both this anecdote and the dialogue in the following pericope.

In v. 19 of the initial interchange, Jesus cites Scripture, that is, the first five commandments given in both Exod. 20.12-16 and Deut. 5.16-20, as well as the prohibition against defrauding the poor found in Sir. 4.1. Here Jesus' scriptural citations are not used as an argument from authority as was the case in 10.2-9. Rather, as a response to the man's inquiry, Jesus provides information by listing major tenets of the Mosaic Law, thus implying that their observation is the basis for the eternal life the man seeks.

The dialogue ends with an action. Instead of offering a counterstatement or stating a verbal rejection, the man's action of 'going away saddened' indicates, in a dramatic way, his refusal of Jesus' invitation. Verse 22b, 'for [γὰρ] he had many possessions', is the narrator's explanation of the man's action. In addition to recording the rich man's response to Jesus, v. 22b serves as another structural element within the story. Mark could have chosen to conclude the report of the dialogue between the rich man and Jesus with the statement by Jesus, just as he ended the dialogue in 10.2-9 with Jesus' words. The additional verse in which the narrator relates the man's action and an explanation of the action provides an 'end moment' for the story, and thus the unit is a διήγημα.[129] The form of the story in

129. In his comments on the διήγημα, Butts draws attention to Mk 10.22 as an indication that Mk 10.17-22 is a διήγημα ('The Voyage of Discipleship', p. 217).

10.17-22 can therefore be classified as a διήγημα. Within this διήγημα 10.17-21 is an anecdote that contains a dialogue.

Closely related to the preceding anecdote about the rich man is the narrative recording Jesus' teaching on wealth found in 10.23-31. This unit is a dialogue consisting of four interchanges between Jesus and his disciples. The elements of this dialogue are a statement by Jesus (v. 23), a response of amazement on the part of the disciples (v. 24a), Jesus' re-statement of his first remark with an argument (vv. 24b-25), the disciples' reaction of astonishment and their question (v. 26), another argument from Jesus (v. 27), the question of Peter (v. 28), and Jesus' reply (vv. 29-30).

I contend that the entire dialogue in vv. 23-31 is an example of one of the preliminary exercises alluded to in Theon's Προγυμνάσματα, the 'advanced confirmation of a saying-χρεία'. According to Theon, the commonplace arguments for an advanced level of the confirmation (κατασκευή) of a saying-χρεία included those he discussed for use in the confirmation of a thesis. Among the arguments for the confirmation of a thesis Theon gives the following, 'that what is being advocated is easy. If it is not easy (but at least possible to do) that it is to be praised so much more than if it were easy' (11.43-48). The dialogue between Jesus and his disciples in Mk 10.23-31 exactly fits the argument for something that is advocated but not easy.

This dialogue, however, is not an argument confirming Jesus' saying, 'How hard it is for a person of wealth to enter the kingdom of God' (v. 32b). The interchange in vv. 28-31 on the rewards of 'leaving everything and following' Jesus make it clear that this dialogue is meant to confirm Jesus' response to the rich man's question on what one must do to inherit eternal life found in the preceding anecdote. The man is told by Jesus, 'Go, sell what you have, give to the poor and you will have treasure in heaven, and come, follow me' (10.21).

The first two interchanges of the dialogue, vv. 23-25, are a commentary on the action of the rich man. Twice Jesus comments that his command and invitation of v. 21 are not easy for a person of wealth; in fact, he gives the example of a camel passing through the eye of a needle to emphasize the difficulty. The fact that Jesus speaks twice, in almost the same words, of the difficulty of fulfilling his command dramatically emphasizes the difficulty. Moreover, the reactions of the disciples to the words of Jesus, that is, that they were first 'amazed', ἐθαμβοῦντο (v. 24a) and then 'greatly astonished' περισσῶς ἐξεπλήσσοντο (v. 26a), dramatize the shocking character and the difficulty of Jesus' saying.

The second interchange, vv. 26 and 27, shows that while it is difficult, nonetheless it is possible to heed Jesus' commands. Jesus answers that it is impossible for humans but not for God. His statement, 'For (γὰρ) all things are possible with God', is an explanation of his answer. Finally, the last interchange (10.29-30), this time between Peter and Jesus, emphasizes the 'hundredfold reward' for those who follow Jesus' commands.

Another argument supporting the claim that this dialogue is an advanced confirmation of v. 21 is the fact that the phrase 'eternal life' occurs in both v. 17 and v. 30. 'Eternal life' forms an inclusion linking the question of the rich man, and hence Jesus' response of v. 21, including the promise of heavenly treasure, with the final words of Jesus.

Finally, 10.31, 'But many who are first will be last, and the last first', continues the promise of future rewards.[130] In its context the verse implies that many who are now first (the rich, represented by the man in vv. 17-22) will be last (because they do not accept Jesus' invitation), whereas many who are now last (the poor, especially those who have made themselves poor voluntarily in response to the invitation of Jesus) will be first (they will receive eternal life; that is, they will enter the kingdom). Moreover, 10.31 echoes the saying of Jesus in 9.35, 'If anyone would be first, he or she shall be last of all and servant of all', and forms an *inclusio* with the anecdote in 9.33-36a. Thus all of the material from 9.33 to 10.31, that is, the contents of Mark's Gospel between the second and third passion predictions, is presented as the teaching of Jesus on a proper understanding of a 'servant-discipleship', and an aspect of this servant-discipleship is the proper relationship to riches.

The saying of Jesus in 10.21, the rich man's response of 10.22 and the dialogue of 10.23-31 are presented here, in schematic form, to summarize the argumentative elements of this advanced confirmation of a saying-χρεία:

130. Verse 31 originally may have been an independent saying. Matthew (19.30) includes the verse in his parallel to the Markan pericope, but Luke omits it. The saying exists, in the reverse order ('the last will be first', and then 'the first will be last'), in two different settings in Mt. 20.16 and in Lk. 13.30, hence it is difficult to posit that the saying is from Q. A Greek fragment of the *Gospel of Thomas*, *POxy* 654.21-27, contains the saying in the same order as Mk 10.31; however, one phrase of the text in *POxy* 654 must be reconstructed. Finally, the Coptic text of the *Gospel of Thomas* 4 contains the statement, 'For many of the first will be last, and will become a single one.' See Kloppenborg, *Q Parallels*, pp. 156-57. Nineham (*The Gospel of St Mark*, p. 276) suggests, but without corroborating evidence, that 10.31 may have been a popular proverb about the 'unpredictable mutability of the human lot'.

Saying of Jesus:
Go, sell what you have and give to the poor, and you will have treasure in heaven; and come, follow me (v. 21).

Advanced Confirmation:

I. It is not easy (vv. 22-25)
   a. The rich man goes away (v. 22)
   b. Jesus comments on the difficulty (vv. 23-25)
      1. Example: 'It is easier for a camel…' (v. 25)

II. It is possible (vv. 26-27)
   a. 'Not for humans but with God' (v. 27b)
   b. Explanation: 'All things are possible with God' (v. 27c)

III. Rewards are greater than what is given up (vv. 28-31)

Thus, the two separate narratives, 10.17-22 and 10.23-31, are woven together since the second, 10.23-31, is an advanced confirmation of the saying of Jesus found in 10.21. Therefore, 'Go, sell what you have, give to the poor, and come, follow me', is a major teaching of the section 8.27–10.45 of Mark.

In regard to this rhetorical unit, Burton Mack argues that 10.21 is a thesis statement. He presents a schematic outline of 10.17-31 based on a pattern of argumentation which he refers to as 'an extended elaboration (ἐργασία)'.[131] However, Mack does not present ancient sources for his pattern of elaboration. He also fails to recognize Theon's 'advanced confirmation', κατασκευή, of a saying-χρεία. Mack includes 10.31 in his thesis argument as a concluding maxim, yet he does not discuss how this maxim relates to 10.17-31. Thus, he incorrectly concludes that the force of the argument in 10.17-31 'must derive from the attractiveness of the social ethos it assumes [Jesus' authority], not from the logic of the argument itself'.[132]

i. *10.32-34: The Third Passion Prediction*

For a third time Jesus predicts the impending death of the Son of Man (10.32-34). Comparing this anecdote with the other two passion predictions in 8.31 and 9.30-32, one sees that this third prediction has been expanded to include more details than are provided in the other two narratives. Here one learns that the imminent events will take place in Jerusalem, that the Jewish authorities will condemn the Son of Man and

131. Mack, *Rhetoric and the New Testament*, pp. 54-56.

132. Mack, *Rhetoric and the New Testament*, p. 56.

then hand him over to the Gentiles. It is the Gentiles who will mock, spit upon, scourge and finally kill the Son of Man.[133] Once again, Jesus predicts that the Son of Man will rise after three days.

While the first two predictions were addressed to the disciples, for this third prediction Jesus takes the twelve aside and addresses his words to them. This focus on the twelve relates 10.32-34 to the following two narratives that involve James and John (10.35-40) and 'the ten' (10.41-45). Thus the third prediction and the teaching on discipleship that follows it and that closes out this section of Mark (8.27–10.45) can be interpreted as teaching directed to early Christian leaders.

The anecdote in 10.32-34, however, is still an independent unit and does not form a διήγημα with 10.35-45. There is no plot or relationship of cause and effect evident in 10.32-45. Rather, the connection between 10.32-34 and 10.35-45 exhibits a paratactic structure that sets the passion prediction and the request of James and John side by side; one incident is not subordinate to another. As noted above, Eric Havelock argues that such a paratactic structure is a feature of oral narratives. Hence, the move from 10.32-34 to 10.35-45 exhibits residual orality in the Markan text.

The third passion prediction in Mk 10.32-34 is therefore identified as an expanded saying-χρεία. It records an unprompted saying of Jesus and is classified as A.1.a according to Theon's typology.

j. *10.35-40 and 10.41-45: The Request of James and John and the Reaction of the Ten*

The final narrative unit in the section of Mark from 8.27 to 10.45 contains two anecdotes, 10.35-40 and 10.41-45. The first anecdote records an incident when James and John, two of the twelve, ask Jesus for places of honor when he is 'in his glory'. The second anecdote narrates the reaction of the other ten when they learn what James and John had attempted to attain. The two anecdotes are combined to form a διήγημα, that is, a story with a beginning, middle and an end. 10.35-40 records the beginning, the request by James and John, and the middle, Jesus' response to them, while 10.41-45 records the ending, in which the other ten learn what has occurred. First, each anecdote is treated separately and then comments are made on the combined unit.

The incident with James and John (10.35-45) is cast in the form of a dialogue. If one were to condense this dialogue to a χρεία, a concise

133. The first prediction, 8.31, mentions the role of the Jewish authorities, while the second prediction, 9.30-32, implicates only 'human persons' (ἄνθρωποι).

version could read, 'When James and John asked Jesus for positions of honor, he responded, "It is not mine to grant, but it is for those for whom it is prepared."' The remaining contents of the dialogue reveal important Markan themes, echoes and forecasts. It is significant that the two brothers address Jesus as 'Teacher'. This title not only highlights the didactic nature of Jesus' forthcoming response, it also serves as praise for Jesus.[134] The dialogue takes the following form: a general request by James and John (v. 35); a clarifying question from Jesus (v. 36); a specific request by James and John (v. 37); a statement and counterquestion by Jesus (v. 38); a simple response by the brothers (v. 39a); a prediction by Jesus and his answer to their specific request (vv. 39b-40).

James and John ask for positions of honor and authority, to sit on the right and the left of Jesus when he enters 'his glory'. The mention of 'glory' echoes the apocalyptic saying in 8.38, 'the Son of Man...when he comes in the glory of his Father with the holy angels'. The disciples misunderstand that Jesus' path to 'glory' is through his suffering and death, which he has just predicted. Jesus reminds them of this path by asking if they can drink his 'cup' and 'be baptized' with his baptism. In the Hebrew Scriptures, 'cup' was used as a metaphor for the judgment of God, a 'cup of wrath' (Jer. 25.15-38; Ezek. 23.31-4), and as such must be drunk (Jer. 25.28; 49.12). 'That God reaches out the cup of wrath to men...accords with Mark's view that the Passion of Jesus is determined by God.'[135] In the first passion prediction the Markan Jesus clearly states that he, the Son of Man, 'must suffer', δεῖ τὸν υἱὸν τοῦ ἀνθρώπου πολλὰ παθεῖν (8.31). Jesus must drink of the cup, must undergo his impending suffering and death as the object of the wrath of God.[136] The mention of the cup also forecasts the cup in the Garden of Gethsemane (14.36). Likewise, 'the baptism with which I am baptized [βαπτισθῆναι]' portends judgment and suffering (Pss. 69.1-2, 14-15; 124.2-4).[137]

James and John assure Jesus that they are able to drink the cup and accept the baptism, and Jesus in turn assures them that they will do just

134. See above on the direct address of Jesus as 'Teacher' in 9.38-40 and the function of the title 'Teacher' as 'praise of the speaker' in an elaboration.

135. Ernest Best, *The Temptation and the Passion: The Markan Soteriology* (SNTSMS, 2; Cambridge: Cambridge University Press, 2nd edn, 1990), p. 153.

136. Best, *The Temptation and the Passion*, p. 153.

137. Taylor notes that in popular Greek, βαπτίζεσθαι was used metaphorically to express being 'flooded or overcome with calamities' (*The Gospel According to St. Mark*, p. 441).

that; however, the positions of prestige and authority that they seek are not his to bestow. Thus the content of the dialogue is rich with Markan themes. The form of the anecdote in Mk 10.35-40 is a dialogue within a διήγημα, that is, within the whole of 10.35-45.

The angry reaction of the other ten disciples, as recorded in 10.41-45, evokes another teaching from Jesus on servant-leadership reminiscent of his response to the quarrel among the twelve over which one was the greatest (9.33-36a). Given this teaching one can assume that the ten were not indignant over the fact that James and John had misunderstood Jesus' passion prediction, but over the fact that the brothers had sought positions of authority that would have placed the two ahead of or over the rest of them.

The teaching of Jesus is cast in the form of an elaborated saying-χρεία. The setting involves Jesus calling the twelve together after James and John have provoked the other ten. Thus, the setting for the teaching of Jesus must include the opening verses of the previous anecdote, that is, 10.35-37, the first three elements in the dialogue, including the specific question posed by James and John. To the quarreling twelve, Jesus first says 'You know that among the Gentiles those who are reputed to be rulers lord it over them and their great ones are tyrants over them' (v. 42). The wording of Jesus' next statement indicates that the example of the Gentiles is presented as a model of behavior *opposite* to what Jesus desires for his followers; Jesus says, 'But it is not so among you' (v. 43a). Then Jesus states what is to be the proper behavior of leaders among the disciples of Jesus, that is, 'whoever wishes to be great among you must be your servant' (v. 43b). Jesus emphasizes his teaching by paraphrasing it as 'whoever wishes to be first among you must be slave of all' (v. 44).[138] Then Jesus follows his teaching and its paraphrase with his rationale, that is, 'For [γὰρ] the Son of Man also came not to be served but to serve and to give his life as a ransom for many' (v. 45). Jesus, whom James and John indicate will be 'in glory' has come to serve not to 'lord it over' others or to act as 'the great ones' of the Gentiles.

If the statements in vv. 42 and 44 had followed v. 45, then the pattern of this teaching would be saying (v. 43), rationale (v. 45), example of the opposite (v. 42) and paraphrase (v. 44). The address of Jesus as 'Teacher' in v. 35 carries over to this second part of the διήγημα and therefore one finds praise of the speaker, Jesus. This revised order of the statements,

138. The saying and its paraphrase provide echoes of the discussion on who is the greatest in 9.34-35.

then, is clearly an elaboration of a χρεία-saying. Mark 10.41-45, as it stands, is still an elaboration. The fact that the order of the statements does not follow the textbook pattern does not change the effect of the argumentation. An inverted order of argumentation in an elaboration is found earlier in Mark's Gospel. Rod Parrott demonstrates an inverted order present in Mk 2.23-28, although the inverted order there is different from the inverted order in Mk 10.41-45.[139] Mark 10.41-45, therefore, is classified as an elaborated saying-χρεία within a διήγημα with the saying arising from a specific situation, A.1.b in the typology of Theon.

The schema of argumentation for the elaborated saying-χρεία within 10.35-45 in its present inverted order, is presented here:

Praise of the speaker:
'Teacher' (v. 35).

Setting:
And James and John, the sons of Zebedee, came forward and said to him, 'Teacher, grant us to sit, one at your right hand and one at your left, in your glory.' When the ten heard they were angry and Jesus called them together and said (vv. 35, 37, 41, 42a):

Example of the opposite:
'You know that those who are supposed to rule over the gentiles lord it over them, and their great ones exercise authority over them' (v. 42).

Saying:
'But it is not so among you. But whoever wishes to be great among you must be your servant' (v. 43).

Paraphrase:
'And whoever wishes to be first among you must be slave of all' (v. 44).

Rationale;
'For [γὰρ] the Son of Man came not to be served but to serve and to give his life as a ransom for many' (v. 45).

Furthermore, the content of 10.45b, that is, that the Son of Man came 'to give his life as a ransom [λύτρον] for many', refers back to the question of Jesus in 10.38, 'Are you able to drink the cup that I drink or to be baptized with the baptism with which I am about to be baptized?' This question by Jesus clearly refers to his impending suffering and death in Jerusalem since it follows so closely the third passion prediction of 10.33-

139. Rod Parrott, 'Conflict and Rhetoric in Mark 2.23-28', in Vernon K. Robbins (ed.), *The Rhetoric of Pronouncement* (Semeia, 64; Atlanta: Scholars Press, 1993), pp. 117-37.

34. Adela Yarbro Collins has shown from a study of epigraphic evidence, especially confessional inscriptions, that 'the word group λύω served to speak of transactions between human beings and gods in which sins were forgiven and offenses expiated'. From this Collins concludes that 'the notion of the Son of Man giving his life as a ransom, λύτρον, for many (Mk 10.45) belongs to the same complex of ideas as the saying over the cup (Mk 14.24)'.[140] Thus, Christians who were acquainted with these Hellenistic traditions would understand 10.45b to mean that the coming death of Jesus was to be an act of expiation on behalf of 'many'. Moreover, when these Christians heard the words over the cup in 14.24, 'This is my blood of the covenant which is poured out for many', there would be echoes of 10.45b present. In 10.45b, then, Jesus offers an interpretation of his 'cup' and the 'baptism with which he is being baptized'.

The two anecdotes of 10.35-40 and 10.41-45 are carefully woven together. Hence, the διήγημα of 10.35-45 is a combination of two anecdotes, the first a dialogue and the second an elaboration of a saying-χρεία. The anecdotes are not as intricately combined as those in 9.33-42, 50d, however, and it is possible to consider them individually.

Finally, the use of the title 'Son of Man' in 10.45 relates this verse back to the passion prediction of 10.33 and thus to the other two passion predictions, 9.31 and 8.31, each of which employ this title. By placing 10.45 as the concluding verse of this pericope, therefore, Mark has provided an inclusion not only for 10.32-45, but also for all of the material from 8.31 to 10.45.

4. *Summary on the Form of the Anecdotes in Mark 8.27–10.45*

The 14 anecdotes of Mk 8.27–10.45 are listed here along with the form of each:

1. 8.27-30: Peter's confession; dialogue within a διήγημα.
2. 8.31-33: first passion prediction and misunderstanding; mixed-χρεία.
3. 8.34-9.1: teaching on discipleship; elaborated saying-χρεία; A.1.b.
4. 9.28-29: private explanation; saying-χρεία within a διήγημα; A.2.b.
5. 9.33-42, 50d: teaching on discipleship; combination of two

140. Adela Yarbro Collins, 'The Signification of Mark 10.45 among Gentile Christians', *HTR* 90 (1997), pp. 371-82 (382).

mixed-χρεῖαι and an elaborated saying-χρεία within an advanced confirmation of the first two sayings.

6. 9.38-40: the other exorcist; elaborated saying-χρεία; A.2.d.
7. 10.2-9: teaching on divorce; debate within a διήγημα.
8. 10.10-12: private teaching; saying-χρεία within a διήγημα; A.2.b.
9. 10.13-16: blessing of children; mixed-χρεία.
10. 10.17-22: rich man; dialogue within a διήγημα.
11. 10.23-31: riches and the kingdom; dialogue within a confirmation of a saying.
12. 10.32-34: third passion prediction; saying-χρεία; A.1.a.
13. 10.35-40: request of James and John; dialogue within a διήγημα.
14. 10.41-45: reaction of the ten; elaborated saying-χρεία within a διήγημα; A.1.b.

In the above discussions of each of the Markan anecdotes, the form of each anecdote was identified. Using Theon's typology as a basis, the following is a typology of the anecdotes in Mk 8.27–10.45 based on their form:

Typology of the Anecdotes in Mark 8.27–10.45 Based on Form

I. χρειαι:			8
A. Saying-χρεία		6	
1. Statement			
a. unprompted	1		
b. from a specific situation	2		
2. Response-χρεία			
a. to a simple question	0		
b. to an inquiry	2		
c. to a question calling for an explanatory response	0		
d. to a remark	1		
3. Double χρεία	0		
B. Action-χρεία		0	
1. active			
2. passive			
C. Mixed-χρεία		2	
II. Other			6
A. Debate		1	
B. Dialogue		4	
C. Combination		1	
Total			14

Of the six anecdotes classified under saying-χρεία, only one, 10.32-34, the third passion prediction, appears as a concise, or slightly expanded, χρεία. Each of the other five saying-χρεῖαι appears as an integral element of another narrative or rhetorical structure. Verses 8.34-38, the teaching on discipleship, and 9.38-40, the incident with the other exorcist, are elaborated saying-χρεῖαι. Both anecdotes recounting private explanations of Jesus to the disciples, 9.28-29 and 10.10-12, take the form of a saying-χρεία within a διήγημα. And the saying-χρεία of 10.41-45, the reaction of the other ten, is elaborated, and this elaboration itself forms a portion of a διήγημα. The two anecdotes that are classified as mixed-χρεία, 8.31-33 and 10.13-16, however, are not elements of another structure. Thus, of the eight anecdotes that are identified as χρεῖαι, only three are what one might term 'textbook examples' of the basic genre.

Moreover, of the six Markan anecdotes that cannot be classified as χρεῖαι, five, the debate (10.2-9) and the four dialogues (8.27-30; 10.17-22; 10.23-31; 10.35-40) are also elements of other narrative or rhetorical structures. The remaining anecdote, 9.33-42, 50d, is a combination of two mixed-χρεῖαι and an elaborated-χρεία containing argumentation that confirms the first two sayings, certainly not an example of the basic or concise χρεία.

This study of the form of the anecdotes in Mk 8.27–10.45 demonstrates that that 'detachable little stories' is not an entirely adequate description of the anecdotes in Mark, at least not in this section of the Gospel. The 'brief stories' of the Gospel must be studied in light of the oral and literary genres of their own time. Moreover, the anecdotes must be studied within the context of the host genre, Mark. That the Gospel is meant as history, not just biography, may indeed affect the form of these stories and is something to be explored further.

As was mentioned above, of the 14 anecdotes in Mk 8.27–10.45, only three anecdotes, two mixed-χρεῖαι and one saying-χρεία, are concise enough to be considered 'brief stories'. The other 11 anecdotes are more developed narrative units, 6 of them built upon or containing χρεῖαι. That 9 out of the 14 anecdotes in this section of the Gospel are χρεῖαι or related to the concise χρεία, allows one to argue that Markan anecdotes are modeled upon the Greek χρεία. One would expect that in a Greek work this would be the case. A full discussion of the anecdotes in the remainder of the Gospel would have to be undertaken to argue this result conclusively.

5. *Function of the Anecdotes in Mark 8.27–10.45*

The 14 anecdotes of Mk 8.27–10.45 are analyzed, first, with respect to their function within the composition of this narrative section and, secondly, for their portrait of their main character, the Markan Jesus.

a. *Compositional Function*

Within 8.27–10.45 the anecdotes function 'compositionally' in one of three ways, that is, when the author of Mark composed this section, he integrated anecdotes into the narrative in one of three ways: either as a free-standing unit, a part of a διήγημα, or a pattern or part of a pattern of argumentation.

As already noted above, only three of the anecdotes (8.31-33; 10.13-16; 10.32-34) are not elements of another structure. These are classified as 'free-standing units'. The remaining anecdotes of this section of Mark are elements of narrative or rhetorical structures. Seven, or one-half, of the 14 anecdotes (8.27-30; 9.28-29; 10.2-9; 10.10-12; 10.17-22; 10.35-40; 10.41-45) are contained within a διήγημα, that is, within a story that has a beginning, middle and ending. Given that these anecdotes appear within the larger narrative or 'story' that is Mark's Gospel, this last statistic is probably to be expected. Finally, five of these anecdotes demonstrate basic argumentation patterns. Three demonstrate the elaboration of a saying-χρεία (8.34-9.1; 9.38-40; 10.41-45), while two (9.33-42, 50d; 10.23-31) are involved in a confirmation of a saying-χρεία. Additionally, one anecdote, 10.35-45, both contains an elaboration of a saying-χρεία and is an element within a διήγημα.

On the level of the composition of this section of the Gospel, then, the 14 anecdotes function in one of three ways according to this typology:[141]

Typology of the Anecdotes in Mark 8.27–10.45 Based on Compositional Function:

I.	'Free-standing units'.		3
II.	Διήγημα.		7
III.	Displaying Argumentation:		5
	A. Elaboration;	3	
	B. Confirmation.	2	

141. The totals exceed 14, since 10.35-45 is classified under both Διήγημα and 'Displaying Argumentation'.

b. *Mark's Portrait of Jesus*

The Jesus of the Markan anecdotes in 8.27–10.45 is portrayed, first and foremost, as a persuasive teacher. Six of the 11 instances within Mark's Gospel wherein Jesus is addressed as 'teacher' by his followers or by others occur in this 'way' material, 5 times within the section and once in the framing story of Bartimaeus.[142] Prior to 8.27, Jesus is only addressed as 'Teacher' once, in 4.38, immediately after the parable sermon and in the midst of the storm at sea; in 5.35 he is referred to as 'teacher' by someone from the household of Jairus. It is only in 14.14, the last use of 'teacher' in the Gospel, that Jesus uses this title for himself when he sends the disciples into Jerusalem to procure a site for the celebration of the Passover meal. 8.27–10.45, then, emphasizes this title for Jesus.

Moreover, the Markan Jesus is a persistent and persuasive teacher. Three times Jesus predicts his coming suffering, death and resurrection, three times the disciples show a lack of acceptance or a misunderstanding of the significance of the impending events in Jerusalem, and three times Jesus teaches attitudes and behaviors that are in harmony with the meaning of these events. Each of these teachings on discipleship, 8.34–9.1, 9.33-42, 50d and 10.35-45, is cast in the form of an anecdote that exhibits an argumentative pattern. Furthermore, in two other anecdotes Mark uses mixed-χρεῖαι, 8.31-33 and 10.13-16, to portray Jesus' teachings. In both anecdotes the action of Jesus along with his saying make the point of his teaching; the action dramatizes the saying, not only clarifying it but heightening its persuasive force. Finally, the two instances where Jesus provides private explanations for his followers, 9.28-29 and 10.10-12, portray a master–disciple or teacher–student relationship between Jesus and his followers. Thus, 7 of the 14 anecdotes studied depict Jesus as engaging in persuasive teaching of his disciples or others; therefore, the Markan Jesus instructs the hearers or readers of the Gospel.

The first two anecdotes studied, 8.27-30 and 8.31-33, reveal the identity of the Markan Jesus, first as the Messiah and then as the suffering Son of Man. In 8.29 Peter identifies Jesus as 'the Messiah' and the text implies that Jesus accepts this identity since he commands his disciples 'to tell no one about him' (8.30). Immediately, Jesus prophesies that he is to be the suffering Son of Man (8.31). Thus, in three verses one hears Jesus identified as Messiah, using the title Son of Man of himself, and speaking as a

142. Jesus is addressed as 'Teacher', διδάσκαλε, in 9.17, 9.38, 10.17, 10.20 and 10.35. In 10.51 Bartimaeus addresses Jesus as teacher using the Aramaic (transliterated into Greek) ῥαββουνί.

prophet. The title 'Messiah' is not attributed directly to Jesus again until 14.62. Hence, the words and actions of Jesus from 8.30 to 14.60 clarify Mark's understanding of Jesus as Messiah.

First, 8.31-33 indicates that 'Messiah' and 'Son of Man' are equivalent; the Markan Jesus as 'Messiah' is the suffering 'Son of Man'. For Mark, Jesus is Son of Man on earth since he must suffer, die and rise; as Son of Man, Jesus already exercises authority on earth as recorded earlier in Mk 2.10 and 2.28. Moreover, Jesus, according to Mark, is also a Heavenly Messiah, since Jesus prophesies that the Son of Man will come 'in the glory of his Father with the holy angels' (8.38).

Secondly, Jesus, the Messiah and Son of Man, functions as a prophet. Three times within this section of the Gospel, he predicts his own arrest, suffering, death and resurrection. Moreover, within the dialogue of 8.27-30, Mark has the disciples relate that some of the people look upon Jesus as though he were John the Baptist raised from the dead (8.28). This mention of John would carry echoes for Mark's audience of earlier references to the Baptist's message, activities and fate. Earlier, Mk 1.9-11 records that Jesus submitted to baptism by John. Adela Y. Collins has shown both that John was a prophet who preached an eschatological message and that 'the baptism of Jesus by John places Jesus in an eschatological framework, both in terms of his social role (first a follower of a prophet, then a prophet in his own right) and his ideas'.[143] Finally, several of the sayings within Mk 8.27–10.45 are prophetic or apocalyptic sayings, that is, 8.38, 9.1 and 10.29-30. For Mark, therefore, Jesus the Messiah is a prophet and Son of Man on earth in his own lifetime, and will be a heavenly Messiah as the Son of Man coming in glory (8.38; 13.26; 14.62).

Finally, the teaching of Jesus on discipleship (8.34–9.1) that follows Peter's rebuke includes the saying referring to the Son of Man coming in glory as an apocalyptic figure (8.38). Thus, the teaching that includes 8.38 is meant to show the meaning of discipleship for the followers of a heavenly Messiah as well as of a suffering Messiah. Since the other teachings on discipleship in the anecdotes of this section of Mark all follow Jesus' predictions of the coming events involving the Son of Man, 9.31 and 10.33, these teachings also describe the disciples of such a Messiah, the Son of Man who suffers now but who comes in glory.

Ten of the anecdotes of this section of Mark, then, either contain Jesus' predictions of the passion, death and resurrection of the Son of Man (8.31-33; 10.32-34) or record teachings on discipleship directly related to mis-

143. Adela Yarbro Collins, 'Jesus the Prophet', *BibRes* 36 (1991), pp. 30-34 (31).

understandings of these predictions (8.34–9.1; 9.33-42, 50d; 9.38-40; 10.13-16; 10.17-22; 10.23-31; 10.35-40; 10.41-45). The contents of these ten anecdotes, are therefore meant to shed light on the meaning of Christian discipleship given God's activity in Jesus, Messiah and Son of Man. Thus, these ten anecdotes function within the host genre of Mark's Gospel, an apocalyptic, historical monograph, to relate the significance of God's activity in Jesus for history and the world in general and for his followers in particular.

6. *Conclusions*

In this chapter the anecdotes of Mk 8.27–10.45 were investigated. First, 8.27–10.45 was shown to be an coherent section of the Gospel; then the anecdotes of this section were identified using the definition of an anecdote developed in Chapter 1 of this book.

Fourteen anecdotes were found in this section of Mark. Since Mark is a Greek work, the forms of the Markan anecdotes were compared to the Greek χρεία, using the definition, typologies and exercises of the ancient προγυμνάσματα, particularly those of Theon and Hermogenes. Of the 14 Markan anecdotes studied, 9 were shown to be types of χρεῖαι (8) or a combination of two χρεῖαι (1). This fact allows one to posit that the majority of the Markan anecdotes are modeled upon the Greek χρεία; however, a study of all the anecdotes of the Gospel would be necessary to confirm this. The 5 other anecdotes of this section of Mark were found to be either dialogues (4) or a debate (1).

The functions of the 14 Markan anecdotes were investigated from two perspectives, that is, their functions both within the composition of the narrative of 8.27–10.45 and as vehicles of Mark's portrait of Jesus. The first investigation showed that three of the anecdotes (8.31-33; 10.13-16; 10.32-34) are 'free-standing units' in contrast to the other 11 anecdotes. Of the remaining anecdotes, 7 are contained within a διήγημα, that is, within a story that has a beginning, middle and ending. Finally, 5 of these anecdotes demonstrate basic argumentation patterns, either the elaboration or the confirmation of a saying-χρεία. One anecdote, 10.35-45, both contains an elaboration of a saying-χρεία and is an element within a διήγημα.

The portrait of the Markan Jesus displayed in these anecdotes is first and foremost that of a persuasive and persistent teacher. Moreover, the Markan Jesus is identified as the Messiah and Son of Man who functions as an apocalyptic prophet in his lifetime, and who will come in glory. As such, the Jesus of these anecdotes persuasively teaches the attitudes and behaviors required of those who would be his followers.

Conclusion

At the outset of Chapter 1, above, the observation of Vernon Robbins was presented, namely 'The brief stories and sayings which Christians used both in speech and writing to communicate their commitment to God's activity through the prophets, John the Baptist, Jesus, and the disciples were a powerful and natural form of communication in Mediterranean culture.'[1] My investigation illustrated this statement in three cultural worlds of the ancient Mediterranean region, that is, the Greco-Roman, the rabbinic and the Christian.

The literary genre 'anecdote', or 'brief story', was identified and then investigated in a literary work from each of these three cultural worlds. Greek anecdotes were examined as they appear in Lucian's *Demonax*, using the definition and typologies for the χρεία found in the ancient προγυμνάσματα. Rabbinic anecdotes were identified, using the general definition of an anecdote from Chapter 1, and investigated in the *Mishnah*, first those of the division *Mo'ed Qaṭan* and then those in the entire *Mishnah* that featured Rabbi Gamaliel II. Finally, the Markan anecdotes of 8.27–10.45 were identified and studied. The comparative results of these three investigations follow here.

1. *Form*

Anecdotes exist in all three literary works and are easily identifiable. In regard to Greek and Roman literature, it was found that both the ἀπόφθεγμα and the χρεία were expressions of the anecdote in these two bodies of literature. The χρεία was chosen as the Greek anecdote because it was a defined rhetorical and literary unit. Theon's definition and typologies for the χρεία were employed as a starting point for the study of the anecdotes in Lucian's *Demonax*.

The anecdotes of the *Demonax* number 52, most of which are found in

1. Robbins, 'The Chreia', p. 22.

the collection of anecdotes which forms the large, middle portion of Lucian's work. Of these 52 anecdotes all but 2 were able to be classified as χρεῖαι. Forty-six were saying-χρεῖαι, 2 were action-χρεῖαι, and 2 were mixed-χρεῖαι. The 2 anecdotes that are not χρεῖαι were both identified as dialogues. Thus, 50 of the anecdotes featuring Demonax recorded his words (46 saying-χρεῖαι, 2 mixed-χρεῖαι and 2 dialogues). Finally, almost all of the anecdotes on Demonax appear as concise χρεῖαι, although some could be condensed and hence their present form may represent slightly expanded forms of a more concise pre-Lucian tradition. There is no other evidence of the exercises with the χρεία present in the *Demonax*.

No definition of a literary unit comparable to the anecdote exists within early rabbinic literature, therefore, the definition of an anecdote developed in this book was used to study the units in the *Mishnah*.[2] The anecdotes that appear either in the division *Mo'ed Qaṭan* or that feature Rabbi Gamaliel II number 64. Of these, 22 contain a saying by a rabbinic authority, 33 record an action, 3 record both a saying and an action, and 4 record dialogues or debates; the 2 other anecdotes cannot be classified in one of the preceding categories. The fact that anecdotes recording actions outnumber those recording sayings points to the didactic function of the lives of the rabbis. The anecdotes that feature Rabbi Gamaliel are classified as 17 sayings, 13 actions, 1 relating both a saying and an action, 2 dialogues, and 2 that do not fit one of these 4 categories. While anecdotes relating Rabbi Gamaliel's sayings outnumber those recording his actions, there are still a significant number of his actions recorded. Again, Rabbi Gamaliel's actions as well as his sayings were used as authoritative.

As with the anecdotes of the *Demonax*, almost all of the rabbinic anecdotes are concise units. However, two longer anecdotes were found, namely *Roš Haš.* 2.8-9 and *Yeb.* 16.7 A-G. These were both shown to be carefully developed narratives, consisting of several anecdotes woven together. Thus, their forms, although different from one another, can both be considered as 'composite' or a 'combination'. In this respect their form is similar to the Markan anecdote classified as a 'combination', that is, Mk 9.33-42, 50d.

Additionally, among the 64 rabbinic anecdotes investigated (36) con-

2. The definition reads: '[A] brief narrative, either oral or written, describing an incident, including its setting, which involves one or more persons and which focuses on an action, saying, or dialogue; the function of an anecdote is to entertain, instruct, relate an historical incident, characterize a person, or authoritatively legitimate a specific opinion, a specific practice, or a broader view of reality.'

tained the formula מעשה, *ma'aśeh.* A study of these anecdotes in conjunction with the work of Arnold Goldberg and Joel Gereboff produced a definition of the מעשה as 'a short narrative consisting of a person(s), a setting, with or without an implicit or explicit question, and a verbal ruling or an action'. Since the anecdotes that contained the formula מעשה were no different in form and function from those without the formula, the term מעשה was adopted in this study for the rabbinic anecdote.

Furthermore, since the above definition of the מעשה and Theon's definiton of the χρεία[3] are very similar, a possible relationship between the מעשה and the Greek χρεία was explored, that is, the possibility that the Greek χρεία influenced the rabbinic מעשה . It was shown that, while the concise expressions of the two genres are very similar, there is no evidence among the Mishnaic anecdotes of the more expanded or elaborated χρεία, except for one anecdote, *'Abod. Zar.* 3.4 A-F, which exhibited a possible partial elaboration. This one example of a possible short elaboration cannot be used to support an assertion that the Greek χρεία influenced the rabbinic anecdotes.

In the third literary study, the narrative of Mk 8.27–10.45 was examined and 14 of the narrative units of that Gospel section were determined to be anecdotes. Like the anecdotes of the *Demonax*, the Markan units were studied and classified according to the discussions of the ancient προγυμνάσματα on the χρεία. Eight of the anecdotes in this section of Mark could be classified as χρεῖαι according to Theon's typology. Another was shown to be a combination of two mixed-χρεῖαι. The remaining five anecdotes were dialogues or a debate. This last result is similar to the classification of the anecdotes in the *Demonax* and in the *Mishnah* where the anecdotes that could not be classified as χρεῖαι were dialogues or debates.

Unlike the majority of both the anecdotes in the *Demonax* and those studied from the *Mishnah*, only 3 of the 14 Markan narratives were found to be examples of the concise anecdote. The other 11 anecdotes, a majority of those studied, are more developed narrative units, 6 of them built upon or containing χρεῖαι. Seven anecdotes are contained within a διήγημα, that is, within a story that has a beginning, a middle and an ending. Five anecdotes demonstrate basic argumentative patterns, that is, 3 demonstrate the elaboration of a saying-χρεία, while 2 are involved in a confirmation of a saying-χρεία. Moreover, one Markan anecdote, 10.41-45, both

3. Theon defined the χρεία as 'a concise statement or action which is attributed with aptness to some specified character or to something analogous to a character' (3.2-3).

contains an elaboration of a saying-χρεία and is an element within a διήγημα. These more developed narrative units distinguish the form of the Markan anecdotes from the form of both the anecdotes in Lucian's *Demonax* and those studied from the *Mishnah*.

Finally, different methods of incorporating the anecdotes within the larger host genre affect the form of the individual anecdotes. Mark's use of the anecdotes within the larger host genre that is his gospel resembles the use that the compilers of the *Mishnah* made of anecdotes. In both of these works, the anecdotes are 'woven into' the text, so to speak, and occur throughout each text from beginning to end.[4] However, although the anecdotes are spread throughout the tractates of the *Mishnah*, they remain relatively concise since the overall genre of each tractate is not narrative. In Mark's Gospel, on the other hand, anecdotes appear as parts of διηγήματα. This phenomenon, the inclusion of one narrative genre that emphasizes a saying within another narrative genre that is primarily a story, reflects the inclusion of blocks of sayings material within the larger host genre, Mark's Gospel, with its narrative framework.

On the other hand, Lucian included a collection of anecdotes whose forms are almost exclusively concise χρεῖαι, related one after the other, as the middle portion of his *Demonax*. Only two anecdotes occur outside this collection; they are found within the closing narrative of the death of Demonax. The fact that the anecdotes of the *Demonax* are mostly concise forms may be reflective of the facts that, first, the overall structure of the work is not a continuous, chronological narrative, and, second, that they do appear together in a collection within the *Demonax*. Lucian may have found this method of depicting characteristics of Demonax most 'useful'. Moreover, it remains a possibility that these anecdotes came to Lucian as a collection or that he himself had compiled them into a collection previously.

2. *Content*

The subject matter or content of the three sets of anecdotes studied is peculiar to each of their respective cultural settings. The sayings and the actions in the anecdotes of Lucian's *Demonax* depict actions and sayings of Demonax, for example, as he attacked the vices of vanity and sham in others, qualities that were looked down upon in the Greek culture. Rabbinic anecdotes present the rabbi's concerns about the proper observance of the

4. Although not included in my study, anecdotes do occur in the opening and closing verses of Mark's Gospel, for example, 1.9-11 and 16.1-7.

Torah and of their legal rulings. Markan anecdotes are concerned, for example, with the attitudes and behaviors of those who would follow Jesus, the Jewish Messiah and Son of Man. Thus, in regard to subject matter, the anecdotes reflect their respective cultural settings and therefore record different concerns.

3. *Function*

In each of the three literary works examined in this study, the anecdotes functioned within the purposes or functions of their respective host genres. Lucian stated that the purpose of his work on Demonax was twofold, that is, to insure that Demonax be remembered and that young persons of Lucian's day have a contemporary model on which to base their lives (2.1-8).

It was shown that within the *Demonax*, the anecdotes functioned as 'revelations' of the character of Demonax by presenting Demonax himself to the reader. They also served as παραδείγματα, illustrating the facts about or character traits of Demonax which Lucian had asserted in his introductory comments on Demonax. As such, the anecdotes advanced the encomiastic function of the *Demonax*, that is, Lucian's desire that Demonax be remembered as the 'noblest of all philosophers' (2.6-7). Furthermore, they aided Lucian's didactic purpose, to present Demonax as a model, παράδειγμα, for youth of Lucian's day. When an anecdote presented Demonax teaching, admonishing or praising a person, the hearer or reader of the *Demonax* was in turn taught, admonished or praised. Thus, the anecdotes taught youth how they should think, speak and behave. Additionally, but secondary to these first two purposes, the anecdotes entertained, were a vehicle for Lucian's own concerns and they provided the reader with background details of life in ancient Athens.

Unlike Lucian in his *Demonax*, the compiler(s) or redactor(s) of the *Mishnah* does not state the purposes of the text. Contemporary scholars do not agree on the genre of the *Mishnah*. Four opinions as to its genre prevail today, namely that it is a collection of legal rulings, a definitive law code, a textbook for teaching possible legal interpretations or a 'philosophical law code'. Each of these proposed genres for the *Mishnah* is directly related to its legal content; one can conclude, therefore, that the *Mishnah* had a legal function.

All but 8 of the 64 Mishnaic anecdotes studied in Chapter 3 had overtly legal functions within the *Mishnah*, that is, they were precedents, proofs or narrative laws. Six anecdotes served only to give the etiology of a practice while the remaining two stories provided only aggadic information. Thus, the principal functions of the Mishnaic anecdotes were legal and reflect the purpose of the host genre itself.

An interesting feature of the Mishnaic anecdotes is that there are 34 stories that are attested, that is, another sage reported the incident, thereby lending his own authority to the legal ruling, etiology or aggadic statement. These testimonies affirm the prominent role of the sages in the establishment of legal rulings. The added testimony of one or more sages also functioned within the *Mishnah* to heighten the portrait of the rabbis as knowledgeable and authoritative leaders.

The 35 Mishnaic anecdotes that feature Rabbi Gamaliel II also have a legal function. Each anecdote about Rabbi Gamaliel functions as a precedent, proof from authority or a narrative law. In addition to this function, these 35 anecdotes reveal aspects of Rabbi Gamaliel's character. The *Mishnah*, within its anecdotes, portrays Rabbi Gamaliel as a highly respected personage, a religious authority and a pious man worthy of imitation.

The anecdotes in the *Demonax* function primarily to emphasize the character of Demonax; through this characterization they provide philosophical teaching. For later readers and scholars they also provide glimpses into the social and cultural background of Demonax's and Lucian's times. Just the reverse is the case with the Mishnaic anecdotes. The rabbinic stories function first and foremost to inculcate legal teachings of early rabbinic Judaism and only incidentally do they reveal aspects of a rabbi's, for example, Rabbi Gamaliel's, character. The primary function of the anecdotes in each text reflects the purpose of the host genre. Thus, the anecdotes of Lucian's *Demonax* and those of the *Mishnah* are similar insofar as they express or contribute to the fulfillment of the objectives of their respective authors.

The 14 Markan anecdotes, a smaller number than the selections found in the *Demonax* or chosen from the *Mishnah*, also function in service of the author's objective. The study in Chapter 5 shows that the Markan anecdotes portray Jesus as a persuasive teacher; five times in this section of Mark, Jesus is addressed as 'Teacher', and 11 anecdotes present teachings of Jesus. He is also depicted as an apocalyptic prophet, suffering Messiah and Son of Man. It was shown that 10 of the 14 anecdotes predict the passion of the Son of Man or record teachings on discipleship directly related to misunderstandings of these predictions. The anecdotes, therefore, shed light on the meaning of Christian discipleship given God's activity in Jesus, the Son of Man. Thus, these anecdotes function within the host genre of Mark's Gospel, an apocalyptic, historical monograph whose purpose is to relate the meaning of God's activity in Jesus for history and the world. In this way, the function of the Markan anecdotes is analogous to that of the anecdotes of Lucian's *Demonax* and that of the *Mishnah*; all three sets of anecdotes function in a manner that directly reflects the function of their respective host genres.

4. *'Usefulness'*

In his Προγυμνάσματα, the grammarian Theon remarked that the entity he had defined as a χρεία was given the name 'χρεία', 'useful', because 'of its excellence, for more than the others it is useful in many ways for life' (3.25-26). This χρεία has been identified as a Greek form of the anecdote. Thus one can say that an 'anecdote is useful in many ways for life'. This has been shown to be the case with the anecdotes in the three literary works studied in this investigation.

One of Lucian's stated purposes for his *Demonax* was to provide the young person of his own day with a contemporary model for their lives. He accomplished his purpose in his text mainly by incorporating a large collection of anecdotes about Demonax. As noted above, when an anecdote presented Demonax teaching, admonishing or praising a person, the hearer or reader of the *Demonax* was in turn taught, admonished or praised. Thus, the anecdotes taught youth how they should think, speak and behave. The anecdotes of the *Demonax* were 'useful for living'.

Jacob Neusner has concluded that the principal concern of the *Mishnah* was the sanctification of life by establishing stability, order and regularity in Israel's life.[5] The anecdotes involving the rabbis presented their actions or rulings on behaviors that were 'useful for' or aided this sanctification of life.

Finally, the anecdotes of Mk 8.27–10.45 portray Jesus, the Messiah and Son of Man, as a persistent teacher. This Jesus is engaged in persuasively teaching his disciples, and therefore Mark's audience, attitudes and behaviors that are necessary to live one's life as his follower, the suffering Messiah, 'on the way'.

5. Neusner, *Introduction to Rabbinic Literature*, p. 100.

Appendix A

ANECDOTES OF DIVISION *MO'ED QAṬAN*

1. *Šabbat 1.4 A-C*
   Form: B.1
   Function: A.1

2. *Šabbat 1.9 A*
   Form: B.2
   Function: A.2; B.1

3. *Šabbat 3.4 A-E*
   Form: [מעשׂה] A.1
   Function: A.3

4. *Šabbat 12.3 G-H*
   Form: B.2
   Function: A.4; B.1

5. *Šabbat 16.7 D*
   Form: [מעשׂה] A.2
   Function: A.3; B.1, B.2

6. *Šabbat 16.8 H*
   Form: [מעשׂה] B.1
   Function: A.2

7. *Šabbat 22.3 H*
   Form: [מעשׂה] A.2
   Function: A.2; B.1

8. *Šabbat 24.5 E*
   Form: [מעשׂה] B.1
   Function: A.2

9. *'Erubin 1.2 E-J*
   Form: D.1
   Function: A.5

10. *'Erubin 4.1 I-L*
    Form: B.1
    Function: A.2

11. *'Erubin 4.2 A-C*
    Form: [פעם אחת] A.1
    Function: A.3

12. *'Erubin 4.4 F*
    Form: [מעשׂה] B.2
    Function: A.2; B.1

13. *'Erubin 6.2 A-B*
    Form: [מעשׂה] B.2
    Function: A.2; B.1

14. *'Erubin 8.7 F*
    Form: [מעשׂה] B.2
    Function: A.2; B.1

15. *'Erubin 10.9 D*
    Form: [מעשׂה] B.2
    Function: A.2; B.1

16. *'Erubin 10.10 D-E*
    Form: [מעשׂה] B.2
    Function: A.2; B.1

17. *Pesaḥim 7.2 B*
    Form: [מעשׂה] B.2
    Function: A.3; B.1, B.2

18. *Šeqalim 1.4 A-C*
    Form: A.2
    Function: A.2; B.1

19. *Šeqalim 3.3 A*
    Form: B.1
    Function: A.5

20. *Šeqalim 6.2 A-D*
    Form: [מעשה] B.1
    Function: A.4

21. *Yoma 2.2 A-D*
    Form: [מעשה] B.1
    Function: A.4

22. *Yoma 3.2 B*
    Form: [פעם אחת] B.1
    Function: A.4

23. *Yoma 6.3 D*
    Form: [מעשה] B.2
    Function: A.2; B.1

24. *Sukkah 2.1 C-D*
    Form: [מעשה] A.2
    Function: A.2; B.1

25. *Sukkah 2.5 A-C*
    Form: [מעשה] C.2
    Function: A.3; B.1, B.2

26. *Sukkah 2.7 D-E*
    Form: [מעשה] B.2
    Function: A.2; B.1

27. *Sukkah 2.8 C*
    Form: [מעשה] B.1
    Function: A.3; B.2

28. *Sukkah 3.8 C*
    Form: [מעשה] B.2
    Function: A.2; B.1

29. *Sukkah 3.9 D*
    Form: B.2
    Function: A.3; B.1

30. *Sukkah 4.9 N-O*
    Form: [פעם אחת] B.1
    Function: A.4

31. *Beṣah 2.6 E-G*
    Form: D.1
    Function: A.3; B.2; A.5

32. *Beṣah 3.2 D*
    Form: [מעשׂה] A.1
    Function: A.3, A.5; B.2

33. *Beṣah 3.5 B*
    Form: [מעשׂה] A.1
    Function: A.2

34. *Beṣah 3.8 D*
    Form: [מעשׂה] B.1
    Function: A.2

35. *Roš haš-Šanah 1.6 A-C*
    Form: [מעשׂה] A.1
    Function: A.2, A.5

36. *Roš haš-Šanah 1.7 E-G*
    Form: [מעשׂה] B.2
    Function: A.2; B.1

37. *Roš haš-Šanah 2.8-9*
    Form: [מעשׂה] E
    Function: A.2, A.5; B.1

38. *Roš haš-Šanah 4.4 B-D*
    Form: [פעם אחת] B.1
    Function: A.4

39. *Ta'anit 2.5 A*
    Form: [מעשׂה] B.1
    Function: A.3

40. *Ta'anit 3.6 A*
    Form: [מעשׂה] B.1
    Function: A.3

41. *Ta'anit 3.9 D*
    Form: [מעשׂה] C.1
    Function: A.2

Appendix B

ANECDOTES INVOLVING RABBI GAMALIEL II

1. *Division Mo'ed Qaṭan**

1. (2) *Šabbat 1.9 A*
   Form: B.2
   Function: A.2; B.1

2. (6) *Šabbat 16.8 H*
   Form: [מעשׂה] B.1
   Function: A.2

3. (10) *'Erubin 4.1 I-K*
   Form: [מעשׂה] B.1
   Function: A.2

4. (11) *'Erubin 4.2 A-C*
   Form: [פעם אחת] A.1
   Function: A.3

5. (13) *'Erubin 6.2 A-B*
   Form: [מעשׂה] B.2
   Function: A.2; B.1

6. (16) *'Erubin 10.10 D-E*
   Form: [מעשׂה] B.2
   Function: A.2; B.1

7. (17) *Pesaḥim 7.2 B*
   Form: [מעשׂה] B.2
   Function: A.3; B.1, B.2

8. (24) *Sukkah 2.1 C-D*
   Form: [מעשׂה] A.2
   Function: A.2; B.1

9. (29) *Sukkah 3.9 D*
   Form: B.2
   Function: A.3; B.1

10. (32) *Beṣah 3.2 D*
    Form: [מעשׂה] A.1
    Function: A.3, A.5; B.2

11. (35) *Roš haš-Šanah 1.6 A-C*
    Form: [מעשׂה] A.1
    Function: A.2, A.5

12. (37) *Roš haš-Šanah 2.8-9*
    Form: [מעשׂה] E
    Function: A.2; B.1

* Number in parentheses is the number of the anecdote in *Mo'ed Qaṭan* listing of Appendix A.

2. *Other Divisions*

13. *Berakot 1.1 G-I*
    Form: [מעשׂה] A.1
    Function: A.2, A.1

14. *Berakot 2.5 C-E*
    Form: [מעשׂה] A.1
    Function: A.2, A.1, A.5

15. *Berakot 2.6 A-C*
    Form: A.1
    Function: A.2, A.5

16. *Berakot 2.7 A-C*
    Form: A.1
    Function: A.2, A.5

17. *Demai: 3.1 B*
    Form: B.1
    Function: A.3

18. *Ma'aser Šeni 2.7 C*
    Form: B.2
    Function: A.2; B.1

19. *Ma'aser Šeni 5.9 C-E*
    Form: [מעשׂה] A.1
    Function: A.2

20. *Yebamot 16.7 A-G*
    Form: [מעשׂה] E
    Function: A.1, A.2; B.1

21. *Yebamot 16.7 H*
    Form: B.2
    Function: A.2, A.5; B.1

22. *Ketubot 8.1 G-H*
    Form: A.2
    Function: A.2; B.1

23. *Ketubot 8.1 M -N*
    Form: A.2
    Function: A.2; B.1

24. *Giṭṭin 1.5*
    Form: [מעשׂה] B.1
    Function: A.2

25. *Baba Meṣi'a 5.8 C-H*
    Form: B.1
    Function: A.2, A.5

26. *'Eduyyot 7.7 I -K*
    Form: [מעשׂה] A.1
    Function: A.2

27. *'Eduyyot 8.3 A-E*
    Form: A.1
    Function: A.2, A.4

28. *'Abodah Zarah 3.4 A-F*
    Form: C.2
    Function: A.3, A.5

29. *Keritot 3.7 A-E*
    Form: A.2
    Function: A.3, A.5; B.1

30. *Keritot 3.8 A-G*
    Form: A.2
    Function: A.3, A.5; B.1

31. *Keritot 3.9 A-F*
    Form: A.2
    Function: A.3, A.5; B.1

32. *Kelim 5.4 B*
    Form: [מעשׂה] B.1
    Function: A.2

33. *Nega'im 7.4 E-F*
    Form: A.2
    Function: A.2; B.1

34. *Yadaim 3.1 K-N*
    Form: [מעשׂה] D.2
    Function: A.2; B.1

35. *Yadaim 4.4 A-L*
    Form: D.1
    Function: A.1

Appendix C

TYPOLOGIES OF THE *MA'AŚEH*

1. *Typology of the* ma'aśeh *Based on Form*

A. Narrative with a Saying:		11
1. Recorded	8	
2. Attested	3	
B. Narrative with an Action:		20
1. Recorded	10	
2. Attested	10	
C. Narrative with Both a Saying and an Action:		2
1. Recorded	1	
2. Attested	1	
D. Narrative with a Dialogue or a Debate:		1
1. Recorded	0	
2. Attested	1	
E. Other		2
Total		36

2. *Typology of the* ma'aśeh *Based on Function*

A. Primary Functions:	
1. Precedent	2
2. Proof from Authority	26
3. Narrative Law	8
4. Etiology	2
5. *Aggadah*	3
B. Secondary Functions:	
1. Testimony	15
2. Contrary Opinion	5

Appendix D

TYPOLOGIES OF GOSPEL ANECDOTES

1. *Martin Dibelius*

Paradigms (18 units):

I. *Pure* (8 units):
Mk 2.1-12; 2.18-22; 2.23-28; 3.1-6; 3.20-21, 31-35; 10.13-16; 12.13-17; 14.3-9.

II. *Less pure* (10 units):
Mk 1.23-27; 2.13-14; 6.1-6; 10.17-22; 10.35-40; 10.46-52; 11.15-19; 12.18-23; Lk. 9.51-56; 14.1-6.

2. *Rudolf Bultmann*

Apophthegms (47 units):

I. *Controversy Dialogues* (13 units):
  A. Occasioned by Jesus' healings (5):
  Mk 3.1-6; Lk. 14.1-6; Lk. 13.10-17; Mk 3.22-30 (par.); Mk 2.1-12 (par.);
  B. Occasioned by other conduct of Jesus or of his disciples (6):
  Mk 2.23-28 (par.); Mk 7.1-23 (par.); Mk 2.15-17 (par.); Mk 2.18-22 (par.); Mk 11.27-33 (par.); Lk. 7.36-50;
  C. An unbelieving person lays claim on Jesus (2):
  Mk 7.24-31 (par.); Mt. 8.5-13 // Lk. 7.1-10.

II. *Scholastic Dialogues* (16 units):
  A. Jesus is questioned by friends (11):
  Mk 10.17-31 (par.); Mk 12.28-34 (par.); Lk. 12.13-14; Lk. 13.1-5; Mt. 11.2-19 // Lk. 7.18-35; Mk 10.35-45 (par.); Mk 9.38-40 (par.); Lk. 17.20-21; Lk. 6.5 (uncial D); Mk 11.20-25 (par.); Lk. 9.51-56;
  B. Jesus is questioned by opponents (5):
  Mk 12.13-17 (par.); Mk 12.18-27 (par.); Mk 10.2-12 (par.); Mk 9.34-40; Lk. 9.51-56.

III. *Biographical Apophthegms* (18 units):
Mk 1.16-20 (par.); Mk 2.14 (par.); Lk. 9.57-62 // Mt. 8.19-22; Mk 3.20-21, 31-35 (par.); Lk. 11.27-28; Mk 6.1-6 (par.); Mk 10.13-16 (par.); Mk 12.41-44 (par.); Lk. 10.38-42; Lk. 17.11-19; Lk. 19.1-10; Lk. 19.39-40 // Mt. 21.15-16; Mt. 17.24-27; Lk. 13.31-33; Mk 11.15-19 (par.); Mk 13.1-2 (par.); Lk. 19.41-44; Mk 14.3-9 (par.); Lk. 23.27-31.

3. *Martin Albertz*

Controversy Dialogues (17 units)

I. *'Trial' Controversy Dialogues* (13 units):
   A. The Galilean collection: Mk 2.1–3.6 (5 units):
      Mk 2.1-12; 2.15-17; 2.18-22; 2.23-28; 3.1-6;
   B. The Jerusalem collection (3 units):
      Mk 11.15-17; 11.27-33; 12.13-40 (par.);
   C. On the obligations of Rabbinic tradition:
      Mk 7.1-23 (par.);
   D. On divorce:
      Mk 10.2-12;
   E. The three-fold dialogue of Jesus with Satan (3 units):
      Mt. 4.1-11 // Lk. 4.1-13.

II. *'Non-trial' Controversy Dialogues* (4 units):
   A. Accusations of demonic origins of Jesus' holiness:
      Mk 3.22-30;
   B. The demand for a messianic sign:
      Mk 8.11-13;
   C. The conditions of salvation:
      Mk 10.17-27;
   D. The person of the 'One to Come':
      Mt. 11.2-6.

4. *Vincent Taylor*

Pronouncement Stories (36 units)
   A. *Mark* (23 units):
      2.3-12; 2.15-17; 2.18-20; 2.23-26; 3.1-5; 3.22-26; 3.31-35; 4.10-12; 7.5-8; 8.11-12; 9.38-39; 10.2-9; 10.13-16; 10.17-27; 10.34-50; 11.27-33; 12.13-17; 12.18-27; 12.28-34; 12.35-37; 12.41-44; 13.1-2; 14.3-9.
   B. *Q material* (2 units):
      Lk. 9.57-62 // Mt. 8.19-22 // and Lk. 7.19-23 // Mt. 11.2-6.
   C. *Special Matthean material*:
      Mt. 17.24-27.
   D. *Special Lukan material* (9 units):
      Lk. 6.5 (variant in Codex Bezae); 11.27-28; 12.13-14; 13.1-5; 13.10-17; 14.1-6; 17.11-19; 17.20-21; 23.27-31.
   E. *John*: late addition of Jn 7.53–8.11.

5. *Arland Hultgren*

Conflict Stories (18 units):

I. *Unitary* (7):
   Mk 2.18-20 (par.); 3.1-5 (par.); 11.27-33 (par.); 12.13-17 (par.); Lk. 7.36-50; 13.10-17; 14.1-6.

II. *Non-unitary* (11):
Mk 2.1-12 (par.); 2.15-17 (par.); 2.23-28 (par.); 3.22-30 (par.); 12.18-27 (par.); Mk 7.1-8 // Mt. 15.1-9; Mk 10.2-9 // Mt. 19.3-9; Mt. 12.22-32; 12.38-42; 22.34-40; 22.41-46 .

6. *Robert Tannehill*

Pronouncement Stories:

I. *Correction stories*:
Mk 3.31-35; 8.11-12; 9.38-40; 10.2-9; 10.13-16; 10.35-45; 11.15-17; 12.18-27; 13.1-2; 14.3-9.

II. *Commendation stories*:
Mk 3.31-35; 10.13-16; 12.41-44; 14.3-9.

III. *Objection stories*:
Mk 2.15-17; 2.18-22; 2.23-28; 3.1-6; 3.22-30; 6.1-6; 7.1-15; 8.31-33; 9.9-13; 10.23-27.

IV. *Quest stories*:
Mk 2.1-2; 7.24-30; 12.28-34; 10.17-22.

V. *Inquiry stories*:
- A. Testing:
  Mk 8.27-30; 10.2-9; 11.27-33; 12.13-17; 12.35-37
- B. Request for Instruction:
  Mk 4.10-20; 7.17-23; 9.28-29; 10.10-12; 11.20-25.

VI. *Description stories*

7. *Wolfgang Weiss*

I. *Controversy Dialogues* (8 units):
- A. On Christian Life Praxis (5):
  Mk 2.15-17 (par.); 2.18-22 (par.); 2.23-28 (par.); 3.1-6 (par.); 7.1-23;
- B. On the Activity of Jesus (3):
  Mk 2.1-12 (par.); 3.22-30; 11.27-33.

II. *Scholastic Dialogues* (5 units):
- A. On General Religious Questions (2):
  Mk 12.18-27; 12.28-34;
- B. On Legal Questions (2):
  Mk 10.2-12; 12.13-17;
- C. Instruction Dialogue:
  Mk 10.17-21.

BIBLIOGRAPHY

1. *Primary Sources*

Unless otherwise noted all Greek and Latin authors are cited from the Loeb Classic Library editions.

Albeck, Ch., and H. Yalon, *Shishah Sidre Mishnah* (6 vols.; Jerusalem: Bialik Institute, 1952–1959).

Aphthonius, *Progymnasmata*, in *Aphthonii Progymnasmata* (ed. Hugo Rabe; Rhetores Graeci, 10; Leipzig: Teubner, 1926), pp. 1-51.

Blackman, Philip (ed.), *Mishnayoth* (7 vols.; Gateshead: Judaica Press, 2nd edn, 1983).

Danby, Herbert, *The Mishnah: Translated from the Hebrew with Introduction and Brief Explanatory Notes* (London: Oxford University Press, 1933).

Hermogenes, *On Types of Style*, in *Hermogenis opera* (ed. Hugo Rabe; Rhetores Graeci, 6; Stuttgart: Teubner, 1913).

—*Progymnasmata*, in *Hermogenis opera* (ed. Hugo Rabe; Rhetores Graeci, 6; Stuttgart: Teubner, 1913), pp. 1-27.

Justin, 'τοῦ ἁγίου Ἰουστίνου Ἀπολογία ὑπὲρ Χριστιανῶν πρὸς Ἀντωνίνον', in *Saint Justin: Apologies* (ed. André Wartelle; Paris: Études Augustiniennes, 1987).

Maximus, Valerius, *Factorum et dictorum memorabilium Libra IX* (ed. Carolus Kempf; 2 vols.; Leipzig: Teubner, 2nd edn, 1888; repr. Stuttgart: Teubner, 1966; ET *Valerius Maximus: Memorable Deeds and Sayings* [trans. Samuel Speed; London: Booksellers, 1678]).

The Mishnah: A New Translation (trans. Jacob Neusner; New Haven: Yale University Press, 1988).

Nestle, Eberhard, Erwin Nestle and Kurt Aland *et al.* (eds.), *Novum Testamentum Graece* (Stuttgart: Deutsche Bibelgesellschaft, 27th edn, 1993).

Nicolaus of Myra, *Progymnasmata*, in *Nicolai Progymnasmata* (ed. J. Felten; Rhetores Graeci, 11; Leipzig: Teubner, 1913), pp. 1-60.

Oxyrhynchus Papyrus 85, Greek text in Taylor, *Groundwork of the Gospels*, p. 82.

Priscan, *Praeexercitamina*, in *Prisciani* (ed. Henricus Keil; Grammatici Latini; 4 vols.; Hildesheim: Georg Olms, 1961), 3.430-40.

Septuaginta. Id est Vetus Testamentum graece iuxta LXX interpretes (ed. Alfred Rahlfs; Stuttgart: Deutsche Bibelgesellschaft, 1935).

Theon, *Progymnasmata*, in James R. Butts, 'The "Progymnasmata" of Theon: A New Text with Translation and Commentary' (PhD dissertation, Claremont Graduate School, 1986), pp. 96-569.

The Tosefta (trans. Jacob Neusner; 6 vols.; New York: Ktav, 1977–86).

2. *Secondary Sources*

Aarne, Antti, and Stith Thompson, *The Types of the Folk-Tale: A Classification and Bibliography* (Folklore Fellows Communications, 184; Helsinki: Suomalainen Tiedeakatemia, Academia Scientaram Fennica, 1961); cited in Dégh, 'Folk Narrative', p. 60 and passim.

Abrams, M.H., *A Glossary of Literary Terms* (Fort Worth: Holt, Rhinehart & Winston, 5th edn, 1988).

Achtemeier, Paul J., '*Omne Verbum Sonat*, The New Testament and the Oral Environment of Late Western Antiquity', *JBL* 109 (1990), pp. 3-27.

Albeck, Chanoch, *Einführung in die Mischna* (Berlin: W. de Gruyter, 1971).

Albertz, Martin, *Die synoptischen Streitgespräche: Ein Beitrage zur Formengeschichte des Urchristentums* (Berlin: Trowitzsch, 1921).

Alexander, Philip, 'Rabbinic Biography and the Biography of Jesus', in Christopher Tuckett (ed.), *Synoptic Studies: The Ampleforth Conference of 1982 and 1983* (JSNTSup, 7; Sheffield: JSOT Press, 1984), pp. 19-50.

Andersen, Øivind, 'Oral Tradition', in Wansbrough (ed.), *Jesus and the Oral Gospel*, pp. 17-58.

Anderson, Graham, *Lucian: Theme and Variation in the Second Sophistic* (Mnemosyne Sup, 41; Leiden: E.J. Brill, 1976).

Anderson, Hugh, *The Gospel of Mark* (London: Marshall, Morgan & Scott, 1976).

Arnim, H.v., 'Agathobulos', PW, I, col. 745.

Atkins, J.W.H., *Literary Criticism in Antiquity: A Sketch of its Development*. I. *Greek* (Cambridge: Cambridge University Press, 1934).

Aune, David E., 'The Apocalypse of John and the Problem of Genre', in Adela Yarbro Collins (ed.), *Early Christian Apocalypticism: Genre and Social Setting* (Semeia, 36; Atlanta: Scholars Press, 1986), pp. 65-96.

—'Greco-Roman Biography', in *Greco-Roman Literature and the New Testament: Selected Forms and Genres* (SBLSBS, 21; Atlanta: Scholars Press, 1988), pp. 107-26.

—*The New Testament in its Literary Environment* (Library of Early Christianity; Philadelphia: Westminster Press, 1987).

—'Septem Sapientium Convivium (Moralia 146B-164D)', in H.D. Betz (ed.), *Plutarch's Ethical Writings and Early Christian Literature* (SCHNT, 4; Leiden: E.J. Brill, 1978), pp. 51-105.

Avery-Peck, Alan J., 'Classifying Early Rabbinic Pronouncement Stories', in Kent H. Richards (ed.), *SBLSP 1983* (SBLSP, 22; Chico, CA: Scholars Press, 1983), pp. 223-44.

—'Judaism without the Temple: The Mishnah', in Harold W. Attridge and Gohei Hata (eds.), *Eusebius, Christianity, and Judaism* (Detroit: Wayne State University Press, 1992), pp. 409-31.

—'Rhetorical Analysis of Early Rabbinic Pronouncement Stories', *HAR* 13 (1991), pp. 1-24.

—'Rhetorical Argumentation in Rabbinic Pronouncement Stories', in Robbins (ed.), *The Rhetoric of Pronouncement*, pp. 49-71.

Bailey, James L., and Lyle D. Vander Broek, *Literary Forms in the New Testament: A Handbook* (Louisville, KY: Westminster/John Knox Press, 1992).

Baldwin, Barry, *Studies in Lucian* (Toronto: Hakkert, 1973).

Baldwin, Charles S., *Medieval Rhetoric and Poetic (to 1400): Interpreted from Representative Works* (New York: Macmillan, 1928).

Bauckham, Richard, 'For Whom Were Gospels Written?', in *The Gospels for All Christians:*

Rethinking the Gospel Audiences (Grand Rapids, MI: Eerdmans, 1998), pp. 9-48.

Ben-Amos, Dan, 'Forward', *Genre* 2 (1969), pp. iii-iv.

—'Introduction', in *Folklore Genres* (Bibliographical and Special Series [Publications of the American Folklore Society], 26; Austin: University of Texas Press, 1976), pp. x-xvii.

—'Narrative Forms in the Haggadah: Structural Analysis' (PhD dissertation, Indiana University, 1967).

Berger, Klaus, *Formgeschichte des Neuen Testaments* (Heidelberg: Quelle & Meyer, 1984).

—'Hellenistisch Gattungen im Neuen Testament', *ANRW*, II.25.2, pp. 1031-432.

Best, Ernest, 'Mark's Narrative Technique', *JSNT* 37 (1989), pp. 43-50.

—*The Temptation and the Passion: The Markan Soteriology* (SNTSMS, 2; Cambridge: Cambridge University Press, 2nd edn, 1990).

Bickerman, Elias J., *The Jews in the Greek Age* (Cambridge, MA: Harvard University Press, 1988).

Black, C. Clifton, *Mark: Images of an Apostolic Interpreter* (ed. D. Moody Smith; Studies in Personalities of the New Testament; Columbia, SC: University of South Carolina Press, 1994).

—'Was Mark a Roman Gospel?', *ExpTim* 105 (1993), pp. 36-40.

Blackburn, Simon, 'dialectic', in *The Oxford Dictionary of Philosophy* (Oxford: Oxford University Press, 1994), p. 104, cols. 1-2.

Bonner, Stanley F., *Education in Ancient Rome: From the Elder Cato to the Younger Pliny* (Berkley: University of California Press, 1977).

Booth, Wayne C., *The Rhetoric of Fiction* (Chicago: University of Chicago Press, 2nd edn, 1983).

Botha, Pieter J.J., 'The Historical Setting of Mark's Gospel: Problems and Possibilities', *JSNT* 51 (1993), pp. 35-37.

Branham, R. Bracht, 'Authorizing Humor: Lucian's *Demonax* and Cynic Rhetoric', in Robbins (ed.), *The Rhetoric of Pronouncement*, pp. 45-46.

Bremond, Claude, 'Le message narratif', *Commmunications* 4 (1964), pp. 4-32.

Breytenbach, Cilliers, 'The Gospel of Mark as Episodical Narrative: Reflections on the "Composition" of the Second Gospel', *Scriptura* S (special issue) 4 (1989; German original, 1985), pp. 1-26.

Brown, Francis, S.R. Driver and Charles A. Briggs, *The New Brown–Driver–Briggs–Gesenius, Hebrew and English Lexicon with an Appendix Containing the Biblical Aramaic* (Peabody, MA: Hendrickson, 1979).

Brown, Raymond E., *An Introduction to the New Testament* (Anchor Bible Reference Library; New York: Doubleday, 1997).

Brownlow, Louis, *The Anatomy of the Anecdote* (Chicago: University of Chicago Press, 1960).

Brozoska, Julius, 'Aphthonius (1)', PW, I, cols. 2797-2800.

Bryan, Christopher, *A Preface to Mark: Notes on the Gospel in its Literary and Cultural Settings* (Oxford: Oxford University Press, 1993).

Bultmann, Rudolf, *Die Geschichte der synoptischen Tradition* (FRLANT, 29; Göttingen: Vandenhoeck & Ruprecht, 2nd edn, 1931 [1921]); ET *The History of the Synoptic Tradition* (trans. J. Marsh; New York: Harper & Row, 3rd rev. edn, 1963).

Burridge, Richard A., *What Are the Gospels? A Comparison with Graeco-Roman Biography* (SNTMS, 70; Cambridge: Cambridge University Press, 1992).

Butts, James R., 'The Chreia in the Synoptic Gospels', *BTB* 16 (1986), pp. 32-38.

—'Passion Apologetic, the Chreia, and the Narrative', *Foundations and Facets Forum* 3 (1987), pp. 96-127.

—'The "Progymnasmata" of Theon: A New Text with Translation and Commentary' (PhD dissertation, Claremont Graduate School, 1986).

—'The Voyage of Discipleship: Narrative, Chreia, and Call Story', in C.A. Evans and W.F. Stinespring (eds.), *Early Jewish and Christian Exegesis: Studies in Memory of William Hugh Brownlee* (Atlanta: Scholars Press, 1987), pp. 199-219.

Butts, James R., and Ronald F. Hock, 'Aphthonius of Tarsus', in Hock and O'Neil (eds.), *The Chreia in Ancient Rhetoric*, pp. 212-22.

Cancik, Hubert, 'Bios and Logos: Formengeschichtliche Untersuchungen zu Lukians "Demonax"', in *Markus-Philologie*, pp. 115-30.

—'Die Gattung Evangelium: Markus im Rahmen der antiken Historiographie', in *Markus-Philologie*, pp. 85-113.

Cancik, Hubert (ed.), *Markus-Philologie: Historische, literargeschichtliche und stilistische Untersuchungen zum zweiten Evangelium* (WUNT, 33; Tübingen: J.C.B. Mohr, 1984).

Capelle, W., 'Timocrates (14)', PW, VI.A, cols. 1266-67.

Carmell, Aryeh, *Aiding Talmud Study* (Jerusalem: Feldheim Publishers, 1988).

Chatman, Seymour, *Story and Discourse: Narrative Structure in Fiction and Film* (Ithaca, NY: Cornell University Press, 1978).

Clark, D.L., *Rhetoric in Greco-Roman Education* (New York: Columbia University Press, 1957).

—'The Rise and Fall of *Progymnasmata* in Sixteenth and Seventeenth Century Grammar Schools', *Speech Monographs* 19 (1952), pp. 259-63.

Clarke, W.K.L., *New Testament Problems* (London: SPCK, 1929).

Coates, George W., 'Introduction: Genres: Why Should They Be Important?', in *Saga, Legend, Tale, Novella, Fable: Narrative Forms in Old Testamant Literature* (JSOTSup, 35; Sheffield: JSOT Press, 1985), pp. 7-15.

Collins, Adela Yarbro, 'The Apocalyptic Rhetoric of Mark 13 in Historical Context', *BR* 41 (1996), pp. 5-36.

—*The Beginning of the Gospel: Probings of Mark in Context* (Philadelphia: Fortress Press, 1992).

—'Daniel 7 and the Historical Jesus', in Harold W. Attridge, John J. Collins and Thomas H. Tobin (eds.), *Of Scribes and Scrolls: Studies on the Hebrew Bible, Intertestamental Judaism, and Christian Origins* (*Presented to John Strugnell on the Occasion of his Sixtieth Birthday*) (College Theology Society and Resources in Religion, 5; Lanham, MD: University Press of America, 1990), pp. 187-93.

—'The Influence of Daniel on the New Testament: The Son of Man Tradition', in John J. Collins, *Daniel: A Commentary on the Book of Daniel* (Hermeneia; Minneapolis: Fortress Press, 1993), pp. 90-105.

—'Introduction', in *Early Christian Apocalypticism Social Setting*, pp. 1-11.

—'Is Mark's Gospel a Life of Jesus? The Question of Genre', in *The Beginning of the Gospel*, pp. 1-38 (repr. of *Is Mark's Gospel a Life of Jesus? The Question of Genre* [The Pere Marquette Lecture in Theology, 1989; Milwaukee: Marquette University Press, 1990]).

—'Jesus the Prophet', *BibRes* 36 (1991), pp. 30-34.

—'Mark 13: An Apocalyptic Discourse', in *The Beginning of the Gospel*, pp. 1-38 (reprint of 'The Eschatological Discourse of Mark 13', in F. Van Segbroeck *et al.* [eds.], *The Four Gospels 1992* [Festschrift Frans Neirynck; BETL, 100; 3 vols.; Leuven: University Press, 1992], II, pp. 1125-40).

—'Narrative, History, and Gospel', in Gerhart and Williams (eds.), *Genre, Narrativity, and Theology*, pp. 145-53.

—'The Origin of the Designation of Jesus as "Son of Man"', *HTR* 80 (1987), pp. 391-407 (reprinted in Adela Yarbro Collins, *Cosmology and Eschatology in Jewish and Christian Apocalypticism* [JSJSup, 50; Leiden: E.J. Brill, 1996], pp. 139-58).

—'The Signification of Mark 10:45 among Gentile Christians', *HTR* 90 (1997), pp. 371-82.

Collins, Adela Yarbro (ed.), *Early Christian Apocalypticism: Genre and Social Setting* (Semeia, 36; Atlanta: Scholars Press, 1986).

Collins, John J., 'Introduction: Towards a Morphology of a Genre', in *Apocalypse: The Morphology of a Genre* (Semeia, 14; Missoula, MT: Scholars Press, 1979), pp. 1-20.

Colson, F.H., 'Phaedrus and Quintilian I.9.2', *Classical Review* 33 (1919), pp. 59-61.

—'Quintilian I.9 and the "Chria" in Ancient Education', *Classical Review* 35 (1921), pp. 150-54.

Crenshaw, James L., 'Education in Ancient Israel', *JBL* 104 (1985), pp. 601-15.

Cuddon, J.A., *A Dictionary of Literary Terms and Literary Theory* (Oxford: Basil Blackwell, 3rd edn, 1991).

Culler, Jonathan, *The Pursuit of Signs: Semiotics, Literature, Deconstruction* (Ithaca, NY: Cornell University Press, 1981).

Danby, Herbert, *The Mishnah: Translated from the Hebrew with Introduction and Brief Explanatory Notes* (London: Oxford University Press, 1933).

Danove, Paul L., *The End of Mark's Story: A Methodological Study* (Biblical Interpretation Series, 3; Leiden: E.J. Brill, 1993).

Daube, David, *The New Testament and Rabbinic Judaism* (London: Athlone Press, 1956).

—'Public Pronouncement and Private Explanation in the Gospels', *ExpTim* 57 (1945–46), pp. 175-77.

Dean-Otting, Miriam, and Vernon K. Robbins, 'Biblical Sources for Pronouncement Stories in the Gospels', in Robbins (ed.), *The Rhetoric of Pronouncement*, pp. 95-115.

Dégh, Linda, 'Folk Narrative', in Richard M. Dorson (ed.), *Folklore and Folklife: An Introduction* (Chicago: University of Chicago Press, 1972), pp. 53-83.

Dewey, Joanna, 'The Gospel of Mark as an Oral-Aural Event: Implications for Interpretation', in Elizabeth Struthers Malbon and Edgar V. McKnight (eds.), *The New Literary Criticism and the New Testament* (JSNTSup, 109; Sheffield: Sheffield Academic Press, 1994), pp. 145-63.

—'The Literary Structure of the Controversy Stories in Mark 2:1–3:6', *JBL* 92 (1973), pp. 397-400.

—'Mark as Aural Narrative: Structure as Clues to Understanding', *Sewanee Theological Review* 36 (1992), pp. 45-56.

—'Mark as Interwoven Tapestry: Forecasts and Echoes for a Listening Audience', *CBQ* 53 (1991), pp. 221-36.

—*Markan Public Debate: Literary Techniques, Concentric Structure and Theology in Mark 2:1–3:6* (SBLDS, 48; Chico, CA: Scholars Press, 1979).

—'Oral Methods of Structuring Narrative in Mark', *Int* 43 (1989), pp. 32-44.

Dewey, Joanna (ed.), *Orality and Textuality in Early Christian Literature* (Semeia, 65; Atlanta, Scholars Press, 1995).

Dibelius, Martin, *Die Formgeschichte des Evangeliums* (Tübingen: J.C.B. Mohr, 1919).

—*Formgeschichte des Evangeliums* (Tübingen: J.C.B. Mohr, 2nd edn, 1933).

—*From Tradition to Gospel* (trans. B.L. Woolf; New York: Charles Scribner's Sons, rev. edn, 1965 [1933]).

D'Israeli, Isaac, *Dissertation on Anecdotes* (facsimile copy; New York: Garland, 1972 [1793]).

Donahue, John R., 'The Quest for the Community of Mark's Gospel', in F. Van Segbroeck *et al.* (eds.), *The Four Gospels 1992* (Festschrift Frans Neirynck; BETL, 100; 3 vols.; Leuven: University Press, 1992), II, pp. 817-18.

—'Recent Studies on the Origin of "Son of Man" in the Gospels', *CBQ* 48 (1986), pp. 484-98.

—'Windows and Mirrors: The Setting of Mark's Gospel', *CBQ* 57 (1995), pp. 1-26.

Dormeyer, Detlev, *Evangelium als literarische und theologische Gattung* (Erträge der Forschung, 263; Darmstadt: Wissenschaftliche Buchgesellschaft, 1989).

Doty, William G., 'The Concept of Genre in Literary Analysis', in Lane C. McGaughy (ed.), *SBL Proceedings*, II (Missoula, MT: Scholars Press, 1972), pp. 413-48.

Dubrow, Heather, *Genre* (New York: Methuen, 1982).

Dudley, Donald R., *A History of Cynicism from Diogenes to the 6th Century A.D.* (London: Metheun, 1937; repr. Chicago: Ares Publishers, 1980).

Ebner, Eliezer, *Elementary Education in Ancient Israel (During the Tannaitic Period 10–220 CE)* (New York: Bloch Publishing Co., 1956).

Edelman, Raphael, 'Some Remarks on a Certain Literary Genre in Talmud and Midrash and Its Relation to the Hellenistic Culture', in *Third World Congress of Jewish Studies [Jerusalem, 1961] Report* (Hebrew; Jerusalem: World Union of Jewish Studies, 1965), pp. 108-110.

Edwards, Walter M., and Robert Browning, 'Lucian', *OCD*, p. 621, cols. 1-2.

Elon, M., 'Ma'aseh', *EncJud*, XI, cols. 641-49.

Epp, E.J., and G.W. MacRae (eds.), *The New Testament and its Modern Interpreters* (The Bible and Its Modern Interpreters, 3; Atlanta: Scholars Press, 1989).

Epstein, J.N., *Introduction to Tannaitic Literature: Mishna, Tosephta and Halakhic Midrashim* (Hebrew; ed. E.Z. Melamed; Jerusalem: Magnes Press, 1957).

Epstein, Joseph, 'Literary Biography', *The New Criterion* 1 (1983), pp. 27-37.

Epstein, Lawrence, *A Treasury of Jewish Anecdotes* (Northvale, NJ: J. Aronson, 1989).

Fademan, Clifton, 'Introduction', in *The Little, Brown Book of Anecdotes* (Boston: Little, Brown, 1985), pp. xii-xxii.

Farley, David J., 'Peripatetics', *OCD*, p. 1141, cols. 1-2.

Fascher, Erich, *Die formgeschichtliche Methode* (BZNW, 2; Geissen: Alfred Töpelmann, 1924).

Feldman, Louis H., *Jew and Gentile in the Ancient World: Attitudes and Interactions from Alexander to Justinian* (Princeton, NJ: Princeton University Press, 1993).

Fine, Elizabeth, *The Folklore Text: From Performance to Print* (Bloomington, IN: Indiana University Press, 1984).

Finnegan, Ruth, *Oral Poetry: Its Nature, Significance and Social Context* (Cambridge: Cambridge University Press, 1977).

Fischel, Henry A., 'A *Chria* on Absentmindedness', in *Rabbinic Literature and Greco-Roman Philosophy: A Study of Epicuria and Rhetorica in Early Midrashic Writings* (SPB, 21; Leiden: E.J. Brill, 1973), pp. 78-89.

—'Story and History: Observations on Greco-Roman Rhetoric and Pharisaism', in *Essays in Greco-Roman and Related Talmudic Literature* (New York: Ktav, 1977), pp. 443-72.

—'Studies in Cynicism and the Ancient Near East: The Transformation of a *Chria*', in J. Neusner (ed.), *Religions in Antiquity: Essays in Memory of Erwin Ramsdell Goodenough* (Leiden: E.J. Brill, 1970), pp. 372-411.

Fitzmyer, Joseph A., *A Wandering Aramean: Collected Aramaic Essays* (SBLMS, 25; Missoula, MT: Scholars Press, 1979) (reprinted in *The Semitic Background of the New Testament: Combined Edition of Essays on the Semitic Background of the New Testament and A Wandering Aramean: Collected Aramaic Essays* [Biblical Resource Series; Grand Rapids, MI: Eerdmans, 1997]).

Fleddermann, Harry, 'The Discipleship Discourse (Mark 9:33-50)', *CBQ* 43 (1981), pp. 46-66.

Fohrer, Georg *et al.*, *Exegesis des Alten Testaments: Einführung in die Methodik* (Uni-Taschenbücher, 267; Heidelberg: Quelle & Mayer, 1976; cited in Hans Peter Müller, 'Formgeschichte/Formenkritik. I: Altes Testament', *TRE*, XI, pp. 271-85 (276).

Fowler, Alastair, 'Concepts of Genre', in *Kinds of Literature: An Introduction to the Theory of Genres and Modes* (Cambridge, MA: Harvard University Press, 1982), pp. 37-53.

Fowler, Robert M., 'The Implied Reader of the Gospel of Mark', in *Loaves and Fishes*, pp. 149-57.

—*Let the Reader Understand: Reader-Response Criticism and the Gospel of Mark* (Philadelphia: Fortress Press, 1991).

—*Loaves and Fishes: The Function of the Feeding Stories in the Gospel of Mark* (SBLDS, 54; Chico, CA: Scholars Press, 1981).

Freyne, Sean, *Galilee from Alexander the Great to Hadrian, 323 B.C.E. to 135 C.E.: A Study of Second Temple Judaism* (University of Notre Dame Center for the Study of Judaism and Christianity in Antiquity, 5; Notre Dame, IN: University of Notre Dame Press, 1980).

Gemoll, W., *Das Apophthegma: Literarhistorische Studien* (Vienna: Hölder, Pilcher, Tempsky, 1924).

Gereboff, Joel, *Rabbi Tarfon: The Tradition, the Man, and Early Rabbinic Judaism* (BJS, 7; Missoula, MT: Scholars Press, 1979).

Gerhardsson, Birger, *Memory and Manuscript: Oral Tradition and Written Transmission in Rabbinic Judaism and Early Christianity* (ASNU, 22; Lund: C.W.K. Gleerup, 1961).

Gerhart, Mary, 'Generic Competence in Biblical Hermeneutics', in Gerhart and Williams (eds.), *Genre, Narrativity, and Theology*, pp. 29-44.

—'Generic Studies: Their Renewed Importance in Religious and Literary Interpretation', *JAAR* 45 (1977), pp. 309-25.

Gerhart, Mary, and James G. Williams (eds.), *Genre, Narrativity, and Theology* (Semeia, 43; Atlanta: Scholars Press, 1988).

Gignon, O., and K. Rupprecht, 'Apophthegma', *LAW*, cols. 222-23.

—'Gnome', *LAW*, cols. 1099-1100.

Gilliard, Frank D., 'More Silent Reading in Antiquity: *Non Omne Verbum Sonabat*', *JBL* 112 (1993), pp. 689-94.

Goldberg, Abraham, 'The Mishna—A Study Book of Halakha', in Safrai (ed.), *The Literature of the Sages*, pp. 211-62.

Goldberg, Arnold, 'Form und Funktion des Ma'ase in der Mischna', *Frankfurter Judaistische Beiträge* 2 (1974), pp. 1-38.

Goldenberg, R., 'The Deposition of Rabban Gamaliel II: An Examination of the Sources', *JJS* 22 (1972), pp. 167-90.

Goldin, Judah, 'Toward a Profile of the Tanna, Aqiba ben Joseph', *JAOS* 96 (1976), pp. 38-56.

Goodman, Martin, *State and Society in Roman Galilee, A.D. 132 to 212* (Totowa, NJ: Rowman & Allanheld, 1983).

Goody, Jack, 'Restricted Literacy in Northern Ghana', in *Literacy in Traditional Societies*, pp. 198-264.

Goody, Jack (ed.), *Literacy in Traditional Societies* (Cambridge: Cambridge University Press, 1968).

Goody, Jack, and Ian Watt, 'The Consequences of Literacy', in Goody (ed.), *Literacy in Traditional Societies*, pp. 27-68.

Grabbe, Lester L., and Ronald F. Hock, 'Nicolaus of Myra', in Hock and O'Neil (eds.), *The Chreia in Ancient Rhetoric*, pp. 238-39.

Green, William S., 'Context and Meaning in Rabbinic "Biography"', in *idem* (ed.), *Approaches to Ancient Judaism*, II (BJS, 9; Chico, CA: Scholars Press, 1980), pp. 81-99.

—*The Traditions of Joshua Ben Hananiah*. I. *The Early Legal Traditions* (SJLA, 29: Leiden: E.J. Brill, 1981).

—'What's in a Name?—The Problematic of Rabbinic "Biography"', in *idem* (ed.), *Approaches to Ancient Judaism*. I. *Theory and Practice* (BJS, 1; Missoula, MT: Scholars Press, 1978), pp. 77-97.

Griffin, Miriam T., 'Demetrius (19)', *OCD*, p. 450, col. 2.

Grothe, Heinz, *Anekdote* (Realien zur Literatur, Sammlung Metzler B, 101; Stuttgart: J.B. Metzlersche, 1971).

Grube, G.M.A., *The Greek and Roman Critics* (London: Methuen, 1965).

Grundmann, Walter, *Das Evangelium nach Markus* (Berlin: Evangelische Verlagsanstalt, 1959).

Gundry, Robert, *Mark: A Commentary on his Apology for the Cross* (Grand Rapids, MI: Eerdmans, 1993).

Gunkel, Hermann, *Genesis, übersetzt und erklärt* (Göttingen: Vandenhoeck & Ruprecht, 3rd edn, 1917).

Güttgemanns, Erhardt, *Candid Questions Concerning Gospel Form Criticism: A Methodological Sketch of the Fundamental Problematics of Form and Redaction Criticism* (trans. W.G. Doty; PTMS, 26; Pittsburgh: Pickwick, 1979 [1971]).

Guttman, Alexander, 'Tractate Abot—Its Place in Rabbinic Judaism', *JQR* 41 (1950), pp. 181-93.

Haight, Elizabeth, *The Roman Use of Anecdotes in Cicero, Livy and the Satirists* (London: Longmans, Green, & Co., 1940).

Havelock, Eric A., *The Literate Revolution in Greece and its Consequences* (Princeton, NJ: Princeton University Press, 1982).

—'Oral and Written: A Reappraisal', in *The Literate Revolution in Greece*, pp. 3-38.

—'Oral Composition in the *Oedipus Tyrannus* of Sophocles', *New Literary History* 16 (1984), pp. 175-97.

—*Preface to Plato*. I. *A History of the Greek Mind* (Cambridge, MA: Harvard University Press, 1963).

Heath, Malcolm, *Hermogenes 'On Issues': Strategies of Argument in Later Greek Rhetoric* (Oxford: Clarendon Press, 1995).

Hein, Jürgen, 'Die Anekdote', in Otto Knörrich (ed.), *Formen der Literatur in Einzeldarstellugen* (Stuttgart: Alfred Kröner, 1981), pp. 14-20.

Hellholm, David, *Das Visionenbuch des Hermas als Apokalypse: Formgeschichtle und Texttheoretische Studien zu einer literarischen Gattung*. I. *Methodologische Vorüberlegungen und makrostrukturelle Textanalyse* (ConBNT, 13.1; Lund: C.W.K. Gleerup, 1980).

—'Die Unterscheidung zwischen Gattung und Form', in *Das Visionenbuch*, pp. 68-69.

—'The Problem of Apocalyptic Genre and the Apocalypse of John', in Collins (ed.), *Early Christian Apocalypticism*, pp. 13-64.

Helm, R., 'Lukianos', PW, XIII, cols. 1725-77.

Henaut, Barry W., *Oral Tradition and the Gospels: The Problem of Mark 4* (JSNTSup, 82; Sheffield: JSOT Press, 1993).

Henderson, Ian H., 'Gnomic Quatrains in the Synoptics: An Experiment in Genre Definition', *NTS* 37 (1991), pp. 481-98.

Hengel, Martin, *Judaism and Hellenism: Studies in their Encounter in Palestine during the Early Hellenistic Period* (trans. John Bowden; 2 vols.; London: SCM Press, 1974; German 2nd rev. edn, 1973).

—*Studies in the Gospel of Mark* (trans. John Bowden; Philadelphia: Fortress Press, 1985; German original, 1983).

Hengel, Martin, with Christoph Markschies, *The 'Hellenization' of Judaea in the First Century after Christ* (trans. John Bowden; London: SCM Press, 1989; German original, 1989).

Hezser, Catherine, 'Die Verwendung der hellenistischen Gattung Chrie im frühen Christentum und Judentum', *JJS* 27 (1996), pp. 371-439.

Hock, Ronald F., 'General Introduction to Volume I', in Hock and O'Neil (eds.), *The Chreia in Ancient Rhetoric*, pp. 10-22.

Hock, Ronald F., and Edward N. O'Neil, 'Aelius Theon of Alexandria', in Hock and O'Neil (eds.), *The Chreia in Ancient Rhetoric*, I, pp. 63-78.

Hock, Ronald F., and Edward N. O'Neil (eds.), *The Chreia in Ancient Rhetoric*. I. *The* Progymnasmata (SBLTT, 27; Graeco-Roman Religion Series, 9; Atlanta: Scholars Press, 1986).

Holloway, Paul A., 'Paul's Pointed Prose: The *Sententia* in Roman Rhetoric and Paul', *NovT* 40 (1998), pp. 32-53.

Holman, C. Hugh, and William Harmon, *A Handbook to Literature* (New York: Macmillan, 6th edn, 1992).

Holtsmark, Erling B., 'Auctor Incertus [*Ad Herennium*]', in Donald C. Bryant (ed.), *Ancient Greek and Roman Rhetoricians: A Biographical Dictionary* (Columbia, MO: Artcraft Press, 1968), pp. 18-19.

Hooker, Morna D., *The Gospel According to Saint Mark* (BNTC; London: A. & C. Black, 1991).

Horna, Konstantin, 'Gnome, Gnomendichtung, Gnomologie', PWSup, VI, cols. 74-87.

Horsley, Richard A., 'The Historical Jesus and the Archaeology of Galilee: Questions from Historical Jesus Research to Archaeologists', in Eugene H. Lovering (ed.), *SBLSP 1994* (SBLSP, 33; Atlanta: Scholars Press, 1994), pp. 129-35.

Hultgren, Arland J., *Jesus and his Adversaries: The Form and Function of the Conflict Stories in the Synoptic Tradition* (Minneapolis: Augsburg, 1979).

Iersel, Bas van, *Reading Mark* (trans. W.H. Bisscheroux; Collegeville, MN: Liturgical Press, 1988; Dutch original, 1986).

Imwood, Brad, 'Epictetus', *OCD*, p. 532, col. 2.

Jastrow, Marcus, *A Dictionary of the Targumim, the Talmud Babli and Yerushalmi, and the Midrashic Literature* (2 vols.; London: Luzac, 1886–1903; repr. NY: Pardes Publishing House, 1950).

Jolles, André, *Einfache Formen: Legende, Sage, Mythe, Rätsel, Spruch, Kasus, Memorabile, Märchen, Witz* (Tübingen: Max Niemeyer, 3rd edn, 1958).

Jones, C.P., *Culture and Society in Lucian* (Cambridge, MA: Harvard University Press, 1986).

Jones, W.H.S., 'Introduction', in *Hippocrates* (LCL).

Kanter, Shamai, *Rabban Gamaliel II: The Legal Traditions* (BJS, 8; Chico, CA: Scholars Press, 1980).

Kasovsky, Chayim, *Otsar lashon ha-Mishnah, Thesaurus Mishnae: Concordantiae verborum quae in sex Mishnae ordinibus reperiunter* (3 vols.; Jerusalem: Massadah Publishing Co., 1956-60).

Kee, Howard C., *Community of the New Age: Studies in Mark's Gospel* (Philadelphia: Westminster Press, 1977; repr. Macon, GA: Mercer University Press, 1983).

Kelber, Werner H., *The Oral and Written Gospel: The Hermeneutics of Speaking and Writing in the Synoptic Tradition, Mark, Paul, and Q* (Philadelphia: Fortress Press, 1983).

Kennedy, George A., *The Art of Persuasion in Greece* (Princeton, NJ: Princeton University Press, 1963).

—*A New History of Classical Rhetoric* (Princeton, NJ: Princeton University Press, 1994).

—*Quintilian* (New York: Twayne Publishers, 1969).

Kent, Thomas, *Interpretation and Genre: The Role of Generic Perception in the Study of Narrative Texts* (London and Toronto: Associated University Presses, 1986).

Klauser, Theodor, 'Apophthegma', *RAC*, I, cols. 546-47.

Kloppenborg, John S., 'Introduction: Forms and Genres', in *The Formation of Q: Trajectories in Ancient Wisdom Collections* (Studies in Antiquity and Christianity; Philadelphia: Fortress Press, 1987), pp. 1-8.

—*Q Parallels: Synopsis, Critical Notes, and Concordance* (Sonoma, CA: Polebridge Press, 1988).

Knight, Douglas A., 'The Understanding of "*Sitz im Leben*" in Form Criticism', in George MacRae (ed.), *SBLSP 1974* (2 vols.; Atlanta: Scholars Press, 1974), I, pp. 105-25.

Köster, Helmut, 'Formgeschichte/Formenkritik. II. Neues Testament', *TRE*, XI, pp. 286-87.

—'Written Gospels or Oral Tradition?', *JBL* 113 (1994), pp. 293-97.

Krupnick, Eliyahu, שערי למוד: *The Gateway to Learning: A Systematic Introduction to the Study of the Talmud* (Jerusalem: Feldheim Publishers, 1981).

Kümmel, Werner Georg, *Introduction to the New Testament* (trans. H.C. Kee; Nashville: Abingdon Press, 17th rev. edn, 1975; German, 17th edn, 1973).

Lane, William L., *The Gospel According to Mark: The English Text with Introduction, Exposition and Notes* (NICNT, 2; Grand Rapids: Eerdmans, 1974).

Langenscheidts Enzyklopädische Wörterbuch: Der Englische und Deutschen Sprache. Teil II. Deutsch-Englisch. 1. Band A–K (ed. Otto Springer; Berlin: Langenscheidt, 1974).

A Latin Dictionary (ed. Charlton T. Lewis and Charles Short; Oxford: Clarendon Press, 1966).

Lausberg, Heinrich, 'Exempla', in *Handbuch der literarischen Rhetorik*, I, §406-26.

—*Handbuch der literarischen Rhetorik* (2 vols.; Munich: Max Hueber, 1960).

—'Sententia', in *Handbuch der literarischen Rhetorik*, I, §1121.

Lee, Brian C., 'genre', in Roger Fowler (ed.), *A Dictionary of Modern Critical Terms* (London: Routledge & Kegan Paul, rev. edn, 1987), pp. 104-105.

Leo, Friedrich, *Die griechisch-römische Biographie nach ihrer litterarischen Form* (Leipzig: Teubner, 1901).

Lerner, M.B., 'The Tractate Avot', in Safrai (ed.), *The Literature of the Sages*, pp. 263-81.

Levine, Diane, 'Eleazar Ḥisma', in William S. Green (ed.), *Persons and Institutions in Early Rabbinic Judaism* (BJS, 3; Missoula, MT: Scholars Press, 1977), pp. 149-205.

Levine, Lee I., 'The Jewish Patriarch [Nasi] in Third Century Palestine', *ANRW*, II.19, pp. 649-88.

—*The Rabbinic Class of Roman Palestine in Late Antiquity* (New York: Jewish Theological Seminary of America, 1985).

Lieberman, Saul, *Hellenism in Jewish Palestine: Studies in the Literary Transmission, Beliefs and Manners of Palestine in the I Century BCE–IV Century CE* (Text and Studies, 18; New York: Jewish Theological Seminary of America, 1950).

—'How Much Greek in Jewish Palestine?', in Alexander Altmann (ed.), *Biblical and Other Studies* (Studies and Texts, 1; Cambridge, MA: Harvard University Press, 1963), pp. 123-41.

Lohr, Charles H., 'Oral Techniques in the Gospel of Matthew', *CBQ* 23 (1961), pp. 403-35.
Lord, Albert B., *The Singer of Tales* (Harvard Studies in Comparative Literature, 24; Cambridge, MA: Harvard University Press, 1960).
Lumpe, A., 'Exemplum', *RAC*, VI, cols. 1229-57.
Mack, Burton L., 'Anecdote and Arguments: The Chreia in Antiquity and Early Christianity', *Occasional Papers of the Institute for Antiquity and Christianity* 10 (1987), pp. 1-48.
—'The Anointing of Jesus: Elaboration within a Chreia', in Mack and Robbins, *Patterns of Persuasion*, pp. 85-106.
—'Decoding the Scriptures: Philo and the Rules of Rhetoric', in F.E. Greenspahn, E. Hilgert and B.L. Mack (eds.), *Nourished with Peace: Studies in Hellenistic Judaism in Memory of Samuel Sandmel* (Denver, CO: University of Denver [Colorado Seminary], 1984), pp. 81-115.
—'Elaboration of the Chreia in the Hellenistic School', in Mack and Robbins, *Patterns of Persuasion*, pp. 31-67.
—*The Lost Gospel: The Book of Q and Christian Origins* (San Francisco: Harper Collins, 1990).
—*A Myth of Innocence: Mark and Christian Origins* (Philadelphia: Fortress Press, 1988).
—*Rhetoric and the New Testament* (Guides to Biblical Scholarship, New Testament Series; Minneapolis: Augsburg–Fortress, 1990).
—'Teaching in Parables: Elaboration in Mark 4:1-34', in Mack and Robbins, *Patterns of Persuasion*, pp. 143-60.
Mack, Burton L., and Edward N. O'Neil, 'Hermogenes of Tarsus', in Hock and O'Neil (eds.), *The Chreia in Ancient Rhetoric*, pp. 153-71.
Mack, Burton L., and Vernon K. Robbins, *Patterns of Persuasion in the Gospels* (Sonoma, CA: Polebridge Press, 1989).
Mandelbaum, Irving, *A History of the Mishnaic Law of Agriculture: Kilayim* (BJS, 26; Chico, CA: Scholars Press, 1982).
Marcus, Joel, 'The Jewish War and the Sitz im Leben of Mark', *JBL* 111 (1992), pp. 441-62.
Marino, Adrian, 'Toward a Definition of Literary Genres', in Joseph P. Strelka (ed.), *Theories of Literary Genre.* III. *Yearbook of Comparative Criticism* (University Park, PA: Pennsylvania State University Press, 1978), pp. 41-53.
Martin, Ralph, *Mark: Evangelist and Theologian* (Grand Rapids, MI: Zondervan, 1972).
Marxsen, Willi, *Mark the Evangelist: Studies on the Redaction History of the Gospel* (trans. James Boyce; Philadelphia: Fortress Press, 1969; German 2nd edn, 1959).
Matera, Frank J., *What Are They Saying about Mark?* (New York: Paulist Press, 1987).
McKnight, Edgar V., 'Form and Redaction Criticism', in E.J. Epp and G.W. MacRae (eds.), *The New Testament and Its Modern Interpreters* (The Bible and Its Modern Interpreters, 3; Atlanta: Scholars Press, 1989), pp. 149-74.
—*What Is Form Criticism?* (Philadelphia: Fortress Press, 1969).
Meier, John P., *A Marginal Jew: Rethinking the Historical Jesus*. I. *The Roots of the Problem and the Person* (New York: Doubleday, 1991).
Momigliano, Arnaldo, *The Development of Greek Biography* (Cambridge, MA: Harvard University Press, 1971).
Morris, Nathan, *The Jewish School: An Introduction to the History of Jewish Education* (London: Eyre & Spottiswoode, 1937).
Moulton, James, and George Milligan, *The Vocabulary of the Greek New Testament Illustrated from Papyri and Other Non-literary Sources* (London: Hodder & Stoughton, 1914–30; repr. Grand Rapids, MI: Eerdmans, 1974).

Mundla, Jean-Gaspard Mundiso Mbâ, *Jesus und die Führer Israels: Studien zu den sog. Jerusalemer Streitgesprächen* (NTAbh, NS, 17; Münster: Aschendoff, 1984).

Murphy, Roland E., 'proverb', in P.J. Achtemeier (ed.), *Harper's Bible Dictionary* (San Francisco: Harper & Row, 1985), pp. 831-32.

Mussies, G., 'Greek in Palestine and the Diaspora', in Safrai *et al.* (eds.), *Jewish People*, pp. 1040-64.

Nadeau, Ray, 'The Progymnasmata of Aphthonius', *Speech Monographs* 19 (1952), pp. 264-85.

Neirynck, Frans, 'Synoptic Problem', in R.E. Brown, J.A. Fitzmyer and R.E. Murphy (eds.), *The New Jerome Biblical Commentary* (Englewood Cliffs, NJ: Prentice–Hall, 1990), pp. 587-95.

Neusner, Jacob, *Are There Really Tannaitic Parallels to the Gospels? A Refutation of Morton Smith* (South Florida Studies in the History of Judaism, 80; Atlanta: Scholars Press, 1993).

—'The Dating of Sayings in Rabbinic Literature', in *Formative Judaism: Religious, Historical, and Literary Studies. Seventh Series: The Formation of Judaism, Intentionality, Feminization of Judaism, and Other Current Results* (South Florida Studies in the History of Judaism, 94; Atlanta: Scholars Press, 1993), pp. 99-119.

—*Development of a Legend: Studies in the Traditions Concerning Yohanan ben Zakkai* (SPB, 16; Leiden: E.J. Brill, 1970).

—*Eliezer ben Hyrcanus: The Tradition and the Man* (SJLA, 3-4; 2 vols.; Leiden: E.J. Brill, 1973).

—*A History of the Mishnaic Law of Appointed Times* (SJLA, 34; 5 vols.; Leiden: E.J. Brill, 1981).

—*A History of the Mishnaic Law of Damages* (SJLA, 35; 5 vols.; Leiden: E.J. Brill, 1983–85).

—*Introduction to Rabbinic Literature* (Anchor Bible Reference Library; New York: Doubleday, 1994).

—*Judaism: The Evidence of the Mishnah* (BJS, 129; Atlanta, GA: Scholars Press, 2nd edn, 1988).

—*Midrash in Context: Exegesis in Formative Judaism* (BJS, 141; Philadelphia: Fortress Press, 1983).

—'The Modern Study of the Mishnah', in J. Neusner (ed.), *The Study of Ancient Judaism*. I. *Mishnah, Midrash Siddur* (New York: Ktav, 1981), pp. 3-26.

—*Oral Tradition in Judaism: The Case of the Mishnah* (Albert Bates Lord Studies in Oral Tradition, 1; New York: Garland Publishing, 1987).

—*The Rabbinic Traditions about the Pharisees Before 70* (3 vols.; Leiden: E.J. Brill, 1971).

—'The Rabbinic Traditions about the Pharisees before 70 C.E.: The Problem of Oral Transmission', in *Early Rabbinic Judaism: Historical Studies in Religion, Literature and Art* (SJLA, 13; Leiden: E.J. Brill, 1975), pp. 73-89 (repr. of 'The Rabbinic Traditions about the Pharisees before 70 C.E.: The Problem of Oral Transmission', *JJS* 22 [1971], pp. 1-18).

—'Types and Forms in Ancient Jewish Literature: Some Comparisons', *HR* 11 (1972), pp. 354-90.

Niederwimmer, Kurt, 'Johannes Markus und die Frage nach dem Verfasser des zweiten Evangeliums', *ZNW* 58 (1967), pp. 172-88.

Nineham, D.E., *The Gospel of St Mark* (Pelican New Testament Commentaries; New York: Seabury Press, 1963).

O'Neil, Edward N., 'The Chreia Discussion of Priscian', in Hock and O'Neil (eds.), *The Chreia in Ancient Rhetoric*, pp. 194-97.

—'Marcus Fabius Quintilianus', in Hock and O'Neil (eds.), *The Chreia in Ancient Rhetoric*, pp. 122-28.

—'Priscian', in Hock and O'Neil (eds.), *The Chreia in Ancient Rhetoric*, pp. 185-88.

—'The Vatican Grammarian', in Hock and O'Neil (eds.), *The Chreia in Ancient Rhetoric*, pp. 271-93.

Ong, Walter, *Interfaces of the Word: Studies in the Evolution of Consciousness and Culture* (Ithaca, NY: Cornell University Press, 1977).

—*Orality and Literacy: The Technologizing of the Word* (New Accents; New York: Methuen, 1982).

—*The Presence of the Word: Some Prolegomena for Cultural and Religious History* (New Haven, CT: Yale University Press, 1967).

—'Text as Interpretation: Mark and After', in *Orality, Aurality and Biblical Narrative*, pp. 7-26.

Orality, Aurality and Biblical Narrative (ed. Lou H. Silberman; Semeia, 39; Atlanta: Scholars Press, 1987).

The Oxford English Dictionary (ed. J.A. Simpson and E.S.C. Weiner; Oxford: Clarendon Press, 2nd edn, 1989).

The Oxford Latin Dictionary (ed. P.G.W. Glare; Oxford: Clarendon Press, 1982).

Painter, John, 'Quest and Rejection Stories in John', *JSNT* 36 (1989), pp. 17-46.

Parrott, Rod, 'Conflict and Rhetoric in Mark 2:23-28', in Robbins (ed.), *The Rhetoric of Pronouncement*, pp. 117-37.

Parry, Milman, *The Making of Homeric Verse: The Collected Papers of Milman Parry* (ed. Adam Perry; Oxford: Clarendon Press, 1971).

Patte, Daniel (ed.), *Kingdom and Children* (Semeia, 29; Chico, CA: Scholars Press, 1983).

Penner, Terry, 'Socrates and the Early Dialogues', in Richard Krant (ed.), *The Cambridge Companion to Plato* (New York: Cambridge University Press, 1993), pp. 121-69.

Perlman, S., 'The Historical Example, Its Use and Importance as Political Propaganda in the Attic Orators', in Alexander Fuks and Israel Halpern (eds.), *Scripta Hierosolymitana*. VII. *Studies in History* (Jerusalem: Magnes Press, 1961), pp. 150-66.

Petersen, Norman R., *Literary Criticism for New Testament Critics* (Guides to Biblical Scholarship, New Testament Series; Philadelphia: Fortress Press, 1978).

—'On the Notion of Genre in Via's "Parable and Example Story: A Literary-Structuralist Approach"', in Robert W. Funk (ed.), *A Structuralist Approach to the Parables* (Semeia, 1; Missoula, MT: Scholars Press, 1974), pp. 134-81.

Pettit, Peter A., 'Shenemar: The Place of Scripture Citation in the Mishna' (PhD dissertation, Claremont Graduate School, 1993).

Porton, Gary G., 'The Pronouncement Story in Tannaitic Literature: A Review of Bultmann's Theory', in Tannehill (ed.), *Pronouncement Stories*, pp. 81-100.

Powell, Mark Alan, 'Literary Criticism and Historical Criticism', in *What Is Narrative Criticism?* (Guides to Biblical Scholarship, New Testament Series; Minneapolis: Augsburg–Fortress, 1990), pp. 6-10.

Price, Bennett J., 'Paradeigma and Exemplum in Ancient Rhetorical Theory' (PhD dissertation, University of California at Berkeley, 1975).

Rabe, Hugo (ed.), *Hermogenis opera* (Rhetores Graeci, 6; Stuttgart: Teubner, 1913).

Rabin, Chaim, 'Hebrew and Aramaic in the First Century', in Safrai *et al.* (eds.), *Jewish People*, pp. 1007-39.

Radermacher, Ludwig, 'Hermogenes (22)', PW, VIII, cols. 865-77.

Ramsaran, Rollin A., 'More Than Opinion: Paul's Rhetorical Maxim in First Corinthians 7:25-26', *CBQ* 57 (1995), pp. 531-34.

Ranke, Kurt, '*Einfache Formen*' (trans. William Templer and Eberhard Alsen), *Journal of Folklore Institute* 4 (1967), pp. 17-31.

Reedy, Charles J., 'Rhetorical Concerns and Argumentative Techniques in Matthean Pronouncement Stories', in Kent H. Richards (ed.), *SBLSP 1983* (SBLSP, 22; Chico, CA: Scholars Press, 1983), pp. 219-22.

Riesner, Rainer, *Jesus als Lehrer: Eine Untersuchung zum Ursprung der Evangelien-Überlieferung* (WUNT, 2.1; Tübingen: J.C.B. Mohr, 1981).

Robbins, Vernon K., 'The Chreia', in David Aune (ed.), *Greco-Roman Literature and the New Testament: Selected Forms and Genres* (SBLSBS, 21; Atlanta: Scholars Press, 1988), pp. 1-23.

—'Chreia and Pronouncement Story in Synoptic Studies', in Mack and Robbins, *Patterns of Persuasion*, pp. 1-29.

—'Classifying Pronouncement Stories in Plutarch's *Parallel Lives*', in Tannehill (ed.), *Pronouncement Stories*, pp. 29-52.

—'Form Criticism, New Testament', *ABD*, II, pp. 841-44.

—'Foxes, Birds, Burials and Furrows', in Mack and Robbins, *Patterns of Persuasion*, pp. 69-84.

—'Introduction: Using Rhetorical Discussions of the Chreia to Interpret Pronouncement Stories', in Robbins (ed.), *The Rhetoric of Pronouncement*, pp. vii-xvii.

—'Picking up the Fragments: From Crossan's Analysis to Rhetorical Analysis', *Forum* 1, pp. 30-64.

—'Plucking Grain on the Sabbath', in Mack and Robbins, *Patterns of Persuasion*, pp. 107-41.

—'Progymnastic Rhetorical Composition and Pre-Gospel Traditions: A New Approach', in Camille Focant (ed.), *The Synoptic Gospels: Source Criticism and the New Literary Criticism* (BETL, 110; Leuven: Leuven University Press, 1993), pp. 111-47.

—'Pronouncement Stories and Jesus' Blessing of Children: A Rhetorical Approach', in Patte (ed.), *Kingdom and Children*, pp. 42-74 (repr. of 'Pronouncement Stories and Jesus' Blessing of Children: A Rhetorical Approach', in Kent H. Richards [ed.], *SBLSP 1982* [SBLSP, 21; Chico, CA: Scholars Press, 1982], pp. 407-300).

—'Pronouncement Stories from a Rhetorical Perspective', *Forum* 4.2 (1988), pp. 3-32.

—'Pronouncement Stories in Plutarch's Lives of Alexander and Julius Caesar', in Paul J. Achtemeier (ed.), *SBLSP 1978* (SBLSP, 13-14; 2 vols.; Missoula, MT: Scholars Press, 1978), I, pp. 21-38.

—'Rhetorical Composition and the Beelzebul Controversy', in Mack and Robbins, *Patterns of Persuasion*, pp. 161-93.

—'A Rhetorical Typology for Classifying and Analyzing Pronouncement Stories', in Kent H. Richards (ed.), *SBLSP 1984* (SBLSP, 23; Chico, CA: Scholars Press, 1984), pp. 93-122.

—'Writing as a Rhetorical Act in Plutarch and the Gospels', in Duane F. Watson (ed.), *Persuasive Artistry: Studies in New Testament Rhetoric in Honor of George A. Kennedy* (JSNTSup, 50; Sheffield: JSOT Press, 1991), pp. 142-68.

Robbins, Vernon K. (ed.), *Ancient Quotes and Anecdotes: From Crib to Crypt* (Sonoma, CA: Polebridge Press, 1989).

—*The Rhetoric of Pronouncement* (Semeia, 64; Atlanta: Scholars Press, 1993).

Ross, Herbert J., 'Acrisius', *OCD*, p. 9, col. 2.

—'Apollonius Rhodius', *OCD*, pp. 124-26.

Ross, Herbert J., and Antony Spawforth, 'Apollonius', *OCD*, p. 128, col. 1.

Rylaarsdam, J. Coert, 'Editor's Foreword', in Tucker, *Form Criticism*, pp. iii-vii.

Safrai, Shmuel, 'Education and the Study of the Torah', in Safrai *et al.* (eds.), *Jewish People*, pp. 945-70.

Safrai, Shmuel (ed.), *The Literature of the Sages. First Part: Oral Tora, Halakha, Mishna, Tosefta, Talmud, External Tractates* (CRINT, 3.1; Philadelphia: Fortress Press, 1987).

Safrai, Shmuel *et al.* (eds.), *The Jewish People in the First Century: Historical Geography, Political History, Social, Cultural and Religious Life and Institutions* (CRINT, 1.2; Philadelphia: Fortress Press, 1976).

Saldarini, Anthony J., ' "Form Criticism" of Rabbinic Literature', *JBL* 96 (1977), pp. 257-74.

—'Reconstructions of Rabbinic Judaism', in Robert A. Kraft and George W.E. Nickelsburg (eds.), *Early Judaism and Its Modern Interpreters* (The Bible and Its Modern Interpreters, 2; Atlanta: Scholars Press, 1986), pp. 437-77.

Saller, Richard, 'Anecdotes as Historical Evidence for the Principate', *Greece and Rome*, 2nd series, 27 (1980), pp. 69-83.

Sanders, E.P., 'The Genre of Palestinian Jewish Apocalypses', in David Hellholm (ed.), *Apocalypticism in the Mediterranean World and the Near East: Proceedings of the International Colloquium on Apocalypticism, Uppsala, August 12–17, 1979* (Tübingen: J.C.B. Mohr, 1983), pp. 447-59.

Schelling, F.A., 'What Means the Saying about Receiving the Kingdom of God as a Little Child (τὴν βασιλείαν τοῦ θεοῦ ὡς παιδίον)? Mk x.15, Lk xvii:17', *ExpTim* 77 (1965–66), pp. 56-58.

Schissel, Otmar, 'Die Einteilung der Chrie bei Quintilian', *Hermes* 68 (1933), pp. 245-48.

Scholes, Robert, and Robert Kellogg, *The Nature of Narrative* (New York: Oxford University Press, 1966).

Schürer, Emil, *The History of the Jewish People in the Age of Jesus Christ (175 B.C.–A.D. 135)* (rev. and ed. Geza Vermes *et al.*; 4 vols.; Edinburgh: T. & T. Clark, 1973–87).

Schwartz, E., 'Apomnemoneumata', PW, II.A.1, cols. 170-71.

Schweizer, Eduard, *The Good News According to Mark* (trans. Donald H. Madvig; Richmond, VA: John Knox Press, 1962).

Scott, Bernard Brandon, *Hear Then the Parable: A Commentary on the Parables of Jesus* (Philadelphia: Fortress Press, 1989).

Senior, Donald, ' "With Swords and Clubs...": The Setting of Mark's Community and His Critique of Abusive Power', *BTB* 17 (1987), pp. 10-20.

Sevenster, J.N., *'Do You Know Greek?' How Much Greek Could the First Jewish Christians Have Known?* (NovTSup, 19; Leiden: E.J. Brill, 1968).

Silberman, Lou H., 'Schoolboys and Storytellers: Some Comments on Aphorisms and *Chriae*', in Patte (ed.), *Kingdom and Children*, pp. 109-15.

Silberman, Lou H. (ed.), *Orality, Aurality and Biblical Narrative* (Semeia, 39; Chico, CA: Scholars Press, 1987).

Smith, Morton, *Tannaitic Parallels to the Gospels* (SBLMS, 6; Philadelphia: Society of Biblical Literature, rev. edn, 1968).

Soulen, Richard N., *Handbook of Biblical Criticism* (Atlanta: John Knox Press, 2nd edn, 1981).

Spencer, Richard, 'A Study of the Form and Function of the Biographical Apophthegms in the Synoptic Tradition in Light of Their Hellenistic Background' (PhD dissertation, Emory University, 1976).

Spoerri, W., 'Gnome', KlPauly, II, cols. 823-29.

Stegemann, W., 'Nikolaos (21)', PW, XVII, cols. 424-57.

—'Theon (5)', PW, V.A.2, cols. 2037-39.

Stevens, Donald, 'Rabbi Yose the Galilean: A Representative Selection of his Legal Traditions' (PhD dissertation, Duke University, 1978).

Stock, Augustine, *The Method and Message of Mark* (Wilmington, DE: Michael Glazier, 1989).

Strack, H.L., and G. Stemberger, *Introduction to the Talmud and Midrash* (trans. Markus Bockmuehl; Edinburgh: T. & T. Clark, 1991; German original, 1982).

Talbert, Charles, 'Once Again: Gospel Genre', in Gerhart and Williams (eds.), *Genre, Narrativity and Theology*, pp. 53-73.

Tannehill, Robert C., 'Attitudinal Shifts in Synoptic Pronouncement Stories', in Richard A. Spencer (ed.), *Orientation by Disorientation: Studies in Literary Criticism and Biblical Literary Criticism. Presented in Honor of William A. Beardslee* (Pittsburgh, PA: Pickwick Press, 1980), pp. 183-97.

—'Introduction: The Pronouncement Story and Its Types', in *Pronouncement Stories*, pp. 1-13.

—'Synoptic Pronouncement Stories: Form and Function', in Paul J. Achtemeier (ed.), *SBLSP 1980* (SBLSP, 19; Chico, CA: Scholars Press, 1980), pp. 51-56.

—*The Sword of his Mouth: Forceful and Imaginative Language in Synoptic Sayings* (Philadelphia: Fortress Press, 1975).

—'Tension in Synoptic Sayings and Stories', *Int* 34 (1980), pp. 138-50.

—'Types and Functions of Apophthegms in the Synoptic Gospels', *ANRW*, II.25.2, pp. 1792-829.

—'Varieties of Synoptic Pronouncement Stories', in *Pronouncement Stories*, pp. 101-19.

Tannehill, Robert C. (ed.), *Pronouncement Stories* (Semeia, 20; Chico, CA: Scholars Press, 1981).

Taylor, Archer, 'The Anecdote: A Neglected Genre', in Jerome Mandel and Bruce A. Rosenburg (eds.), *Medieval Literature and Folklore Studies: Essays in Honor of Francis Lee Utley* (New Brunswick, NJ: Rutgers University Press, 1970), pp. 223-28.

Taylor, Christopher C.W., 'Aristippus (1)', *OCD*, p. 161, col. 1.

Taylor, R.O.P., 'Form-Criticism in the First Centuries', *ExpTim* 55 (1943–44), pp. 218-20.

—'Greek Forms of Instruction', in *Groundwork of the Gospels*, pp. 75-90.

—*The Groundwork of the Gospels with Some Collected Papers* (Oxford: Basil Blackwell, 1946).

Taylor, Vincent, *The Formation of the Gospel Tradition* (London: Macmillan, 2nd edn, 1953).

—*The Gospel According to St. Mark: The Greek Text with Introduction, Notes and Indexes* (London: Macmillan, 2nd edn, 1966).

Telford, W.R., *Mark* (New Testament Guides; Sheffield: Sheffield Academic Press, 1995).

Thaniel, Kathryn M., 'Quintilian and the Progymnasmata' (PhD dissertation, McMaster University, 1973).

Theissen, Gerd, *The Gospels in Context: Social and Political History in the Synoptic Tradition* (trans. Linda M. Maloney; Philadelphia: Fortress Press, 1991; German original, 1989).

Thomas, John D., 'The Exemplum in Ancient Rhetorical Theory' (MA thesis, University of Florida, 1960).

Todorov, Tzvetan, 'The Origins of Genres', *New Literary History* 9 (1976), pp. 159-70.

Tolbert, Mary Ann, *Sowing the Gospel: Mark's World in Literary-Historical Perspective* (Philadelphia: Fortress Press, 1989).

Trapp, Michael B., 'Favorinus', *OCD*, p. 590, col. 1.

Trittle, L.A., 'Plutarch's "Life of Phocion": An Analysis and Critical Report', *ANRW*, II.33.6, pp. 4258-97.

Tucker, Gene, *Form Criticism of the Old Testament* (Guides to Biblical Scholarship, Old Testament Series; Philadelphia: Fortress Press, 1971).

—Review of *Was is Formgeschichte? Neue Wege der Bibelexegese* (Neukirchen–Vluyn: Neukirchener Verlag, 1964) by Klaus Koch, in *Dialog* 5 (1966), pp. 145-47.

Tuckett, Christopher, 'Genre', in *Reading the New Testament*, pp. 68-77.

—*Reading the New Testament: Methods of Interpretation* (Philadelphia: Fortress Press, 1987).

Turner, Martha, *The Gospel According to Philip: The Sources and Coherence of an Early Christian Collection* (NHS, 38; Leiden: E.J. Brill, 1996).

Turner, Nigel, *A Grammar of New Testament Greek*. IV. *Style* (ed. J.H. Moulton and F.W. Howard; 4 vols.; Edinburgh: T. & T. Clark, 1949–76).

Utley, Francis Lee, 'Oral Genres as Bridges to Written Literature', *Genre* 2 (1969), pp. 91-103.

Vielhauer, Philipp, *Geschichte der urchristlichen Literatur: Einleitung in das Neue Testament, die Apokryphen und die Apostolischen Väter* (Berlin: W. de Gruyter, 1975).

Votaw, C.W., 'The Gospels and Contemporary Biographies', *American Journal of Theology* 19 (1915), pp. 45-73, 217-49 (repr. as *The Gospels and Contemporary Biographies in the Greco-Roman World* [Facet Book; Philadelphia: Fortress Press, 1970]).

Wansbrough, Henry, 'Introduction', in *Jesus and the Oral Gospel* (JSNTSup, 64; Sheffield: JSOT Press, 1991), pp. 9-15.

Wansbrough, Henry (ed.), *Jesus and the Oral Gospel* (JNTSup, 64; Sheffield: JSOT Press, 1991).

Wardman, Alan, *Plutarch's Lives* (Berkeley: University of California Press, 1974).

Wartensleben, G. von, *Begriff der grieschischen Chreia und Beitrage zur Geschichte ihrer Form* (Heidelberg: Carl Winter, 1901).

Webster's New Collegiate Dictionary (Springfield, MA: G. & C. Merriam Company, 1981).

Webster's New Third International Dictionary of the English Language Unabridged (editor-in-chief Philip B. Gove; Springfield, MA: Webster, Inc., Publishers, 1986).

Weiner, David, 'A Study of Mishnah Tractate Bikkurim Chapter Three', in W.S. Green (ed.), *Approaches to Ancient Judaism*. III. *Text as Context in Early Rabbinic Literature* (BJS, 11; Chico, CA: Scholars Press, 1981), pp. 89-104.

Weiss, Wolfgang, '*Eine neue Lehre in Vollmacht': Die Streit- und Schulgespräche des Markus-Evangeliums* (BZNW, 52; Berlin: W. de Gruyter, 1989).

Wellek, René, and Austin Warren, 'Literary Genres', in *The Theory of Literature* (New York: Harcourt Brace Jovanovitch, 3rd edn, 1977), pp. 226-37.

Wiesel, Elie, *The Gates of the Forest* (trans. Frances Frenaye; New York: Holt, Rinehart & Winston, 1966; French original, 1964).

Wilson, Walter T., 'The Ancient Genres of Gnomic Wisdom', in *The Mysteries of Righteousness: The Literary Composition and Genre of the 'Sentences' of Pseudo-Phocylides* (Texte und Studien zum antiken Judentum, 40; Tübingen: J.C.B. Mohr [Paul Siebeck], 1994), pp. 15-41.

—'The Gnomic Saying in Antiquity', in *Love without Pretense: Romans 12.9-21 and Hellenistic-Jewish Wisdom Literature* (WUNT, 2nd series, 46; Tübingen: J.C.B. Mohr [Paul Siebeck], 1991), pp. 9-39.

Zahavy, Tzvee, '*Kannanah* for Prayer in the Mishnah and Talmud', in Jacob Neusner *et al.* (eds.), *New Perspectives on Ancient Judaism*. I. *Religion, Literature, and Society in*

Ancient Israel, Formative Christianity and Judaism (BJS, 206; Atlanta: Scholars Press, 1990), pp. 35-48.

—'The Psychology of Early Rabbinic Prayer', in *Studies in Jewish Prayer* (Studies in Judaism; Lanham, MD: University Press of America, 1990), pp. 111-19.

INDEXES

INDEX OF REFERENCES

BIBLE

OTHER ANCIENT REFERENCES

OTHER ANCIENT AUTHORS

Index of Authors

JOURNAL FOR THE STUDY OF THE NEW TESTAMENT
SUPPLEMENT SERIES

70 J. Webb Mealy, *After the Thousand Years: Resurrection and Judgment in Revelation 20*
71 Martin Scott, *Sophia and the Johannine Jesus*
72 Steven M. Sheeley, *Narrative Asides in Luke–Acts*
73 Marie E. Isaacs, *Sacred Space: An Approach to the Theology of the Epistle to the Hebrews*
74 Edwin K. Broadhead, *Teaching with Authority: Miracles and Christology in the Gospel of Mark*
75 John K. Chow, *Patronage and Power: A Study of Social Networks in Corinth*
76 Robert W. Wall and Eugene E. Lemcio (eds.), *The New Testament as Canon: A Reader in Canonical Criticism*
77 Roman Garrison, *Redemptive Almsgiving in Early Christianity*
78 L. Gregory Bloomquist, *The Function of Suffering in Philippians*
79 Blaine Charette, *The Theme of Recompense in Matthew's Gospel*
80 Stanley E. Porter and D.A. Carson (eds.), *Biblical Greek Language and Linguistics: Open Questions in Current Research*
81 In-Gyu Hong, *The Law in Galatians*
82 Barry W. Henaut, *Oral Tradition and the Gospels: The Problem of Mark 4*
83 Craig A. Evans and James A. Sanders (eds.), *Paul and the Scriptures of Israel*
84 Martinus C. de Boer (ed.), *From Jesus to John: Essays on Jesus and New Testament Christology in Honour of Marinus de Jonge*
85 William J. Webb, *Returning Home: New Covenant and Second Exodus as the Context for 2 Corinthians 6.14–7.1*
86 Bradley H. McLean (ed.), *Origins and Method—Towards a New Understanding of Judaism and Christianity: Essays in Honour of John C. Hurd*
87 Michael J. Wilkins and Terence Paige (eds.), *Worship, Theology and Ministry in the Early Church: Essays in Honour of Ralph P. Martin*
88 Mark Coleridge, *The Birth of the Lukan Narrative: Narrative as Christology in Luke 1–2*
89 Craig A. Evans, *Word and Glory: On the Exegetical and Theological Background of John's Prologue*
90 Stanley E. Porter and Thomas H. Olbricht (eds.), *Rhetoric and the New Testament: Essays from the 1992 Heidelberg Conference*
91 Janice Capel Anderson, *Matthew's Narrative Web: Over, and Over, and Over Again*
92 Eric Franklin, *Luke: Interpreter of Paul, Critic of Matthew*
93 Jan Fekkes III, *Isaiah and Prophetic Traditions in the Book of Revelation: Visionary Antecedents and their Development*
94 Charles A. Kimball, *Jesus' Exposition of the Old Testament in Luke's Gospel*
95 Dorothy A. Lee, *The Symbolic Narratives of the Fourth Gospel: The Interplay of Form and Meaning*

96 Richard E. DeMaris, *The Colossian Controversy: Wisdom in Dispute at Colossae*
97 Edwin K. Broadhead, *Prophet, Son, Messiah: Narrative Form and Function in Mark 14–16*
98 Carol J. Schlueter, *Filling up the Measure: Polemical Hyperbole in 1 Thessalonians 2.14-16*
99 Neil Richardson, *Paul's Language about God*
100 Thomas E. Schmidt and Moisés Silva (eds.), *To Tell the Mystery: Essays on New Testament Eschatology in Honor of Robert H. Gundry*
101 Jeffrey A.D. Weima, *Neglected Endings: The Significance of the Pauline Letter Closings*
102 Joel F. Williams, *Other Followers of Jesus: Minor Characters as Major Figures in Mark's Gospel*
103 Warren Carter, *Households and Discipleship: A Study of Matthew 19–20*
104 Craig A. Evans and W. Richard Stegner (eds.), *The Gospels and the Scriptures of Israel*
105 W.P. Stephens (ed.), *The Bible, the Reformation and the Church: Essays in Honour of James Atkinson*
106 Jon A. Weatherly, *Jewish Responsibility for the Death of Jesus in Luke–Acts*
107 Elizabeth Harris, *Prologue and Gospel: The Theology of the Fourth Evangelist*
108 L. Ann Jervis and Peter Richardson (eds.), *Gospel in Paul: Studies on Corinthians, Galatians and Romans for Richard N. Longenecker*
109 Elizabeth Struthers Malbon and Edgar V. McKnight (eds.), *The New Literary Criticism and the New Testament*
110 Mark L. Strauss, *The Davidic Messiah in Luke–Acts: The Promise and its Fulfillment in Lukan Christology*
111 Ian H. Thomson, *Chiasmus in the Pauline Letters*
112 Jeffrey B. Gibson, *The Temptations of Jesus in Early Christianity*
113 Stanley E. Porter and D.A. Carson (eds.), *Discourse Analysis and Other Topics in Biblical Greek*
114 Lauri Thurén, *Argument and Theology in 1 Peter: The Origins of Christian Paraenesis*
115 Steve Moyise, *The Old Testament in the Book of Revelation*
116 C.M. Tuckett (ed.), *Luke's Literary Achievement: Collected Essays*
117 Kenneth G.C. Newport, *The Sources and Sitz im Leben of Matthew 23*
118 Troy W. Martin, *By Philosophy and Empty Deceit: Colossians as Response to a Cynic Critique*
119 David Ravens, *Luke and the Restoration of Israel*
120 Stanley E. Porter and David Tombs (eds.), *Approaches to New Testament Study*
121 Todd C. Penner, *The Epistle of James and Eschatology: Re-reading an Ancient Christian Letter*
122 A.D.A. Moses, *Matthew's Transfiguration Story in Jewish–Christian Controversy*
123 David Lertis Matson, *Household Conversion Narratives in Acts: Pattern and Interpretation*

124 David Mark Ball, *'I Am' in John's Gospel: Literary Function, Background and Theological Implications*
125 Robert Gordon Maccini, *Her Testimony is True: Women as Witnesses According to John*
126 B. Hudson Mclean, *The Cursed Christ: Mediterranean Expulsion Rituals and Pauline Soteriology*
127 R. Barry Matlock, *Unveiling the Apocalyptic Paul: Paul's Interpreters and the Rhetoric of Criticism*
128 Timothy Dwyer, *The Motif of Wonder in the Gospel of Mark*
129 Carl Judson Davis, *The Names and Way of the Lord: Old Testament Themes, New Testament Christology*
130 Craig S. Wansink, *Chained in Christ: The Experience and Rhetoric of Paul's Imprisonments*
131 Stanley E. Porter and Thomas H. Olbricht (eds.), *Rhetoric, Scripture and Theology: Essays from the 1994 Pretoria Conference*
132 J. Nelson Kraybill, *Imperial Cult and Commerce in John's Apocalypse*
133 Mark S. Goodacre, *Goulder and the Gospels: An Examination of a New Paradigm*
134 Larry J. Kreitzer, *Striking New Images: Roman Imperial Coinage and the New Testament World*
135 Charles Landon, *A Text-Critical Study of the Epistle of Jude*
136 Jeffrey T. Reed, *A Discourse Analysis of Philippians: Method and Rhetoric in the Debate over Lierary Integrity*
137 Roman Garrison, *The Graeco-Roman Context of Early Christian Literature*
138 Kent D. Clarke, *Textual Optimism: A Critique of the United Bible Societies' Greek New Testament*
139 Yong-Eui Yang, *Jesus and the Sabbath in Matthew's Gospel*
140 Thomas R. Yoder Neufeld, *Put on the Armour of God: The Divine Warrior from Isaiah to Ephesians*
141 Rebecca I. Denova, *The Things Accomplished among Us: Prophetic Tradition in the Structural Pattern of Luke–Acts*
142 Scott Cunningham, *'Through Many Tribulations': The Theology of Persecution in Luke–Acts*
143 Raymond Pickett, *The Cross in Corinth: The Social Significance of the Death of Jesus*
144 S. John Roth, *The Blind, the Lame and the Poor: Character Types in Luke–Acts*
145 Larry Paul Jones, *The Symbol of Water in the Gospel of John*
146 Stanley E. Porter and Thomas H. Olbricht (eds.), *The Rhetorical Analysis of Scripture: Essays from the 1995 London Conference*
147 Kim Paffenroth, *The Story of Jesus According to L*
148 Craig A. Evans and James A. Sanders (eds.), *Early Christian Interpretation of the Scriptures of Israel: Investigations and Proposals*
149 J. Dorcas Gordon, *Sister or Wife?: 1 Corinthians 7 and Cultural Anthropology*
150 J. Daryl Charles, *Virtue amidst Vice: The Catalog of Virtues in 2 Peter 1.5-7*
151 Derek Tovey, *Narrative Art and Act in the Fourth Gospel*

152 Evert-Jan Vledder, *Conflict in the Miracle Stories: A Socio-Exegetical Study of Matthew 8 and 9*

153 Christopher Rowland and Crispin H.T. Fletcher-Louis (eds.), *Understanding, Studying and Reading: New Testament Essays in Honour of John Ashton*

154 Craig A. Evans and James A. Sanders (eds.), *The Function of Scripture in Early Jewish and Christian Tradition*

155 Kyoung-Jin Kim, *Stewardship and Almsgiving in Luke's Theology*

156 I.A.H. Combes, *The Metaphor of Slavery in the Writings of the Early Church: From the New Testament to the Begining of the Fifth Century*

157 April D. DeConick, *Voices of the Mystics: Early Christian Discourse in the Gospels of John and Thomas and Other Ancient Christian Literature*

158 Jey. J. Kanagaraj, *'Mysticism' in the Gospel of John: An Inquiry into its Background*

159 Brenda Deen Schildgen, *Crisis and Continuity: Time in the Gospel of Mark*

160 Johan Ferreira, *Johannine Ecclesiology*

161 Helen C. Orchard, *Courting Betrayal: Jesus as Victim in the Gospel of John*

162 Jeffrey T. Tucker, *Example Stories: Perspectives on Four Parables in the Gospel of Luke*

163 John A. Darr, *Herod the Fox: Audience Criticism and Lukan Characterization*

164 Bas M.F. Van Iersel, *Mark: A Reader-Response Commentary*

165 Alison Jasper, *The Shining Garment of the Text: Gendered Readings of John's Prologue*

166 G.K. Beale, *John's Use of the Old Testament in Revelation*

167 Gary Yamasaki, *John the Baptist in Life and Death: Audience-Oriented Criticism of Matthew's Narrative*

168 Stanley E. Porter and D.A. Carson (eds.), *Linguistics and the New Testament: Critical Junctures*

169 Derek Newton, *Deity and Diet: The Dilemma of Sacrificial Food at Corinth*

170 Stanley E. Porter and Jeffrey T. Reed (eds.), *Discourse Analysis and the New Testament: Approaches and Results*

171 Stanley E. Porter and Anthony R. Cross (eds.), *Baptism, the New Testament and the Church: Historical and Contemporary Studies in Honour of R.E.O. White*

172 Casey Wayne Davis, *Oral Biblical Criticism: The Influence of the Principles of Orality on the Literary Structure of Paul's Epistle to the Philippians*

173 Stanley E. Porter and Richard S. Hess (eds.), *Translating the Bible: Problems and Prospects*

174 J.D.H. Amador, *Academic Constraints in Rhetorical Criticism of the New Testament: An Introduction to a Rhetoric of Power*

175 Edwin K. Broadhead, *Naming Jesus: Titular Christology in the Gospel of Mark*

176 Alex T. Cheung, *Idol Food in Corinth: Jewish Background and Pauline Legacy*

177 Brian Dodd, *Paul's Paradigmatic 'I': Personal Examples as Literary Strategy*

178 Thomas B. Slater, *Christ and Community: A Socio-Historical Study of the Christology of Revelation*

179 Alison M. Jack, *Texts Reading Texts, Sacred and Secular: Two Postmodern Perspectives*

180 Stanley E. Porter and Dennis L. Stamps (eds.), *The Rhetorical Interpretation of Scripture: Essays from the 1996 Malibu Conference*

181 Sylvia C. Keesmaat, *Paul and his Story: (Re)Interpreting the Exodus Tradition*

182 Johannes Nissen and Sigfred Pedersen (eds.), *New Readings in John: Literary and Theological Perspectives. Essays from the Scandinavian Conference on the Fourth Gospel in Århus 1997*

183 Todd D. Still, *Conflict at Thessalonica: A Pauline Church and its Neighbours*

184 David Rhoads and Kari Syreeni (eds.), *Characterization in the Gospels: Reconceiving Narrative Criticism*

185 David Lee, *Luke's Stories of Jesus: Theological Reading of Gospel Narrative and the Legacy of Hans Frei*

186 Stanley E. Porter, Michael A. Hayes and David Tombs (eds.), *Resurrection*

187 David A. Holgate, *A Prodigality, Liberality and Meanness: The Prodigal Son in Graeco-Roman Perspective*

188 Jerry L. Sumney, *'Servants of Satan', 'False Brothers' and Other Opponents of Paul: A Study of those Opposed in the Letters of the Pauline Corpus*

189 Steve Moyise (ed.), *The Old Testament in the New Testament: Essays in Honour of J.L. North*

190 John M. Court, *The Book of Revelation and the Johannine Apocalyptic Tradition*

191 Stanley E. Porter, *The Criteria for Authenticity in Historical-Jesus Research. Previous Discussion and New Proposals*

192 Stanley E. Porter and Brook W.R. Pearson (eds.), *Christian–Jewish Relations through the Centuries*

193 Stanley E. Porter (ed.), *Diglossia and other Topics in New Testament Linguistics*

195 Stanley E. Porter and Dennis L. Stamps (eds.), *Rhetorical Criticism and the Bible: Essays from the 1998 Florence Conference*

196 J.M. Holmes, *Text in a Whirlwind: A Critique of Four Exegetical Devices at 1 Timothy 2.9-15*

197 F. Gerald Downing, *Making Sense in (and of) the First Christian Century*

198 Greg W. Forbes, *The God of Old: The Role of the Lukan Parables in the Purpose of Luke's Gospel*

199 Kieran O'Mahony, O.S.A., *Pauline Persuasion: A Sounding in 2 Corinthians 8–9*

200 F. Gerald Downing, *Doing Things with Words in the First Christian Century*

202 Gustavo Martín-Asensio, *Transitivity-Based Foregrounding in the Acts of the Apostles: A Functional-Grammatical Approach*

203 H. Benedict Green, CR, *Matthew, Poet of the Beatitudes*

204 Warren Carter, *Matthew and the Margins: A Socio-Political and Religious Commentary*

206 David Edgar, *Has God Not Chosen the Poor? The Social Setting of the Epistle of James*

207 Kyu Sam Han, *Jerusalem and the Early Jesus Movement: The Q Community's Attitude toward the Temple*

208 Mark D. Chapman, *The Coming Crisis: The Impact of Eschatology on Theology in Edwardian England*

209 Richard W. Johnson, *Going Outside the Camp: The Sociological Function of the Levitical Critique in the Epistle to the Hebrews*

210 Bruno Blumenfeld, *The Political Paul: Democracy and Kingship in Paul's Thought*

211 Ju Hur, *A Dynamic Reading of the Holy Spirit in Luke–Acts*

212 Wendy E. Sproston North, *The Lazarus Story within the Johannine Tradition*

213 William O. Walker Jr, *Interpolations in the Pauline Letters*

214 Michael Labahn and Andreas Schmidt (eds.), *The Teaching of Jesus and its Earliest Records*

215 Barbara Shellard, *New Light on Luke: Its Purpose, Sources and Literary Context*

216 Stephanie L. Black, *Sentence Conjunctions in the Gospel of Matthew: και, δε, τοτε, γαρ, οὐν and Asyndeton in Narrative Discourse*

217 Alf Christophersen, Carsten Claussen and Jörg Frey (eds.), *Paul, Luke and the Graeco-Roman World*

218 Paul L. Danove, *Linguistics and Exegesis in the Gospel of Mark: Applications of a Case Frame Analysis and Lexicon*

219 Iutisone Salevao, *Legitimation in the Letter to the Hebrews: The Construction and Maintenance of a Symbolic Universe*

220 Alan R. Kerr, *The Temple of Jesus' Body: The Temple Theme in the Gospel of John*

222 David Neville, *Mark's Gospel—Prior or Posterior? A Reappraisal of the Phenomenon of Order*

224 J. Arthur Baird, *Holy Word: The Paradigm of New Testament Formation*

227 Marion C. Moeser, *The Anecdote in Mark, the Classical World and the Rabbis*

229 Stan Harstine, *Moses as a Character in the Fourth Gospel: A Study of Ancient Reading Techniques*

231 Eric Eve, *The Jewish Context of Jesus' Miracles*

232 Thomas R. Hatina, *In Search of a Context: The Function of Scripture in Mark's Narrative*